Walter Rodney's Intellectual and Political Thought

Walter Rodney's Intellectual and Political Thought

Rupert Charles Lewis

The Press University of the West Indies
●Barbados ●Jamaica ●Trinidad and Tobago

Wayne State University Press
Detroit

The Rodney family in Tanzania. From left, Kanini, born 28 March 1969 in Tanzania; Shaka, born in London 5 July 1966; Asha, born 22 March 1971 in Tanzania; and parents Pat and Walter Rodney.

The Press University of the West Indies
1A Aqueduct Flats Mona
Kingston 7 Jamaica

© 1998 by Rupert Lewis
All rights reserved. Published 1998

Published simultaneously in the United States of America by
Wayne State University Press, Detroit, Michigan 48201

Printed in United States of America

ISBN 976-640-044-X (The Press University of the West Indies, pbk.)
ISBN 0-8143-2743-5 (Wayne State University Press, cloth)
ISBN 0-8143-2744-3 (Wayne State University Press, pbk.)

02 01 00 99 98   5 4 3 2 1

Library of Congress Catalog Card Number 97-61422
A publication in the African American Life Series

CATALOGUING IN PUBLICATION DATA

Lewis, Rupert
 Walter Rodney's intellectual and
 political thought / Rupert Charles Lewis.

 p. cm.
 Based on the author's PhD thesis presented at the
 University of the West Indies, Mona, Jamaica, 1995.
 Includes bibliographical references.

 ISBN 976-640-044-X

 1. Rodney, Walter, 1942-1980 – Political and social views. 2. Rodney, Walter, 1942-1980 – Contributions in political science. 3. Black nationalism. 4. Caribbean area – history. 5. Africa – History. 6. Guyana – Politics and government. 7. Ras Tafari movement. 8. Historians – Caribbean, English-speaking – Biography.
 I. Title.

 F2385.R62L47 1998   988.03-dc-20

Set in 11/13pt Times Roman with Switzerland display
Book design by Prodesign Ltd, Red Gal Ring, Kingston

This book has been printed on acid-free paper

For my wife Maureen,
and children Yewande and Jide.

Also in memory of our African ancestors,
who 160 years ago, were emancipated
from slavery in the British Caribbean

Table of Contents

Ackowledgments *ix*

Abbreviations *xii*

Introduction *xiii*

Chapter 1   **EARLY YEARS**   1

Chapter 2   **UNIVERSITY YEARS 1960–1966**   13

Chapter 3   **ENGLAND 1963–1966**   31
             Rodney's Marxism ● *Doctoral thesis*

Chapter 4   **WALTER RODNEY AND THE WRITING OF AFRICAN HISTORY**   47
             Evolution as African historian ● *The Cambridge essays*
             The African diaspora ● *History and politics*
             How Europe Underdeveloped Africa ● *Conclusion*

Chapter 5   **RODNEY AND THE CULTURAL POLITICS OF RASTAFARI AND RUDE BOY**   85
             Lifestyle and politics ● *Black Consciousness in Jamaica*
             Grassroots connections ● *Groundings* ● *Ras Negus and*
             Planno ● *Rastafarian creativity* ● *Rudie culture*
             Rodney's writings ● *The State and the intelligentsia*
             Conclusion

| Chapter 6 | **RODNEY'S ACADEMIC AND POLITICAL AGENDA IN TANZANIA** | 124 |

Dar es Salaam: Defining an intellectual role African students ● *Rodney on Arusha* ● *Shivji's intervention* ● *Rodney's response* ● *Revolutionary pedagogy* ● *Teaching and research* ● *Dar es Salaam historiography* ● *Conclusion*

| Chapter 7 | **RODNEY'S PAN-AFRICANISM** | 167 |

| Chapter 8 | **CARIBBEAN HISTORIAN AT WORK** | 182 |

Politics and professorship ● *Writing Caribbean history*

| Chapter 9 | **RODNEY'S PERSPECTIVES ON CARIBBEAN AND GUYANESE POLITICS** | 202 |

Jagan's critical support and Rodney's critical exposure Study group and theoretical work ● *The Working People's Alliance and race* ● *Left wing ideology* ● *Political crisis, 1978–1980* ● *Death*

Conclusion 254

Bibliography 257

Index 277

Acknowledgments

I am very grateful to Professor Rex Nettleford, Vice Chancellor of the University of the West Indies, founder of the National Dance Theatre Company and scholar for his close reading and comments on the text. His encouragement has been unwavering and his intellectual example, as writer, thinker, choreographer and institution builder, puts him among the leaders of postcolonial thought and creative expression. He has stressed the importance of understanding and giving expression to the specifics of our experience in the Caribbean and moving from there to an articulation of the general or the 'universal'.

My special thanks go to Walter Rodney's widow, Dr Pat Rodney, who shared her experiences with me and allowed me access to his personal papers. Their children Shaka, Kanini and Asha spoke to me about their father. Among other family members who assisted me were, Edward Rodney, Walter Rodney's eldest brother, who sent me clippings from the Guyanese press, and his sister Kathleen Scott. I am grateful to Andaiye who spent many hours with me while undergoing chemotherapy treatment in Barbados, and who put me on to many other informants in Guyana. Eusi Kwayana is among the most knowledgeable concerning Guyana's history in the last fifty years of this century and is an exceptional political personality. His political ethics helped to shape Rodney's ethical point of view. Nigel Westmaas, Jocelyn Dowe, Bonita Harris, Wazir Mohammed, Ogun, Frank Fyffe, Kwesi Afrani, Colin Cholmondeley, Professor Ewart Thomas of Stanford University, Dr Omawale, Karen de Souza, Rickey Singh, Claremont Kirton and Professor Clive Thomas of the University of Guyana, were all very supportive. Rupert Roopnarine's critical reader's report was highly appreciated and helped me to improve chapter 9. But the political judgements are of course my own and in instances differ from his own. I hope that Guyanese political activists in that period will write more substantially on the politics of the period. I am grateful to Elvin McDavid, who worked closely with the late President Forbes Burnham, for speaking with me and to the late President Cheddi Jagan, who was then opposition leader, for providing me with an unpublished essay of his on Walter Rodney.

Among those who helped with my work in Tanzania in the summer of 1990 are Professor Horace Campbell, who introduced me to his former colleagues at the University of Dar es Salaam, and June Ward, who helped with accommodation and transportation. I am grateful to Professors Haroub Othman, Issa Shivji, Wamba-dia-Wamba, Anse Tambila and Fred Kaijage of the University of Dar es Salaam. Walter Bagoya of the Tanzania Publishing House (TPH) provided me with valuable information concerning the Tanzanian edition of *How Europe Underdeveloped Africa*. Professor Joe Kanywanyi of the University of Dar es Salaam corresponded with me, Professor Julius Nyang'oro of the University of North Carolina, made comments and passed my chapter on Tanzania to Professor Severine Rugumamu of the University of Dar es Salaam who critiqued it. Abdul Babu was very helpful and spent several hours with me in London talking about his political experience in Tanzania and his relations with Walter Rodney. The work of Professor Joseph Inikori of the University of Rochester, in the United States, was very important because it overlapped with many of the academic concerns in African history which engaged Rodney.

Many people in Jamaica deserve mention but I would like to single out Robin and Richard Small. Robin Small enabled me to recapture the undocumented politics among urban youth and Rastafarians in the 1960s. Richard Small, who was Rodney's lawyer and friend, provided valuable information on his activities in London during his student years. Kathleen Drayton provided me with hospitality in Barbados and with access to her papers and correspondence with Rodney. Dr Harold Drayton also helped with a penetrating interview.

Professors Ali Mazrui and Edward Ferguson, who were members of the panel on Walter Rodney at the African Studies Association panel in Baltimore in 1990, not only made stimulating and informative presentations but spoke to me at length afterwards. Caribbean novelists, George Lamming and Jan Carew, gave excellent interviews.

This study would not have gotten off the ground without the institutional and financial support from the University of the West Indies. This support enabled me to travel to Guyana and Trinidad in 1989 and to Tanzania, Zimbabwe and England in 1990. While on a Fulbright Fellowship at the Center for Latin American Studies, University of Florida in 1991/1992, I did the first draft of this book. I also benefited from the comments of those who attended a seminar I gave on Walter Rodney at the Center for African Studies at the University of Florida in 1990.

My students in Caribbean Political Thought and Garveyism in the Americas and Africa have forced me to come to terms with Rodney's contribution in this area and to them I am grateful for questions and comments in tutorials. I thank Lynette Josephs and Denise Leander, two Guyanese students at the time of writing, who loaned me tapes from their radio documentary on Walter Rodney. Thanks also to Barry Chevannes, Brian Meeks, David Scott, Anthony Bogues, Clinton Hutton, Marion Bernard and Christine Cummings who took an interest in this work and encouraged its completion.

Special thanks to the librarians of the University of the West Indies at St Augustine and Mona, the University of Dar es Salaam, the National Humanities Center in North Carolina, the University of Guyana and the University of Florida, Gainesville.

From the conception of the study through to its completion my wife, Dr Maureen Warner-Lewis, has been very supportive. Her critical reading of the drafts and final version has been invaluable. My son Jide, and Maureen made timely interventions which enabled me to better utilise my word processing programme. I thank my children, Yewande and Jide, for giving moral support and understanding my extended absences from home. They have had to put up with parents wrapped up in the research and writing of books and papers.

Abbreviations

ANC	African National Congress
ASCRIA	African Society for Cultural Relations with Independent Africa
CIA	Central Intelligence Agency
DUSO	Dar es Salaam University Students' Organisation
EWF	Ethiopian World Federation
FRELIM	Front for the Liberation of Mozambique
GNFA	Guyana Nationals and Friends Alliance
IMF	International Monetary Fund
IPRA	Indian Political Revolutionary Association
JAH	Journal of African History
JCHR	Jamaica Council for Human Rights
JLP	Jamaica Labour Party
KANU	Kenya African National Union
LACAP	Los Angeles Committee for Academics in Peril
MAO	Movement Against Oppression
MPLA	Popular Movement for the Liberation of Angola
NATO	North Atlantic Treaty Organisation
NDTC	National Dance Theatre Company
OAU	Organisation of African Unity
PAC	Pan African Congress
PAIGC	African Party for the Index of Guinea and Cape Verde
PLO	Palestine Liberation Organisation
PNC	People's National Congress
PNM	People's National Movement
PNP	People's National Party
PPP	People's Progressive Party
PRO	Public Relations Office
RUWIS	Regional Union of West Indian Students
SNCC	Student Nonviolent Coordinating Committee
SOAS	School of Oriental and African Studies
SWAPO	South West Africa People's Organisation
TANU	Tanganyika African National Union
TPH	Tanzania Publishing House
UCWI	University College of the West Indies
UF	United Force
UNIA	Universal Negro Improvement Association
USARF	University Students' African Revolutionary Front
UWI	University of the West Indies
WLL	Workers' Liberation League
WPA	Working People's Alliance
WPJ	Workers' Party of Jamaica
ZANU	Zimbabwe African National Union
ZAPU	Zimbabwe African People's Union

Introduction

Part of my concern in writing about Walter Rodney is to develop a political dialogue with my students in Caribbean Political Thought and my children who were born in the 1970s. The biographical format adopted tries to facilitate this method of analysis so that readers are aware of some of the personalities with whom Rodney interacted, the choices made, the negations, affirmations, the errors, the ideas and activism in their social, economic and political context.

This study sets out to trace and discuss the evolution of Walter Rodney's intellectual and political thought. In the discussion of Caribbean political thought, Rodney is remembered largely as an activist who posed issues concerning race, class and ethnicity in Jamaica in 1968 during the Black Power era (Benn 1987). His pioneering work on African history and politics and his Pan-African activism in Tanzania are virtually ignored. On the other hand, those who are familiar with his African activities are vague about his work in the Caribbean. There is a need, therefore, to bring together his African and Caribbean intellectual and activist contributions for they constitute a whole. When seen in this light Rodney's work forms part of a larger tradition of West Indian involvement with continental Africa and represents a milestone in the efforts of Caribbean intellectuals to understand the modern origins of the region. It is to this task of understanding the unity of his African and Caribbean concerns, in the early years after political independence, that this study is dedicated.

Most people know Rodney through his famous text *How Europe Underdeveloped Africa*. However, he was the author of many other academic and polemical works, of which some are out of print and others were never published. My intention is to introduce readers throughout the narrative to the wide range of his writings from his high school years in Guyana until his assassination in 1980. An important area of Rodney's intellectual work was reconstructing the political economy of the Atlantic slave trade and analysing its consequences for Africa, Europe and the Americas. Rodney's work in this area continues to receive critical attention and has been the subject of work done by the Nigerian historian, Joseph Inikori (1992a, 1992b, 1993a, 1993b, 1994; Inikori and Engerman 1994). The depth of his historical research and analyses was integrally linked to what he considered the practical tasks of decolonisation. This study therefore hopes to provide a basis whereby Rodney can be seen as someone whose intellectual and political thought is rooted in the history and politics of Africa and the African diaspora. At this stage I am not seeking to develop a political theory of Walter Rodney's ideas but am concerned with tracing the evolution of his political ideas through biography, analysis of his writings on Africa and the Caribbean, and his political practice.

I have benefited considerably from work that has already been done on Rodney as an intellectual and activist. Foremost among these studies is the 1982 collection, *Walter Rodney – Revolutionary and Scholar: A Tribute* edited by Edward A. Alpers and Pierre-Michel Fontaine, which set the agenda for analysing his legacy and which included C.L.R. James' critical essay "Walter Rodney and the Question of Power". The Tanzanian collection, which appeared in 1980 at the University of Dar es Salaam in the special issue of the radical journal *Cheche*, the essay by the Tanzanian historian, Bonaventure Swai (1981, 1982), entitled "Rodney on Scholarship and Activism", and the collection by Nigerian scholars in the booklet *And Finally They Killed Him* (1980), were adulatory, and were consequently less critical, but the statements provided evidence of his significant impact on African intellectuals. Eusi Kwayana's (1988) pamphlet entitled *Walter Rodney* is an indispensable source because of the grasp he has of Rodney's political thought as well as of his political activities in Guyana during 1974–1980.

Horace Campbell's (1991) article "The Impact of Walter Rodney and Progressive Scholars on the Dar es Salaam School" identified the key elements in Rodney's academic and intellectual work. These are the roles intellectuals play in the production and reproduction of social knowledge and Rodney's determination to critique colonial and bourgeois approaches to history and social life. Rodney contributed to the development of an intellectual culture linked to the self-emancipation of the working people. Campbell argued that the theoretical requirements of reconstruction remained the task of committed intellectuals. But this task was necessarily bound up with the freedom, skills, knowledge and intellectual culture of the broad masses in the process of becoming active agents in the making of their own history. For in relation to the fate of oppressed classes in a given country, Rodney believed that they must discover themselves in order to understand their historic mission in their own emancipation (Campbell 1991: 102–103).

Horace Campbell (1991), Trevor Campbell (1981) and Biodun Jeyifo (1980) have employed Gramsci's useful concept of the "organic" intellectual to apply to Rodney's work and have done so quite convincingly. In so doing they distinguish him from traditional intellectuals. For Gramsci, traditional intellectuals were literary, scientific, and religious persons "whose position in the interstices of society has a certain inter-class aura about it but derives ultimately from past and present class relations and conceals an attachment to various historical class forms" (Hoare and Smith 1978: 3). On the other hand, the organic intellectuals were "the thinking and organising elements of a particular fundamental social class. These organic intellectuals are distinguished less by their profession, which may be any job characteristic of their class, than by their function in directing the ideas and aspirations of the class to which they organically belong" (Hoare and Smith 1978: 3). If Rodney is to be situated on this terrain, it is to his own notion of the working people coming out of a history of slavery and colonialism to which he must be tied, rather than to a schema based on the evolution of the Italian intelligentsia.

Coming closer to the Caribbean, Manning Marable (1986, 1987) has located Rodney in the radical black intellectual tradition. Marable's discussion follows Cedric Robinson's (1983) positioning of C.L.R. James, Richard Wright and W.E.B. DuBois in a similar juxtapostion with Marxism. Anthony Bogues' *Caliban's Freedom – The Early Political Thought of C.L.R. James* is also in this mould. While Rodney can be located here with greater legitimacy than afforded by Gramsci's Italian cultural history, my intention is to try to follow the trajectory of Rodney's intellectual and political course as a West Indian or Anglophone Caribbean intellectual. In order to understand this intellectual trajectory one must turn to C.L.R. James' interpretation of Walter Rodney.

C.L.R. James wrote the most perceptive comments on Rodney and was the first to locate him within a certain intellectual genealogy that was West Indian, Pan-African and also Marxist.

> Walter grew up in an atmosphere where for the first time a generation of West Indian intellectuals was able not only to study the revolutionary and creative works that had been created in Europe but also to benefit from and be master

of what had been done in the same tradition in direct reference to the Caribbean
... He was able to look upon the revolutionary ideas, perspectives, and analysis of the Caribbean as something natural, normal, fixed, written, and beyond dispute. That is what sent him along the path he followed to Africa (James 1982: 134).

A. W. Singham (1990) has quite correctly credited James with helping to shape a Caribbean intellectual tradition. The present study is guided by both James' sense of an intellectual tradition that evolved in the context of British colonial rule, and in which he could claim paternity, and Rodney's own theorising about himself and his work. This is far richer for our purposes than Gramsci's comments, as the latter are based on a class paradigm which is centred on a vision of Italian and European socialism, while Rodney seeks to understand the complex of relationships between Africa, Europe and the Caribbean and to examine their consequences for decolonisation. The centre of Rodney's vision is Africa and the Caribbean, thus Gramsci's privileging of class cannot be done at the expense of race. Rodney attempts to work through the relationships between these two interconnected conditions of class exploitation and racial oppression.

James regarded Rodney as one of his intellectual sons, and as is the case with father-son relationships, there is some tension between them. These tensions emerged on issues of Pan-Africanism as well as the risks attendant on Rodney's intervention in the politics of Guyana. They reflect some theoretical differences especially concerning the role of the petty bourgeoisie as well as different political judgements and temperaments. This process of arriving at his own intellectual identity is evident in Rodney's work on Africa and the Caribbean, and in the many debates with other scholars and with activists in liberation movements. At this point I am not comparing James with Rodney. I am interested in looking at a West Indian postindependence intellectual functioning in Africa and the Caribbean. James is a pathfinder from the colonial generation and in a sense he is always there intellectually for us to draw on, but his political work in Trinidad and Tobago in the 1950s and 1960s notwithstanding, he cannot be described as a political activist in the Caribbean and Africa in the way that Rodney was. He was a senior political intellectual who some deferred to and many criticised but respected.

Rodney's own theorising on his role, which he sets out in his writings on the Caribbean and Africa, will be drawn on extensively in this study for critical analysis. Rodney set himself rigorous standards and this shows up in his nondogmatic approach to Marxism. Wole Soyinka, the Nigerian writer and 1986 Nobel prize winner for literature, summed up the nondogmatic quality of Rodney's Marxism when he wrote:

in an intellectual world rendered increasingly turgid by ideological mouthers and phrase-mongers, Walter Rodney stood out for lucidity, relevance, a preference for actuality, its analysis and prescription over and above a slavish cant. He proceeded from attested facts to analysis, not like many others, commencing with worn and untested frameworks – usually made up of someone else's summary, thesis, or even a bare out-of-context quotation – onto which existing facts are then stretched, pruned, tortured and distorted to obtain a purely theoretical semi-fit. Walter Rodney was not the latter kind.

No one remotely acquainted with his work, his thinking or his person would be surprised that he carried the same kind of approach into active politics. His activities in Guyana since his return were inspired by courageous assessment of the actualities of Guyana. Walter Rodney was no armchair rhetorician, he was no captive intellectual playing to the gallery of local or international radicalism. He was clearly one of the most solidly ideologically situated intellectuals ever to look colonialism and its contemporary heir – black opportunism and exploitation – in the eye, and where necessary spit in it (Soyinka 1980: 10).

This is an accurate assessment of Rodney's approach and I try to evaluate his work in the spirit of these observations, especially Soyinka's emphasis on Rodney's "preference for actuality, its analysis and prescription over and above a slavish cant" as well as the recognition of his "courageous assessment of the actualities of Guyana". These characteristics are evident in his efforts to think hard about Africa and the diaspora.

While following a biographical framework, this is not a biography or life of Walter Rodney,[1] but an attempt to situate his intellectual and political evolution in the transatlantic diasporic locations of Guyana, Jamaica, London and Tanzania. These geographically dispersed locations were, of course, linked by the history of the British Empire and capitalism. What emerges from Rodney's work is not only a critique of empire and capitalism in general but a dissection of the domestic political elite that assumed political authority from the colonisers in Africa and the Caribbean as well as an analysis of the processes of recolonisation. Rodney tried to understand why the moment of independence was also a moment of recolonisation. This was due not only to the strength of international capitalism and the Western political alignment in the years following the Second World War, but also to the weaknesses of the social forces in the ex-colonial countries and of their political elite.

This study is a response to the need to explore the Caribbean intellectual tradition[2] through the life and work of one of its important postindependence thinkers. Rodney functioned in the intellectual tradition of Henry Sylvester-Williams,[3] George Padmore[4] and C.L.R. James, all of Trinidad and

Tobago, Theophilus Scholes[5] and Marcus Garvey of Jamaica[6] and the collective cultural force of the Rastafarian movement[7] in Jamaica during the 1960s and 1970s.

The first three chapters follow a biographical sequence from his birth in British Guiana in 1942 until the completion of his doctoral dissertation and the start of professional life as a historian at age 24. The remaining six chapters cover significant issues in his research into African and Caribbean history and vital moments of his political activism from 1966 to his murder in 1980 at age 38.

Notes

1. See Arnold Gibbons (1994) who has written *Walter Rodney and His Times*. Vol. 1. This work (and a second volume has been promised) is about aspects of his ideas and not so much about his life.
2. The pioneering and most comprehensive work in the field of Caribbean political thought is Arthur Lewis (1983).
3. See James Hooker (1975) and Owen Mathurin (1976).
4. See the very useful biography of George Padmore by James Hooker (1967). See also La Guerre (1982) for discussion of Padmore as a colonial intellectual.
5. See Patrick Bryan's (1991a) essay on Dr Theophilus E.S. Scholes, a Jamaican intellectual writing in the late nineteenth century on Africa and the British Empire.
6. For a discussion of Marcus Garvey's anticolonialism see Rupert Lewis (1988).
7. See Smith, Augier and Nettleford (1967); Nettleford (1970); Chevannes (1989).

CHAPTER 1

Early Years

Walter Rodney was born on 23 March 1942 in Georgetown, Guyana. He was the second son of Edward Percival Rodney and Pauline Rodney. Walter's father made his living as a tailor and his mother was a housewife and seamstress. Walter described his father as a member of "the independent artisan class" (Rodney 1990: 1). However, when his father experienced economic difficulties, he went to work for a "big tailoring establishment . . . and was simply assigned jobs and was paid a wage each week" (Walter Rodney 1990: 1). Percival Rodney had travelled abroad and had worked in Curaçao and the Dominican Republic in the 1930s. As a result of his travels in South America and the Caribbean he learned to speak Spanish, Portuguese and Papiamento (Eddie Rodney 1989). An intelligent and hard-working man, he joined the nationalist movement in Guyana in the 1940s which was led by the young Indo-Guyanese dentist, Cheddi Jagan, then in his early thirties, and his American wife, Janet. The Jagans were later joined by the young Afro-Guyanese lawyer, Forbes Burnham. Cheddi Jagan and Forbes Burnham were to dominate Guyanese politics throughout Rodney's life. The only possible breach in the political space dominated by Jagan and Burnham was for a few months in 1979–1980 when Rodney and the Working People's Alliance (WPA) rose to political prominence.

The decade of the 1940s was one of child bearing and rearing as Pauline Rodney mothered six children. Lawrence Albert, the first boy, was born in 1940; Walter, affectionately called Wally, followed in 1942; Hubert in 1944; Keith in 1946; the only girl, Kathy, came in 1949 and Donald, who was in the car in 1980 when the bomb exploded killing Walter, was born in 1951.

The 1940s were also important for the Rodney family because of political developments in Europe and in the British colonies. The 1940s saw the defeat of fascism and a victory for the Allied Forces of the United States, the Soviet Union, England and France. West Indian soldiers were involved in the war effort as the islands supplied soldiers and food for the war effort. Churchill, the Conservative Party leader, won the war and lost the peace in that the British Labour Party came to power and formed the first postwar government. The left wing of the anticolonial movement in the English-speaking Caribbean was influenced by British left wing social democracy through the British Labour Party and was encouraged by its electoral victory. Contrary to Winston Churchill's hope that the sun would never set on the British Empire, it was indeed setting: the British Empire faced mass movements against colonial rule in Asia, especially India, in Africa and in the Caribbean.

In Rodney's youth the People's Progressive Party (PPP) led the struggle against British colonial rule, had multiracial support and was the country's first mass party. In 1953 the PPP won 18 out of 24 seats to the Legislative Council but after 100 days in power the British suspended the constitution because they were faced with a party that was genuinely for decolonisation and democracy. Reflecting on this period in the mid 1970s Walter Rodney described the PPP "as the only party in the West Indies which had any pretensions about having a scientific socialist outlook or Marxist outlook or working class outlook" (Walter Rodney 1990: 5). Speaking of the impact of the radical 1940s and 1950s in Guyana on his adult life, Rodney said that it raised in his mind:

> a conviction about the seriousness and potentiality of our own people. My parents, particularly my father, were involved in the early formation of the PPP. I knew those individuals who would come to our house or to whose house my father would go to discuss political organization. As a youngster, I was given the sort of humdrum task to distribute party manifestos which one doesn't necessarily understand, but you come up against certain things. How does a person react when you say to them, here is a PPP manifesto? Do they take it with sympathy? Do they buy a rosette or one of the things that you're trying to sell for the party? Do they chase you away? Do they take it contemptuously? Do they, as happened in one instance, set their dog on you so that you run out of their house? After a while, without knowing anything about class, I knew that there were certain kinds of Guyanese into whose yard one did not go to carry a PPP manifesto. You could tell from the kind of house or the shade or complexion of the lady reclining, sipping her tea, or whatever she may be doing. You don't intervene in that situation and say, "read a PPP manifesto, we're asking for workers to do this and that". That was it at age

eleven. You just have to have a sense of survival, rather than class consciousness, because they might have a Alsatian dog under the house, and they may let it loose on you. This was my first real introduction to the class question (Rodney 1990: 6–7).

Through the involvement of his parents in politics Walter was introduced to the reality of class relations in Guyana as well as the potentiality of the working people in social transformation which was a central theme of his intellectual labour and writings.

If at age 11 he was introduced to class, his introduction to race would have come earlier. Walter Rodney grew up in a racially divided society comprising Asiatic Indians, Africans, Portuguese, native Americans (Amerindians) and Chinese

> in which the majority of one's day to day contacts were with one's own ethnic group. There was a certain isolation, but I did not regard it as a condition of hostility. One inter-related with Indian families and with Indians at school. They were just other Guyanese. But there was that sense that they were out there and that there was potential rivalry and that one had to be on guard. The images that were common in the black community were images, for instance, which set one to thinking that one must of necessity maintain certain standards because the alternative would be the threat of being overcome by Indians. It was a curious kind of double-standard. In one way it was anti-Indian in another sense it raised the Indians to a position of the ideal almost. Black people had a way of saying: you see those Indian students. They go to school and they go back home and they help their parents. So you must help your parents. You see that Indian fellow there, he isn't spending his time round some jukebox joint. He's studying hard. So one must study. It was in a sense competitive and contradictory, but it was almost an idealization (Rodney 1990: 2).

Rodney honestly summarises some of the predispositions of the aspiring Afro-Guyanese middle class towards the Indo-Guyanese population highlighting its competitiveness in the sphere of education, its idealisation of Indian family ties which could lead either to harmless competition or to racial conflict depending on the political or social embers that were being fanned and by whom. This certainly was but one expression of Afro-Guyanese perception of the hard-working Indian youth with a great deal of family devotion. This type of idealisation would have been mixed with other sentiments that would not have been as positive. It all depended on the circumstances, moment in time and the situation for a complex of ethnocentric psychological responses to come into play.

In the late 1940s and early 1950s the nationalist movement struggled for racial harmony, but by the mid 1950s it became politically divided along racial lines, and Forbes Burnham led his own party with the support of the Americans and British. Burnham appealed to the African population as a Guyana Scholar who had been successful in his studies and had returned from London as a lawyer with strong anticolonial views. He had initially thrown in his lot with the People's Progressive Party run by the formidable Jagan couple who had strong support among the Indo-Guyanese population. But the political effort at racial unity in politics faltered and eventually led to the racial riots of 1963–1964. Rodney was then doing postgraduate work in London and was therefore absent from Guyana during those traumatic years. However, his commitment and efforts at promoting multiracial political unity were pursued both in his research and writing on Guyanese history and in his political philosophy which helped to shape the outlook of the Working People's Alliance in the 1970s.

Moreover, the interrelationship between race and class was a central theme of much of his later writings: What factors account for these two social categories of class and race and how are they interconnected in reality? This remained a critical question that Rodney tackled in his writings and political practice; the origins of this crux lay in his early formation as well as in Guyanese nationalist politics.

Walter's brilliance, which was evident from his earliest years in school, gave him some privilege in determining the balance between personal time for study and self-advancement as against domestic chores. Rodney was the second son and appears to have been favoured by his mother especially in being given the lighter household chores. His mother knew the others felt that she treated him differently and defended herself much later on to his wife, Pat Rodney, saying she treated Walter differently "because he treated me differently. Boys who win 11+ scholarships to go to Queen's College don't normally go to the market for their mothers before going to school" (Pat Rodney 1989). On the other hand, Eddie, Walter's older brother, had the responsibility of going to the market and the shop, weeding the yard and doing the gardening. He remembered that "Walter created his own area to be free of household routine and nagging. He would leave minor issues to be dealt with by other persons and concentrate on political or academic issues" (Eddie Rodney 1989). This meant that the burden of domestic chores fell on Eddie and this may have led to sibling rivalry. Walter had the devoted attention of his parents and elder brother. Eddie recalled that as a result of his academic brilliance Walter became 'special', with his father sewing his school uniforms – khaki pants and white shirts – and his mother giving priority to having his meals on time each day before he went to school. After

40 years Eddie remembered that breakfast consisted of porridge with condensed milk and buttered toast, boiled egg and cheese with bread.

Walter's mother, Pauline Rodney, was a hard-working Christian woman whose dressmaking helped to supplement the small income of her husband. She was the quiet centre of the home. She survived Walter by almost nine years, dying in March 1989. Walter's only sister, Kathleen, remembered her father as being somewhat aloof.

> He didn't live too close to us. He was not the fond type of father. His background was a very strict one and he had that same kind of strictness with his children . . . he was very concerned that his family should be in a home. So even if there was not a lot of money we were never scattered about or sent to live with relatives. We never had the feeling of uncertainty that Daddy was not around. He maintained the home (Scott 1989).

Politics was a part of the household as discussions took place with friends about Burnham, Jagan, the race issue and British and American involvement. Percival Rodney's circle of friends also included sportsmen as he had a keen interest in cricket and boxing. Very often when boxers came from Santo Domingo or Brazil he would be asked to act as an interpreter. He did not go to church and Eddie remembers him as an atheist. Their parents were married in a Catholic Church and some of the children were baptised there. Pauline Rodney was confirmed as an Anglican. Kathy recalls her mother being attached to a breakaway group from the Anglican Church known as Mr Bailey's church. The Rodney household was not staunchly religious and when Mr Rodney died in June 1979 the funeral in Georgetown was not a very sacred occasion and the service was performed by Mr Bailey.

Kathy recalled Walter being the only child that had a bicycle and that he would take herself and Donald to the sea wall which was a recreational centre for teenagers. Walter was favoured but was not spoilt, neither was he selfish. A good education was the legacy his parents intended to give their children but given the financial problems facing a working class family it was not easy to do so. It was not possible for them to pay for education through high school so the children had to win scholarships. The more scholarships you won the further you went. Walter gained scholarships all through his academic career from primary school to high school through to his doctorate in England.

The other children were not as fortunate as Walter. Eddie dropped out of high school for economic reasons; Keith dropped out because his father got ill and there were financial problems; Hubert didn't attend high school; and Kathleen's five years at Central High School were partially funded by some of Walter's scholarship money while he was studying in Jamaica and London from 1960 to 1966. Donald, the youngest, did well in high school, was university trained and became a surveyor.

Walter, as was the case with his brothers and sister, attended St Stephen's Church of Scotland School before going on to high school. He studied under the headmastership of Mr C.D. Giddings and was placed in the scholarship class from the third standard class and was taught by him. From St Stephen's he won a scholarship to Queen's College. Entering Queen's was not an easy transition. His parents and brother had to pool resources to ensure that his needs were met. The sacrifices paid off as Walter was an academic success. Describing their entry into Queen's College in 1953 Rohlehr wrote:

> He and I were only two of over 100 scholarship winners to enter Queen's College in 1953, the first and only year of the original PPP (People's Progressive Party) government. In 1952 there had been only 12 scholarships for the entire country, and in previous decades fewer still. Such narrowness of opportunity, normal throughout the Caribbean, bred our bitter mixture of intellectual brilliance and crippled elitism. Our best minds often received an invisible education in the art of creating and preserving distance between themselves and ordinary people, which carried over into their politics (Rohlehr 1980: 3).

Rodney's adult life was evidence of a successful struggle against this invisible education, but in 1953 he could not understand the significance of that process. The year 1953 was significant for three reasons. First, it was the year when the PPP led by Cheddi Jagan won 51 percent of the votes and secured 75 percent of the seats in the Legislative Council and for 133 days formed the government of British Guiana (Greene 1974: 22). Then the British government suspended the constitution and sent in troops to "prevent Communist subversion of the government and a dangerous crisis both in public order and in economic affairs" (Jagan 1972: 125). It was the period of the Cold War and Jagan was seen as a communist politician so British Guiana's domestic politics became enmeshed with the Cold War interests of Britain and the United States. The second reason was the impact of nationalist politics on Rodney's generation. Rohlehr described 1953 "as a moment of original release and opening" (Rohlehr 1980: 3). Rodney's later life was to deal with the negation of this optimism and the degeneration of nationalism. The third significant aspect of 1953 was the expansion of scholarships and the widening of educational opportunities for local youth. For Rohlehr:

> The generation of 1953, then, was something special in that it represented the first attempt in Guyana's history to broaden the popular base of the educated elite, to proletarianize the elite and elitism. Rodney attended Queen's College

between 1953 and 1960 when he won an Open Scholarship to read History at UCWI (University College of the West Indies), Jamaica. I attended between 1953 and 1961 when I won a similar scholarship, also to read History. We were classmates between 1954 and 1960, part of a remarkable class which, though it concentrated on language, classics and history produced students who were equally able at mathematics, physics and chemistry. Indeed, some left the Fifth classical and went straight into the Science Sixth. One was to become distinguished in Mathematics, and I can think of two brilliant surgeons and a score more professional men scattered all over the world (Rohlehr 1980: 3).

Rodney entered Queen's College in 1953, the year when additional scholarships were given in honour of the coronation of Queen Elizabeth II, and was placed in the second form along with Ewart Thomas[1] who became a close friend and scholastic competitor at Queen's College. Walter and Ewart were in the classical stream and Walter outshone everyone in history. He was by then a voracious reader. Indeed, before Walter entered the sixth form he used to go to the public library in Georgetown to read the history books that the Advanced Level students were working on. His essays and examination papers therefore had depth (Thomas 1989).

In 1958 Walter passed ten subjects in the General Certificate of Education (Ordinary Level) set in London. In his next two years at school, history remained his strong subject. But he also loved languages and got a distinction in Spanish at 'A' Levels. He eventually spoke Spanish well, later researched in Spanish, Portuguese and Italian archives, knew Kiswahili, and towards the end of his life was trying to find his way through German. He thus excelled both scholastically and in extracurricular activities. At Queen's College he was President of the Historical Society, Vice President of the Debating Society and editor of the school magazine – *The Lictor*. In 1959 he became a Lance Corporal in the cadet corps and on the basis of excellent performance in his Advanced General Certificate of Education won an Open Arts Scholarship to enter the University College of the West Indies in 1960. At Queen's College he won the Luckoo Memorial debating trophy and Wishart Memorial prize for English. Walter also won several form prizes.

Yet he never had the image of a 'bookworm' as he also excelled in sports. In 1955 he was awarded the prize for the under thirteen high jump; he was third in the under fifteen age group and regained first place in the under seventeen (McGowan 1993).[2] Ewart Thomas, his good friend, came second. In 1959, during Guyana's History and Culture Week, Walter led a debating team for Queen's College which won a motion that "the average Guyanese in the latter half of the nineteenth century enjoyed greater happiness than his counterpart in the early part of the twentieth century" (Thomas 1989). Walter

Rodney and James Croal constituted a formidable debating team for Queen's College. Both boys excelled in their work and won scholarships to the University College of the West Indies.

Walter had in fact been influenced by the early graduates from the University College of the West Indies in the 1950s. One of these was Robert Moore whom Gordon Rohlehr said introduced them to West Indian history and the writings of Eric Williams, Elsa Goveia, Philip Sherlock and Roy Augier (Rohlehr 1980: 3). Moore not only taught history but inculcated in his bright students a love for the idea of the West Indies and its newly formed regional university in Jamaica, with its intellectual atmosphere, its beautiful campus and the pioneering work that was being undertaken in the new discipline of Caribbean history. Given the British bias in education during the colonial years, this new vision was very important in shaping nationalist commitment among the intellectual elite in the region who would have been predisposed to take up scholarships in Britain. In Ewart's case he had the best of both worlds. An outstanding mathematician, he won the Guyana scholarship to Cambridge University and a scholarship to the University College of the West Indies. He went first to Jamaica and then on to England for postgraduate work.

At Queen's College Walter and Ewart formed part of a study group. After school ended they would go home and return to school to study and then they would 'lime'[3] on the streets on their way home. Walter, Ewart and their gang also limed together after the twice a week cadet parade, especially on Friday. They went to a lot of fêtes and spent time together listening to their favourite music such as the Platters from the US and Trinidadian calypso. This close group was mainly Afro-Guyanese. Ewart Thomas' recollections stressed the lighter boyish aspects of growing up in the fifties in Georgetown.

On the other hand, Gordon Rohlehr[4] recalled the turbulence of this period when he wrote:

> I seem to have lived life always on the edge of upheavals, the borders of catastrophe. My early high-school days at Queen's College in Guyana of 1953–1954, took place opposite Eve Leary, a military camp which housed British peace-keeping troops – Royal Welsh Fusiliers, Black Watch, Argyle and Sutherland Highlanders – whose bag-pipe energies failed to prevent racial and political fracture and friction, and civil war in the early sixties. Second term first-year lectures at UCWI, Mona, Jamaica in 1962, were often punctuated by news of looting and burning at home. Wood burns well, and by the time I set out in 1964 for the neuter void of three years at an English University, a good part of the business area of Georgetown had been erased by fire (Rohlehr 1992: i).

Rodney, Rohlehr and others like them were on their way up the social ladder through education and were to spend most of their adult lives out of Guyana. Similar groups of young men and women could be found in the region's best high schools.

Judging from an editorial Walter wrote in *The Lictor – The Queen's College Magazine,* 1958/59, the concerns and aspirations of the young Rodney were not very different from the Guyanese and West Indian middle classes in the middle of the twentieth century. In the editorial entitled "What Price Patriotism?" Rodney bemoaned the plight of the well educated young Guyanese who were expected to lead Guyana into the

> Promised Land of political autonomy and economic self sufficiency, and to bequeath her a cultural identity. But the important question now is what does BG have to offer these students on their return – or rather, if they return . . . earlier this year the three UCWI lecturers who were in BG (British Guiana) to interview prospective students of the University led a discussion which touched on the same subject. For the science students the prospects are quite good and will probably remain so for some time but for the Arts students (who are still in the majority) the future is not very rosy. Young men who return home can find employment in the Civil Service at a salary of $240 per month while females are even more unfortunate and must be prepared to accept $147.00 (Rodney 1958/1959).

Rodney went on to complain about the poor chances of promotion in the civil service and to point to the necessity for financial inducements to encourage Guyanese to return home. Rodney himself when he left British Guiana in 1960 did not return to settle permanently until fourteen years later in 1974. The article ends with a glimmer of two themes that would feature in Rodney's writings and activism. These are the struggle against the fear of victimisation and links between the intellectuals and the people. Of the Guyanese who returned home after studying abroad he wrote:

> Guyanese who returned home with optimism in their breasts were speedily disillusioned in their country's future and were quite satisfied with a modicum of social and economic security. Others became narrowminded and refrained from any agitation for improvement for fear that they would get a black mark against their names and perhaps hamper their chances of further promotion, forgetting that their biggest black mark is their skin and their history. Lastly, there are a few who lose the common touch and eventually identify themselves with the master race. Independence would go a long way towards dispelling these various attitudes of fear, apathy and hostility; since the country is

independent, by itself, and the chances are that the instinct of self-preservation would assert itself (Rodney 1958/1959).

Rodney's sanguine hopes for independence were reflected in the fact that he appears to have been active in the campaign for Forbes Burnham in the 1961 election since, according to Ewart Thomas, he returned to Guyana from Jamaica to campaign for Burnham (Thomas 1989). This is not surprising as Burnham "was an idol for Black Guyanese" and some parents named their sons Forbes Burnham in his honour. Having come from a poor background, Burnham had succeeded as an eloquent lawyer and political leader who had a way with words and people. Like most nationalist politicians of the mid twentieth century he, like Jagan, embodied the hopes of many as the colonial years receded.

Pat Rodney recalled that one of the big influences on her early life was Jessica Burnham, sister of Forbes Burnham, who taught her at primary school. Jessica was "very brilliant, also a very brave woman. And I can remember trying to be like her, she was somebody I liked very much and we had a very good relationship" (Pat Rodney 1989).

Rodney's political opposition to Burnham seemed to have developed while studying in London in the mid 1960s. Yet at that time and certainly well into the 1970s Burnham's credentials in the progressive movement in and outside of Guyana remained strong. But by the mid 1970s cracks had started to appear in Burnham's shield inside of Guyana while outside he remained an anti-imperialist figure in the eyes of the leaders of some Third World states in Africa and the Caribbean. He was seen as an ally by the regime of Fidel Castro, and was classified in Washington as such.

By the time his years at Queen's College – 1953–1960 – had ended Walter had been shaped and his talents were already apparent. He knew what he wanted academically and would advance towards his doctorate in six years. A stable and very supportive family had sacrificed for him and he in turn would contribute financially to his family from his scholarship funds. By this time he had also met Pat Henry who later became his wife.

Pat Henry's parents were also of working class background. Her father, Wilfred Henry, was a unionised stevedore and her mother Louisa Henry was a housewife who reared hens, sold eggs and a few things that she baked. There were ten children, six girls and four boys, and Pat was the second-to-last child. She went to high school in Guyana in preparation for a career in nursing. Her father was very strict.

> My father didn't approve of things like you standing on a corner to talk to boys. If we had to go to a party my father wanted you to inform him like two weeks

before . . . When boys visited the house, sometimes it was embarrassing . . . He would always come downstairs to fetch his clock as a signal it was time for them to leave . . . I remember when Walter and I went home for the first time in 1967 . . . Daddy said it was because of him I got such a good husband, because he protected me (Pat Rodney 1989).

It was a typical West Indian patriarchal set-up. Pat was partial to her father because "you knew where you stood with him, he would either say yes or no, but my mother would say, go and ask your father . . ." (Pat Rodney 1989). Recalling her acquaintance with Walter in British Guiana, Pat revealed:

I knew of Walter a long time because I had friends, a particular friend, I think she was Walter's girl friend at primary school and Walter's name was well known in Guyana, even when he was at secondary school, so I would go with other friends, listen to him debate for the debating society, so I knew of him but in a very casual way (Pat Rodney 1989).

In the summer of 1960 the relationship moved from a casual affair to a serious one. It was not long before she left to study nursing in London and he to enter the University College of the West Indies. They corresponded and he visited London in the summer of 1962 before going there in 1963 to do his doctorate. Pat and Walter got married in 1965.

Walter Rodney was a bright scholarship boy who through academic success achieved social mobility and intellectual standing in a society where many placed a high premium on education as a means of social and economic advancement. With the end of colonialism and the political advances of the nationalist movement, opportunities opened up in an unprecedented way for the better-off sections of the African population to enter middle class occupations and attain relative privilege and status. Rodney's short adult life was a challenge to the apparently normal trajectory of secure tenure as a university professor with an international reputation as a historian and development theorist and with numerous options for good positions in North America or Europe. The choice he made was essentially a political one and that meant gearing his talents towards effecting an agenda of radical decolonisation in Africa and the Caribbean, and constantly clarifying what it meant to put himself at the service of his people from both an academic and political standpoint. This shaped his approach to African and Caribbean history as much as did his determination not to leave Guyana after his return in 1974 in the face of political victimisation arising from the dictatorial rule of President Forbes Burnham.

A product of colonial education in the twilight years of British colonial rule, Rodney became part of the intellectual elite who pioneered the rethinking and rewriting of African and Caribbean history. Influenced by Frantz Fanon, Amilcar Cabral and C.L.R. James, Rodney embraced Marxism and brought to it a critical approach rooted in actual historical processes which made his theorising as well as political practice different from the dogmatic and partisan pro-Soviet or pro-China currents that dominated the Third World left in the 1960s and 1970s.

Notes

1. Ewart Thomas was a close friend from childhood. See Thomas (1982) for his tribute to Walter Rodney. When he wrote this piece Thomas was professor of psychology at Stanford University.
2. Walter's athletic skills were to be emulated by his daughter Kanini at the University of the West Indies, Jamaica campus, in the 1980s.
3. 'Liming' is a Trinidadian term for passing time with a group of people.
4. Gordon Rohlehr is the distinguished Caribbean literary scholar who has published on Edward Braithwaite and written on the early history of the calypso in Trinidad and Tobago. His essays have been collected in two volumes – (1992a and 1992b). See Rohlehr (1980) for an essay on Rodney.

CHAPTER 2

University Years 1960–1966

Coming from the best high schools in the British Caribbean colonies in the twilight years of colonial rule and having gained distinctions in their sixth form subjects, scholarship winners could compete academically with any 17 or 18 year old in any part of the world. They were the cream of the crop and would become the elite, stepping into the political and bureaucratic positions vacated by the British. There was no question of racial inferiority when it came to books and book learning. There was a strong commitment to academic success for it was a ticket not only to knowledge but to social mobility. The competition for scholarships had been stiff, as Eric Williams related in his autobiography *Inward Hunger*, and only one or two were able to go to England to pursue a university education. With the coming of a regional university,[1] the best from the high schools at first went to the Mona campus in Jamaica, later St Augustine in Trinidad and then the Cave Hill campus in Barbados. So many more students were now able to pursue a university education.

The University of the West Indies at Mona was established in 1948 as a college "in relationship with the University of London. It achieved university status in 1962, becoming a degree granting institution in its own right" (Public Relations Office [PRO] 1987: 1). The Medical Faculty started in 1948 with 33 students, the Natural Sciences followed in 1949, Arts in 1950, and eight years later the Faculty of Social Sciences was established. The second campus was founded in 1960 when the Imperial College of Tropical Agriculture "was incorporated into the University College, thus becoming the first Faculty of the College outside of Jamaica. The Faculty of

Engineering was established at St Augustine in the following year, 1961" (PRO 1987: 1).

The third campus was established in 1963 at Cave Hill in Barbados, "offering courses in Arts and Natural Sciences which were also introduced at St Augustine. In 1970 the Faculty of Law was established at Cave Hill" (PRO 1987: 1).

Walter Rodney entered the University College of the West Indies in 1960 and graduated from the University of the West Indies in 1963. At that time the Mona campus had a genuinely regional student body with a Caribbean atmosphere. The region's brightest young women and men from Barbados, Antigua, Trinidad and Tobago, St Lucia, Grenada, St Vincent and Guyana met Jamaican students for the first time, and the cultural interchange helped to smooth out some of the rougher edges of nationalism among Jamaican students. With the development of the other two campuses the Mona campus was robbed of its regional flavour and interaction and settled into becoming a Jamaican rather than a Caribbean campus. However, by that time the Trinidadian students had successfully introduced a version of their carnival to the Mona campus with calypso, steel pan music, masquerade bands and fêtes.

The Jamaican campus was well situated and lived up to the expectations of the new students who had heard about the Mona plains spreading over 600 acres, protected by a picturesque mountain range. Then there were the aqueduct ruins of the old sugar estate and the chapel, the stones of which had been taken from an eighteenth century Georgian building on a sugar-producing slave estate in the parish of Trelawny. Not many students saw any significance in these stones that built the chapel. But occasionally preachers in the chapel reminded worshippers that the stones that once symbolised the burden of slavery now represented freedom.

Nation building and independence, optimism and rationalism were central themes in the period of institutional redesign which marked the end of three centuries of British rule. The university itself was one such institution which reflected regional aspirations that hopefully would coalesce the different island nationalisms into a force for decolonisation.

Dr Arthur Lewis, the first Vice Chancellor of the University of the West Indies and later a Nobel prize winner in economics, argued in support of a West Indian orientation.[2] He said:

> Britain is an industrial, urbanised, racially homogenous community, with small closely knit families, while the West Indies is agricultural, rural and racially mixed, with a unique family system. No amount of modification could produce a social science syllabus which fitted both Britain and the West Indies. Or if

you take medicine, the London medical degree includes neither Public Health nor Psychiatry, since in Britain both these fields are left to specialists. But in the West Indies we train a doctor who goes out into the country for his first job and may find himself doing both Public Health work and Psychiatry, so we need these subjects in our medical training (Lewis 1962: 13).

Lewis placed a lot of emphasis on developing the research capability of the university and in attracting funding. He said:

We have an obligation to the West Indies to do first class research into West Indian problems of all kinds, social, medical, engineering, linguistics, agricultural, and so on. Research and teaching are intimately linked both ways. You don't get first class teaching staff unless you are doing first class research, and if you are doing first class research the standards of teaching will be high. Given the amount of money that is pouring into the University from research foundations for research of all kinds, there is much more danger that our standards may be too high than that they may be too low (Lewis 1962: 13, 15).

The academic values implicit in these statements shaped the recruitment of staff and the philosophy of the university. They were shared to some extent by Walter Rodney who, as a revolutionary intellectual, did not fundamentally challenge these principles insofar as his own commitment to academic excellence was concerned. In this sense Rodney was very much in the intellectual tradition of Eric Williams and Arthur Lewis. It was C.L.R. James who was to teach him Marxism. But James shared similar intellectual values with both Arthur Lewis and Eric Williams. Moreover, all four – C.L.R. James, Arthur Lewis, Eric Williams and Walter Rodney – were strong Caribbean regionalists.

Eric Williams and Arthur Lewis were the outstanding West Indian intellectuals trained in British universities who returned to provide leadership in the transition to independence and to shape the region's new institutions. They pinned their hopes on the evolution of a West Indian nation comprising all the English-speaking territories and governed through a federal parliament. Many students from the Mona campus went on speaking tours in support of federation and Rodney was among them. On positions such as this he was sympathetic towards Norman Manley and the People's National Party (PNP), especially the young people who were active in the Young Socialist League. The Federation was launched in 1958. However, in 1961 Jamaica voted against staying in the West Indian Federation and after that referendum Eric Williams was to say that after Jamaica's vote, "One from ten leaves nought."

After the Jamaican vote against federation in 1961 Arthur Lewis continued his advocacy for a federation of the Eastern Caribbean. There is a memorable description of Lewis' abilities and commitment in John Mordecai's book, *The West Indian Federation*:

> After long argument the (British) Secretary of State asked that a document be produced containing their idea, also on the subject of a caretaker organization ... the Chief Ministers ... asked Professor Lewis to prepare a memorandum giving the outlines of a constitution, a budget and the financial structure of a federation of Eight. This formidable document would be required next day ... Having no fear of the impossible, Lewis completed the document overnight and circulated it next morning (quoted in Sherlock and Nettleford 1990: 117).

Sherlock and Nettleford noted that Lewis

> was harder on himself than on others, demanded high standards and hard work, made no parade of patriotism and gave more than those who did. He need not have come to the University; the need to keep the University strong, independent and West Indian pulled him back. He need not have tried to preserve an Eastern Caribbean federation after Jamaica's secession but his concern for the future of the West Indian people compelled him to do so (Sherlock and Nettleford 1990: 117).

As Principal, Lewis had introduced the system whereby officers of the Guild Council, the executive of the student body, "should meet with him every fortnight to discuss plans and problems" (UCWI 1960/61: 9) and the Guild Council was very pleased with this development. Lewis served as Principal and Vice Chancellor of the university from 1959 to 1963, and it is not surprising that before he left to take up an offer from Princeton University as Professor of Economics, Rodney was one of the campaigners for Lewis to remain as head of the University of the West Indies.

Another important intellectual and political shaper of those years was Eric Williams[3] who addressed the graduating class on 16 February 1962. Trinidad and Tobago, of which he was Premier, was then only six months away from independence. Williams' opening remarks were cryptic:

> Your university came on the scene too late. In conception it was too narrow. It was too rapidly overtaken by the political evolution in the area that it served. It grew too slowly. Its period of tutelage lasted too long, but the checkered career, Ladies and Gentlemen, is behind you (Williams 1963: 4).

Speaking in the context of Jamaica's secession from federation Williams refashioned the motto of Jamaica "Out of many, one people" and devised

"Out of many Governments, one University"; in other words, he saw the regional university as a symbol of intellectual unity (Williams 1963: 4). For Williams this intellectual unity was broader than the English-speaking area and ought to have embraced the Dutch, French and Spanish subregions. Williams' speech was full of optimism and rationalism. Having graduated from Oxford in 1935, he was probably the only person in his "graduating class who didn't regard colonialism in the West Indies as one of the eternal verities" (Williams 1963: 7).

Williams and Lewis were lone rangers intellectually who studied and obtained academic honours very much like the African-American scholar, W.E.B. Dubois,[4] in white dominated academic establishments where racism prevailed. Lewis and Williams belonged to the generation of preindependence nationalist intellectuals who were regarded as the exception rather than the rule as far as blacks were concerned. Furthermore, they never had the possibility of a Caribbean intellectual community which a regional university afforded. Drawing on a cricket anecdote, Williams related:

> Not so many years ago I believe that the West Indians went to England for the first time and somebody asked them why they had come, and one of the great West Indian cricketers said, 'Sir, we come to learn.' I am sure that in 1963 we go to teach (Williams 1963: 7).

Indeed, the West Indian intellectual community was to be defined, not only by its identification with the successes of the West Indian cricket team and its university, but also by its artists and writers, many of whom had migrated to England. The 1950s and 1960s had seen the emergence of a generation of West Indian writers who were to excel in the craft of writing fiction and creating poetry and drama. Among the prominent authors were Edgar Mittelholzer and Wilson Harris of Guyana, Roger Mais, Andrew Salkey and John Hearne (Jamaica), Sam Selvon and Vidia Naipaul (Trinidad), George Lamming and Edward Braithwaite (Barbados), Derek Walcott (St Lucia). The Jamaican cultural scene was being shaped by Rex Nettleford in dance,[5] in painting by Albert Huie,[6] and in sculpture by Edna Manley.[7] Derek Walcott,[8] 1992 Nobel prize winner for literature, had been on the Mona campus in the 1950s writing poetry and plays, and so had Rex Nettleford who had started his career as a scholar and dancer. Among Rodney's colleagues in Chancellor Hall was the sociologist and novelist Orlando Patterson.[9]

In 1962 the Literary Society at the university celebrated the work of West Indian writers with an evening of readings from Wilson Harris, Vidia Naipaul, George Lamming, John Hearne, Edgar Mittelholzer and Samuel

Selvon. The Dancing and Gymnastic Society presented the National Dance Theatre Company (NDTC) with co-directors Rex Nettleford and Eddy Thomas. The presentation featured Nettleford's "Roots and Rhythms" as well as Lavinia Williams' Haitian dances. Marjorie Whylie, composer, drummer and pianist, was then an undergraduate in the Faculty of Arts and a musician with the NDTC.[10] Dennis Scott,[11] who was a dancer, was then active as poet and playwright in a manner that mirrored Derek Walcott's creative work on the Mona campus in the 1950s.

Rodney came to Mona in 1960 to study history. However, his friend, Ewart Thomas, thought he would have done a degree in the social sciences as this was a new area suitable for someone who had such a strong interest in development. But history was what Rodney loved, what he did best, and the History Department had excellent Caribbean scholars such as Elsa Goveia, Douglas Hall, and Roy Augier. Elsa Goveia was herself from Guyana and was appointed in her thirties in 1960/61 to the newly created Chair of West Indian History.

Franklin Knight, History Professor at Johns Hopkins University, who was Rodney's junior and companion debater in Chancellor Hall and who edited and prepared Rodney's *History of the Guyanese Working People* for publication following his death, recalled:

> Elsa Goveia's influence was critical. She encouraged research. She had an incisive mind. You never got away with sloppy thinking. She instilled in you the confidence that what you were doing could stand up with the best. She liked research and set high standards and encouraged her students to set high standards for themselves (Knight 1988).

Walter continued his wide reading at Mona where the library was much better stocked than in Georgetown and where he had access to the personal libraries of staff members. Moreover, books that were not available in the Caribbean could easily be purchased or borrowed from the University of London. His skills as a debater were further developed as he represented not only Chancellor Hall, his hall of residence, but the university. In the academic year 1960–1961, Walter, then a first year student, was elected President of the Debating Society. Walter Rodney and Selwyn Walter from Antigua were chosen to represent the university in its annual debate with Pittsburgh University. In Pittsburgh the 'two Walters' won themselves speaking awards. The return debate was held in Kingston and the Pittsburgh Debating Union opposed the moot "Be it resolved that the United Nations is justified in refusing membership to Red China" (Knight 1988). The team of the 'two Walters' won again. Walter Rodney was a guest debater of the Sixth Form

Association and he also participated in a West Indian debating tour. The most intense debates were the interhall debates between Chancellor, Taylor, Irvine and Mary Seacole Halls. Chancellor Hall's team of Walter Rodney and Franklin Knight won the Alcan trophy in 1961/62. This was the second year that Rodney was on the winning team. Knight described Rodney as "having an almost singular quality of mind. He was the smartest guy I ever knew. In a minute Rodney could demolish the argument of his opponent. He would have made an absolutely brilliant lawyer. He also had a good sense of humour" (Knight 1988).

One of the memorable events of the Debating Society was a 'raft' debate held in February 1963

> where it was surmised that four prominent leaders (a capitalist, communist, evangelist and a Rastafarian) were on a slow-sinking raft. A helicopter would rescue the one who could best argue his continued existence. The speakers were Richard Fletcher – Jamaican third year student in Economics – the capitalist; Ronny Manderson-Jones – Jamaican first year History student – the communist; Walter Rodney – 3rd year History – the Rastafarian and Colin Moore – Guyanese 3rd year Economics student – the evangelist (University of the West Indies 1963: 2).

That debate formed part of a week of celebrations from 11 to 16 February commemorating the university's independence and was won by the evangelist, Colin Moore,[12] a Guyanese student.

Having made a name for himself on campus as an intellectually gifted student and debater and a very sociable person,[13] it was not surprising that Rodney should participate in electoral student politics. However, his two attempts at the presidency of the Student Guild were unsuccessful. In 1961/62 Aidan Layne, a Barbadian student, was elected and in 1962/63 Gloria Lannaman, a talented Jamaican student, won the presidency. Having lost a no-confidence vote, Gloria Lannaman did not serve her full term and was succeeded by Selwyn Walter from Antigua. Having failed at the presidency, Walter served in the Guild Council in the academic year 1961/62 as Director of Guild Press. Then in 1962 the Extrenal Affairs Commission of the Guild sponsored a visit to Cuba which was a very bold step given the anticommunist atmosphere in Jamaica. Members of the delegation included Richard Fletcher, Winston Davis and Walter Rodney. As a result of this visit Winston Davis had passport troubles for most of the 1960s and Walter Rodney came to the attention of the Jamaican Special Branch which dealt with matters affecting national security. Rodney later spoke of his trip to Cuba and recalled the excitement of those days. He said "I was fortunate in visiting Cuba twice, only for brief periods, but long enough to get that fire and dynamic of the Cuban Revolution" (Rodney 1990: 18). In 1962 he visited Leningrad, representing the University of the West Indies at a conference of the International Union of Students. In Leningrad he met Richard Small, then a law student who was representing the Federation of West Indian Students Union in Britain and who was later to become a personal friend and family lawyer. Rodney therefore had some contact with the Cuban Revolution, which was then independent of Moscow, and of the Soviet Union during its Krushchev and Brezhnev years. His lectures[14] on the Russian Revolution, given at the University of Dar es Salaam in the late 1960s and early 1970s, show how familiar he was with the literature on it and how much he had mastered Marxist historical methodology in studying revolutionary processes. Thus by his early twenties he was already fairly well travelled but had many more miles to go.

In a pen sketch, written by Norman Girvan, for the university's student publication, *Pelican Annual* 1961–1962, Walter Rodney's spirit and character as well as his intellectual abilities and relationship to his community were summed up quite accurately:

> To have been beaten twice in the race for the Presidency of the Guild is a record about which few would boast but to which one student does lay claim. But those who think that Walter Rodney would have been crushed (in any sense) by this unique experience underrate the profound self-assurance and capacity for detachment that he possesses.
>
> Rodney has never enjoyed the halo of the charismatic leader, nor has he ever sought it out. Rather he has always put his faith in speaking and in writing, in rigorous analysis and inflexible logic. When he has arrived at a conclusion or has come to hold an opinion, he articulates it publicly and persuasively with a sometimes arrogant disregard for the consequences in terms of his own personal popularity. Thus it was that he debated for the UCWI at Pittsburgh but two months after his arrival; and still in his freshman year, mobilised overwhelming support for Prof. Lewis when he threatened to resign.
>
> But fate and the student body have strange ways of dealing with those whose abilities bring them into prominence. In a society which should value intellectualism, the greatest crime a student can commit is to appear to be intellectual. Although elected to RUWIS (Regional Union of West Indies Students), Rodney was beaten on both tries for the Presidency by persons conservative by temperament and opinions. On the first occasion, the charge against him was that he was a dictator because of an innocent (but impolitic) remark on election eve. On the second, he was called a communist, because of a visit to Cuba, and the literature with which he returned.

Walter's defeat was thus not only a personal one – it was a defeat for the intellectual spirit itself. He is not the first to be martyred on the altar of anti-intellectualism on this campus, nor will he be the last. As a symbol only, he deserves to be called a personality. And as a person, his abilities, and his fundamental honesty, can never be called in question (Girvan 1961–1962: 110–11).

This "fundamental honesty" was to mark his entire career as a historian and political activist. Rodney shared the Student of the Year prize in 1962 with Gloria Lannaman. Norman Girvan, who became a well-known economist, shared the coveted prize with Grace Jackson in 1961. James Croal, Rodney's debating partner, won it in 1963. As Girvan had indicated, electoral defeat did not stop him from pursuing his academic and extra-curricular activities.

Rodney's publications included contemporary issues. The search for an identity and the efforts at self-definition were key themes during the early sixties (Nettleford 1970). The thinking out of political and economic alternatives complemented the cultural quest. The character of Caribbean societies that had been shaped by slavery, sugar plantations and colonial rule was analysed by historians and social scientists, and new paradigms were being developed. It is in the intellectual environment of the University that Rodney took up issues that he later developed. In the *Pelican Annual* 1961–1962 he co-authored a thoughtful article with Earl Augustus entitled "Some Political Aspects of Independence". It is a concentrated piece that brings together a number of interesting propositions. First, Augustus and Rodney take the view that:

> in the West Indies there has been plenty of 'political trickstering' but little sincere attempt to expose the population to arguments which may enable them to make rational and informed decisions. Having begun along these lines the worthy Premier of Trinidad and Tobago, Dr Eric Williams, has apparently given up the effort (Augustus and Rodney 1961–1962: 10).

The role of the masses in the making of history and in government and their political education became central issues in Rodney's academic research, writing and political practice. In a sense he was to emulate Eric Williams who, at the euphemistically termed 'University of Woodford Square', had in the 1950s educated a generation of Trinidadians in West Indian history, politics and contemporary issues.

Augustus and Rodney were not taken in by the symbols of independence but looked critically at its substance. For them "democracy can only work when the people are given clear alternatives and when the machinery is present so that the masses can participate in the decision-making process" (Augustus and Rodney 1961–1962: 90).

On the question of ideology, Augustus and Rodney were naturally critical of colonial values and attitudes but "they also felt that one should not view the region from the standpoint of the British Labour Party Socialist, or even a Marxist-Leninist" (Augustus and Rodney 1961–1962: 91). These two trends were strong in the Young Socialist League which was made up of a group of radical intellectuals connected to Norman Manley's People's National Party. Augustus and Rodney eschewed "looking outside for the solutions to internal problems" and took the eclectic position, "it may well be that we can adopt some fundamental way of looking at the world from other communities, and that we can borrow various techniques used by countries in a similar position" (Augustus and Rodney 1961–1962: 91).

The authors, in taking up the question of the role of the middle class, contended that:

> Since 1938 a middle-class elite group has ruled in most of the islands. The members of this group are experts at making and breaking constitutions, but in so far as values are concerned they have little to offer the community, and their departure would be welcome even if they all have to be pensioned off. The only replacement for the present 'establishment' are those who can be counted on to define clear goals in a more objective manner. That is to say while this new elite may be middle class it will not share middle class biases. One has only to consider by way of example that the middle class intelligentsia is more susceptible to revolutionary ideas than the proletariat, to realise that the idea of such leadership is by no means strange. The emphasis is laid on group leadership rather than on the elevation of a single individual, since, although the charisma of a particular leader is useful and virtually inevitable in a small community it is unwise to perpetuate the personal cultism which now exists in West Indian politics. It is not over-optimistic to suppose that the University can produce such an elite group (Augustus and Rodney 1961–1962: 92).

This quote sums up many of the key concerns in Rodney's political assessment. First, there is the attempt to analyse the West Indian middle classes, coupled with an idealistic wish that the university could be a cradle for the creation of middle class leaders who would be revolutionary. Augustus and Rodney did not write off the middle class but looked to the more enlightened and progressive sections, among which the authors would obviously count themselves. The writers also tried to deal with the problem of West Indian charismatic leaders who arrogated unto themselves supreme power and who cultivated a following loyal to them. The party machinery became their instrument and did not evolve as a democratic institution. Looking at the role of the University and the middle class, the authors came out against "the urbane detachment of the British University", arguing that it was a luxury that could not be afforded and opted instead for the dynamic role of the Latin American universities. The role of the university and of the intellectuals were themes Rodney returned to in 1968 in many talks on the Mona campus as well as on the Dar es Salaam campus in the 1960s and 1970s.

Augustus and Rodney felt very strongly that C.L.R. James had a major role to play in the postcolonial Caribbean. James had visited the campus in 1959 to give a series of lectures which had been cut short by a car accident. His work with the People's National Movement (PNM) in Trinidad and his editing of its organ, *The Nation*, had put him in an active political relationship with the West Indian population. His erudition, lecturing skills and political outlook endeared him to young West Indian intellectuals and it is not surprising that some of them within the university tried unsuccessfully to get him on the staff. According to Lloyd Best, "James was denied the Research Fellowship (which had been endorsed by the whole college of scholars at the Institute of Social and Economic Research) on the interesting ground that he was only a pamphleteer" (Best 1990: 17).[15] Political opposition to James' radicalism, academic snobbery based on his lack of university degrees, would have combined to frustrate the efforts of the younger academics. Like them, Augustus and Rodney contended that:

> gifted individuals in the society must always be wooed since their insights can be of great help in formulating policy. One is minded to cite C.L.R. James whose contribution to Trinidad and the West Indies has not been inconsiderable. It shall be the function of such individual thinkers, of the planners, and of the political leaders, constantly to reassess the national situation (Augustus and Rodney 1961–1962: 95).

The overall tone of this article bore no trace of cynicism. Rather it was full of positivist idealism, so typical of the optimism of the early independence years and of political thinkers in their twenties, but it was not naive about political realities. Rodney had an excellent mind that had been challenged and stimulated by faculty in the humanities such as Elsa Goveia and Roy Augier and in the social sciences by Lloyd Braithwaite, Raymond Smith, Michael Smith, Chandra Jayawardena, David Edwards, Archie Singham, Lloyd Best and students at Mona in the early sixties, but more importantly by the pressing issues of decolonisation which independence had put on the agenda.

He had as strong an interest in contemporary issues as he did in history and he was well read in the literature of the social sciences. This emerges in his paper, "The Role of the Historian in the Developing West Indies". Here he argued that "there is no essential difference between history and the social sciences... I always insist on telling my colleagues in the social science faculty that history is the father of the social sciences" (Rodney 1963: 13).[16] He elaborated on this link, claiming that the

> first task of the social scientist in the West Indies is really to augment his own forces. There is so much to be done and so few people to do it... The second important task of the historian and the sociologist, especially the former, is to look at West Indian society from within rather than from without. It is one of the tasks of the historian of the West Indies to approach the society in a different manner and to lay emphasis on precisely what was going on within the region. This would certainly lead to the presentation of new heroes with whom the West Indian people would identify themselves – an important psychological necessity... In determining where we go from here, there are three broad points to be noticed. Firstly although for convenience social problems are arbitrarily split up into social, political and economic spheres everyone is aware that the inter-relationships cannot be broken. It follows therefore that if social scientists are involved in planning each specialist would not work in isolation. Secondly the area of the West Indies is meant to have more than just geographical significance. Culturally and historically it is an entity and it is likely that at some time the dictates of economic rationality will overcome political shortsightedness. Finally the social scientist is not working in a vacuum but with and for a particular public. It is not as though many of the problems outlined so far have not already been tackled by historians, sociologists and anthropologists, but their findings are well known only to a few. It is not too much to ask the University to assume the responsibility for popularising such knowledge. At an early stage the people must be informed so as to be better able to define their image of the good society (Rodney 1963a: 16).

This perception of the close relationship between history and the social sciences bore fruit in Rodney's classic 1972 text *How Europe Underdeveloped Africa* and informed many of his lectures and academic papers.

In fact, Lloyd Best lists Rodney among a group of students whose work influenced the seminal New World Group of the 1960s.

> It was only in 1961 that the West Indian Society for the Study of Social Issues emerged out of the cross-fertilization between a rare collection of talents including Walter Rodney, David Beckles, Adlith Brown, David Dabydeen, Orlando Patterson, Norman Girvan and Eric Abrahams. It was the first

incarnation of what came to be called the New World Group after the quarterly journal issued by kindred spirits in Georgetown in March 1963 just about the time that British Guiana was breaking away from the UWI and establishing a campus of its own (Best 1990: 13).

So at Mona Rodney had become a Caribbean nationalist with a strong regionalist perspective. Yet within this framework his preoccupation with Guyana's development remained strong. In an article entitled, "B.G. – Some New Dimensions" written for the *Pelican*, he analysed the political situation in his homeland in a detached manner, not betraying any idea of the side he supported. It may be that he was re-examining his own position which would have been close to that of Burnham. He was critical of the right wing in British Guiana but as between Jagan and Burnham he was objective. He observed that Jagan, who was then in government, was being propelled more towards the East (i.e., the communist world) and the People's National Congress (PNC) more towards the West.

> The PNC has been most unsuccessful in the attempt to project a socialist image. On the one hand Dr Jagan has always been the darling of the socialists and the left-wing elements both in the West and the East often stigmatise Burnham as the betrayer of the national movement. On the other hand the moderates and the conservatives have never been quite convinced that a distinction could really be made on ideological grounds between Burnham and Jagan and with the rise of D'Aguiar the right-wing has been provided with a genuine champion. Burnham has been more concerned of late with drawing the line between himself and Jagan and establishing his probity in the eyes of the West. That a coalition with D'Aguiar should have been given serious consideration is evidence of this fact. Now more than ever the PNC seems likely to shape its policy with an eye on the US and an ear for the local US officials (Rodney 1963b: 9).

This was an accurate analysis of the orientation of the two main contenders in Guyanese politics in the 1960s in the context of the Cold War superpower rivalry between the USA and the Soviet Union.

But among Rodney's student essays was an article coauthored with Earl Augustus called "The Negro Slave" that was published in *Caribbean Quarterly* in 1964, thereby initiating a career of distinguished academic writing. Rodney's involvement with Caribbean history under the guidance of Roy Augier, Douglas Hall and Elsa Goveia led him to his interest in understanding the background of the slaves in Africa. There is a particular experience he recalled with one of his professors who had given an assignment to look at Europe and Africa and their relevance to the Caribbean. Rodney said:

> I attempted to answer that by suggesting that both Europe and Africa were equally important. But, as I recall it, I could readily illustrate why I thought that Europe was important. I had a facility for drawing upon a range of common historical assumptions which I shared with the British at that time, and still do actually, to indicate why Europe was relevant. But I could only say Africa was relevant at a sort of intuitive level. Outside of some vague generalizations, I couldn't articulate why Africa was relevant. So eventually it was necessary to move in that direction (Rodney 1990: 14).

Rodney's inability was one that was shared by virtually everyone else in the Caribbean. It was known that Africa was one of the chief ancestral sources of the region's peoples. But mention of Africa was shunned and nowhere within the educational system was there factual treatment of the continent and its peoples, either historically or in the modern era. It remained a vague entity, thoughts of which were believed best abandoned on the basis of visual images of 'barbarity'.

After graduating with first class honours in history in 1963, Rodney went on to fill that emotive and cognitive gap that he had perceived as an undergraduate. He pursued doctoral research in African history at the School of Oriental and African Studies (SOAS) in London, and became one of the outstanding scholars in African history in the 1960s and 1970s. This intellectual excursion into Africa had important historical and ideological significance in the Caribbean, given the denigration and self-denigration of people of African descent in the region and the thirst for knowledge that existed in some quarters.

Another ideological underpinning of his work was his Marxism to which his Guyanese experience had made him receptive. But another impetus was his Jamaican experience which was to prove important in developing his sense of the Caribbean's regional potential as well as his own personal, intellectual and career trajectories. With regard to Jamaica he commented:

> there is a different pace of life in Jamaica, probably due to the fact that the population is larger and more concentrated. But there definitively is a greater pace. Trinidadians try to assume the role of city slickers almost, and are clever and fast, but for staying power, for sheer energy, Jamaican people seem to have us all beat. It's not surprising that there should be a universalising tendency when different Caribbean people get together to fall into certain Jamaican idioms, certainly to use the swear words. Jamaicans can curse more proficiently

than any other Caribbean people. They have such a range of words describing phenomena so neatly and I think this is a testimony to their combativeness. So that I always felt that there must be tremendous revolutionary potential in that island.

One also saw it when one went to London. The Jamaicans were the largest group in London and they were also the most important group. I would really say that their sense of combativeness nipped British racism in the bud. Jamaicans had a way of striking back that did not brook too much playing about . . . Jamaicans would take on a whole railway station if necessary and would move forward to single out a white man, snatch him and hit him. The lesson was learnt. After a while when you met people in England and you said you were from the West Indies, they would say, oh you're a Jamaican (Rodney 1990: 10–11).

Several factors differentiated Jamaica from the rest of the English-speaking Caribbean. First, Jamaica had emerged from slavery and colonialism with a more violent social history and rugged past than most of the other islands. Evidence for this is the large-scale slave revolts in the eighteenth century, the small settlers' revolt of 1865 in St Thomas and its brutal suppression.[17] Twentieth century Jamaica has continued to be a volatile polity and the intensity and scale of its political violence has been unsurpassed in the West Indian region. Secondly, Jamaica was more economically developed and in the 1950s and 1960s had experienced economic growth, due to the investment of North American capital in the bauxite/alumina industry and tourism, coupled with a fairly thriving export agriculture in sugar and bananas. This had positive implications for government revenue, for local business, the expansion of the middle classes and the growth of the working class, especially in construction and the new economic sectors. But there was also an underbelly of extreme poverty in the rural and urban areas. Far too many people lived in squalor.

Social differentiation in Jamaica was more marked than anywhere else in the English-speaking Caribbean and this would have been obvious to students coming to Jamaica from other territories. It is true that Port of Spain had its Woodbrook middle class residential areas, but moving out of that area there was considerable residential overlap between middle and lower income social groups. The same was true generally speaking of Bridgetown in Barbados and Georgetown, Guyana. Residential differentiation had become more marked in Kingston with the development of middle income housing estates. This social and class differentiation had given Jamaica a middle class that had achieved social mobility and status, but was at the same time somewhat paranoid about colour in its preference for lighter complexions.

Sections of the middle class were socially pretentious and abusive towards household helpers and gardeners, thereby reproducing the master/servant stereotype of colonial society. The Kingston middle class certainly felt it was better off than its counterparts elsewhere in the region. Jamaica also had a more sophisticated and experienced business elite drawn from the racial minorities – Chinese, Jews, Syrians, Europeans etc., who were, probably, less integrated into the social fabric at the time than their counterparts elsewhere in the Caribbean. The conflicts and tensions of social relations were played out in the politics of the two main political parties, with the Jamaican rural workers and peasants following Alexander Bustamante, a near-white, charismatic and pragmatic founder of the Jamaica Labour Party (JLP) and the middle class following his cousin, the mulatto Rhodes Scholar, Norman Manley,[18] who had a reputation as legal luminary and went on to found the People's National Party. The middle class worshipped at the Manley shrine and their servants voted for Bustamante. Manley's PNP had harboured the Marxist left whose leaders had been purged in 1952. But by the 1960s there was a revival of a younger grouping in the Young Socialist League under the leadership of the lawyer, Hugh Small. However, by the 1960s the most dynamic social force which owed no allegiance to any party, which was partly religious and quite definitely radical in its challenges to all aspects of the legacy of colonialism was the Rastafarians (Chevannes 1989).

UWI sociologist, Orlando Patterson, made his way down to Western Kingston where he took notes for his first novel *The Children of Sisyphus*. Rodney also went to visit the Rastafarians but did not see them through the defeatist lenses of the Sisyphean myth. He instead gleaned their potential for social transformation and viewed their efforts as part of the process of self-emancipation. He was preparing for his final exams when the Coral Gardens incident of April 1963 took place. Rastafarians were reported to have attacked a gas station ten miles from Montego Bay, on Jamaica's northwest coast (Nettleford 1970: 79). The incident left eight people dead including two policemen and three Rastafarians. There was an extensive campaign against Rastas in some rural parishes leading to the detention of 150 (Nettleford 1970: 79).

Three years before in 1960 M.G. Smith, F.R. Augier and Rex Nettleford had produced their report, "The Rastafari Movement in Kingston, Jamaica". The university team "had found that ganja and the easy translation of the Rastafarian dialectic into orthodox Marxism were ready attractions for middle-class youths and Jamaicans of a leftist persuasion" (Nettleford 1970: 95). This connection between socialists and Rastafarians[19] was a potentially volatile mix for Jamaican society although it was to be successfully harnessed and tamed by Norman Manley's son, Michael, in the run-up to the 1972 elections and during the tumultuous 1970s as part of the PNP's ideology of democratic socialism.

Rastafarianism was one of the forms that Black Nationalism took among poorer sections of the population in the years after the demise of the Garvey movement in the 1930s. Rodney understood this and sought to utilise its political potential in a radical direction in 1968. When in the raft debate he took the position of the Rastafarian he was already familiar with the movement and some of its central urban figures like Mortimo Planno. It is not far-fetched to suggest that the Jamaican experience contributed to his determination to go beyond the plantation to study the origins of its African population.

Notes

1. For an authoritative history of the University of the West Indies see Sherlock and Nettleford (1990).
2. Lloyd Best is of the view that Arthur Lewis' greatest failing has been as an educator.

   I don't think he had anything like the right idea of what was required of a University of the West Indies at the juncture of hope when he was induced to take it over just when the West Indies Federation had been launched. He was confident of the model he had inherited. The work that he embarked upon with admirable resolution and incomparable vigour was a work of expansionist and not intrinsic development. Lewis had returned with an armoury of tried formulas; this is my recollection from those days of elevated promise at Mona. He never made a vital connection with the young; the romance was lacking and when Guyana broke away from UWI in search of another dispensation, all that Mona could offer was the materialist promise of its own campus – fully funded from outside (Best 1993: 17).

   The question remains unanswered as to what is meant by intrinsic development in the first place and, following on that, what is the appropriate institutional response to intrinsic development. This opinion requires careful evaluation as it treats with some of the epistemological issues at the heart of the transplant of British institutions to the Caribbean.
3. See Paul Sutton (1992) for an interesting comparative analysis of Walter Rodney and Eric Williams.
4. See David Lewis (1993) for discussion of the early life and education of W.E.B. Du Bois.
5. See Rex Nettleford (1985) for a history of the National Dance Theatre Company of Jamaica.
6. Albert Huie is regarded as one of the masters of Jamaican painting. See Nettleford (1978: 38); also Shirley Maynier-Burke (1988).
7. See Rachel Manley (1989) for an intimate portrait of Jamaican cultural and political life.
8. See Derek Walcott (1993) for an exploration of his recollections of the University College of the West Indies in the 1950s. Also Edward Baugh (1993) for discussion of Walcott's literary work in Jamaica in the same period.
9. Orlando Patterson is a distinguished authority on slavery. See Patterson (1967, 1982, 1991). He is also the author of three novels.

10. See Nettleford (1985).
11. See Mervyn Morris (1992) for a remembrance of Dennis Scott (1939–1991).
12. See editorial in *Rising Star* 27 October 1963: 1, for a report on the banning of Colin Moore by the Jamaican government. The report suggests that Moore's ban was due to his fraternisation with the Rastafarian community and his criticisms of the Jamaican government.
13. In conversation with Anthony Abrahams he recalls Rodney living on Block B Chancellor Hall and described him as being "a serious book-beater. He would take off his shirt and pull his desk into the middle of his room and beat some heavy books . . ." To 'beat books' means "to study assiduously". Trevor Munroe recalled representing the UWI team along with Rodney and defeating the debating team from Columbia University sometime in 1962 (conversation with Anthony Abrahams and Trevor Munroe, 10 December 1992, Kingston).
14. Photocopies of Walter Rodney's lecture notes on the Russian Revolution were kindly made available to me by Professor Robin Kelley.
15. Best (1990) suggests that Arthur Lewis blocked James' appointment.
16. Rodney's paper "The Role of the Historian in the Developing West Indies" was presented at a seminar, "The Role of the Social Sciences in the West Indies", held in celebration of University Independence week, 11–16 February 1963.
17. See Clinton Hutton (1992) for an insightful study of the ideological origins of the Morant Bay rebellion.
18. See Vic Reid (1985) for a biography of Norman Manley written with the eye of a novelist.
19. See Trevor Munroe (1992: 43–47) for discussion of the political attitude towards Rastafari in the 1950s on the part of British colonial officials, on the one hand, and the Jamaican left, on the other.

CHAPTER 3

England 1963–1966

Walter Rodney went to London in 1963, when he was 21 years old, to pursue his doctorate in African history at the School of Oriental and African Studies. His relationship with Pat Henry had started before he went to the University College of the West Indies. She went on to England in 1960 to study nursing, the relationship was maintained through correspondence and it blossomed when he went to London in 1963. Pat described Walter as leading a very active life, politically and socially. Both of them participated in functions at the West Indian Students' Union and socialised a lot. Hyde Park became a weekly Sunday slot in Walter's political itinerary. Pat recalled him speaking on African and Caribbean politics, racism in Britain and the civil rights movement in the United States. Among their close circle were the Guyanese Al Parkes, Ewart Thomas and Gordon Rohlehr. Rohlehr, nicknamed 'Boscoe', was then doing his doctorate in literature at the University of Birmingham, and Eddie,[1] Walter's elder brother, was then in the Royal Air Force. Walter lived with Eddie for a time. Pat recalls that

> Walter was very proud of his brother Edward and I think he was like a role model for Walter or a mentor at times. Walter always looked up to him because I think Eddie was a self-made person. Eddie left home very early, I think at either age 16 or 17, went off to England, got into the Air Force and Walter always talked a lot about his brother that time, even before I met Edward in London (Pat Rodney 1989).

Eddie shared an apartment with Walter and Pat in London in the 1960s and also lived with them for some time in Dar es Salaam in the 1970s. In the late 1970s, in Guyana, Walter was very solicitous of Eddie's health and economic circumstances. Walter's London 'mother' was Virgil Duncan, a Guyanese called 'Mums' who adopted Walter and Pat as her own. Other acquaintances in London were a group of Jamaican students among whom were the brothers Hugh and Richard Small studying law, Norman Girvan reading economics, and Orlando Patterson doing sociology.

Walter was not a strict person in family life but Pat recalled that one definitely knew where one stood with him and he knew what he wanted. Speaking of what attracted her to Walter, Pat said:

> His simplicity. I think he was a very sincere person. I think he was a very attractive man. He was a very interesting person, a very intellectual person but he did not behave in that way that most people who had higher education behaved. He wasn't arrogant, he was a very simple person who could talk about anything, could associate with any and everybody. He was somebody I always felt very comfortable with, and I think we enjoyed a lot of the same things. He liked dancing, he liked music (Pat Rodney 1989).

They were married on 2 January 1965 in a civil ceremony and the witnesses were Al Parkes, their close friend, and Virgil Duncan. This was followed by a small reception with friends among whom were Ewart Thomas and Gordon Rohlehr. The ceremony was indicative of their modest lifestyle and personal taste as West Indian weddings at home or overseas do tend to be elaborate affairs with a lot of people, food and toasts, which sometimes involve the couple in debt. The form of the wedding was itself an ideological and personal statement that marriage vows were a simple, yet complex, expression of love and commitment between two people. Other weddings of Rodney's friends in the 1960s reflected Black Power sentiments in hairstyle and dress, forms which broke with the traditional wedding, except when parental intervention was overpowering. Pat recalled that they had decided "not to get married in the church because Walter felt strongly that what was important was living together, being two people who cared, you didn't have to do it in a church, in fact you didn't have to go to church to do good things" (Pat Rodney 1989). These opinions on the church were shared by Walter's father and were not therefore solely a product of the West Indian student-intellectual milieu of the 1960s. It also indicated harmony between his public critique of the West Indian middle classes and his own modest and non-acquisitive lifestyle.

Walter shared in the domestic tasks throughout the marriage although Pat remained the anchor of the family. In London when Pat was on night duty at the hospital and needed to rest in the days Walter would cook on returning home from the archives.

He would always cook the dinner and he never liked Al (Parkes) to cook because Al would always burn the food . . . So either I would cook or Walter would cook and I would do the washing up . . . He was a very good cook. Walter taught me to cook. He loved Chinese food and he is very good at Chinese food . . . Coming from a large family I didn't have to cook and I never had to cook, so really he did a lot of that (Pat Rodney 1989).

What was important about Pat's perception of him was the congruence between what she saw and valued and what working class people especially in Jamaica and Guyana saw and valued.

Walter's experience as a colonial travelling to London was not that of the typical West Indian migrant, because he was a scholarship student sent for higher education. But his living in London did have a

> touch of what it meant to go to doors in answer to an advertisement and knock and be told that it was already taken once the landlady perceived the colour of my face . . . My experience of English society, of its racism, and of its exploitation was in a sense second-hand. Yet I understood, because I lived among West Indian workers and I understood what it meant to be part of the most exploited section of the working class. Even though I was in school, my brother was at work and my room-mate was at work. My wife worked later on when we got married. The person with whom I lived was a Guyanese woman, Virgil Duncan, whom we called "Mums." She was a surrogate mother for a lot of younger people and she was a worker in the broad sense of the word: part-time housekeeper, part-time day-carer for children, and part-time seamstress working as an extension of London's sweating trade at a very low rate. So I was part of that working community. Very quickly, but largely through my brother, who already had very rich experiences in being a member of the British Air Force (he had served in Cyprus) and who was already involved in political life, I moved immediately into trying to learn from the mass of migrant workers (Rodney 1990: 20–21).

Rodney's Marxism

While working on his dissertation Rodney devoted time to public speaking in Hyde Park. He recalled:

> In those years a lot of West Indians turned up at Hyde Park. It was, of course, a place where a number of freak shows were also held, a place where things were said that weren't serious. But quite a number of West Indians did go there

> as a meeting place, as an expression of the fact that they were under pressure and they wanted to find ways of talking and dealing with their exploitation and with racism. Thus I was involved there for three years, every summer. From the time it got warm enough to speak until the time when it was too cold to speak, I would be on the platform at Hyde Park. In this period of my life and with the necessity to relate to working people, I was consciously beginning to read Marxism more extensively (Rodney 1990: 21).

At these gatherings he spoke on a wide range of historical and political themes and continued honing his talents for public speaking and developing his aptitude for presenting difficult issues in a manner comprehensible to working people.

He had done a course in the History of Political Thought as an undergraduate but his exposure to Marxism at the university had been largely an academic one. The foundation of his Marxism was his Guyanese experience of the early 1950s but that had not been based on independent reading but had been shaped by the political education of Jagan's People's Political Party. In London he realised that

> this was not just material within a course, or a segment within the totality of bourgeois knowledge, but that it had something fundamentally different to offer. Also one began to look more closely at the Marxist experience per se, at transformational experiences such as China, which had an important emotional appeal because it was a non-white country at a time when one's racial consciousness was very high (Rodney 1990: 21–22).

His development as a Marxist was growing with his political activism, limited as it was to his regular Hyde Park speeches, his meetings with Guyanese and other Caribbean students and workers who were concerned about the deterioration in interethnic relations in Guyana and the future of the region. Rodney's intellectual mentor during these London years was C.L.R. James, the venerable Marxist theoretician. James had returned to Trinidad in 1958 after an absence of 26 years and had undertaken the editorship of *The Nation*, the paper of the People's National Movement, and the secretaryship of the West Indian Federal Labour Party. He resigned both posts in 1960 after political differences with Eric Williams and went to England to resume his writing and socialist activity. The political significance of James' involvement with the federation, his work with the People's National Movement (PNM) and the break with Williams are summed up in James' (1962) insightful work on West Indian politics entitled *Party Politics in the West Indies*. James' politics could not have survived in the PNM for very long and from the outset some of the members on the party's General Council were opposed to him on the ground of what Eric Williams called "his notorious political record",[2] which simply meant his Marxist political reputation. In this book, as well as in *Modern Politics*, James (1960) was able to draw on his knowledge and experience of modern politics in Europe and the United States to situate the West Indies and to assess the prospects for its democratic evolution. He was also able to start shaping West Indian intellectuals[3] of a generation younger than Eric Williams, who heard him lecture and read his books. His work with the PNM and *The Nation* had given him a temporary political base. After his break with Williams he published *Party Politics in the West Indies* (1962) in which he critiqued the PNM, explained the reasons for his resignation and discussed some of the central issues in Trinidad's political life such as the role of the middle classes, the role of culture and the political implications of race. He was also concerned with the role of the mass party in decolonisation and felt that no personality – not even the captain of the team, Eric Williams – should ride roughshod over the party. Together with this volume there were his fascinating lectures, collected in the volume entitled *Modern Politics* and published in Trinidad in 1960. This collection located the region in the context of the development of modern civilisation. James covered the Greek city-state, showed the genesis of the idea of democracy and representative government, and discussed modern philosophy inclusive of Kant, Hegel and Marx, the twentieth century socialist movement, and modern literature and the arts. James' intellectual work demonstrated his belief in the transformatory powers of the ordinary people and the necessity for democracy in effecting real change. James, then in his sixties, was not yet past the height of his intellectual powers. His reconnection with the Caribbean after nearly 30 years of exile in England and the United States was fruitful as it put him in touch with a new generation of Caribbean intellectuals and writers. He was highly regarded by Derek Walcott, Vidia Naipaul, Kamau Brathwaite, Andrew Salkey, among many others. His works were being reprinted and were being read, and his lectures on a variety of cultural and political subjects ranging from Greek political thought to West Indian federation, from the calypsonian Sparrow to the West Indian literary renaissance of the 1950s, the game of cricket and regional decolonisation, were very well attended in the Caribbean.[4] James' encyclopaedic knowledge of modern history, literature and philosophy and his ability to synthesise and present his material in memorable lectures put to shame his contemporaries and younger scholars who had been university trained.

The volume, however, which gave him his widest audience after *Black Jacobins* was *Beyond a Boundary*, which linked the game of cricket to autobiographical narrative, Western culture and politics and West Indian nationalism. James had earlier on gained a reputation for historical scholarship and excellent writing with *The Black Jacobins*, his classic study of the Haitian Revolution. Its re-publication in 1963 in a paperback edition by Vintage Books made it available once more to a generation of students and general readers eager to learn not only about the Haitian Revolution but about general problems of decolonisation. With this generation in mind James wrote a long essay entitled "From Toussaint L'Ouverture to Fidel Castro" which he added as an appendix.

In many respects, as an intellectual working outside the formal academic establishment, James appealed to the rebel intellectual within Rodney whose entire training and livelihood were derived from within academic institutions. It was the rebel-intellectual within Rodney which made him write *How Europe Underdeveloped Africa*. In a letter to his publisher on 17 July 1971 Rodney said his purpose was "to upset and not to please the deans of African History in London and Wisconsin".[5]

Walter Rodney was a second generation West Indian Marxist. George Padmore and C.L.R. James were among the first. Although Rodney was a victim of political persecution he did not know the frustrations of James' generation and the difficulties of surviving as an intellectual without institutional support. In his tribute to Rodney, James sums up the intellectual essence of the generational difference when he stated:

> In 1936, Dr W.E.B. Du Bois had written his superb book *Black Reconstruction*. I know no finer single-volume history of any episode or any territory than *Black Reconstruction*. Two years later, by some accident of the time, I had written *The Black Jacobins*, the first statement of revolutionary policy and instructions for the revolutionary development of the colonial countries. At just about that time, Aimé Césaire had written *Return to My Native Land*. Around the same time, in 1934, Learie Constantine, with my help, had published a book, *Cricket and I*. A West Indian, for the first time, spoke to the world at large and to the Caribbean about an event in which many people of the world were interested. In 1936 I published my novel, *Minty Alley*, the first West Indian novel published in Great Britain. I emphasize that all this took place before Walter was born.
>
> Now I, Aimé Césaire, George Padmore, Dr Du Bois, and others were faced with a particular challenge. As we grew up and went along, we had to fight the doctrines of the imperialist powers in order to establish some Caribbean foundation or foundations for the underdeveloped peoples. *Walter did not have to do that*. The aforementioned works were written before he was born. Walter grew up in an atmosphere where for the first time a generation of West Indian

intellectuals was able not only to study the revolutionary and creative works that had been created in Europe but also to benefit from and be master of what had been done in the same tradition in direct reference to the Caribbean (James 1982: 133–34).

It was the study group around C.L.R. James and his wife, Selma James, that had a significant impact on Walter Rodney. Richard Small and Norman Girvan were the organisers of this study group which met at No. 20 Staverton Road in North London. Among the members of the group of West Indian students, were Orlando Patterson, Adolph Edwards, Joan French and John Maxwell from Jamaica, Margaret Carter Hope from Barbados, Stanley French from St Lucia, and Walton Look Lai from Trinidad (Girvan 1990: viii).

Rodney's assessment of this group indicates its importance in his intellectual growth:

> Meeting over a period of two to three years on a fairly regular basis afforded me the opportunity that I, and a number of other people were seeking – to acquire a knowledge of marxism, a more precise understanding of the Russian Revolution, and of historical formulation. One of the most important things which I got out of that experience was a certain sense of historical analysis, in the sense that C.L.R. James was really a master of the analysis of historical situations. It was not enough to study Lenin's *State and Revolution*. It was important to understand why it was written and what was going on in Russia at that precise point in time. It was not enough to study Lenin's *What Is To Be Done?* One must understand the specific contextual nature of the discussions that were going on in Russia at that time . . . One thing is certain about C.L.R. James – he has mastered a whole range of theory and historical data and analysis . . . The group might do some reading and try to understand what a text says. But James gave it that added dimension which nobody else in the group could easily acquire in being able to say: this is what Lenin was about; this is what Trotsky was doing; he had just come from this conference or this debate, or this was his specific programmatic objective when he was writing, and so on. That was a very important experience which I am still pondering. I see its significance more as one goes along and I recognize the necessity for us to do much more work of that type (Rodney 1990: 28–29).

Rodney was equally impressed by James' wife, Selma, and was enthusiastic on recalling her.

> What a very unusual woman! She sometimes, even more than C.L.R., had this habit of taking a foolish position and really indicating why that position was

foolish. When Selma was finished indicating why it was foolish, one had very little doubt about its foolishness. She did, along with C.L.R. exemplify the power of Marxist thought (Rodney 1990: 29).

This study group had a profound influence on Rodney's writing and this can be seen especially in the manner in which he conceived his lectures on the Russian Revolution, as well as the way he wrote *How Europe Underdeveloped Africa*. Girvan, in a memorial tribute to C.L.R. James, recalled that

> James' prescribed texts ranged from Marx's *18th Brumaire of Louis Napoleon*, to the chapter in *Das Kapital* on "The Working Day", and the booklet on the Hungarian revolt of 1956 produced by James and his associates ("Facing Reality"); and many others. He gave us his unique interpretation of the subtleties of Hegel, Heidegger, and Wilson Harris. At a subsequent stage we ourselves prepared papers: my own thinking on Caribbean economic thought was first stimulated by a paper I wrote for this group. Walter Rodney further honed his views about the relationship between Marxism and democracy in a review of "Facing Reality". And Adolph Edwards' booklet on Marcus Garvey, one of the first of its kind, was a direct result of his paper for that group (Girvan 1990: viii–ix).

Marxist study groups have a mixed history and depend very much on the political-ideological line of the organisation, the person guiding the study and the pedagogical approach. James' group was obviously not toeing a party line but rather helped to stimulate independent thinking and creative work. Rodney's expertise in guiding study groups in Tanzania and in Guyana are remembered by many as unique learning experiences (Kwayana 1988; Bagoya 1990). Marxist study groups developed in the Anglophone Caribbean in the 1970s and were often accompanied by mimeographed publications and involvement in public debate on national issues through the mass media. In some cases they led to the formation of small left wing political parties. With the development of political parties and the requirement of adhering to a political line, study groups became ideological appendages and lost the sharp edge of intellectual inquisitiveness involved in the discovery of new ideas and their application to postcolonial countries. Dogmatism replaced creative thought. Nowhere else in the English-speaking Caribbean was this more applicable than in the ideological deterioration in the New Jewel Movement whose study programme was copied and shaped by the pro-Moscow Workers' Party of Jamaica (WPJ),[6] and this in no small way contributed to the rot within the leadership of the New Jewel Movement and the subsequent loss of touch with political reality.

While in London Rodney appeared not to have had much interest in the British left. He was very dismissive of the Communist Party of Great Britain, the Trotskyites and the intellectuals around the journal, *New Left Review*. The British communists he met seemed to be still debating the 1930s and were living out the factional ideological debates of Stalinism and Trotskyism. Of the New Left and radicals around the London School of Economics he concluded:

> from my brief meetings with some of them and my readings of their materials, my impression was that they tended to be very facile, within a tradition of attempting to be clever – the idea was who could put forth clever formulations. I was never convinced of any depth or of any seriousness of purpose among these people. In fact, I found a couple of them that I met to be upsetting even in the kinds of relationship one had with them. And there was always that latent racism, sometimes coming out in paternalism, sometimes coming out in hostile manifestations (Rodney 1990: 31).

On the other hand, Rodney's Marxism was shaped by his early Guyanese political experience, by his efforts at applying it to his historical research on the Caribbean and Africa, by C.L.R. James' own decisive mentorship as historian, theoretician and political activist, and by African Marxists such as Amilcar Cabral and Samir Amin. Dogmatic Marxism was alien to him and so he did not go around proclaiming catch phrases. Rather, Rodney's Marxism was independent of the Soviets and the Chinese, whose ideas and material assistance won many a Third World Marxist to a rote learning dogmatic adherence to ideological cliches. Although he was not pro-Moscow, in the sense that Cheddi Jagan was, Rodney's own considerable knowledge of the Russian Revolution had been gained from wide reading, teaching and political discussions. The Russian Revolution was an important source for comparing revolutions and a point of departure in analysing issues concerning the role of social classes, the state, and economic transformation. His teaching on the Russian Revolution, the French Revolution and the English Civil War reflected his interest in the area of Comparative Revolutions which he pursued at Dar es Salaam. This area of his research is not reflected in his curriculum vitae as he had no publications on these topics. In an undated letter written in the early 1970s to his friend Ewart Thomas he said:

> I've given the occasional seminar on Cuba and I've helped with seminars on China, but my main field has been Russia. My publications obviously do not

provide evidence of expertise in European History, but I really have done a great deal of work on the Russian Revolution. This year I was about to start on a monograph covering the 1917 Revolution and the period up to World War II and I put it aside only because the African material had to be given higher priority (Rodney 1972f).

George Padmore and C.L.R. James had more intimate contact with the Russian Revolution than most West Indian Marxists, especially Padmore who had worked with the Comintern in Moscow, had known Stalin and had broken with him on political grounds. James had written an authoritative book on the Communist International movement[7] which critiqued Stalinism, had been a Trotskyite and had broken with Trotsky.[8] Padmore became an astute organiser of the anticolonial movement and of Pan-Africanism and was a big influence on Kwame Nkrumah whose political advisor he became in the 1950s.[9] By contrast, Rodney's Marxism was to grow and mature in the 1960s and 1970s under the influence of the decolonisation movement in Tanzania and the armed struggle for liberation from Portuguese rule in Southern Africa. Yet Rodney belongs to the radical Pan-African intellectual and political tradition, of which Padmore and James themselves are two foremost West Indian figures. For all three Marxism became an intellectual instrument to better understand and change subject nations to free ones.

Doctoral thesis

Rodney had gone to London to do his doctoral research and writing and this he did successfully. However, when he went to the School of Oriental and African Studies:

> The question was raised as to whether or not I had to take some qualifying exams or do some papers in their undergraduate work. Now, I had always understood that somebody who got first-class honours at a University was entitled to continue to do postgraduate research. And I had this naive impression that since the University College of the West Indies (which it was when I started my degree) was one of the constituent colleges of the University of London then there could be no question that it was just as though I had come from down the road at King's College or somewhere else. But this was not so.
>
> I had come from the colonies. You may call UCWI a college of the University of London, but their missionaries had set that up and it doesn't necessarily mean that it had the same standards as that which they claim to possess. This was the attitude of some people. In other words, the issue had to

be debated. Ultimately it was said, 'oh well, the University College of the West Indies, the first class honours, we can accept this' (Rodney 1990: 22).

Walter described his psychological response to this colonial situation as one where the

> colonial had to show that colonized people had the same capacity . . . The moment you go there you're under that load, that you're not just you, but you are a representative of a whole people who have been victimized, and who not only have been victimized but who are also regarded as the agents of their own victimization and that something is somehow wrong with them. The outcome was that I was forced to try and formulate something that was intellectually different and yet in a sense acceptable to the academic establishment. And I really was among the establishment. SOAS had at that time the two most important British scholars on Africa, Roland Oliver and John D. Fage. Fage then left to found the Center [of West African Studies] at [the University of] Birmingham but he came back for seminars (Rodney 1990: 23).

Rodney saw SOAS as having been set up to train colonial administrators, but with decolonisation it had to be refashioned. He perceived SOAS as being

> very involved in the defense of bourgeois ideology. We had weekly seminars, every Tuesday afternoon, the most urbane seminars that you could think of, led by all these deans of knowledge on Africa, who had this tremendous flair for keeping everybody at a lower level. Even if one were an African or a West Indian and one wanted to talk about the questions (raised) in the seminar, they could dominate partly because of their greater expertise, and familiarity with the paper, and partly because, after all, they had been at this for a long time. They represented the outgrowth of centuries of an intellectual tradition, and this is just not to be scoffed at (Rodney 1990: 24).

This critical response to the School of Oriental and African Studies was, in a sense, typical of the radical intellectual Rodney was by the 1960s. But the historical sense which he applied to everything made him understand the importance of, what he termed, the bourgeois intellectual process in Britain's development and its importance for his own development. It enabled him to avoid a naive and pointless anarchic critique which saw nothing of relevance in the British tradition. Instead, Rodney engaged the British establishment on an intellectual terrain, using well the tools he had acquired. His thesis and subsequent writings and the response of the academic establishment to his work are testimony to the seriousness with which he assumed the role of radical-scholar. In order to do so he had to master the tools of his profession as a historian.

Dr Richard Gray, his supervisor at SOAS, was very supportive. This was very important as in the British system the graduate student had a supervisor and not a committee as in the American graduate school. Rodney described Gray

> as a liberal bourgeois historian who had . . . certain basic skills as well as integrity. And he made a lot of effort, I would say, even went out of his way, to accommodate my own development and my own view. Perhaps if this was not so, I might have been forced to take another stand. But I thought he was very helpful (Rodney 1990: 24).

Gray developed a close relationship with Rodney during his doctoral research and maintained contact with him while he was at the University of Dar es Salaam, inviting him to contribute two essays to the *Cambridge History of Africa*. Vol. 4. *c.1600–c.1790*. Gray was also to write Rodney's obituary in the London Times of 21 June 1980 in which he described Rodney as "one of the most significant Third World historians of his generation". Rodney, for his part, paid tribute to Gray's supervision of his thesis which was published in 1970 and bore the same title as the thesis, A History of the Upper Guinea Coast 1545–1800, when he wrote that

> The specific choice of the Upper Guinea Coast was due to the direction of my tutor, Dr Richard Gray of the School of Oriental and African Studies, who possesses vast knowledge of the location of source materials for African History. I benefitted not only from his technical skill but also from the personal warmth of his assistance. Under his guidance, I have sought to ensure that the integrity of the evidence was respected at all times, for this has always to be demanded from those who practise the writing of history (Rodney 1970a: ix).

The SOAS seminars were important in shaping his empirical sense, but there were no Marxist historians there to engage him on theoretical issues, unlike the London School of Economics where there were "Marxist elements from time to time" (Rodney 1990: 26). He therefore read Marxism on his own and started to apply it to the historical data. The uses to which he put Marxist ideas, as well as the emendations to that body of ideas, will be discussed in the assessment of his principal writings on Africa and the Caribbean. Rodney's research took him to archives in Lisbon, Seville, Rome and London. His Spanish served him well and he developed an ability to read Portuguese and Italian. He had the political experience of living in fascist

Portugal and Spain, and this gave him a better appreciation of the kind of opponents the liberation movements in Portugal's African territories had to face. It also broadened his understanding of the national complexions of European colonialism. Rodney completed his thesis, of 614 typewritten pages, and submitted it in May 1966. He had specialised in the colonial history of West Africa and his idea was to teach there for a brief period and then return to "the University of the West Indies to teach African history and to relate to our people on the African question. Specifically, I was returning to the Caribbean by way of Africa. This is how I always saw it" (Rodney 1990: 33).

Rodney's choices of teaching location were heavily influenced by political questions. He eliminated Guinea for "cultural and historical reasons". On the other hand, he didn't think he "could have learned anything from participation in the kind of politics that was being developed in Nigeria, or at that time in Ghana after Nkrumah. Hence the choice was to go to Tanzania" (Rodney 1990: 33). He applied to the British Ministry of Overseas Development to get into the university at Dar es Salaam. On political and academic grounds Tanzania turned out to be an excellent choice. He had a contract for less than two years and was negotiating with the University of the West Indies for an appointment.

So after gaining his doctorate in 1966, Rodney's first teaching assignment was at the University College of Dar es Salaam. On 30 November 1965 he had written to Professor T.O. Ranger, then head of the History Department, applying for a job as lecturer in West African history. His referees were Professor Roland Oliver and Dr Richard Gray. His letter to Ranger provides an academic profile of the young historian at age 23. Rodney wrote:

> The History courses of the University College of the West Indies (as it was until 1963) were based on the general pattern of the University of London. There were nine final papers, to be written after three years. Two of these were in English History between 1487 and 1945, and there was a similar arrangement for European History. The West Indies and the Americas accounted for two further courses of the usual kind. 'Reconstruction' after the Civil War in the USA was the special topic which introduced the use of source materials, and this comprised two papers. Finally there was a translation paper, involving two languages.
>
> The courses in New World history occasioned a very marginal interest in West Africa, so that I have done most of my reading in that subject since my arrival at the School of Oriental and African Studies in October 1963. My thesis is entitled 'A History of the Upper Guinea Coast: 1545–1800'. It covers the coastal area between the Gambia and Cape Mount, and seeks to reconstruct

the society of that region, and to measure the impact of external forces acting from the interior and from the Atlantic. Both the wide time-span and the general nature of my enquiries have led me to reflect upon the Upper Guinea Coast in the context of the whole West African littoral.

I have prepared from my own research material two seminar papers as well as an article on 'Portuguese Attempts at Monopoly on the Upper Guinea Coast' which has been accepted for publication by the *Journal of African History*. Away from SOAS, I have also been engaged in lecturing on African History, including a series of lectures given to a class of the Oxford University Delegacy for Extra-Mural Studies. My main committment [sic] is to the University of the West Indies, to which I will return in October 1967 to help start a programme in West African studies. My interest, therefore, is in a temporary post at the University College, for which I would be available after completion of my thesis in June 1966 . . . (Rodney 1965a).

Meanwhile Tanzania was experiencing a postindependence radical reform under Nyerere's Arusha Declaration, which had been declared in 1966. Thus Tanzania afforded Rodney

> the opportunity to grow in conjunction with the total movement of a society, and to grow in conjunction with other comrades, younger and older, though mainly younger, who were also grappling with the same perspective on African history (Rodney 1990: 35).

Ranger's response was positive. As it turned out, the University College of Dar es Salaam was to be the principal institutional base that Rodney had in his short life. The Jamaican government was to ban Rodney from re-entering Jamaica in October 1968, thus thwarting his efforts to develop a serious African studies programme for the first time in the English-speaking Caribbean. After his expulsion from Jamaica in October 1968, he decided in 1969 to return to Tanzania and his second application to Ranger for a job was, again, met with a positive response. He worked there from 1969 to 1974. Those years were very important for him as a historian and for his political and personal growth. Pat Rodney described the Tanzanian years as the "happiest period of our lives". Rodney returned to Tanzania in his twenty-seventh year and remained there for five years. He returned to Guyana in 1974, at age 32, to take up a professorship in the Department of History but Forbes Burnham, the country's president, brought political muscle to bear on the University of Guyana and a professorship was denied him. From that time until his death in 1980 Rodney lived hand to mouth, doing teaching stints in German and North American universities and going on many speaking tours so that he could sustain his family and maintain his political work in the Working People's Alliance of Guyana. As an independent scholar he did an incredible amount of academic work while conducting intensive political activity. It was as if the political and academic spheres of activity nourished each other.

Notes

1. Eddie Rodney is a member of the People's Progressive Party which was founded and led by Cheddi Jagan who died in office as Guyana's president on 6 March 1997. His wife Janet Jagan succeeded him as party leader. Rodney writes for the the *Mirror*, the PPP's newspaper, and became a parliamentarian in the 1992–1997 PPP-led administration.
2. See Eric Williams' (1969: 267–68) response to C.L.R. James' tenure where he argued that the General Council of the People's National Movement "objected to his admittance into the Party on the ground of his notorious political record", that James abused his position as editor of The Nation to promote himself, and that he had mismanaged the PNM Publishing Company.
3. The impact on West Indian intellectuals can be seen in the fact that Orlando Patterson dedicated his first major academic publication, *The Sociology of Slavery – An Analysis of the Origins, Development and Structure of Negro Slave Society in Jamaica*, to C.L.R. James. The tributes to James after his death in 1989 saw Trinidadian intellectual, Lloyd Best (1990), placing James in the context of a West Indian intellectual tradition and Gordon Rohlehr (1989) referring to him as our truest ancestor. Another Trinidadian scholar, Selwyn Cudjoe organised a conference in James' honour at Wellesley College, 19–21 April 1991 and among the speakers were West Indian intellectuals Sylvia Wynter, Paget Henry, Winston James, Orlando Patterson and Derek Walcott. A selection of the papers appeared in Cudjoe and Cain (1995). James' influence will grow with the re-issuing of his writings and the publication of theses and books on him. His influence is, of course, broader than that of the West Indies and covers Britain, the United States and Africa.
4. See C.L.R. James (1962) for discussion of his political break with Eric Williams and (1960) for a series of lectures on modern politics given at the Trinidad Public Library, in its Adult Education Programme. See also biography of James by Paul Buhle. For a scholarly collection of essays on James see Paget Henry and Paul Buhle (1992) and for a recent collection of James' writings see Anna Grimshaw (1992). There are two documents written by James in 1958 and 1962 in my possession. The first is a photocopy of a document, written in July 1958, entitled "An Analysis of the Political Situation in Barbados". In this document James analyses the "strength and the vitality of the split from the Barbados Labour Party of the Democratic Labour Party". The second is a letter dated 16 July 1962 from C.L.R. James to Carlton Warner, a supporter of the PNM from a well-known Tunapuna family. It is a cover note for the gift of a book, most likely, *Party Politics in the West Indies*. In it James says, "this book makes it clear that there are wide political differences between me and the party you support. I am leaving on August 8. I do not have and have never had any political aspirations in the WI . . ."

5. Reference to African historians, anthropologists and others at the School of Oriental and African Studies in London and the University of Wisconsin.
6. For discussion of the ideological numbing of the New Jewel Movement, see Gordon Lewis (1987), Charles Mills (1990) and Brian Meeks (1993). An interview the author conducted with Maurice Bishop in 1982 and which was published in a Russian academic journal on Latin America showed the extent to which he had mastered the language of Soviet theorists on the Third World such as Karen Brutents and Rostislav Ulyanovsky. Books by these Soviet writers had come via the influence of the Workers' Party of Jamaica, which had relations with the Communist Party of the Soviet Union. Bishop was not comfortable during the interview but did his best over two sessions to sound right and to use the appropriate ideological terms. He asked me to edit it in that light. I made no changes. See Bishop (1984).
7. See C.L.R. James (1993).
8. See chapters 2 and 3 of Paul Buhle (1988) for discussion of James' involvement with Trotskyism.
9. See Hooker (1967) and James (1992).

CHAPTER 4

Walter Rodney and the Writing of African History

This chapter discusses the political content and significance of Rodney's work as a historian of Africa. Walter Rodney belonged to the generation of postcolonial historians of Africa and the Caribbean who embarked on the project of rewriting the history of the regions affected by the Atlantic slave trade from the standpoint of those whose voices had been muted in the historical record. It was pioneering work and it was, as well, a pioneering time coming as it did at the end of European colonial rule in Africa and the birth of independent African regimes. Roland Oliver and J.D. Fage in the preface to the sixth edition of their book, *A Short History of Africa*, stated that in 1961 when it first appeared:

> the academic study of African history was less than fifteen years. There were four named posts in the subject in Britain, of which we held two. The first learned journal devoted to the publication of the results of new research in African history had been founded in the previous year with ourselves as the editors (Oliver and Fage 1989: ix).

With regard to the United States, Jan Vansina has observed that

> the focus of research on Africa lay in this country from the later 1960s through the 1970s. According to Professor P.D. Curtin, 350 historians of Africa were active here in the United States in 1970 and there were some 600 by 1980. Even though some of them were not really involved in research, they

outnumbered all other specialists in African history all over the world (Vansina c.1987: 13).

Having been trained as a historian in the 1960s at the School of Oriental and African Studies in London, Rodney was in on the formative stage of the discipline of constructing postcolonial African history. He was able to engage his colleagues in very sharp debates about the nature of their project as historians and to publish in the *Journal of African History*, and the *Cambridge History of Africa* and the *UNESCO General History of Africa*. He wrote his well-known study *How Europe Underdeveloped Africa* at the University of Dar es Salaam, as well as trained and influenced a generation of historians and social scientists whom he taught. In addition to all that, he made a name for himself as a Caribbean historian with what was his best written work, *A History of the Guyanese Working People, 1881–1905*.

In African historiography Rodney has been seen as the historian who applied Latin American dependency theory to African history (Temu and Swai 1981; Freund 1984; Vansina 1986; Jewsiewicki 1989; Slater 1986). Other assessments have looked at his work as being central to scholarship on the Atlantic slave trade and African underdevelopment (Inikori and Engerman 1994; Inikori 1992a, 1992b, 1993a, 1993b, 1994). He is also assessed as a Marxist or Pan-Africanist historian (Emeagwali 1981; Ferguson 1982; Kaba 1982).[1] Others see him as a neo-Marxist working in the tradition of the Annalistes (Thornton 1992: 6).[2]

Rodney was a Marxist historian in the Jamesian sense of the term. C.L.R. James' classic study *Black Jacobins* and his approach to the history of the colonised world was Rodney's model, and to the Jamesian method Rodney added a more rigorous analysis of the place of Africa within contemporary history[3] and the world capitalist economy. The strength of dependency theory lay in its basic concern with the relations of the global economic system and its impact on the Third World. But Rodney's concern with macro-historical issues was balanced by his empirical studies of specific countries and regions in West and East Africa from the initial period of the slave trade and into the era of colonialism. This combination of approaches certainly applied to his years in Dar es Salaam where *How Europe Underdeveloped Africa* was accompanied by studies of Tanzania's political economy; regional and class stratification in Tanzania; coercive labour regimes in the German and British colonial periods; internal migration; problems in the development of the modern state and democracy. These issues were elaborated in a number of seminar papers or appeared in journals that were not widely circulated and hence have escaped historiographical reflection. His work in Dar es Salaam is discussed in chapter 6. In this chapter I will be reviewing some of Rodney's principal writings on African history while paying special attention to the social and political themes that were of concern to him.

Evolution as African historian

There is a tendency to superficially trace Rodney's writings in a linear way from bourgeois historian trained at the London School of Oriental and African Studies to a Dar es Salaam Marxist historian (Lawi 1986). His evolution was more complex than that.[4] Rodney's discussion of his growth as a historian does not suggest this kind of linear development (Rodney 1991: 22–27). Reflecting on *A History of the Upper Guinea Coast 1545–1800* in the mid 1970s, he said:

> Looking at that work now, I would certainly not see it as a strong statement of Marxian scholarship by any means. It was just strong enough, let's say, to upset some members of the establishment who perceived the direction in which I was trying to move. As far as those at SOAS were concerned, so long as it met their own criteria for being a work of scholarship, it didn't do any harm (Rodney 1990: 27).

The book was based on his doctoral thesis at the School of Oriental and African Studies in London which was submitted in May 1966. The preface to the book was written in June 1969 and it was published by Oxford University Press in 1970 and dedicated to his parents. His reputation as a scholar of African history started with this work and with it he launched his professional career. He had published essays in the *Journal of African History* based on his thesis and scholars had started to pay attention to his work. His three early articles in the *Journal of African History* were "Portuguese Attempts at Monopoly on the Upper Guinea Coast, 1580–1650" (1965b); "African Slavery and Other Forms of Social Oppression on the Upper Guinea Coast in the Context of the Atlantic Slave Trade" (1966b); and "A Reconsideration of the Mane Invasions of Sierra Leone" (1967b). Philip Curtin had observed that:

> Walter Rodney's study of the upper Guinea coast has been eagerly awaited since 1967 when his 'Reconsideration of the Mane Invasions' appeared as an article in this Journal (*JAH*). That and his other articles suggested that he had something important to say about West Africa in the era of the slave trade, and in many respects the work lives up to the advance billing . . . His treatment of the Mane invasions as a single episode also remains a brilliant reconstruction (Curtin 1970: 453).

The article on the Mane invasions which was developed in the book demonstrated Rodney's mastery of Portuguese sources on sixteenth century West Africa and his skills in reconstructing an important element in the ethnic formation of Sierra Leone.

Rodney described *A History of the Upper Guinea Coast 1545–1800* as being concerned "with the relatively small section of the West African Coast between the Gambia and Cape Mount" (Rodney 1970a: vii). This is an area which included Guinea-Bissau, Guinea and Sierra Leone. Rodney's study established the outline for a much larger canvas and the discussion of broader issues concerning the devastating impact of the European slave trade on Africa and the role of the African ruling groups – including traditional chiefs, Muslim leaders and the mulatto elite. These were themes he later developed with greater polemical vigour in *How Europe Underdeveloped Africa*.

Rodney started his study with an examination of the precolonial period, describing in his first chapter "The Land and the People". In the second chapter he discussed "The Era of the Mane Invasions (1545–1606)". He examined the social and political cultures of the populations and the nature of their economic activities. He wrote in full recognition of the social differentiation and status systems within African society and did not idealise these social formations.[5] In underscoring the importance of this he argued that

> The prevalent communal image of African society may serve to obscure the decisive differences between the masses and nobility. It is true that a village chief might be related to most of the residents of the village, but even though for certain purposes he acted as family head, there remains little doubt that his level of subsistence was markedly superior to that of his poorer relations. The noble was a social being apart from the masses of the people, and a recognition of this fact is basic for an understanding of much that occurred in the Upper Guinea Coast between 1545 and 1800 (Rodney 1970a: 37–38).

Rodney's doctoral thesis was written within the British tradition of historical empiricism but it was influenced by his evolving sense of a Marxist approach to history. However, he did not impose rigid schemes on the data but interpreted the way in which the Atlantic slave trade drew Africa into the international capitalist order and how the African elite facilitated that process. Rodney was very pointed when he argued:

> The responsibility for the slave trade, as far as Africans themselves bear part of this responsibility, lies squarely upon the shoulders of the tribal rulers and elites. They were in alliance with the European slave merchants, and it was upon the mass of the people that they jointly preyed (Rodney 1970a: 114).

While supporting Rodney's thesis on the slave trade and African underdevelopment, Inikori argues that Rodney exaggerated the extent to which the African elite participated in the trade (Inikori 1993b: 28) The important point here is that Rodney's work set the agenda for some of the fundamental issues in African history and development. Debates on these issues will continue for some time to come as new material comes to light and new interpretations and judgements are made. In his *History of the Upper Guinea Coast*, Rodney therefore tried to understand the way social differentiation developed in Africa and the relationship between that process and the slave trade. Rodney stressed the hostile aspects of the relationship between ruler and ruled as well as the predatory aspects of rulership. He wrote in his doctoral thesis, "The Kings Were Just as Likely to Rob their Own People as to Attack their Neighbours" (Rodney 1966: 231). In the book, based on the dissertation, that sentence is replaced by one which commented on this issue as well as on the part played by tribalism in the area under investigation.

> Tribal divisions were not, then, the most important. When the line of demarcation is clearly drawn between the agents and the victims of slaving as it was carried on among the littoral peoples, that line coincides with the distinction between the privileged and the unprivileged in the society as a whole (Rodney 1970a: 117).

The rest of the paragraph read:

> The Atlantic slave trade was deliberately selective in its impact on the society of the Upper Guinea Coast, with the ruling class protecting itself, while helping the Europeans to exploit the common people. This is of course the widespread pattern of modern neo-colonialism; and by the same token the period of slave trading in West Africa should be regarded as protocolonial. Though on the one hand there was no semblance of European political control over the African rulers, on the other hand it was the Europeans who were accumulating capital (Rodney 1970a: 117–18).

He therefore brought together the themes of class, ethnicity and international trade which were later developed in *How Europe Underdeveloped Africa*.

Rodney was sharply critical of those colonial-minded historians such as Christopher Fyffe who argued the advantages accruing to Africa from the slave trade:

Only the rulers benefited narrowly, by receiving the best cloth, drinking the most alcohol, and preserving the widest collection of durable items for prestige purposes. It is this factor of realised self-interest which goes some way towards explaining the otherwise incomprehensible actions of Africans towards Africans (Rodney 1970a: 253).

Rodney pointed out that:

In modern capitalist society, rules are drawn up to protect members of the possessing class from devouring each other raw; but on the Upper Guinea Coast and the West African littoral as a whole, capitalism paraded without even a loin-cloth to hide its nakedness. With no restraints on either side, the confrontation of the two cultures which produced the Atlantic slave trade was neither peaceful nor orderly, contrary to the exploratory revision, and it proved entirely detrimental to African society, which was the weaker party (Rodney 1970a: 254).

The consequence of this was the undermining of customary law, wars, loss of life, reduction of the labour force, disruption of economic activities, and the development of new social forces as seen in the emergence of the mulatto traders of Afro-Portuguese origin. The intermediary position and role of the latter group is very reminiscent of social relations in the Caribbean. The mulatto is like a lizard changing skin, as an observer of eighteenth century slave trading noted: "with a White Man he is a White Man, with a Black Man a Black Man" (Rodney 1970a: 222). Rodney discussed the role of important female mulatto traders but did not develop a gendered analysis of the topic. He did attempt, however, to address the gender question in *How Europe Underdeveloped Africa*.[6]

Through the Atlantic slave trade Africa was forcibly brought into the developing world capitalist economy and contributed significantly to the shaping of Western capitalism.

The expanding markets for slaves as a result of European investment in plantations in North America and the Caribbean triggered a vigorous demand for African labour power, and bankers were prepared to lend money for this profitable business. The plantation owners, the slave traders and allied banking interests were the main players but "the great agents of the Atlantic Slave trade, the Mande and the Fulas", other African chiefs, Muslim leaders and the mulatto elite all had their fingers in the blood of the trade. Rodney does not therefore paint an idyllic picture of Africa nor an evil one of Europe but tries to assess the relationships that emerged with their contradictions on the north and south sides of the equator.

Curtin's 1970 review of Rodney's first book was hostile. The first two paragraphs of the review recognised Rodney's promise and the rest of it carefully cut away at his professionalism. Curtin did not engage the major issues raised by Rodney about long-term processes of ethnic and state formation, class differentiation in the Upper Guinea Coast in the precolonial period, or how the African ruling groups fought and facilitated the Atlantic slave trade. Curtin credited Rodney for his use of archival deposits in Lisbon, Seville, Rome and London but criticised him for having an "overdependence on contemporaneous sources. Much of the recent work by ethnographers, economic anthropologists, and economic historians was not consulted, though it could have led to far better analysis" (Curtin 1970: 454). Curtin criticised Rodney for overestimating the export of slaves as well as details of ethnographic description. Curtin had just published his book, *The Atlantic Slave Trade: a Census* (1969), and naturally defended his position. The debate on the issue of the numbers of captives sold into the slave trade was of course taken up by other scholars who supported Rodney's point of view. Prominent among them was the Nigerian historian Joseph Inikori (1992a, 1992b, 1993a, 1993b, 1994).[7] Joseph Inikori in his estimate of the volume of the Atlantic slave trade has increased Curtin's figure of approximately ten million. Drawing on research done on transatlantic slave exports in the last 20 years Inikori suggests that Curtin's figures underestimate the volume of captives by about 40 percent and put the estimate at 15 million captives (Inikori 1992a: 12–13). The Du Bois Institute Slave Trade Data Base at Harvard University, that has accounted for approximately 27,000 slaving voyages, will enable researchers to make better informed statistical estimates of the number of Africans moved across the Atlantic as well as facilitate more sophisticated analyses on age and gender characteristics of the African captives as well as their ethnic and regional sources (Lovejoy 1997).[8] The debate over the numbers and the significance for African underdevelopment and the growth of European capitalism remains highly controversial.[9]

As for Curtin's review, it ended: "this is a book that might well have been a brilliant contribution to African history but is seriously weakened by insufficient knowledge of the literature and by careless presentation" (Curtin 1970: 455). Moreover, the tone of the review sought to discredit Rodney's version of history.

Another historian, E.A. Alpers, pointed out how Curtin and other critics had missed Rodney's essential contribution.

> Almost everyone who has written about pre-colonial African trade has nodded in the direction of European initiative and economic exploitation, but to date only a handful of scholars have successfully managed to balance African

initiative with a fully aware realization of constant European initiative and with a clear-sighted recognition that the pre-colonial relations led directly to the colonial subjugation of Africa by Europe. One of these is Rodney himself, whose pioneering volume on the Upper Guinea Coast has been sharply reviewed by major scholars who have not – however valid their specific criticisms of his book – apparently seen this most important point . . . The willingness of Western scholarship to ignore the argument presented by Rodney and Suret-Canale concerning pre-colonial West Africa apparently arises from the fact that they are both recognizably Marxist (Alpers 1973: 166).

Rodney's Marxism was subdued in his *History of the Upper Guinea Coast* but his Marxist approach to African history became more explicit and intellectually combative in his later writings.

It was not surprising therefore that the British historian George Shepperson wrote in a review of Rodney's *Groundings With My Brothers*:

Historians have beliefs as much as other people. But they are too prone, perhaps, to cram their credos under narrow decks of 'objectivity' in the hope, conscious or unconscious, that the directions in which they are sailing will escape notice. Dr Walter Rodney, however, is not afraid to nail his colours to the mast (Shepperson 1972: 173).

Shepperson is right in that much of the debate around Rodney's work in African history is ideological and this becomes very evident in the debates over *How Europe Underdeveloped Africa*. In his paper "African History in the Service of Black Revolution", which was a chapter in the title under review by Shepperson, Rodney argued that "the work of self-revaluation in terms of our African past is taking place within a milieu of social upheaval, and the mechanics of upheaval have first priority on the energy of black people" (Rodney 1969c: 51). Rodney's conception of his role as a historian was linked to his role as a political activist involved in the processes of decolonisation in Africa and the Caribbean. What he brought to his political activism was an in-depth historical understanding of contemporary economic and political circumstances that was similar to Eric Williams' use of history in the anticolonial struggles in Trinidad and Tobago in the 1950s (Sutton 1992; Cudjoe 1993).

Rodney identified two functions that linked his academic work to the struggles for decolonisation. The first of these was to contend with the colonial view of African history with its racist constructions. Connected to this, was the second function, which he identified as the need to portray the elements of African everyday life and to comprehend the culture of all Africans irrespective of whether they were resident in the empires of Mali or in an Ibo village. In reconstructing African civilisations, the concern is to indicate that African social life had meaning and value, and that the African past is one with which the black man in the Americas can identify with pride (Rodney 1969c: 52).

Although Rodney does not idealise this past there is a tension between the nationalist and the materialist impulses in his historical reconstructions. The nationalistic impulse led him to bring out the elements or features in African history that would enhance self-esteem while the materialist led him to a rigorous presentation of African social structures and the critique of African elites. Indeed it is often hard to distinguish between the severity of his exposure of African elites and their European counterparts though the latter bore the brunt of his critique.

This critique appeared in his pamphlet entitled "West Africa and the Atlantic Slave Trade"[10] where he contended that

> for nearly the whole of the period of the Atlantic slave trade in West Africa (and in East Africa also), there were many Africans who were prepared to sell their fellow men in exchange for European manufactures such as cloth, pots and pans, beads and fire-arms . . . It must be emphasised that the rulers in West Africa were in full political control during the period of the Atlantic slave trade. This was true even in areas where European forts were established, because forts were usually built with the permission of the African rulers, and the Europeans were forced to pay rents and taxes for being there. To a large extent, therefore, the Europeans conducted their slave trading on the West African coast under conditions laid down by the Africans (Rodney 1967a: 6–7).

But the corollary to this was that

> the Atlantic slave trade was organised and financed by Europeans, who had already reached a capitalist stage of development. Africans had absolutely no control over the European side or the American side of the slave trade. Only the European capitalists had such world-wide power, and they used Africans for their own purposes (Rodney 1967a: 6–7).

This was Rodney the materialist avoiding the dangers of a black and white, cut and dried, good and evil, European versus African, binary interpetation of history.

The tension between the nationalistic and materialist dimensions characterised his reconstruction of African history and is evident in *How Europe Underdeveloped Africa* as well as in two long essays he wrote for the *Cambridge History of Africa* which appeared in 1975.

The Cambridge essays

These two essays entitled "The Guinea Coast" and "Africa in Europe and the Americas" were written for *The Cambridge History of Africa*. Vol. 4. *c.1600–c.1790* which was edited by Richard Gray, Rodney's professor at the School of Oriental and African Studies. Those who propound that *How Europe Underdeveloped Africa* dealt too much with the impact of external factors on Africa and insufficiently with the internal relations which contributed to underdevelopment need to look at these essays which are less well known.[11] They show Rodney's knowledge of pre–slave trade Africa and the network of slave trade relations involving Africa, Europe and the Americas. I have quoted extensively from these two essays as contributions to the volume in which they were included as they are not a well-known part of Rodney's works.

The focus of the long essay on the Guinea Coast is on the process of state building in Africa and the relationship between the maturation of African city-states and slave trading. Rodney reconstructed the social, political and economic systems of West African societies that existed contemporaneously with the Atlantic slave trade. The base from which the African ruling elite played a crucial role in slave raiding and facilitated the huge transatlantic trade was carefully set out. State formation, social differentiation within Africa as well as subordination to Europe were speeded up by the slave raiding and trading practices. The expansion of plantations in the Americas created a demand for African labour which grew exponentially with the investment of European finance in the colonies. The other essay "Africa in Europe and the Americas" showed the diaspora that was created on the other side of the Atlantic and its impact on those shores.

Rodney's approach in the essay on West Africa was to examine the different cultural zones on the Guinea Coast, focusing on the Yorubas, the Ibos, the Upper Guinea Coast, with its strong Mande influence, and the Gold Coast Akan culture. State formation was a complex process. Referring to Oyo, Benin and Dahomey, Rodney wrote:

> Traditions in Oyo and Benin mention the same founding dynasty of Oranmiyan, and there were a large number of Yoruba under Benin's authority. Political relations between Oyo and Dahomey were substantial, the former

exercising some degree of control over Aja country throughout the eighteenth century (Rodney 1975b: 223).

He also pointed out that the

> existence of internal trade and of taxation and tribute mechanisms attests to the integration of resources, with cowries serving as a medium of exchange. The field of comparative religions has been more fully investigated, and there is no doubt about the fundamental religious ties between these peoples (Rodney 1975b: 226).

Benin, on the other hand, was far-flung and defined as:

> a central nucleus plus a large number of tributary states. In the nucleus of the state, the oba alone could inflict the death penalty. Differences in dialects and facial marks were among the clues which provided ready identification concerning both regional origins and position on the social hierarchy (Rodney 1975b: 226–27).

The oba was said to be capable of raising an army of 80,000 to 100,000 men. Power was decentralised through local civil and military representatives and trade was quite well developed:

> Metropolitan Benin manufactured brass utensils and iron implements; coastal areas produced salt; while cloth was the most valuable commodity originating in the near interior. Other domestic resources which entered into the cycle of local trade included ivory, coral beads, leather, beans and palm products (Rodney 1975b: 229).

The kingdom of Oyo spread through military conquest in the seventeenth and eighteenth centuries and it was known for its expert cavalry. It overpowered Dahomey in the eighteenth century and achieved the subordination of the Yorubas in the nineteenth century. Rodney's interpretation was that real power

> had passed to Oyo, in the sense of the capacity to make and implement decisions, based ultimately on military strength. Ife had to recognize this military and political power, but it counterposed its "authority" as father of the Yoruba – the said authority being exercised in the constitutional and military spheres (Rodney 1975b: 230).

He discussed the relationship between the royalty and nobility and the power play which ensued. In the case of Oyo, so strong were the nobility that the mode of succession had been changed from primogeniture to election by the major nonroyal lineages:

> The path was therefore clear for the nobility to rule with nominal reference to the alafin, and this happened during the ascendancy of Basorun Gaha (c. 1754–74). Gaha was called a dictator, but he must have been representative of most of the Oyo Mesi and other powerful interests. Otherwise he would have had no base on which to stand in opposition to the Alafin's lineage (Rodney 1975c: 241).

The basis for the undermining of the Alafin was the strengthening of the nobility through its record of military conquest as a result of which its political power grew as the empire expanded.

The slave trade transformed some African rulers into slave raiders. Some opposed the trade but even the well intentioned got drawn into it. One such was the Dahomean King Agaja Trudo[12] who, as was the case with the Kongo kings[13] in their contacts with the Portuguese, wanted to import European skills. According to Rodney:

> Agaja offered invitations to European craftsmen such as tailors, carpenters and blacksmiths. However, these overtures to establish relations with Europe other than those of slave trading evoked no positive response; and by 1730 Agaja was forced to come to terms with the European slave buyers. Apparently, his only successful stipulation was that the trade should come under exclusive royal control (Rodney 1975b, 246–47).

In the case of the Ibos, who were a dominant force in eastern Nigeria, the growth in the slave trade coincided with a relatively highly developed set of city-states among them:

> Their agriculture allowed major trade in surpluses; they were proficient in iron-working; their commercial activity extended throughout this region; and they had devised judicial and religious institutions which partially transcended the boundaries of their village governments. Over a wide area, large numbers of people spoke the various dialects of the Ibo people. Obviously, the fundaments of their way of life had been preserved and extended over a very long period (Rodney 1975b: 253).

Discussing slave raiding or captive taking for the internal economies of parts of West Africa, especially the Niger-Delta, Rodney noted that it transformed the descent-based Houses, especially in the delta. The House, as it developed in the eighteenth and nineteenth centuries, was as much a commercial firm as an extended family. It owned assets such as trading canoes; it controlled the labour and property of its members; it conducted credit operations and it organized agricultural plantations. The man power that became available as part of the slaving operations also contributed to the rise of 'Canoe Houses' in Bonny and Kalabari during the latter part of the eighteenth century . . . A few slaves, or the children of such, achieved great distinction within the city-states, especially during the late eighteenth century and subsequently. But, apart from the occasional 'success story,' the non-freeborn remain the most disprivileged section of the commonalty, some being very close to the status of chattel slaves (Rodney 1975b: 261).

Not only was the institution of the House disfigured but the secret societies, such as the 'ekine' or 'sekiapu', the masked dancing societies in the delta, and the famous Efik ekpe society dedicated to forest spirits, were also brought into the service of enslavement. Foreign trade helped build up ekpe into a powerful institution. Thus the slave trade had a profound impact on a wide range of political and cultural institutions in African society. And some of the political institutions moved from loose and decentralised systems to more centralised, hierarchical and oppressive structures. According to Rodney:

Ekpe as an association was far more important than any single individual, but its top positions were also the objects of the most important political posts, because these were the Houses that built up the greatest material resources and the largest population by retaining slaves for domestic use (Rodney 1975b: 268).

Contact between Africa and Europe was done through the ruling class in Africa. African raiders organised by the ruling class were mainly responsible for captives whether through war or piratical expeditions. As such, the impact on the rulers was profoundly negative for Africa. Rodney wrote:

Rulers and the upper class in general displayed a pattern of consumption which accorded the highest priority to European goods, regardless of quality or utility. European manufactures were part of their regalia; trade goods were buried underground to be stored for prestige; European houses were built for ostentation; and the dress to which city-state rulers were attached was invariably that cast off by Europeans. The king of Bonny in 1699 was described as wearing an old-fashioned scarlet coat, laced with gold and silver, very rusty, and a fine hat on his head. When the records provided a description of the Efik ruler in 1762, it was virtually identical with that given for the Bonny king. All the rulers in the Bight of Biafra had a partiality for gold-laced caps and stained European finery. Besides, the very names of the monarchs and other dignitaries were rendered as European – being either translations or more usually approximations to Ijo and Efik names. Often the choice was mundane to the point of 'Tom', 'Dick' and 'Harry'; and it was always incongruous, being no different from the slave names imposed on those Africans that the worthy House heads were helping to dispatch to the Americas (Rodney 1975b: 268–69).

Slave raiding worsened the quality of social relations and in Mande-dominated Upper Guinea coast and other areas there was a "marked increase in the servile and caste sectors" (Rodney 1975b: 283).

Under the impact of the slave trade the Gold Coast became the Slave Coast in the eighteenth century as slave extraction had become more profitable for some Akan groups than gold mining. Rodney observed that:

state building on the Gold Coast was up to the eighteenth century still essentially a process of agglomerating people rather than territory . . . Asante became more involved with the European slave trade as the eighteenth century progressed. Yet, at all times it defended and increased the population of metropolitan Asante at the expense of the provinces and more so at the expense of tributaries and areas on the frontiers of their empire (Rodney 1975b: 322–23).

The Asante ruling class might have protected its own citizens from sale into slavery but it preyed on others and contributed to the large-scale export of captives from Africa to the Americas.

The Guinea Coast analysis was one of Rodney's important essays in which he came to terms with the internal relations of West Africa and the way the slave trade transformed them in a fundamentally negative direction with dire consequences for a long historical period. My interest in "The Guinea Coast" is in Rodney's political and social reconstructions of the period contemporaneous with the slave trade, and the formation of the plantation economies in the Caribbean.[14] Rodney's work on the Guinea Coast facilitated a better understanding of the cultures, politics and state systems out of which the enslaved populations came. The state systems were not particularly large, neither were they strong and Inikori has proposed that:

African political systems had been undergoing evolutionary processes since the eleventh century as they responded to forces such as population pressure, religious ideologies and external trade from Asia, the Middle East and North Africa. The process of state formation over large populations and large geographical areas, with ruling classes and exploited lower classes cutting across lineages, clans and ethnic groups was still in the early stages in many areas (Inikori 1993b: 23).

It was in this general political context that the Atlantic slave trade took place and contributed to political fragmentation in the interest of securing captives for the plantations of the Americas.

The African diaspora[15]

The second Cambridge essay entitled "Africa in Europe and the Americas" was in part an analysis of the African diaspora and a synopsis of modern racism. It drew on Rodney's experience in teaching a course on the Black Diaspora at the University of Dar es Salaam. He reminded his readers that European writers did not always have a negative view of Africa. The views on Africa held by Europeans had been informed by old Greek legends, direct contact between North Africa and Europe, travel collections and scholarly works such as those by Leo Africanus that were published in several languages in the sixteenth and seventeenth centuries. He quoted Philip Curtin who wrote that "relative to their knowledge of the world in general, eighteenth century Europeans knew more and cared more about Africa than they did at any later period up to the 1950s" (Rodney 1975c: 580).[16] Rodney adds that this knowledge was restricted by class barriers such as:

> the illiteracy of the majority of the population, and by a matrix of preconceived ideas. There were only a few individuals with a professional interest in Africa: namely, administrators of overseas affairs, merchants and missionaries. In our own time, detailed knowledge about Africa in the hands of a minority of Europeans is compatible with crass ignorance on the part of the rest of the population. This is so in spite of widespread literacy and the availability of mass communications media. It was ignorance rather than knowledge which characterised Africa's image within Europe, so that novelists, poets, painters and playwrights catered to the new awareness of Africa mainly at the level of the exotic (Rodney 1975c: 581).

The African presence in Europe was strongest in Spain and Portugal where Africans were in domestic servitude before the heyday of the Atlantic slave trade (Pike 1972; Saunders 1982). In fact, the first African slaves sent to the New World were said to have come from Spain. For Rodney the main historical significance of the African presence in Portugal and Spain is the miscegenation which took place. Africans disappeared as a separate and distinct section of the population, but their large numbers ensured a lasting impact. Throughout the seventeenth and eighteenth centuries, it was common to refer to the Portuguese as dark, swarthy, Negroid, Moorish; and the mulatto element ran throughout all classes of the society (Rodney 1975c: 583).

He also discussed the African presence in England and France. In trying to explain modern racism he followed the positions taken by C.L.R. James and Eric Williams that it was the slave trade and plantation slavery that consolidated modern racism.[17] Plantation slavery in the Americas gave rise to political, legal and social institutions which legitimised racism not only in the Americas but in the Western world that profited from enslavement.

Rodney discussed the importance of the resistance of African peoples in ending slavery, and in the debate concerning the role of economic factors versus humanitarian values in the process of abolition, came down squarely on the side of economic factors. Analysing the impact of the French Revolution on the Caribbean, Rodney pointed out that it was only a minority of its leaders who were against slavery and it took the Haitian Revolution to end slavery and abolish a "major sector of the slave trade, and they were doing so many years before European nations passed abolitionist legislation of varying degrees of effectiveness" (Rodney 1975c: 597). Rodney assessed the enormous contribution of Africans to the creation of the Americas and the enrichment of Europe as well as the decisive stamp on modern music, dance and languages. He concluded the essay by advancing that

> Africans were carried to the Americas for the single though multi-faceted purpose of labouring in the interests of European capitalism. But the significance of their presence in this part of the world extended far beyond the aims and dispositions of the masters (Rodney 1975c: 622).

This essay focused on the African diaspora and the history of African peoples forcibly dispersed to become slaves and frontiersmen in creating a 'New World' for others. It produced a history of suffering as well as an overcoming of suffering. Critical to this survival was the "heritage of social organisation" of the enslaved Africans which enabled them not simply to survive but contributed to the remaking of the culture and social life of the regions created, in no small measure, out of the labour resulting from the Atlantic slave trade. Although he overstated the comparison with the indigenous populations of the Americas, Rodney pointed out that

Africans came from their mother continent with a heritage of social organization and solidarity at a level which was sufficiently high to allow them to survive collective labour at its most rigorous. The obverse of this is that Indians of settled agriculture were absolutely bewildered when imposed upon by the Europeans. For this and other reasons they failed to survive. Africans survived (Rodney 1975c: 605–606).

Rodney certainly overstated the comparison in relation to the indigenous populations of the Americas but the importance lies not in the comparison between the survival ratings of the two peoples but the recognition of the heritage of social organisation in the survival of African peoples in the diaspora.[18]

History and politics

In many of his writings Rodney probed a range of important topics which showed the relationship between compelling contemporary issues of decolonisation as he saw them and African history. One such issue was that of the history of African resistance to colonial rule. In his article "The Year 1895 in Southern Mozambique: African Resistance to the Imposition of European Colonial Rule" Rodney explored the Portuguese involvement in the late nineteenth century scramble for Africa. This article was published in Nigeria in 1971 when the war against Portuguese colonialism would not have allowed him to tap oral sources in Southern Mozambique. He was therefore forced to rely on Portuguese sources and wrote:

> The attempt to analyse the Afro-European confrontation from an African perspective reveals in an acute form some of the problems of African historiography. The written record comprises almost exclusively the reports of Portuguese army officers. Such reports are extremely jingoistic, even by imperialist standards. The orally-preserved record on the African side is hardly likely to be tapped in the present period of revolutionary war in Mozambique; and consequently the nationalist historian has willy nilly to wrestle with Portuguese accounts (Rodney 1971c: 509).

He discussed the Gaza monarchy and its empire and complex structure of inter-ethnic relations. He also analysed the battles fought by the Portuguese to defeat this developed political formation that had feudalistic features. He examined class and ethnic formation among the peoples of Southern Mozambique and wrote:

The point here is both to emphasize the existence of class lines running horizontally throughout the Gaza society and at the same time to emphasize the fuzziness of demarcation. The first aspect can be underestimated and ultimately lost in any analysis which takes ethnic groups as its basic referrent [sic], while the second is testimony to the slow rate of change in a process of dialectical evolution – bearing in mind that it was only in the capitalist phase of human development that contradictions sharpened to produce revolutionary change and well-delineated class-societies (Rodney 1971c: 518).

This gave some indication of the way in which Rodney approached the complex issue of class formation and ethnicity which he later developed in his writings on Guyanese history.

Rodney also showed how Europeans exploited the contradictions among different African ethnic groups in order to deploy Africans in the colonial army. Angolans played a key part in the Portuguese colonial army in the wars of conquest against other Africans. Rodney pointed out:

There were blacks from Angola who were being used as Portuguese troops in Mozambique as early as 1879. They were always placed in the most exposed positions and ran the greatest risks – being issued with less ammunition than white troops. At Marakwene, there were 200 Angolans out of 850 troops, and yet only three whites were killed and nine wounded, while more than thirty of the black soldiers were killed and twenty wounded (Rodney 1971c: 522–23).

Rodney did not dismiss these African soldiers in the colonial army as collaborators. Rather, recognising the association of the word with the idea of Nazi collaborators during World War II, he took the position, which is certainly open to debate, that "even the most benign conception of 'collaboration' involves unanimity with respect to objectives; and this could not have been present when Africans were unaware of European intentions and were indeed deliberately misled on that issue" (Rodney 1971c: 535). He went on to posit:

The most important and immediate consequence of Marakwene was that Africans lost the military initiative, and were unlikely to regain it, for Portuguese strength was derived from the strength of Western Europe, and the access which they had to the technological and organisational skills of European capitalism in the epoch of imperialism (Rodney 1971: 523).

The key weapon for the Portuguese was one of Europe's best rifles called the Kropatschek. In his Dar es Salaam seminar paper on "Resistance and

Accommodation in Ovimbundu/Portuguese Relations", he set out some of the basic ideas which are found in his African and Caribbean writings concerning the complex process of resistance and accommodation. He schematically laid out five phases of resistance to Portuguese domination. These were: phase 1 – Ovimbundu accommodation of Portuguese trade (eighteenth century to 1890); phase 2 – External aggression and conquest (1890–1900); phase 3 – Mass exploitation and mass resistance (1900–1904); phase 4 – Ovimbundu incorporation within a new political economy (1904–1967); phase 5 – The resurgence of resistance (1968 to the present) (Rodney 1972c: 1). Rodney concentrated on the second and third phases which coincided with the European scramble for Africa. Interestingly, he did not idealise African resistance even in the heady days of African nationalism when new states were being created and new myths being made. Accommodation concerned him as much as the heroic moments of resistance. The creation of the conditions for resistance were in a sense dialectically related to accommodation. Conquest meant subordination and incorporation and new contradictions emerged which formed the base for the resistance movements. In this respect he suggested that

> the evidence from various parts of the continent is mounting to indicate that the military conquest was almost invariably achieved by European-led but not European troops. In this regard it follows an observable trend in other colonial contexts and indeed from a class perspective it is always from among the oppressed that the oppressor selects his military force (Rodney 1972c: 6).

He concluded his paper by stating that

> Angolan freedom fighters themselves affirm a connection between their wars of national liberation and previous resistances, and that (on their authority) the mass of the people are said to recall positively the spirit of such events as the Bailundu[19] war. Idle academicians are in no position to challenge this (Rodney 1972c: 9).

Unlike historians who had ignored oral sources and for whom historical events were discrete, even disparate, Rodney's perspective of the past was that it illuminated the present. This enabled him to make connections that were not obvious to the individual concerned with an interpretation of the present that was narrowly empirical. Rodney was concerned in the 1960s and 1970s with what he considered the final phase of the struggle against Portuguese colonialism in Southern Africa and the issue of the support which the Portuguese had been obtaining ever since the nineteenth century struggles from their Boer allies. The structure of this paper therefore indicated the connections he made between the past and present.

In examining the implications of technology for colonial warfare Rodney wrote:

> Today, we are aware of how modern NATO weapons are used by Portugal against African peoples. It would be worthwhile to illumine the period of imperialist conquest by tracing the facilities by which Portugal obtained technological assistance and used this in Africa. The new technology certainly radically altered the balance of power both in Angola and Mozambique (Rodney 1972c: 3).

Thus Rodney pointed to the overall significance of technology in the success of colonialism, noting the role of the telegraph and railway which made a major difference in the quality of communications and in the coordination of effective military campaigns. According to a Portuguese source in the late nineteenth century, the time in organising troop reinforcements was significantly reduced (Rodney 1972c: 3).

In his essay "European Activity and African Reaction in Angola" Rodney succinctly presented many of the themes that are to be found in his better-known writings and lectures. The framework within which Rodney worked was the relationship between precapitalist Africa and the development of commercial capitalism in Europe. Rodney stated:

> The period of the world-wide development of European commerce, which began in the fifteenth century with the voyages of Portuguese and Spanish sailors to Africa, Asia and the New World, meant for Africa the beginning of the terrible experience of the Atlantic slave trade. Considering European slave-trading activities in Angola as part of the broader theme of slave-trading in central Africa, one finds that Angola occupies a special but unfortunate position. Angola and the Congo must be bracketed together as the principal slave-exporting sections of central Africa, both of them having made a tremendous contribution to the Atlantic slave trade (Rodney 1968a: 50).

He therefore showed the centrality of Angola in the slave trade and its importance to Portuguese trade especially to Brazil. Whereas the other European countries relied more on trade with African chiefs, greater violence was used in the case of Angola. Rodney argued that this was due to the uneven development of capitalism in Western Europe, which had left Portugal behind. As such, she was "not able to offer trade goods to the African in competition with other Europeans" (Rodney 1968a: 51). Slave raiding therefore became central to Portuguese slave trading. Circumstances in

Africa facilitated the barbarism of the slave raiding and trading practices as in most parts of the continent "Africans existed in small competing groups at little above subsistence level when they were thrown into a relationship with the commercial world of Europe" (Rodney 1968a: 54). Each political grouping fought their own battles against the Portuguese. Rodney pointed out that before the arrival of the Portuguese

> The Bangalas, Jagas and Sossos were both aggressors against the Mbundu and fighting among themselves. The Jagas and Bangalas were at that time particularly warlike and restless. Their whole life was organized for fighting and raiding under the leadership of a warrior chief or soba. Many migrations had not yet settled down and, particularly in eastern and southern Angola, tribes were still in the process of formation when the Portuguese arrived. That is to say, out of an intermixture of peoples of different tribes and clans, new tribes were being formed. Not even the Mbundu kingdom of Ndongo was a united whole, nor were the Ovimbundu to the south. In the nineteenth century, there were supposedly twenty-two Ovimbundu chiefdoms, about half of which paid tribute to one or other of the larger groups. Under these circumstances, it proved easy for the Portuguese to exploit existing enmities and gain allies and puppets (Rodney 1968a: 55).

At times different African groups made what they considered to be strategic and tactical linkages with the colonial invaders against other groups but these agreements contributed to long-term erosion of African sovereignty and the triumph of European domination. Rodney pointed out that if a

> soba (warrior chief) thought that the Portuguese newcomers would capture his war camp or threaten the way of life of his people, he would fight bitterly; but if instead the Portuguese offered him further profitable reasons to go on raiding his neighbours, then he would do so, with the additional factor now that his warriors would seize individuals from the raided villages to sell to the European slave-ships . . . It must be stressed that the small African political units were being loyal to their own petty interests and in most cases considered that they were employing the Portuguese rather than the other way around (Rodney 1968a: 56).

Rodney further showed that in addition to this fragmentation there was the appeal of European goods, as

> throughout Africa, European goods started off as luxuries, but rapidly came to be regarded as necessities. Africans were prepared to go to great lengths to obtain European goods, and this proved detrimental to their society and to their economic and political independence (Rodney 1968a: 54).

The consequences of this

> involvement of the African and European economies inevitably brought about major changes leading to the disappearance of the small political units, to the creation of a wider unity and to considerable modifications in the system of production. Those who noticed this trend at an earlier date than most of their fellows and those who sought the means of ensuring the welfare of the greatest number of Angolans are to be placed among the heroes of Angola and Africa (Rodney 1968a: 56).

Rodney identified Nzinga Nbandi, a Queen of Mbundu origin, as one such heroine of Angola. She is credited with being a founder of an independent state in Matamba in 1630 and as having created alliances with other groups in order to be stronger in the struggle against the Portuguese.

> Her pride, courage and resourcefulness both in military matters and in negotiations impressed even the Portuguese. However, no single individual can change the direction of history. Because she had great foresight, Queen Nzinga could point the way to the future when Angola would achieve unity in the face of the enemy, but the rate of change was determined by the impact of the European capitalist economy on the Angolan situation (Rodney 1968a: 57).

The emergence of Angolan mulattoes – referred to as 'pombeiros' – is also mentioned, and reflected Rodney's attention to the issue of colour and social stratification. Under commercial capitalism their numbers remained small and of course Portuguese colonialism restricted their development.

Rodney moved from discussing the relationship between European commercial capitalism and precapitalist Africa to the emergence of industrial capitalism and its impact on Africa. He wrote that the

> main impact of industrial capitalism on Africa was, firstly, to bring large sections of the population within the limits of the European money economy. More and more people would earn money from commerce, by working for wages and by selling crops; while they would use the money in making purchases and paying taxes. In the second place, industrial capitalism led to imperialism, one of whose features was the political domination of Africa by several European states (Rodney 1968a: 61).

Employing Eric Williams' thesis concerning the role of industrial capitalism in undermining slavery in the British colonies, Rodney repeated his argument that the historical backwardness of Portugal meant that she held on to the old forms of exploitation and oppression. She clung to the Atlantic slave trade until 1885 when slavery was abolished in Brazil and maintained slaves in Angola in Portuguese agricultural businesses even at the beginning of the twentieth century (Rodney 1968: 62).

How Europe Underdeveloped Africa[20]

Rodney made his name with *How Europe Underdeveloped Africa* which was published in 1972. It is interesting to observe that three other Guyanese scholars of Africa were to make noteworthy contributions to the study of Africa. There was George James' very controversial book *Stolen Legacy. The Greeks Were Not the Authors of Greek Philosophy, but the People of North Africa, Commonly Called the Egyptians* (1985) first published in 1954; then there was Denis Williams' *Icon and Image: a Study of Sacred and Secular Forms of African Classical Art* (1974) which analysed the Yoruba aesthetic idiom in clay and metal; and Ivan Van Sertima's *They Came before Columbus* (1976) dealt with the African presence in ancient America. To one extent or the other these works have become part of the Afrocentric canon.

How Europe Underdeveloped Africa continued in this tradition of West Indian scholarly investigation of Africa. In addition, it augments the West Indian intellectual tradition of three Trinidadians – J.J. Thomas' nineteenth century work *Froudacity*, and the twentieth century classics – C.L.R. James' *Black Jacobins* and Eric Williams' *Capitalism and Slavery*. Furthermore, what is interesting about these four personalities is the relationship between their scholarly work and political activism. Their research and writing provided the intellectual basis for their political activism which in the case of Thomas concerned the postemancipation status of Blacks as citizenry; with C.L.R. James and Williams it was geared towards the anticolonial struggle and in that of Rodney toward radical decolonisation.

Rodney tried to do for Africa what the dependency theorists, especially Andre Gunder Frank, had done for Latin America. In a public lecture on "Strategies of Development" given in Toronto in 1975 he said that *How Europe Underdeveloped Africa* was not just a foray into the past but in it he had tried to come to grips with problems of underdevelopment and the role of colonialism in that process (Rodney 1975f). Rodney was a critic of the school of thought which saw colonialism as having had more positive than negative social and economic consequences for Africa. There were other African historians who regarded the "colonial impact as skin-deep and maintained that colonialism did not constitute any break with the African past" (Boahen 1990: 337). However, *How Europe Underdeveloped Africa* was also shaped by Rodney's experience at the University of Dar es Salaam and the intellectual ferment there in the late 1960s and early 1970s among his fellow academics, a minority of them of a critical Marxist persuasion (Campbell 1986). Then there was the interaction with his students, many of whom were in his age group, the questions they were asking and his involvement in popular education in Tanzania as well as in Jamaica in 1968.

His intention in writing[21] *How Europe Underdeveloped Africa* is set out in a letter to his publisher:

> The main request which you made is that the manuscript should be passed on to an African historian, because you felt yourself unequal to the task of judging its worth as 'serious history'. It is an ideological challenge. Unfortunately, there is scarcely anyone about, who combines my own world-view with data about the African past. My procedure has been to try as hard as possible to let the work be scrutinised by progressive individuals. To pass it on to a serious bourgeois historian would be a sheer waste of time. Under the circumstances, I will have to be authority for whether a given fact, date, name, etc. is correct. Beyond that, it is a matter of interpretation, logical and internal consistency. The text aims at a strata of literate Africans in universities, secondary schools, the bureaucracy and the like. They will have to judge whether it makes sense in the light of present conditions in Africa (Rodney 1971a).

In other words, his decision to write in this way was political, and was influenced by the fact that as an intellectual leader at the University of Dar es Salaam he was deeply involved with Tanzania's "attempt to chart a course of development beyond the classical neo-colonial path" (Campbell 1986: 14).

Rodney had completed writing *How Europe Underdeveloped Africa* at age 29 and it was published in his thirtieth year. This work marked the transition to writing directed at a wider audience of African readers about Africa. Rodney developed the theme of the impact of the European slave trade and colonialism on Africa, at greater length, and with greater polemical and theoretical vigour than was possible in a doctoral dissertation. It was a revolt against established academic scholarship on Africa and it was unencumbered by the footnoting rituals of the thesis and the genuflections to the authorities whose views one opposes but in whose hands one's academic future and tenure lay.

Theoretically the work combined a Marxist method of historical analysis with Latin American dependency theory. It was multidisciplinary in focus, drawing on his expertise in historical research and his wide reading in the social sciences. In addition, Rodney's approach to development was not narrowly economistic. He started out by defining development in a broad and universalist manner, considering it both at the individual and societal levels.

"At the level of the individual, it implies increased skill and capacity, greater freedom, creativity, self-discipline, responsibility, and material well-being." At the level of social groups, "development implies an increasing capacity to regulate both internal and external relationships" (Rodney 1983: 9–10). In discussing development at its most general level Rodney was intent on establishing the viewpoint of the universal character of this process.

> Development was universal because the conditions leading to economic expansion were universal. Everywhere man was faced with the task of survival by meeting fundamental material needs; and better tools were a consequence of the interplay between human beings and nature as part of the struggle for survival. Of course human history is not a record of advances and nothing else. There were periods in every part of the world when there were temporary setbacks and actual reduction of the capacity to produce basic necessities and other services for the population. But the overall tendency was towards increased production, and at given points of time the increase in the quantity of goods was associated with a change in the quality or character of society (Rodney 1983: 11).

The dialectical relationship between development in Europe and underdevelopment in Africa as a result of centuries of the slave trade and colonialism is a central thesis of this work. At the heart of Africa's underdevelopment therefore is Europe's development. This could lead some critics to argue that Rodney understated the internal factors responsible for underdevelopment. While the emphasis in this book is on the external factors Rodney is at pains to point out that there were social forces within Africa which facilitated the process of underdevelopment or maldevelopment but they were not the key players in the larger game. In analysing this relationship Rodney focused on issues of comparative development between Europe and Africa. In opening up this discussion Rodney took on colonial historiography that had been characterised by assumptions based on racist views about the inherent superiority of whites as well as religious and pseudohistorical views which basically justify the status quo. He was also sharply critical of those who presented the slave trade and colonialism as having significant advantages for Africa. The issue as to what alternative approaches and social forces could create genuine development for the African peoples lay at the heart of many of his speeches and articles. He had a socialist perspective but was critical of the state centred socialism in the Soviet Union and Eastern Europe as well as China, and his writings on Tanzania and the Caribbean in the 1970s showed that he did not expect much from either existing African or Caribbean political leaderships.

In order to adequately understand Africa's postcolonial predicament Rodney was intent on establishing the historical process that was responsible for Africa falling behind so badly.

Rodney was also concerned with issues of uneven development within Africa as well as within Europe. In his dissertation he had discussed the reasons which made the Iberian countries lose out to competing European nations. Uneven development was itself a consequence of the social and economic forces at work in Africa before and during the long and oppressive years of the slave trade and colonialism.

One of the basic issues in Marxist theory related to the historical modes of production. Many crude Marxists writing in the period employed the categories Marx had developed for Europe as it proceeded from communalism, ancient slavery, feudalism to capitalism and they imposed this schema on Africa. Rodney tried to map out his own paradigm of the evolution of the African continent. On this issue he wrote:

> Marx himself recognized that the stages of development in Asia had produced a form of society which could not easily be fitted into a European slot. That he called 'the Asian mode of production'. Following along those lines, a number of Marxists have recently been discussing whether Africa was in the same category as Asia or whether Africa had its own 'African mode of production'. The implications of the arguments are very progressive, because they are concerned with the concrete conditions of Africa rather than with preconceptions brought from Europe. But the scholars concerned seem to be bent on finding a single term to cover a variety of social formations which were existing in Africa from about the fifth century A.D. to the coming of colonialism. The assumption that will underlie this study is that most African societies before 1500 were in a transitional stage between the practice of agriculture (plus fishing and herding) in family communities and the practice of the same activities within states and societies comparable to feudalism (Rodney 1983: 46).

These are the transitional forms in existence at the moment that the encounter between emergent capitalist Europe and precapitalist Africa took place. Africa's development was retarded, distorted and in some cases suppressed by the slave trade and colonialism. Rodney contended:

> if the low figure of ten million was accepted as a basis for evaluating the impact of slaving on Africa as a whole, the conclusions that could legimately be drawn would confound those who attempt to make light of the experience of the rape of Africans from 1445 to 1870 (Rodney 1983: 96).

Rodney pointed out that "the colonisation of Africa lasted for just over 70 years in most parts of the continent" (Rodney 1983: 244). It was a much shorter period than that of the slave trade but from the evidence marshalled in *How Europe Underdeveloped Africa* no less devastating. It was an intensive period of exploitation, extracting far greater surpluses and repatriating them to Europe, thus intensifying the gap between a developed Europe and underdeveloped Africa. Rodney provided examples of the vast difference in wages between African and European workers, the exploitation of the peasantry not only by the colonial landowners but a whole chain of intermediaries including usurious creditors and marketing boards which bought cheap. There were no sickness and death benefits and workers who died in mining accidents were simply replaced by a new set eager for employment. Compensation was not obligatory and when payments were made these amounted to a pittance. The colonial state played an important role in facilitating this exploitation through its coercive role as well as through its marketing boards, land policy and tax system. As a result of colonial expansion Europe continued to leap ahead of Africa.

Of the transition from colonialism to imperialism Rodney wrote:

> Ever since the fifteenth century, Europe was in strategic command of world trade and of the legal and organizational aspects of the movement of goods between continents. Europe's power increased with imperialism, because imperialism meant investments, and investments (with or without colonial rule) gave European capitalists control over production within each continent (Rodney 1983: 193).

Rodney also examined the scientific and technological changes resulting from production and trade in the colonies such as the invention of machinery for processing agricultural produce, shipping design, refrigeration and even the development of synthetics to reduce dependency on the colonies. Rodney identified the changes in the qualitative character of capitalism:

> European capitalism achieved more and more a social character in its production. It integrated the whole world; and with colonial experience as an important stimulus, it integrated very closely every aspect of its own economy – from agriculture to banking. But distribution was not social in character. The fruits of human labour went to a given minority class, which was of the white race and resident in Europe and North America. This is the crux of the dialectical process of development and underdevelopment, as it evolved over the colonial period (Rodney 1983: 197–98).

How Europe Underdeveloped Africa remains a devastating critique of colonial historiography of Africa. Rodney did not spend too much time in a point by point refutation of this historiography but concentrated on clarifying the way in which Africa had been drawn into a world economy that had reduced it to continental underdevelopment. Rodney had particular contempt for the balance sheet approach to colonialism with its accounting imperative requiring one to see the pluses and minuses of the process of subjugation. For Rodney colonialism was a malignant cancer and not a benign growth. The final chapter in this book is subtitled "The Supposed Benefits of Colonialism to Africa". Commenting on the balance sheet approach Rodney wrote:

> On that balance sheet, they place both the credits and the debits, and quite often conclude that the good outweighed the bad. That particular conclusion can quite easily be challenged, but attention should also be drawn to the fact that the process of reasoning is itself misleading. The reasoning has some sentimental persuasiveness. It appeals to the common sentiment that 'after all there must be two sides to a thing'. The argument suggests that, on the one hand, colonial governments did much for the benefit of Africans and they developed Africa. It is our contention that this is completely false. Colonialism had only one hand – it was a one-armed bandit (Rodney 1983: 223).

In arguing his case Rodney showed how little was done in education, health, communications and other areas during the colonial period.

While colonialism therefore facilitated the development of capitalism in Europe it retarded its development in Africa. Rodney contended that

> it is essential to distinguish between capitalist elements and capitalism as a total social system. Colonialism introduced some elements of capitalism into Africa. In general terms, where communalism came into contact with the money economy, the latter imposed itself (Rodney 1983: 235).

European colonialists preferred to assist minorities such as the Asians to emerge as middlemen while the way up for African businessmen was blocked by legal, financial and social barriers. Colonialism needed African labourers not African capitalists. The African working class that emerged in the colonial era was largely unskilled and had a low level of modern industrial skills.

> By its very nature, colonialism was prejudiced against the establishment of industries in Africa, outside of agriculture and the extractive spheres of mining

and timber felling. Whenever internal forces seemed to push in the direction of African industrialisation, they were deliberately blocked by the colonial governments acting on behalf of the metropolitan industrialists (Rodney 1983: 237).

Given the fact that the emergence of an African bourgeoisie was frustrated by colonialism, Rodney failed to seriously consider the prospects for its development as part of developmental options in the postcolonial era. Such consideration was in opposition to his strong anticapitalist position. The issue of the development of forms of capitalism that are consistent with national goals in the context of the strengthening of the global capitalist system has been forcibly put back on the agenda since the late 1980s.

Previously, however, in the political strategy of the left wing of the anticolonial movement capitalism and colonialism were seen as twin evils. Some of the radical leaders of the independence movement were influenced by socialist theory and sought to develop socialist strlopment based on the Soviet and Chinese experience. Theories of noncapitalist development and socialist orientation were appealing to some Third World states where capitalism was most under-developed. The policies of socialist orientation, as the African experience indicated, meant the development of state to state relations with the former Soviet Union and the development of a party and state-economic bureaucracy to run the economy. However, the socialist experiments of the 1970s and 1980s have had negative economic consequences. Pressure from the IMF and the World Bank, the major brokers of the international capitalist economy, political changes in Eastern Europe as well as domestic opposition have led to a swing to market oriented policies and the mouthing of multiparty approaches to democracy in a number of African countries. But the issue of the African bourgeoisie and the extent to which the state can be used as a means to help create such a class remains an issue notwithstanding the fact that some political scientists see the ruling class in Africa to date as exhibiting predatory characteristics (Nyang'oro 1989: 135; Fatton 1992).[22]

The political consequences of colonialism included the suppression of large and small traditional polities, it meant the denial of civil and constitutional liberties and the exclusion of the colonised people from politics on grounds of race and class. Rodney observed:

> Jules Ferry, a former French colonial minister, explained that the French Revolution was not fought on behalf of the blacks of Africa. Bourgeois liberty, equality, and fraternity was not for colonial subjects. Africans had to make do with bayonets, riot acts and gunboats (Rodney 1983: 244).

Colonialism thus denied bourgeois liberty to the colonised. Just as colonialism underdeveloped capitalism as an economic system within the colony it did the same thing in the political sphere. However the contempt with which many of the radical leaders held bourgeois democracy was sometimes misplaced insofar as it identified forms of colonial autocracy with bourgeois rule. When socialist experiments were tried ideas of individual liberty, freedom of the judiciary, the press, etc. were seen as bourgeois and identified with the reactionary colonial past. Rodney was not guilty of this as is shown in my discussion in chapter 9 of his political involvement in Guyanese and Caribbean politics in the 1970s. His political activism and his critique of the left-authoritarian positions of Burnham and Bishop showed his concern for the creation of the conditions for civil society and political freedom.

In sum, *How Europe Underdeveloped Africa* remains a tour de force of theorising backed up by wide-ranging empirical knowledge and good writing. It achieved what the author set out to do and remains a classic of historical research and synthesis both for general and specialist readers on Africa.

Many of the themes in *How Europe Underdeveloped Africa* were developed in the lectures given at the University of Hamburg in the summer of 1978. These lectures constitute another fine example of his ability to link African history to current issues of socioeconomic development. He was against history as the study of antiquarianism and criticised some of his colleagues for being more concerned "with bones and artefacts and with things that have crumbled" than with "living history that reflects itself in the present, with what one historian has called the 'present as history'" (Rodney 1984: 19–20). The Hamburg lectures are significant because they point to some of the methodological approaches Rodney used in his research and writing such as the importance of understanding, as C.L.R. James had demonstrated, the "particular historical conjuncture in a society" (Rodney 1984: 7), his emphasis on the interrelationship between particular local economies and the world capitalist economy and his exposure of racially based assumptions about human history. Taking as his example the Gambia, he illustrated what one could call the economic conjuncture of that country:

> if we are examining the economy of the Gambia we have to ask ourselves: what does the Gambia produce? Our answer is: a monocrop, groundnuts. The Gambia produces groundnuts and the groundnuts enter into world trade mainly because they will produce edible oil and fats, margarine in particular. But somehow, in our analysis of the processes of development and under-

development in the Gambia, we omit to mention that the principal buyer of its groundnuts will be Unilever. Now you and I know that if you want to find out about Unilever you will have to go down the road here in Hamburg; you will never find out much about Unilever in the Gambia, because Unilever's operations in the Gambia are an insignificant part of its worldwide operations. To understand the nature of groundnut pricing you have to take a broader framework than the Gambia: you have to look at the groundnuts coming from other areas; at Unilever's buying and selling policies with respect to groundnuts and palm-oil; and at the worldwide implications of the fact that the Gambia is engaged in an international specialisation. This is the critical point: the specialisation in groundnuts is an international specialisation; it is part of an international system. If you do not look at the international system your analysis is inadequate; it is partial (Rodney 1984: 11).

Rodney had identified the way in which concession companies had used forced labour and had created labour reserves for the production of crops such as cocoa and groundnuts. Rodney argued that the latter two mechanisms were the most important and that the use of concession companies was a feature of the early stage of colonialism:

when the colonial state had not yet been formed, when a particular colonial power still did not have either the capacity to establish nor the interest in establishing a colonial state . . . The German East African Company, for example, was a very powerful company as concession companies went, but ultimately it was the German state which had to intervene at the time of the Maji Maji wars and it was the German state which later had to be responsible for actual conquest of the territory and for establishing what would have been called the 'colonial peace': the order of stability required for the extraction of surplus (Rodney 1984: 65).

In Southern Africa and other areas of white settlement Rodney pointed out that what white landowners needed was cheap labour. So therefore once the whites controlled the land they looked for labour. Rodney drew two important theoretical conclusions. First, he was of the view that "land alienation and the creation of labour as a commodity went hand in hand" (Rodney 1984: 70). His other key conclusion was that labour reserves in Africa meant the creation of a working class and colonial trade meant the development of a peasant class.

Rodney's focus on Africa's incorporation into the world capitalist system mirrored the experience of so many third world economies. While accepting the concept of a single world capitalist system he rejected the view that change depended primarily on struggles at the centre and argued that struggles in the periphery were just as important. This kind of intellectual work showed how he had positioned himself as a historian concerned with the relationship between history and the social sciences. In this regard, Rodney valued the work of the economist Samir Amin. Commenting on Amin's work Rodney said:

> it is precisely because he has a materialist and Marxist world outlook that for him, the integration of history into analysis is a normal thing, it is the first thing that he must do . . . It is impossible to discuss African development without discussing African history; this has been proved by individuals like Samir Amin (Rodney 1984: 22).

In *How Europe Underdeveloped Africa* he had demonstrated how important the historical dimension was to an understanding of the current issues of underdevelopment. These points were repeated in the Hamburg lectures, and in papers such as "The Historical Roots of African Underdevelopment" (1970b) and "African History and Development Planning" (1973c) which were done at the University of Dar es Salaam. Rodney gave us an understanding of the genesis of his own work when he stated:

> my own work initially came about precisely through an awareness that neither the historian nor the economist in the traditional schools, in places like the School of Oriental and African Studies in London which was supposed to be a leading centre of African history, had sought to understand why the present was the way it was . . . This analysis had of course been carried out for Latin America, India and other parts of Asia before the new perception that underdevelopment was a historical force, that underdevelopment came about because of the specific relationships of international production which had been established between different parts of the world. The initial hypothesis might be crude; one must always be self-critical enough to see that when one challenges an old methodology and attempts to substitute it with a new starting point, one's own approach might have certain weaknesses which others coming along in the field will have to clarify. But however crude the hypothesis might be, it seems to me to be now beyond the shadow of a doubt that we can no longer discuss African history or the present without locating them within this trajectory of underdevelopment and dependency (Rodney 1984: 22–23).

In his lecture "A Century of Development in Africa", Rodney dismissed the racist notion of the British historian Hugh Trevor-Roper who had said that Africa had no history other than the history of Europeans in Africa (1984: 34). This conception had led to the view that African development started with colonialism. Rodney identified two other positions on the meaning of colonialism in Africa. The first of these contended that "Colonialism did not last for very long, did not affect Africans very much, and now that it is over, Africans can return to their natural selves." The other position was that "Europe's intervention into Africa was a profound intervention which is still living with us: the colonial past is very much a part of the present" (Rodney 1984: 35). It was the latter thesis that Rodney supported. He contended that in his research

> which began with slavery, one of the things that struck me quite early was that the slave trade was antecedent to colonialism and that colonialism in fact reinforced tendencies that had already begun with the slave trade ... for those parts of the African continent involved in the slave trade, the slave trade represented their first major involvement in the world economy; and that with colonialism, that involvement was intensified in many ways. For one thing, colonialism directly exploited the land and labour of African people inside Africa while the slave trade, of course, took that labour outside of the African continent (Rodney 1984: 38–39).

Rodney went on to emphasise the role of violence in this process and African resistance to it. He looked at the many-sided nature of the resistance – from that of centralised sociopolitical formations to that of small groups. There was the resistance of African middlemen to the takeover of their economic role by Europeans. He provided the example of how the Europeans tried to take over the trade in slaves and ivory from Arab Swahili traders of East Africa. Rodney also highlighted cultural resistance. He saw the conflict not primarily as a racial one but as a conflict between precapitalist and capitalist social formations and modes of production. Linking this conception to the contemporary period, Rodney maintained that "One of the illusions created by modern social science is that the commodity relations which exist among us today constitute the normal, natural, primordial way in which society was always organised." He therefore underscores the historicity not only of the past but the present.

A study of the reception and critical references to *How Europe Underdeveloped Africa* has its own intellectual value. In a review published in the Dar es Salaam *Sunday News* 22 November 1972, the book was hailed "as probably the greatest book event in Africa since Frantz Fanon". Horace Campbell (1973), a Jamaican political scientist, writing from Makerere University in Uganda, referred to it as "a major breakthrough in its thorough analysis of the impact and results of European exploitation of Africa." In 1973 the African Studies Association of the West Indies at the University of the West Indies in Kingston sponsored a symposium on *How Europe Underdeveloped Africa* and presentations were made by historian and poet, Edward Kamau Brathwaite (1973), economist, Norman Girvan (1973), historian, Ken Hall (1973), and political scientist, Rupert Lewis (1973) and published in the *Bulletin of the African Studies Association of the West Indies*, vol. 6. Brathwaite's presentation entitled "Dialect and Dialectic" concluded by stating that the work needed to have some "dialect to go along with the dialectic". In other words, Rodney was being criticised for not going beyond protest literature into the exploration of an alternative African-derived discourse as to how to emerge from underdevelopment.

Other critics accused Rodney of being too nationalistic. Bill Freund argued that although Rodney "betrayed much of the influence of the earlier idealist and romantic Afro-American nationalist understanding of Africa, his book represented a powerful and effective break with the positivism of the Africanists" (Freund 1984: 11–12). John Thornton saw Rodney as belonging to a group of scholars who used the French Annalistes tradition with a neo-Marxist focus. Among the scholars were André Gunder Frank, Immanuel Wallerstein and Eric Wolf. Thornton argued that these writers

> agreed that the non-Western world, including Africa, had played a passive role in the development of the Atlantic. Although their radical perspective and their advocacy of Third World causes tend to make them sympathetic to Africa, the effect was simply to reinforce the tentative conclusions of the French pioneers that Africa was a victim, and a passive victim at that, for it lacked the economic strength to put up an effective resistance (Thornton 1992: 4).

Thornton's reading of Rodney seems ideologically motivated to fix Rodney within the group of scholars mentioned above. There is ample evidence in Rodney's writings, and which I refer to in this chapter, that he did not see Africa simply as a passive victim.

In a critical introduction to the sixth edition of *How Europe Underdeveloped Africa* Robert Shenton (1983) noted that his own introduction had been done originally as a review in 1974 which had its origins in frustration. His frustration arose from the fact that Rodney's book seemed to him to have been a major breakthrough, yet it was largely ignored by the African history establishment. "It was as if the political and scholarly importance of the book could be killed by a conspiracy of silence and polite laughter in University corridors and 'Africanist' conferences" (Shenton 1983: ii). This frustration was certainly not shared by Rodney whose readership in Africa made *How Europe Underdeveloped Africa* become the flagship book for Tanzania Publishing House (Dar es Salaam) and Bogle L'Ouverture (London). Four reprints by Bogle L'Ouverture appeared before Rodney's death in 1980. A seventh edition, also by Bogle L'Ouverture appeared in 1988. Howard University Press did an American edition in 1974. A French edition appeared in 1986 and a German one in 1980 (Rodney 1980f, 1986). There are Japanese and Spanish translations as well.

How Europe Underdeveloped Africa has been widely referenced by historians and social scientists working on Africa. They use it as a point of departure to develop their own theses and ideas either in affirmation or in opposition to Rodney.

Conclusion

Rodney wrote as a Marxist historian in the tradition of C.L.R. James. His work on precolonial Africa illustrated the diverse social, ethnic structures and state systems in Africa, the relationship between African and European slave traders and the way in which this trade fuelled commercial capitalism in Europe while retarding Africa's growth. Commercial capitalism laid the basis for European colonial expansion and late nineteenth century imperialism. This was the history that postcolonial Africa and the Caribbean faced and for Rodney the agenda of decolonisation could not be elaborated and tackled without a profound grasp of the intersection of African and European history. This intellectual work informed his political activism in Africa and the diaspora.

Notes

1. There is a large body of work on the Atlantic slave trade. C.L.R James, Eric Williams and Walter Rodney can be regarded as scholars who pioneered work on the Atlantic economic and political relations that arose out of the slave trade. Eric Williams' 1944 study *Capitalism and Slavery* as well as Rodney's *How Europe Underdeveloped Africa* are frequently referred to in contemporary debates on the slave trade. C.L.R. James was a mentor to both Williams and Rodney. As Selwyn Cudjoe (1993) has pointed out, James' Marxist ideas had an impact on Williams' work *Capitalism and Slavery*.

    I have found useful the volume by Inikori and Engerman (1994) and their essay entitled "Introduction: Gainers and Losers in the Atlantic Slave Trade". They write that the "issues fall into three broad groups: (1) the social cost in Africa of forced migration; (2) Atlantic slavery and the rise of the Western world; and (3) Atlantic slavery, the world of the slaves and their enduring legacies."

2. Thornton provides this snapshot: "The Annaliste school, named after its principal journal, *Annales: Economies, Sociétés, Civilisations*, was founded on the initiative of

Fernand Braudel and Lucien Febure after the Second World War. It sought to integrate social and economic history as the focal point for historians and de-emphasised traditional themes of political, military, and diplomatic history" (Thornton 1992: 4 fn 11).

3. Certainly one of the weaknesses of *The Black Jacobins* is its failure to account for the fact that the majority of the slave population was born in Africa and to discuss the political and military significance of these fresh imports. While the French Revolution obviously was the central event in creating the conditions for a successful revolt and the ideas of liberty had a politicising impact on the slave population, the latter were more than black Jacobins. They had their own ideas of freedom, they brought with them military and political experience etc. which any rewrite of the Haitian Revolution would have to account for. One is, however, mindful of the fact that in making the Africans in Haiti the centrepiece of his analysis of revolution, James was attacking racist attitudes which denied their role as makers of history.

4. For useful discussions of Rodney as a historian, see Alpers (1982) and Ferguson (1982).

5. Some critics still maintain that Rodney romanticised precolonial Africa. "I think it is fair to say that, at least subconsciously Rodney was a romantic, falling for the myth of the 'noble savage', believing in an ideal and idyllic precolonial 'Merrie Africa'" (Fage 1989: 128).

6. Gender issues, marginally dealt with in the colonial historiography of Africa, are also raised in *How Europe Underdeveloped Africa*. Rodney contended that

> A realistic assessment of the role of women in independent pre-colonial Africa shows two contrasting but combined tendencies. In the first place women were exploited by men through polygamous arrangements designed to capture the labour power of women. As always, exploitation was accompanied by oppression; and there is evidence to the effect that women were sometimes treated like beasts of burden, as for instance in Moslem societies. Nevertheless, there was a countertendency to insure the dignity of women to greater or lesser degree in all African societies. Mother-right was a prevalent feature of African societies, and particular women held a variety of privileges based on the fact that they were keys to inheritance.
>
> More important still, some women had real power in the political sense, exercised through religion or directly within the politico-constitutional apparatus. In Mozambique, the widow of an Nguni king became the priestess in charge of the shrine set up in the burial place of her deceased husband, and the reigning king had to consult her on all important matters. In a few instances, women were actually heads of state. Among the Lovedu of Transvaal, the key figure was the Rain-Queen, combining political and religious functions. The most frequently encountered role of importance played by women was that of 'Queen Mother' or 'Queen Sister'. In practice, that post was filled by a female of royal blood, who might be mother, sister, or aunt of the reigning king in places such as Mali, Asante, and Buganda. Her influence was considerable, and there were occasions when the 'Queen Mother' was the real power and the male king a mere puppet.
>
> What happened to African women under colonialism is that the social, religious, constitutional, and political privileges and rights disappeared, while the economic exploitation continued and was often intensified (Rodney 1983: 247–48).

See Robertson and Klein (1983) *Women and Slavery in Africa.*

7. See also Inikori and Engerman (1994) for an extensive discussion of the impact of the Atlantic slave trade. See Hair (1978) for a view from Britain opposed to Rodney's interpretation of the impact of the Atlantic slave trade on Africa.

8. Paul Lovejoy says that in the late 1990s:

    the focus has shifted from the total number of slaves to gender, age, regional and temporal variations in the source and flow of people. This has allowed a whole bunch of new questions that relates to issues of ethnicity, a reconsideration of the centrality of political will, and the recognition that there was a much more open and flexible trans-Atlantic community, not just between Europe and the Americas but between Africa and the Americas (Lovejoy 1997).

9. In her review of the literature on slavery and the slave trade in Africa, Janet Ewald (1992) distinguishes between Islamic Africa and Atlantic Africa. Atlantic Africa refers to "those parts of sub-Saharan Africa that sustained an intercontinental exchange of goods or slaves via the Atlantic". Islamic Africa comprised "those parts of the continent south of the Sahara where Muslims exercised significant cultural, economic, or political influence; Islamic Africa was not a homogenous bloc" (465 fn 1). She quotes estimates from Paul Lovejoy claiming that there were a total of 11,612,000 slaves crossing the Red Sea, Indian Ocean and Sahara Desert from 650 to 1900; from 1500 to 1900, he estimates that 11,656,000 crossed the Atlantic. She also quotes the findings of Ralph Austen who suggested that 17,000,000 African slaves crossed the Eastern oceans (466 fn 2).

10. See also Rodney (1967c) for a similar discussion on the slave trade. This essay was included in the book edited by Roland Oliver with the curious title *The Middle Age of African History*.

11. In the introduction to the 1983 edition of *How Europe Underdeveloped Africa* Robert Shenton criticised Rodney for not paying sufficient attention to the impact of the slave trade on class relationships in Africa (1983: vii). Shenton had not done his homework in this regard.

12. Professor Richard Gray portrayed Agaja as a leader with military and diplomatic skill. His "creation of an original and highly organized intelligence service and system of military apprenticeship, enabled the state to survive the crises of his reign and to emerge as a tightly centralized unit" (Gray 1975: 9).

13. See Thornton (1983) and Hilton (1985) for discussion of the kingdom of Kongo.

14. While Rodney worked from Africa back to the Caribbean other scholars have worked from the Caribbean back to Africa using African language retentions. See Maureen Warner-Lewis (1991 and 1996a).

15. The study of the African diaspora is now a growing field. A useful survey article is Edmondson (1985). Among valuable collections are Crahan and Knight (1979), Bonnett and Watson (1990), Joseph Harris (1992), and an interesting research project is Hamilton (1990). Professor Ruth Simms Hamilton is director and principal investigator of the African Diaspora Research Project.

16. Much more work has been done on this topic of Africa's cultural and scientific impact on Greece. For example, there is Cheik Anta Diop (1991) and Martin Bernal (1987, 1991).

17. The emphasis in Rodney is not so much in tracing the origins of modern racism but in understanding how it became a central ideological factor in Western culture. In his introduction to the 1968 reprint of Richard Jobson's book *The Golden Trade*, which was first published in 1623, Rodney noted that notions of "African barbarity were already part of Europe's intellectual baggage, given the technical and commercial

disparity which was both apparent and growing since the first significant Afro-European contact in the middle of the fifteenth century" (Rodney 1968e: viii).

18. For work illustrating this point, see Bascom (1972); Crahan and Knight (1979); Cabrera (1986); Sosa Rodríquez (1982); Schuler (1970); Warner-Lewis (1991).
19. The Bailundu war started in 1902 and was effectively crushed by the Portuguese in 1904.
20. An early version of *How Europe Underdeveloped Africa* is evident in a lengthy paper entitled "The Historical Roots of African Underdevelopment" that Rodney (1970b) presented to the Universities of East Africa, Social Science Conference in 1970.
21. Rodney completed writing *How Europe Underdeveloped Africa* in 1971 and it was published jointly by Tanzania Publishing House in Dar es Salaam and Bogle L'Ouverture in London a year later in 1972 (Rodney 1971e). By 1973 he was discussing a reprint with his West Indian publisher in London, Bogle L'Ouverture (Huntley 1973).
22. One political scientist has argued, "For African rulers, the disorganization of the state and its resulting bureaucratic incompetence is clearly of secondary significance to its continued ability to impose the insidious mechanisms through which subordinate classes remain subordinate" (Fatton 1992: 22).

CHAPTER 5

Rodney and the Cultural Politics of Rastafari and Rude Boy

This chapter is concerned with Rodney's political activism in 1968 within the context of a pre-existing social movement in Jamaican urban communities of the poor that were very heavily influenced by Rastafarianism. Rodney's expulsion by the Jamaican government was based on fears that his interaction with the leading figures at the grass roots could lead to the emergence of a radical political ideology taking hold among them and that instability would ensue if such a political movement became an oppositional force threatening the political system of independent Jamaica that was barely six years old. The possibility of a link between the intellectuals and the masses seemed to be a source of paranoia in the ruling Jamaica Labour Party, but so far no hard evidence of Rodney trying to overthrow the Jamaican government has emerged. What emerges is hostility by the political elite to black nationalism coupled with cold war anticommunism, and narrow-minded Jamaican nationalism which portrayed Rodney as a foreigner from Guyana who was interfering in national politics. Rodney symbolised these fears and insecurities within the political elite. The latter feared more than anything else that Rodney could give some coherence to the disparate expressions of resistance to the political status quo and for them it was a question of either squashing that type of criticism or, in the case of the People's National Party, then in parliamentary opposition, co-opting and subordinating it politically. The Rodney ban in 1968 saw the playing out of these fears.

Lifestyle and politics

Rodney came to embody the aspirations of politically aware young people from the middle and lower classes who were alienated socially, economically and politically. People saw in Rodney qualities they admired. He was well educated, well informed, articulate, yet different from his peers in ways that were personal and ideological. The clues to Rodney's appeal may be found not simply in the status derived from his academic achievements, but in his personal conduct, ability to connect history and contemporary politics, and his articulateness. He was not an intellectual posturer, neither did he use his immense knowledge of Africa and the Caribbean to show off his brilliance but helped to clarify the past and challenge the interpretations of colonial and bourgeois historians. Rodney's personal and political life were intertwined in such a way that what grass roots people perceived in private political interaction was what came out in public. Many people commented on Rodney's genuineness. To them he became Brother Wally. The same appeal to the grass roots in Jamaica in 1968 was evident in Tanzania in 1969–1974 and in Guyana, particularly in 1979–1980, the last two years of his life. Moreover the appeal was also based on the extent to which he embodied the unfulfilled aspirations of a large number of people at a particular moment in their social and political life. Rodney[1] spent eight and a half months lecturing at the University of the West Indies in 1968. The mid sixties had seen him making decisions that resulted in his rejection of much of what was considered conventional West Indian middle class values – the striving for status, the distancing from one's social background, the imitation of an English accent, the marrying of an English wife or marrying what was considered the next best, a light-skinned woman. Rodney never embraced a conventional West Indian middle class lifestyle and the politics that went with it because he chose not to and was comfortable with that decision.

Political attraction to or repulsion from a personality is often based on very small personal things. The fact that his education had not alienated him made a big impression on students in the 1960s because he was setting an example that was so unlike the posturing and radical chic behaviour of some campus radicals. Rodney was of average height and had the look of a 1960s black radical though unexaggeratedly so. He wore dashikis, had an Afro hairstyle and a slight beard. Pat, his wife, wore a low haircut and dressed in African print wraps. In the past the Mona campus had grown accustomed to the brightest young black male intellectuals returning from London with their PhDs and white wives. This had been the expectation but the existence of a vibrant university and the growing number of female students widened male spouse options. The relationship students and friends observed between Walter and Pat seemed very healthy. She travelled with him whenever she had time off from her job as a nurse at the University Hospital and she took their son Shaka on the rural trips. Pat was very fascinated by Jamaica, how beautiful it was. But Walter cautioned her: "There are two sides to Jamaica and I will show you both sides" (Pat Rodney 1989). Walter introduced her to the two Jamaicas and this left a very deep impression on her mind:

> because Walter took me down to Trench Town and I met a lot of his friends. I saw the poverty, I saw the other side of Jamaica. It upset me a lot because I saw people rummaging through dustbins. But Walter said he never wanted me to get a false image at any time of wherever we lived, or what life was really like for the majority of the people (Pat Rodney 1989).

He was a well educated black man who was very comfortable in a social sense around ordinary people and so was Pat. There seemed to be some congruence between his personal and political ideals. People sensed this and warmed to them.

His decision to live off campus was deliberate as he loathed what he perceived as the philistinism of those of his colleagues whose lives revolved almost exclusively around the lecture room, laboratories, libraries, students, other lecturers and the Senior Common Room bar.[2] He lived in Trafalgar Park, then a newly built middle class suburb from which he reacquainted himself with the "dungles"[3] of Kingston that Orlando Patterson had portrayed so tellingly in his 1964 novel *The Children of Sisyphus*. But for Rodney, unlike Orlando Patterson, the struggle was not seen in terms of the Sisyphean myth but from the standpoint that the people of the "dungle" had to become their own liberators.

Rodney's impact on young people is evident in Robin Small's first encounter with him in early 1968.

> I remember Peter Phillips[4] and I think Michael Morgan[5] told me that there was this young history teacher who just come from Africa and who was very interested in the liberation struggles. He had a lot of personal contact with the liberation struggle in Africa and had contacts with the OAU. They arranged for me to meet him. I think it was around by the History department one day, Peter carried me around there and I met this man, Walter Rodney, and I was struck you know, the smallness of his features, almost a kind of little boy look, not looking really hard and tough and aloof (Robin Small 1989).

Robin Small, Garth White[6] and Peter Phillips formed the core of a group of Jamaica College radicals from middle class background who became Rastafarians. They were bright, articulate, and rebellious. Robin Small's alienation from his own family, which was one of Jamaica's most prominent black professional families, mirrored a sense of disquiet with racial prejudice and social oppression in Jamaica among sections of the middle class. Robin Small was the younger brother of Hugh Small, a well-known lawyer and the key figure in the Young Socialist League which housed the PNP's left wing. Richard Small was another brother who was a close friend of Rodney's and his lawyer in the 1979–1980 arson trial in Guyana. Walter had met Richard in Leningrad in 1962 and they had been members of the C.L.R. James study group in London in the early 1960s. Walter later developed a close relationship with Robin Small who had leadership qualities. Among his peers Robin was the most articulate and widely read, and was very determined to pursue his own way of being, shunning his middle class upbringing and halting his own education past high school in an act of rebellion which led him to immerse himself into Rastafarianism and Twelve Tribes[7] and radically change his lifestyle. He became a dreadlocks and lived in the communities of the poor to the dismay of his family.

Robin recalled the cumulative impact of Millard Johnson's[8] call for 'Black Man Time Now' at independence, the appointment of Clifford Campbell, a rural school teacher, as the first black Jamaican to be chosen as governor general, the 1963 bus strike, the strike at the Jamaica Broadcasting Corporation in 1963,[9] the formation of the Organisation of African Unity in 1963 and the Coral Gardens incident, discussed below, of the same year. He remembered that he and his teenage friends

> were very introspective and very reflective about black people situation and Jamaica ... But especially after independence when the high expectations of everybody was being tested, young people like ourselves 13, 14, 15 and 16 were starting to realise that this independence wasn't really living up to black people expectations (Small 1989).

Rastafarians placed the racial question, the character of Jamaica's multiracialism, and the island's relationship with Africa all on the national agenda. At Jamaica College Robin Small was influenced by the ideas of Marcus Garvey and he remembered that

> I never even start to defend Rasta movement at that time, but you know I was strong on Marcus Garvey and people like that. I remember that morning I cut out a heart out of a piece of black paper I find in front of the old lady [mother] Bible and pin pon me shirt (Small 1989).

The American civil rights and Black Power movements had a strong impact on Caribbean youth in the 1960s. Small connected the growth in political consciousness among some high school students to a wider radicalisation which brought new political ideas to high school youths and university progressives.

Between the time of Martin Luther King and the SNCC (Student Nonviolent Coordinating Committee) rising up in the early 1960s and Malcolm X getting prominent and even Kennedy's assassination there was a lot of debate among high school students about Black People's rights. JC (Jamaica College) was a place where it used to go on a lot, especially because of a large white population in the school which was so favourably treated by the headmaster (Small 1989).

Robin Small's perception of a white bias in Jamaica College was not surprising given the colonial legacy of the school and its elite status at the time.

Black Consciousness in Jamaica

Rodney was a political figure in a larger picture that was not of his making. The main social character in that larger picture was the somewhat disparate black consciousness social movement in Jamaica whose ideas and values the political elite had tried to marginalise. The turbulence of the 1960s was a response to this policy of marginalisation and it was fuelled by information about the United States civil rights and black power movements but was quite independent of them. Among the major events of this turbulent period were the Henry protest of 1960;[10] the activities of Millard Johnson's Garveyite People's Political Party; the Coral Gardens disturbance of 1963; the anti-Chinese riots of 1965; and the national state of emergency of 1966–1967.

Rev Claudius Henry came to public attention when he was charged with fraud and disturbing the peace in 1959 (Meeks 1996). As "God's Anointed, Anointed Prophet and Repairer of the Breach", he was said to have "issued to thousands of the faithful, membership tickets for his Africa Reform Church at one shilling per head and had promised a return trip to Africa on October 5, 1959" (Nettleford 1970: 83–84). It was in April 1960 however that police raids on his premises in Kingston revealed a "shot-gun, a .32 calibre, 18 sticks of dynamite, a large quantity of machetes, sharpened on both sides, swords, batons, conch shells filled with cement, a club and a spear" (Nettleford 1970: 84). Claudius and his son Reynold, who operated the First Africa Corps, out of New York, were charged with planning to launch an armed insurrection against the Jamaican government. Claudius was arrested along with 14 of his followers and charged with treason, with being in possession of weapons, and with possession of a letter addressed to Fidel Castro soliciting the Cuban revolutionary's advice (Nettleford 1970: 84–85). Henry was tried, sentenced and was incarcerated for most of the decade of the 1960s. On his release from prison he formed the New Creation Peacemakers' Association but continued to be subjected to military and police raids although his work was geared to peaceful cooperative ends. Henry, although imprisoned under the regime of Norman Manley,[11] went on to support his son Michael Manley when he became Prime Minister[12] and mobilised national support around Manley's democratic socialist ideas in the 1970s as well as the Workers' Party of Jamaica[13] in the 1980s. Henry represented a black and radical evangelical trend in the Jamaican indigenous church.

In addition to the already established Jamaica Labour Party and the People's National Party, Millard Johnson had formed a third grouping in 1961 called the People's Political Party. It did badly in the elections just before independence but contributed to the determination of the framers of the Independence Constitution of Jamaica to entrench the two-party system (Munroe 1972: 163–66). This ensured that there would be only two players in the political game as third players were not recognised in the constitutional provisions.

The Coral Gardens incident of 1963 was one of a number of events that triggered off mass repression of Rastafarians in Jamaica. At the root of the incident was the long-standing demand for land by the rural poor and the resort to squatting which many had taken up as well as the intense discrimination against Rastafarians in all areas of social life. According to the newspaper reports, the leader of the group, Rudolph Franklin, had been shot and sentenced to a prison term in 1962 after a land dispute in the Rose Hall area. Coral Gardens is located near Montego Bay, a main tourist area. The attack by Rastafarians on a gas station resulted in eight people being killed – among them two policemen and three Rastafarians. The incident created panic in the country and led to the arrest of 150 Rastafarians in four parishes (Nettleford 1970: 79).[14]

In 1965 there were the anti-Chinese riots arising from a black female employee being beaten by three Chinese brothers as a result of a dispute over the payment of instalments on a radio. Outraged citizens in downtown Kingston burnt and looted Chinese property (Lacey 1977: 86).

Then in 1966 Haile Selassie's visit to Jamaica highlighted the enormous social and cultural influence of the Rastafarian movement at the time. In the Jamaican context of the 1960s Ethiopia's monarch became a symbol of a reverential counterpoint to the British throne. The counter-culture of Rastafari had constructed in-group values based on appropriation of Ethiopian aristocratic orthodoxy and rejection of the more recent British monarchy that had been associated with the subjugation of parts of Africa and black enslavement. In what amounted to religious frenzy Rastafarians converged on the tarmac when Selassie's plane arrived and totally disrupted official protocol in their enthusiasm to greet the King of Kings. It was the eminent Rastafarian leader Mortimo Planno[15] who parted the throng so the Emperor could descend with his entourage in safety and not the Jamaican protocol officers loyal, through the government, to the Queen of England. No other event in the 1960s, not even the Independence celebrations of 1962, had had such a catalysing effect on grassroots Jamaica as did that visit.

Haile Selassie visited a number of educational institutions including Jamaica College but the students had not been informed. A visit by a member of the British royal family would have seen the red carpet being rolled out and the boys being involved months before in preparation for the welcome. It was by chance that Robin Small found out about the visit.

> When I reach up JC the afternoon about 3.30 p.m. I can see all the school youth leaving the school, hundreds of them streaming through the gate. When I ask them where them going, they said they are being sent home, the headmaster and staff tell them must go home. So I said, you don't know that there is an official visit by a visiting head of state up here this evening? Most of them did not know it (Small 1989).

Small and some of the boys who stayed behind saw Haile Selassie arrive for his visit. Security police tried to remove him from the premises but he was allowed to remain due to the intervention of a press officer. Haile Selassie's April 1966[16] visit gave Rastafarians a sense of legitimacy and vindication and their following grew among both working class and middle class youth.

The middle class was ambivalent, confused and somewhat hostile to the visit and some of the lower classes shared those attitudes. But there was no doubt that among large numbers of the poor in Jamaica influenced by Rastafarianism[17] and driven by curiosity there was intense positive feeling about the visit. Small, probably with some exaggeration, said:

> almost every house in West Kingston, from Coronation Market go right back to Six Miles used to have a red, black and green or red, gold and green flag flying ahead. And when you walk them place there, is just almost like you a little town, a market town in Africa, because is just red, black and green flag

and pure sign mark up pon people house and slogan, black militancy in every form. Worse now the expressions of solidarity with Selassie mixed with the abuse hurled at government officials as the train passed through West Kingston (Small 1989).

This was a period when politically controlled communities were being set up including the garrison[18] constituencies of Jamaica's postindependence politics. In June and July 1966 the homes of over 3,000 people were bulldozed (Jamaica Council for Human Rights [JCHR] 1967: 2). Following Selassie's visit the bulldozing of Western Kingston's slums continued. The bulldozers, protected by armed soldiers, became hated objects and they symbolised the creation of the modern low income housing estates, access to which was based on political party affiliation. The PNP later responded with its own residential enclaves and this marked the transition of party tribalism into its armed phase. Political protests against this kind of turf politics, which the youths called "politricks", saw the discrediting among a minority of radicalised youth and intellectuals of the political parties as vehicles for social and political change. So in 1966–1967 political violence entered its modern phase with the formalisation of garrison constituencies, and fierce trade union and party rivalry led in October 1966 to the declaration of a state of emergency in Western Kingston. (Lacey 1977: 87; Munroe 1989: 76–107).

Although the Jamaican economy in the 1960s had experienced some of its best years compared to the 1970s and 1980s, the share of the poorest 40 percent of the population in personal earned income

> had declined from 7.2% in 1958 to 5.4% in 1968. Illiteracy, poor housing and unemployment remained the lot of vast numbers of Jamaicans. The level of unemployment and underemployment in the society had increased hugely, doubling from 12 per cent to 24 per cent during the very period of fast economic growth (Payne 1988: 15).

But Anthony Payne's analysis of the Rodney riots in 1968 tended to underestimate the importance of black nationalist activity by stressing principally the socioeconomic conditions underlying the riots.

On the other hand, in his study *Class, Race and Political Behaviour,* Carl Stone linked growing economic deprivation with increasing levels of racial and class militancy among the poorer classes in Kingston and St Andrew. Stone pinpointed the intersection of history, socioeconomic deprivation, race, class and the reproduction of cultural psychology rooted in racial stereotypes and provided an accurate gauge of the elements which went into Black Power in the late 1960s. He reasoned that strong feelings of black solidarity within the black working and lower classes in urban Jamaica is [sic] not surprising in a society which has given birth to the Garvey and Rastafari movements. The ideological thrust of these movements has attempted, with some manifest success, to counter the history of black denigration . . . Poverty, unemployment, low educational opportunities, and the hopelessness and parasitic paternalism they breed in political life, force poor blacks into a bitter struggle for survival in which the closest enemy is another struggling poor black. The persistence of both anti-black stereotypes and negative stereotypes about the nature of the Jamaican people is partly due to this factor. In addition, white affluence encourages pro-white attitudes as appropriate role playing. Deference and instrumental cultivation of white paternalism are perceived as potentially yielding material rewards. Beyond these factors, however, the class arrogance of the black middle class alienates working and lower class urban blacks by weakening the tendency towards black solidarity. This black middle class arrogance is critical precisely because poverty, unemployment, state paternalism and low educational opportunities force the less skilled blue collar and lower classes to depend on the black middle class, among others, for menial personal service, employment, patronage, excessive bureaucratic favours and services, and other arbitrary hand-outs of welfare assistance; all of which are bestowed with an appropriate display of contempt for poor blacks (Stone 1973: 112).

Stone's political diagnosis pointed to the symptoms of the colonial legacy at the psychological level and the way in which black middle class social mobility and privilege perpetuated values of servility and self-deprecation within the black majority. Much of Rodney's political activism in the Caribbean and Africa was a critique of the black Caribbean and African middle class who were primarily located within the political, regulatory and administrative seats of power. According to Robin Small:

coming down to the end of 1967, the whole of the black conscious movement decided, the majority of people especially the little group of youth that I used to move with, that 1968 is Human Rights year[19] and there is a definite opportunity to pressure the forces along the lines of human rights consciousness (Small 1989).

This was the larger picture with which the Jamaican government and its security forces had to work. In this scenario Rodney was seen as a political troublemaker who was fuelling the embers of a potential social rebellion. He came into Jamaica at a time of growing black awareness and facilitated the radicalisation of that awareness but, contrary to government propaganda, he did not create it. His relationship with the group around Robin Small was the most important political relationship of Rodney's Jamaican months. It is to this group and others like it that Rodney addressed much of what was later published in *Groundings With My Brothers*. Small's narrative[20] shows Rodney's approach and style which won him the love and admiration of the socially conscious youth of the 1960s. According to Small:

> The news spread about this young African doctor, everybody describing him as an African doctor who come to get involved in the black struggle. Him was a doctor of philosophy but people just used to refer to him as African doctor, and you know how powerful a title that is (Small 1989).

Rodney's popularity was due to the fact that he had deserted the middle class politically and was able to develop alternative political and ideological positions which spoke to the psychological and material interests of the majority in the population. Moreover, socioeconomic conditions cried out for individuals who would speak out in favour of amelioration. One did not have to look far in Kingston, Jamaica's capital city, to see desperation. The unemployed

> numbered some 150,000, approximately a quarter of the population of Kingston. Of these, at least one-third can be said to have comprised a lumpenproletariat, permanently detached from the labour market. The latter survived mainly through petty and organised crime, gambling, prostitution and trade in illegal commodities such as ganja. Many were involved in the Rastafarian movement (Payne 1988: 17).

Rodney sought out and tapped into these sectors of resistance and his strength lay in forging links with the urban youth in the poor communities, Rastafarians, and radicalised middle class students and intellectuals.[21]

It was to the urban youth radicalised by Rastafarians that Rodney directed much of his attention in an almost Fanonist belief in their revolutionary potential. That potential did exist and was to be absorbed by Michael Manley into the democratic socialist PNP in the 1970s as well as by the much smaller Marxist-Leninist Workers' Party of Jamaica. The urban youth responded not only to class issues but to racial issues in the broad sense of the term, addressing the position of blacks in Jamaican society, the Black Power movement in the US and the Caribbean, and the liberation struggles especially in Southern Africa. Rodney dealt with these questions in ways that did not form part of conventional left wing class wisdom in and outside of the PNP. The question of racism in Jamaica had always been tricky for the mulatto-led PNP and at best they dealt with it either by denial that race was an issue in Jamaican life or by advocating a multiracial vision that appeared fine on the surface but in reality had all the sores and scars of prejudice against the black majority. But denial never got rid of the racial problem and it reappeared in national debates each decade in a new form over new issues. In the 1960s it grafted on the rhetoric of Black Power in the United States and in their music radicalised youth and Rastafarians protested discrimination.

Grassroots connections

Walter Rodney had contacts with Rastafarians and left wing individuals from the early 1960s when he was an undergraduate at the University of the West Indies, and he renewed these contacts in 1968. His groundings[22] in the urban ghettoes of East and West Kingston and in the countryside acted as catalysts to the growth in social and political consciousness. The oppressive conditions of life for the poor and the determination of groups of activists to initiate social protest were ongoing in the early 1960s. Such resistance was not a result of communist subversion as right wing voices in the press and government believed.

Rodney had a very sharp mind and was an exceptionally gifted speaker with a mild but very endearing manner. Young people felt that he was someone with whom they could reason. A brilliant lecturer, in the few months he taught at Mona he made a deep impression on his students. His lectures were attended not only by history students but those from other faculties. His talks at the UWI Students' Union on Black Power had both campus and off-campus support. He was not connected to any organisation neither did he build any. He would accept invitations from youth and community groups, Rastafarian groups and high school students. Groundings took place anywhere people wanted to hear about African and Caribbean history and politics or discuss the black power and civil rights movements in the United States. It was his expertise on Africa and his ability to relate this knowledge to the traditions of resistance of black people which consolidated a youthful Jamaican audience.

On 17 August 1968 he spoke at Garvey's shrine on the eighty-first anniversary of his birth. On that day I noted in my diary.

> It was drizzling in George VIth Park[23] and a youth was distributing copies of a resolution to be sent to the government protesting the ban on books by Stokeley Carmichael, Elijah Mohammed and Malcolm X. It was a motley

gathering of youth, Rastas, University students, UNIA Garveyites, New Creation Tabernacle members connected to Rev Henry, curious individuals, Babylon – seamed[24] and in plain clothes, attending this protest meeting at the Marcus Garvey shrine (Lewis 1968).

Rodney addressed the gathering, saying he did so not in his capacity as a University lecturer but as a black man from Guyana. He was very critical of his colleagues at the University for their failure to initiate direct dialogue between people at the grassroots and academics. While he spoke the special branch men in attendance took detailed notes. Also speaking at Garvey's shrine was Rev Claudius Henry.

Claudius Henry had over the years shifted his position from "Back to Africa" to one of "building Africa in Jamaica" (Nettleford 1970: 101). I recall going with Walter in mid 1968 to visit Rev Claudius Henry,[25] the black nationalist evangelist who had been released from prison in November 1966 and whose church in Clarendon was a religious and entrepreneurial centre with a blockmaking factory, a bakery, a farm and several homes.

Henry's lieutenants gave Rodney a tour of the premises. The church was packed and the drumming was powerful. Henry was not a moving speaker but he was held in respect and the fact that he had been to prison and remained a target of political harassment gave him standing as a persecuted prophet among his followers. At that time Henry claimed some 4,000 followers, of whom 1,000 were active members in his organisation. During this visit Rodney did not speak at the church; he simply listened. An important aspect of Rodney's activity in Jamaica was doing this – listening and observing and trying to understand the specific qualities of mass activity. This deepened his knowledge of indigenous radical forms in Jamaica, intermixed as they were with strong religious sentiment. In his "Message to Afro-Jamaica Associations" written after he was forced to leave Jamaica, Rodney commented at length on the significance of the Rev Claudius Henry.

> I must ask you to turn your attention also to another unique individual who champions the cause of the Black Man in Jamaica and he is the Rev Claudius Henry R.B. The government has charged me with the crime of consorting with Rev Henry which means that he is a criminal. It is unnecessary here to refute those wild charges. One must understand that such accusations come from a set of frightened men alarmed by a massive demonstration of black solidarity.
>
> Rev Henry's name is mentioned here specifically in connection with the question of economic re-awakening, for although his organization is basically religious, it carries out a policy of economic co-operation and self-reliance among black people.

At Kemp's Hill, in the middle of a most depressed area which is the Prime Minister's (Hugh Shearer) constituency, Rev Henry has gathered together a number of black brothers and sisters, and they have turned themselves into an independent black economic community. In less than a year they built themselves an attractive church and several dwelling houses – all of concrete for they make the concrete blocks. They have proper plumbing and electricity, and in case the local supplies are inadequate they have their own water tanks and electrical generator. They operated a fish shop from the outset and later they set up a bakery. In spite of massive persecution by the government, the police and the army, the Henry community has extended to several other parts of the island and at Cross they are doing the same thing all over again except that this time they are achieving it all in a matter of weeks instead of months. The importance of the above example of economic re-awakening is that it proves the great capacity of our people once they are resolved to strike out for themselves (Rodney 1969d: 16).

Rodney's conclusions are very much in the tradition of C.L.R. James' political thinking in that he looked at the capacities of the ordinary people and how these were manifested in different ways. Study of grassroots self-mobilisation made for better understanding of the nature of political life and the ability to draw conclusions about the character of political action.

Groundings

One of the meeting places frequented by Rodney was Brother Single's[26] home in Eastern Kingston near the McGregor Gully area. Audvil King,[27] the poet and author of several pieces in the Bogle L'Ouverture collection of prose and poetry entitled *One Love*, also lived there and participated in many of the groundings. There was Frank Hasfal who published the small magazine *Our Own* and who also moved with that circle and was well known among the youth in East Kingston. The Ethiopian World Federation (EWF) had always been a focal point for Africa-conscious individuals and Hasfal and Small had been active in Local 37 of the EWF since the mid 1960s. Among the other places frequented by Rodney were 50 Anderson Road in Allman Town, together with George's Lane, Salt Lane, Majesty Pen at Three Miles, Ras Planno's yard and Neville Howell's beer joint in Trench Town; several yards in August Town including Robin Small's place; Dunkirk, Wembley Sports ground in East Kingston and a number of open spaces used as football fields where young people gathered for games and reasoning. The fact that some of them were drawn to serious reasonings is an indication of the influence of Rastafarianism as well as the impact of the Black Power movement in the United States. In this climate small publications had an audience and were an index of radical politicisation among young people.

Robin Small's publication *Black Man Speaks* was influenced by the Garvey tradition in journalism as well as by *Muhammad Speaks*, the Black Muslim publication from the US. Worn out copies of *Muhammad Speaks* would pass from hand to hand as it was a banned publication. According to Small:

> *Muhammed Speaks* had a great impact on us, not religiously because we never subscribe to Muslim talking in any way but the militancy of the paper and the powerfulness of the medium had an impact on us, so the combination of the *Black Man*[28] that Marcus Garvey used to have and the idea of speaking out won out and after much reasoning *Black Man Speaks* was born and the first issue came out in 1968 (Small 1989).

Black Man Speaks had a strong Selassie orientation mixed with left wing ideas and black nationalist views. Rodney and some of the youth tried to make the line of the paper more radical by saying that it should not provide only Rastafarian views. He tried to infuse black nationalism with social and class analysis and an understanding of power relations within the world and twentieth century imperialism. But his point of view, though influential, was one among many. Jamaican Selasseism was varied with some Rastafarians focusing on the religious aspects of their beliefs and waiting for deliverance from Jamaica through repatriation. For Rastafarians Garveyism was back to Africa and Selassie was God. Others were prepared to listen to and embrace more radical political positions on African liberation and political change in Jamaica. But for them too Selassie was the central figure in their religious outlook and repatriation was non-negotiable. Involvement in the politics of Jamaica was at best a form of activity most would want to avoid unless it got them to Africa. The young people who published *Black Man Speaks* held many discussions with the Rastafarian elders to justify their putting out a publication and the content of that publication was the subject of many exchanges.

A lot of reasoning took place over the kind of publication *Black Man Speaks* should become in the context of its youth constituency and the Jamaican situation. Differences emerged around who were the "true ghetto youth" and around who was becoming or had become authentic revolutionary youth. It was decided that the paper must be edited every week by a different group and the tone of the paper would vary accordingly. Small said, "A certain group of man edited the paper who used to fight against too much of the kind of black image and too much of Rasta oriented thing." Walter supported Frank Hasfal then known as Abraham,[29] in publishing *Our Own* – the first issue of which appeared in August 1968. Small indicated that Rodney gave more support to *Our Own* run by Frank Hasfal.[30] The name *Our Own* was associated with an early twentieth century nationalist publication in Kingston (Lewis 1988: 42–45). *Our Own* had eight pages and on its front page was a picture of shackled slaves leaving West Africa and on the back was one of Ras Daniel Heartman's beautiful faces of a young dreadlocks entitled "Prince Man-I". In that issue the editor started serialising Rodney's article "African History and Culture" which made up chapter 4 of *Groundings With My Brothers*. Another piece by Rodney dealt with slavery and the slave trade. The second issue of *Our Own* appeared in September and had a photograph of an angry Rastafarian "blooding Babylon and calling down fire and brimstone". The Rastafarian looked as if he had been modelled on Ras Negus from East Kingston. *Our Own* promoted a more radical critique than *Black Man Speaks* – but within the ambit of Rastafarianism which had different trends – some religious and cultural in focus, others drawn to political involvement such as Sam Brown,[31] and some represented by the Fanonists like Ras Negus. Rodney shared the passion of Rastafarian brethren like Ras Negus from East Kingston and Ras Mortimo Planno from West Kingston for political liberation in Africa. Ras Negus and Ras Planno were both in their own way as intriguing as Rodney and certainly as brilliant with words and ideas.

Ras Negus and Ras Planno

Negus was a politically oriented Rastafarian who was intelligent, articulate, and penetrating in his analyses of the Jamaican power structure. Being in his presence and reasoning with him was to be intellectually and personally challenged especially if one was an aspiring political activist from the middle class. He had obviously read whatever literature he could find on Africa and was well informed about the anticolonial liberation movements in West and East Africa during the time of Kwame Nkrumah and Jomo Kenyatta. He was a role model for youths in Eastern Kingston and it was inevitable given Rodney's movements that he would meet Negus. It was Small who took Walter to Negus.

> Negus is one of the man who me carry him go meet. Now Negus used to be in Brown's Town, where they called Dunkirk, and Negus is a very militant, dreadlocks man, very articulate, very volatile and very revolutionary in every

> sense of the word. That man kind of sceptical too, him don't just accept everybody him meet. Walter and him had a very good relationship. Remember when Shearer made the speech after him ban Walter, that evening at a meeting up at university, one Rastaman got up and say in reference to the academics led by Walter 'You have the brains, we have the brawn, just give us the guns and we will do the rest.' Remember that? Well Negus was the one. That speech actually was made right at Students' Union, and Negus was the man who never fraid to talk that way, police or no police (Small 1989).

Prime Minister Hugh Shearer used this quote in Parliament to justify declaring Rodney persona non grata. The quote Shearer manipulated from his security report was "We have the brawn, you have the brains, all we need are the guns" (*Jamaica Hansard* 1968–1969: 392). These words bore no relationship to political action and reflected social anger and desperation. But Negus' statement was used to implicate Rodney as a political subversive bent on a Castro-like takeover of the Jamaican state. The anger contained in that statement was a reflection of the socially inflammable 1960s in which Rastafarianism and black nationalist militancy had come under ferocious state repression. Negus was later involved with the radical *Abeng*[32] newspaper group in 1969 (Lewis 1997).

Negus was born in Port Morant, in the parish of St Thomas in 1934 and at age 14 he met two Rastafarians who led him to the consciousness of Rastafarianism. Negus' conversion indicated the impact of Rastafarianism and its strong spiritual dimension, on which foundation its secular political and social activities were conducted.

> While I was there going among them as a small boy I get to find that they prove some form of genuineness in them. When I say genuine I mean something humanitarian, that is, they teach love. My mother was a Methodist but my father didn't defend any form of religion. He was a fisherman and my mother boiled oil and was a higgler. At 14 I didn't stop trimming my hair as I was developing the concept on the reality surrounding my religion. The fact that really surround the religion was the dignity of black people. I came to town (Kingston) and then first lived with my sister. From then I started every night to go to West Kingston mostly Rose Town and Denham Town where the Rastas generally meet. I started locksing at 22. I sit down for three days before I could come to the true conviction whether I should locks or not. Because, I had seen what it really means, what it really stands for and I was considering a way of survival. After these three days I come to a consciousness within myself that it is better for a man to suit his God more than to suit myself because God will then provide in every way. Before I come to the state of locks I worked as a painter doing work with Public Work contractors. I moved to the Wareika Hills

and I lived there for about five years. In 1963 we were burnt out under the Bustamante government. Well, I still build back a next shack there and lived for eighteen months. After that I came down from the hills. As for now, I hardly have a way of survival. I work £30 (British currency) in December but hardly any more after that (Ras Negus 1969).

Another personality who was a leader of the Rastafarian community and the urban poor was Mortimo Planno who lived at 5½ Brook St off Salt Lane which ran parallel to the Spanish Town Road in Western Kingston and was the headquarters of the local EWF.[33] While Negus' voice tended to be high-pitched, Planno had a deep bass and both spoke with a keen sense of timing, with pauses and without haste, almost as if they were talking on a musical scale.

The chief thing why people listened to him in the past, you know, is that Planno wasn't really talking for himself but was talking on behalf of a whole generation, that is what make him a person that you want to hear and listen to. And that is why people come to him. I go to him yard and sit down under the tree and listen to him talk and sometimes him ignore you and get up and walk away, but you still go back because you feel he has something to say (Small 1989).

Planno had visited five African states – Ethiopia, Nigeria, Ghana, Liberia and Sierra Leone – as a member of the 1961 Mission to Africa that had been set up by Premier Norman Manley. This mission set out to probe the prospects for setting up relations between Jamaica and independent countries in Africa and was also a response to the demands for repatriation to Africa that Rastafarians had always made. Other Rastafarian delegates were Filmore Alvaranga and Douglas Mack and they were known as the three wise men because they filed a minority report (Mulvaney 1990: 66). Also included in the delegation were members of the Universal Negro Improvement Association, the Afro-Caribbean League, the Ethiopian World Federation Inc. and the Afro-West Indian League.

Planno had a big influence on Bob and Rita Marley among many others and it was under Planno's tutorship that Bob became a locksman and started performing at the shows marking Selassie's birthday. Planno wrote articles in the press and even wrote a poem on the Rodney events of October 1968. Planno's passport was seized in 1964 and Rastafarian leaders joined the Government's list of radicals who were unable to travel. Planno, Negus and other Rastafarians were to Kingston's urban youth what Malcolm X and others were to their counterparts in the United States. The difference was that the work done by Planno and others got no media coverage and there is no record of the speeches and talks given or the reasonings that took place.

Rastafarian creativity [34]

It was in this context that the creativity and militancy of the music of Bob Marley, Peter Tosh, Bunny Wailer and many others blossomed. Ras Daniel Heartman had done some of his best drawings of Rastafarian heads and Don Drummond, "steeped in the agonies and hopes of the Rasta man", had used his trombone to make tunes like "Beardman Ska", "Addis Ababa" and "Marcus Garvey Jnr" to create a brooding sound which, according to the literary analyst Gordon Rohlehr, carried a message of "despair, rebellion and the longing to travel further East, back to the Fatherland" (Nettleford 1970: 98). And Count Ossie's drums could be heard in Wareika Hills laying the ska music rhythms, beating down Babylon and giving praises to Jah Rastafari. Rodney knew Count Ossie and had arranged for him to play at the Senior Common Room. In recalling this experience with the Rastafarians Rodney said:

> I got knowledge from them, real knowledge. You have to speak to Jamaican Rastas, and you have to listen to him, listen very carefully and then you will hear him tell you about the Word. And when you listen to him, and you can go back and read *Muntu*,[35] an academic text, and read about Nomo (Nommo), an African concept for Word, and you say, Goodness the Rastas know this . . . You have to listen to them and you hear them talk about Cosmic Power and it rings a bell. I say, but I have read this somewhere, this is Africa. You have to listen to their drums to get the Message of the Cosmic Power. And when you get that, know that you get humility, because look who you are learning from. The system says they have nothing, they are the illiterates, they are the dark people of Jamaica. Our conception of the whole world is that white is good and black is bad, so when you are talking about the man is dark, you mean he is stupid (Rodney 1969: 66).

Given the strength of this culture that was reshaping the language, music and lifestyle of many Jamaicans and challenging the status quo, it is not surprising that the middle class rebels and Small who embraced Rastafarianism did not feel they were losing much by not following a conventional career path. Their rebellion was against the racial and social prejudices of Jamaican society and the institutions that reinforced these negative values. Rastafari was idealistic in its desire to change the world they knew, challenging the assumptions they had grown up with. Furthermore, it was communitarian in its approach to daily living. Gaining access to the Rastafarian structures did not come easy. Even the *Black Man Speaks* was treated sceptically "as a lot of the elder Rastaman was very touchy and very funny especially when it come to so-called educated youths and especially when it come to anything printed or what they call 'papercy'" (Small 1989).[36] It took some time to get acceptance from the Rastafarian and ghetto community who were sceptical of these middle class drop-outs who could drop in back home where the parents of their ghetto friends worked as maids and gardeners. The radicalised middle class often lived a double life even when they grew locks. Some abandoned this escape hatch when times changed to a more conservative climate in the 1980s and when their youth had passed and pragmatism dictated the return to middle class ways. By this time Rastafarianism had become an important but past phase of their youth. By the 1980s the Rastafarian role model of the 1960s was to be tragically replaced by political gunmen, drug dons and criminals.

Rudie culture

Our Own, *Black Man Speaks* and many of Rodney's talks were directed at the urban youth known as rudies or rude-boys living in the economically depressed areas of Kingston and sporting ratchet knives in their waists. These weapons were soon to be replaced by the gun. Many were itinerant workers sifting and loading sand onto trucks bound for construction sites or selling sno-cones, pants lengths or picking pockets. In general rudies were hustling whatever could be hustled. Ska[37] music defined them and was their expression. Noted Jamaican musicologist, Garth White, observed:

> Rude bwoy was heralded on a selection from Studio One (recording studio of Clement Dodd) by Roland Alphonso as early as late 1962. But another musical ode, this time by the 'Wailers' in late 1965 signalled that rude bwoy was no passing indulgence but a very real element . . . The number of rudie tunes on the air-waves reflect the increased status accorded Rudies . . . radio requests are often from middle class youths, who to some extent are acquiring the symbols of rudie culture . . . Sound systems, for example, are being used by the traditionally conservative and Victorian school-boards . . . Prior to middle class acceptance, these systems supplied dance music in halls, lawns and the like . . . The music played is ska, although American negro pop music enjoys some popularity. Notable among this 'pop' music are records of the people like the Impressions, Shirley and Lee. It must be noticed that before the

emergence of ska, music supplied by the sound-system medium was usually from this source and old names like Fats Domino, Bill Doggett and Louis Jordan are one-time stars. Ska is one of the means of expression of the 'lower class'. It is a propagandistic music and with increasing force it has acquired the role of commentator on the society. It is now reflecting the increased militancy of the class it generally represents. 'Good Good Rudie' and 'Let Him Go' are tunes related to West Kingston. A tune by the 'Ethiopians' in its opening lines says:

I'm gonna take over now
For I know that
Our time has come
And I know
We must wear that crown (White 1967: 41–42).

Peter Tosh's[38] music best reflected this militant and revolutionary style. The rude-boy culture claimed the ear of the middle class youth in the 1960s and together with Rasta culture and lifestyle constituted the two principal cultural reference points of that generation of radicals.

Ras Dizzy, who did some of his best work as a painter, poet and prose writer in the 1960s and 1970s, captured the rude-bwoy ethos when he wrote:

It was on Wednesday last, walking through Kingston 12 – a section of the West. It was now night-break. I found myself on a dry and overcrowded city style corner. It was 9th Street – the sign for the eye-sighters. The fix-wheel bicycles, instead of cars, came regularly behind one another as the riders exceptionally cruised through the combat. A night-joint saloon was in its swing of music and fun as the rudies go in and out the dance. But if you had ever listened to Rudies' reggae tunes like 'Just Another Girl' by Ken Boothe and 'Sweet n' Dandy' by Toots and Maytals, then Glady and Stranger Cole's creation and tunes like 'Dr No-Go' and 'Bongo Nyah' – then you could tell why the youths want to listen to them and watch the human emotions behind the effect. The youths dance and as they creep up in numbers they like to greet and toast one another.

The way they drink the beer and then how they dance to the beat of the blues show that they are sophisticated human beings searching for freedom and recreational facilities free from fear of force . . . as soon as about a half-a-dozen beer bottles were thrown to splinters not in the street but against the walls – then you could feel a heart of brokenness in pocket; so they smashed a few pints and left the spot. And where did they go? No one knows. And why do they leave the spot? No money of course, and no dole. No way to drive away the thinking of crime and the planning of what maybe bigger than even the morality of both myself and you . . . no envelopes on Fridays – they decide to hold up the pay-roll. The law later turns them in and the Resident Magistrate in court is not interested in asking them what is wrong with their house, their life and why they want to hold-up Mr So and So or Mr He and She. Instead, the court is interested in guilty or not guilty. But does that stop them from holding up another pay-roll? (Dizzy 1969: 25–26).

Prince Buster made the popular song about Judge Dread where the Judge sentences rude-boys to hundreds of years in jail. Prince Buster, the ska singer and Muslim convert, sharply criticised Prime Minister Shearer for the ban on Rodney and had his business place and home raided by the police.[39] Prince Buster used to take copies of *Black Man Speaks* for his record shop but he destroyed the issue which had a picture of Fidel Castro on the back with the quotation, "The exploitation of man by man has to be dug out by the roots." Buster destroyed those issues because he was opposed to any white man appearing in such a prominent position in the paper. Obviously in response to this, Rodney in one of his Black Power lectures repeated Stokeley Carmichael's claim that Fidel was one of the blackest men in the Americas (Rodney 1969c: 31).

This incident indicated some of the strain and conflict between a dogmatic kind of black nationalism and socialist thinking which had a multiracial class orientation. In the 1970s when Marxism had an impact on the Caribbean left, many of the leading thinkers did not discuss race and culture except as epiphenomena while the class reductionist analysis prevailed. As early as February 1969 Trevor Munroe was to give a lecture on "Black Power as a Political Strategy in Jamaica" that was reprinted in *Bongo-Man*.[40] In it black culturalism was attacked and the cultural-political significance of race, Africa and popular youth culture was totally missed (Munroe 1969). This was the beginning of the thinking that led to Marxism-Leninism becoming the dogma of sections of the Jamaican middle class left that had previously been influenced by Rodney.

Edward Brathwaite, the distinguished Caribbean poet, historian and cultural critic, in a perceptive essay noted that there was a conflict within *Bongo-Man* and *Abeng* "between those who were willing to tolerate and even encourage what Trevor Munroe called 'black culturalism' and those (like Munroe) who saw it as a possible distraction and division" (Brathwaite 1976: 23). Brathwaite identified one of the major errors of Caribbean Marxism in the 1970s which was the misreading of culture and ethnicity. He wrote:

> one can see the danger that Comrade Munroe is worried about, especially when he perceives the mere move back to blackness as a superficial fad and therefore something selfish and individualistic. But Munroe, I think, under-estimated

the real deep instinct for Africa which our people carried in themselves, and mistook the dashiki and the afro for divisive fashions, when in fact they were/are the awakenings to a new style, a real alternative aesthetic possibility, creating not a sense of individuation, as 'press hair' does, but of the very collective solidarity that he calls for. And with the style and the new-found confidence, went the desire to know more: hence the popularity of Rodney's lectures in African history, the formulation of an Afro Women's Study Group after the scandals of headmistresses in certain secondary schools turning girls away because they dared enter the precincts in their afros, and reverberations of the 'Africa Night' held at Mary Seacole Hall (Mona Campus) in November, 1968. This was the first time that our students had been exposed in any serious way to African art, music, dress, poetry (Brathwaite 1976: 23).

Issues of self-respect, racial dignity so important to the construction of personhood in postcolonial societies, tended to be ignored by the left, and were seen as soft issues, while economic questions were the hard issues that contained the key to liberation. It was a fatal flaw in political thinking, given the history of the region, to ignore the psychosocial and psychopolitical dimension of the colonial experience which were embodied in national debates about culture and identity. For those on the left who were influenced by Fanon,[41] they had virtually ignored the psychological dimension of race in his work and focused narrowly on his class analysis.

Another key issue was that of repatriation. Some Rastas did not want to have anything to do with Jamaican politics which was dubbed 'politricks'. As is evident in his groundings, Rodney made the connection between African and Caribbean liberation in the way that Garvey had done and he understood the historic roots of the claim for repatriation to Africa in Jamaica which the Rastafarians had made one of their main calls and which they had learnt from previous generations of the African population of Jamaica.[42] Many Rastafarians had made their voices felt on a wide range of issues and were human rights activists when it came to the defense of freedom of religion, the right to be groomed differently, the right to pursue alternative lifestyles and the right of Rastafarian children to attend regular schools. Their walk and dance moves, their recognition of the forms of beauty among black people influenced the aesthetic and choreographic work of artists such as Rex Nettleford and others.

In the area of gender the Rastafarians as well as the black radicals, including Rodney, in different ways embraced traditional male values. It was only in the post–Black Power phase that Rastafarian women and radical black women continued the process of challenging male dominance within the realms of political discourse and social practice.

The community of Rastafarians, youth and middle class radicals was not one that was intimidated by Rodney's academic status. He was always being tested and this testing was not only based on what he said but on his manner and conduct among them, the vibrations they felt and discussions about his motives. Some middle class radicals thought they could disguise the negative vibes they gave off by talking like the dreads and smoking like them. Rodney neither smoked nor did he change his style of speech. He remained himself. Young people in the urban communities were impressed that he spent so much time among them and that he brought his knowledge and experience to share with them. Some disagreed with what they perceived as his impatience about the level of political struggle and, as with many other left wing intellectuals, he believed in timetables for the escalation of the class struggle. On one occasion during a reasoning Ras Single "lick out saying why him trying to push certain things so fast, asking him if is because him have a two year or three year contract at the University him want see things done within that period of time" (Small 1989). Small recalled that Rodney was flabbergasted at the open remark. Some of the dreads were more politically experienced than he was and had been through the difficult Coral Gardens period and the bulldozing which had destroyed their communities and were more cautious. They had a much better grasp of the Jamaican realities than Rodney whose political experience was limited and whose expertise was that of a scholar of African history.

Rodney's writings

Rodney's writings in 1968 can be divided into four categories. First, there were his academic writings on African history which he continued in Kingston and which I have discussed in chapter 4. Secondly, there were his popular articles for *Our Own* on African history and culture which looked at classical African civilisations in precolonial Africa and which were collected in chapter 4 of *The Groundings With My Brothers*. These articles were also collected in an "Africa Youth Move" mimeographed collection and widely distributed by Small and his group. His paper "African History in the Service of Black Revolution" which he read at the Black Writers' Congress in Montreal in October 1968 made up chapter 5 of *Groundings* and was published in *Bongo-Man* in December 1968. Thirdly, there were his lectures on Black Power which were given at the Students' Union and which made up chapters 2 and 3 of *Groundings*. Rodney's Black Power lectures were published in *Bongo-man*.

In Jamaica Rodney attempted to interpret Black Power in the light of the Caribbean experience. His analyses of Jamaica's neocolonial politics should also be included in this area. Fourthly, there was his article "The Tanzanian Revolution" which was published in the *Social Scientist*, 1968–1969 – the journal of the Economics Society of the University of the West Indies – and which I discuss in chapter 6.

Rodney's lectures were attended by many students who were not registered in his courses but simply wanted to follow them. He was active in the African Studies Association of the West Indies comprising campus-based and off-campus persons with an interest in Africa and was elected to its executive as treasurer. The sharp debates he had with Eurocentric Africanists such as John Hatch[43] on postindependence developments on the continent were characteristic of his style.

My own recollections as a student connected to the campus Black Power group were noted in my diary:

> Students are talking about Black Power and assessing the validity of the concept to the WI and themselves. The pro–Black Power students argue the need to be valid in one's own terms. Dr Rodney, a history lecturer, has been responsible for bringing this debate in the open. Students have no doubt about his sincerity and commitment. They fear the implications of this creed which does not mean the symbolic attainment of political power by a black executive but a socialist revolution restructuring the society which presently oppresses a black population. For him Asians, Latin Americans and Africans are black. Rodney's wife has a Makeba haircut and wears African style dresses. This saves him from the criticism often made against black radicals that they have married white. The women naturally, are most offended by this ambiguity . . . Outside his office bearded men, Rastafarians await entrance to speak with him as students leave . . . The police and military have raided Claudius Henry's outpost again. Four times now . . . I don't doubt that he'll soon be deported and made persona non grata. This young Guyanese is aware of the threat and this has increased the intensity of his living (Lewis 1968).

Rodney's lectures on Black Power were organised by a group of UWI students. In these lectures Rodney's focus was on the racial question as it had developed from slavery to independence. He was sharply critical of the false middle class multiracialism of independence in a country whose population was made up of well over 90 percent of African descent and exposed the neocolonial character of the Jamaican state. An important characteristic of Rodney's Black Power lectures was the rejection of race supremacist notions of any kind and this was especially important in the context of the Caribbean with its large Indian populations in places like Guyana, Trinidad and Suriname. Rodney reworked the notion so that Black Power covered other oppressed ethnic groups.

Rodney's message in 1968 was Garveyite in its link between the class and race questions. After he was declared persona non grata he sent a "Message to Afro-Jamaica Associations" in which he challenged:

> it is on the very question of Garvey that most work needs to be done in the educational and cultural spheres. Garvey lives on in the hearts of a certain generation of black people in Jamaica. For that reason, the government was forced to recognise him as a national hero. They brought Garvey's bones but not his philosophy. They named a street after him and built a statue in his likeness, but on October 16th they tear-gassed black people who were gathered around the statues of Paul Bogle and Marcus Garvey – how symbolic! The task of bringing Garvey to the black youth must be shouldered by all organizations which are interested in the cultural re-awakening of the Afro-Jamaicans. African youth in Jamaica today are waging a struggle in their own way against ignorance, unemployment and starvation. They will immediately understand how Garvey's thoughts and deeds relate to their own way of life and they themselves will create new methods of dealing with the oppressors.
>
> Besides, Jamaicans are extremely fortunate in still having amongst them Mrs Amy Jacques Garvey, wife of Marcus Garvey, and a black revolutionary fighter in her own right. She must be protected and the best use made of her services. It will be interesting to see whether the government will be brazen enough to move openly against the Garvey family and the Garveyite philosophy when it is fully propagated. Then, even the blind will see (Rodney 1969d: 15–16).

Amy Jacques Garvey was very active in 1968. She knew Rodney and supported his work. She was quite outspoken in her condemnation of the government's ban on Rodney and the restriction placed on books by Stokeley Carmichael and Malcolm X. In 1968 programmes that she had done for the Jamaica Broadcasting Corporation were banned as was the case with Rodney's Black Power lecture. In 1968 Amy Garvey published her collection of essays on "Black Power in America", "Marcus Garvey's Impact on Jamaica and Africa" and "The Power of the Human Spirit". On the other hand, she did not allow Garvey's name to be exploited by either the Jamaica Labour Party or the People's National Party without making a public intervention.

Obika Gray, in reflecting on the parallel streams of black nationalism and Marxism in Jamaican radicalism, noted that

> Rodney's articulation of Black Power expressed both global – and local-level critiques of class rule and antagonistic racial themes – and this without falling

into the illusions of popular ideologies or the orthodoxies of an automatic Marxist outlook . . . Rodney's activism was remarkable not for his founding of a political organization, since he created none; but for his twofold contribution: he transcended the barriers which hitherto had prevented the alliance of radical intellectuals and the militant unemployed, and he reconciled the previously estranged ideologies of socialism and cultural nationalism in Jamaica (Gray 1991: 157).

Rodney was able to transcend these social barriers because of his strong class identification with the working people in the Caribbean, a class from which he had come. He did not allow his education to cut him off from social and political interaction with those at the grass roots. Less of his time in Jamaica in 1968 was spent as a soapbox orator than moving in the ghettoes of Kingston, reasoning with people, and sharing their lives at a Rastafarian nyabinghi, a dance hall or at a communal meal in a yard. But when he did speak he brought to these groundings a perspective based on the role of the people as the makers and shapers of history. Rodney absorbed as much of Jamaica as he could through his old and newly made contacts in the lower and middle classes: Rastafarians, middle class professionals with whom he had studied at university, political comrades and others. He never pulled intellectual and academic rank and with each person he met he developed trust. Indeed, although at times there were sharp political disagreements, people opened up to him in recognition of a bond of trust that had been created. In 1968, therefore, Rodney learnt more about Jamaica and its people than he had during his undergraduate years. In return, he brought to Jamaica his knowledge of African history and Marxism, but more importantly his experience of Tanzania as it started out its experiment with Nyerere's radical reforms.

In a letter written to Gordon Rohlehr who was lecturing in English at the UWI campus in Trinidad just two weeks before he was declared persona non grata by the Jamaican government we get a close-up of his social attitudes. Rodney wrote:

> Over the past few months I have had cause to think and talk about you even a little more than one usually does with reference to an old pardy. The reason is simple. Being here at Mona, I constantly run across mutual acquaintances of ours, and during the course of the ST,[44] either myself or the party involved would mention yourself. Quite a fair sprinkling of our contemporaries are still around, mainly at the hospital, but I have also run across a few Jamaicans who are out in civvy street. Incidentally, I also met Aggrey[45] (of Birmingham) who is now working at the University Hospital.

However, I must hasten to add that there is no continuity in my life with respect to old acquaintances. We meet; I try to be pleasant; and I move on. For our generation too is adding its quota to the frightening sterility of the society. Living off-campus is a great boon, for it reduces my contact with rum-sipping, soul-selling intellectuals of Mona. I do resort to such elements to play bridge and dominoes, those being the HCF of our respective ideologies. In due course, I will probably change even that. Meanwhile, I try to find some meaning among the mass of the population who are daily performing a miracle – they continue to survive! Kingston is meaner than when you left it, and when you left it you probably did not know how mean it was. Indeed, I doubt whether there is yet a further gap between what I perceive and what our black brothers experience.

Today, all that matters is the question of action: determined, informed and scientific action against imperialism and its cohorts. Just as Leonardo da Vinci was the archetype of Renaissance Man, so Che Guevara is the ideal of Revolutionary Man. All that is required is that one should extract the essence of his life's experience, rather than attempt to embrace his suggestions concerning guerrilla warfare. The latter course has the serious limitation of being irrelevant to many objective situations (as Che knew). Right now I am grappling with the problem of the appropriate revolutionary line within a Jamaican context.

I doubt whether the situation is explosive, and I doubt whether I will be here long enough to witness the explosion; but as a matter of integrity I must address myself to that question so long as I am here. Otherwise what will distinguish me from the Philistines? I live in the petty-bourgeois area of Trafalgar Park in a three-bedroomed house; I buy and eat goodies from the capitalist supermarket; I drive to work etc. This is a distinction which I must draw to have any self-respect and if it is seen to be a difference by my black brothers, then this means that we are already on our way towards defining the revolutionary line.(vague) If I come up with any answers I'll try to communicate. Pat is keeping fine and joins me in sending love (Rodney 1968d).

The letter summed up how he lived and thought about those months of 1968 and some of the principles he had developed for his political and social conduct; his differences with the middle class and resistance to being absorbed by it; his approach to Che Guevara and efforts to find an appropriate revolutionary line for the Jamaican situation. There is nothing in *Groundings With My Brothers* that speaks to this issue in an explicit way and nothing that he published subsequently elaborated on what was an appropriate revolutionary line for the Jamaican situation but it was a question that he was thinking about. Rodney's ideology in the late 1960s could be described as being radical populist, but eschewing political demagoguery, taking a nondogmatic view of Marxism as a method of analysis, but recognising that political action had to be arrived at through the specifics of a country's history, social and ethnic relations and other factors that could not be deduced from the classics of nineteenth century Marxist texts. He did not enter the Jamaican situation with ready-made solutions but his travels throughout the country and groundings with so many groups led to the government of the Jamaica Labour Party deciding to declare him persona non grata. Rodney was one of a number of intellectuals in the 1960s against whom the Jamaican government took action because their ideas, travel destinations, and political connections were deemed to be subversive of the national interest.

The State and the intelligentsia

The Jamaican state had targeted progressive intellectuals and used measures such as the seizure of passports, banning orders on individuals and literature to restrict their influence.[46] On 18 July 1968 Roy McNeil, the Minister of Home Affairs, banned "all the publications of which Stokeley Carmichael is the author or coauthor; all publications of which Malcolm X (otherwise called Malcolm Little) is the author; all publications of which Elijah Muhammad (otherwise called Elijah Poole) is the author".[47] On 30 January 1968 he had banned *The Crusader* which was edited by the African-American nationalist, Robert Williams. A year before in May 1967 the Undesirable Publications Law had been revised to include all English-language publications coming from Moscow and the international organisations financed by the USSR, Peking and Cuba. The publications by Stokeley Carmichael and Malcolm X were widely available in the United States so they were easily accessed by Jamaicans who had travelled to the United States or who had family living there but police raided the homes of activists associated with Black Power activities and Walter Rodney and seized this literature.

The intelligence section of the state harassed progressives. Among those Jamaican intellectuals who had their passports seized in the 1960s were Winston Davis,[48] Leroy Taylor[49] and George Beckford[50] who had visited Cuba; among Caribbean intellectuals who were banned from Jamaica were Harold and Kathleen Drayton,[51] and C.Y. Thomas;[52] among the non–West Indian expatriates were political scientist Bertell Ollman[53] and economic historian Jay Mandle.[54] In early 1966 the economist George Beckford had his passport seized when he was at the airport on his way to Barbados and the Windward Islands. The immigration officer gave no reason and only informed Beckford that he was acting on the instructions of the Superintendent of Police in charge of Immigration. Prior to this, on 21 October 1965, a high-ranking member of the police force had visited his home saying that he had been sent to collect his passport. Beckford refused to surrender his document. Taylor had the same experience and also refused to surrender his passport. Beckford and Taylor had visited Cuba and were members of the New World Group.

Rodney's visits to Cuba and the USSR as a student were part of the charges brought by Prime Minister Shearer to justify the banning order. Roy McNeil, the Minister of Home Affairs, in the debate following the exclusion order on Rodney had said, "I have never come across a man who offers a greater threat to the security of this land than does Walter Rodney."[55] Frank Davis, who worked with the Special Branch in Kingston and was directly involved with the Rodney case, admitted that the reason for banning Rodney was that he "was charismatic at the grassroots level and had a following among intellectuals" (Davis 1991). It was this relationship with the working people that constituted the main fear of the Shearer regime which was shaken by the demonstrations following the ban on Rodney. It was the circumstances surrounding the ban on Rodney which provoked widespread protests but the conditions for the protests had been in the making throughout the 1960s.

> The aircraft which brought Rodney back from Montreal where he was attending a Congress of Black Writers[56] landed at 2.20 p.m. on Tuesday 15th October. However it was not until 9.00 p.m. that the students learnt that he was refused re-entry and confined to the aircraft . . . a meeting of students on the campus was advertised for 11.00 p.m. in Mary Seacole Hall. The meeting of some 900 students unanimously accepted a resolution to march the following day on the offices of the Minister of Home Affairs and the Prime Minister and to deliver two petitions (Gonsalves 1979: 3–4).

The students originally intended to hire buses to go to the Office of the Prime Minister to lodge their protest. But when the buses did not turn up on the morning of 16 October the students decided to walk into town. Neither the students when they set out nor Prime Minister Shearer appreciated the significance of their actions. The students never expected nor did they intend their actions to lead to rioting and to the closure of the University. Shearer expected protests from a section of the University community but certainly not any large-scale protest. The students set out quite innocently wearing their undergraduate red gowns to distinguish themselves and their protest. Their actions were largely a response to the victimisation of a lecturer and his family.

Ralph Gonsalves who was President of the UWI Student Guild wrote a detailed account of the march and the political decisions he had to make (Gonsalves 1979). One of the most important decisions was not to follow the silly advice of those who wanted to march into West Kingston as that would certainly have led to political violence and considerable loss of life. As it turned out, the student march and demonstrations were joined by urban youth who in response to police repression did considerable damage. The mass response to the Rodney ban took the government by surprise and the violence and destruction of property played into their hands to the extent that it fuelled views that the 26-year-old Walter Rodney was a bogeyman who had a plot to overthrow the Jamaican government. The *Gleaner* of 18 October reported the death of two people. Many buses were seized and used to block roads, 13 buses were destroyed, 72 damaged, in addition to over 90 buildings, 11 policemen injured and about 23 people were arrested on various charges (Munroe 1989: 98–99). In the parliamentary debate on the following day Rodney was depicted as the evil mind behind the violent resistance and was made out to be the mastermind of both student unrest and mass protest. He was called a communist and black power advocate, and as a non-Jamaican was villified as a foreigner. The JLP tended to blame the incident on non-Jamaican university students and lecturers and the fact that the Guild President Ralph Gonsalves, who led the student march, was from St Vincent added fuel to the antiforeigner fire. Edward Seaga, who represented the Jamaican government on the University Council, took a very hard line against non-Jamaican students and staff who were involved in the protests.[57] The 1968 riots and the attention paid to Walter Rodney were a result not so much of economic disaffection but the failure of the brown middle class-led nationalist movement and the propertied ethnic minorities to come to terms with the fact that Jamaica was predominantly a country of people of African descent and its national substance and image had to come to terms with reversing centuries of racial oppression and denigration. As Rodney pointed out, in 1968 the racial question[58] was out in the open "in spite of all the efforts to maintain the taboos surrounding it" (Rodney 1969c: 14).

The demonstrations were the clearest indication of growing mass opposition to the JLP that had been elected in 1967 for a second term. Large sections of the urban youth were to be drawn into the PNP by Michael Manley who in 1969 succeeded his father as leader of the PNP. It was a period that was to lead to the renewal of the political parties with the entry of middle class radicals such as D.K. Duncan, Arnold Bertram and others into the PNP, Bruce Golding and Pearnel Charles into the JLP, the formation of the Workers' Party of Jamaica and the ideologisation of Jamaican politics along Cold War lines in the 1970s.

But as indicated at the start of this chapter, Rodney's influence was regional. Caribbean radicalism in the postindependence years made its mark by putting on the agenda a range of economic, social, cultural and racial issues that formal independence had not really touched. The February Revolution in Trinidad 1970, in which the National Joint Action Committee and progressive military officers were key players, was the most dramatic protest and challenge to the postindependent regimes (Brian Meeks 1977; Selwyn Ryan 1989). Newspapers such as *Tapia* and *Moko* were published by New World theoreticians Lloyd Best and James Millette. In the Windward Islands several forum groups similar to the group around the *Abeng* newspaper emerged; in Antigua there was the Afro-Caribbean Liberation Movement around *Outlet*; in Guyana there was the Movement Against Oppression around *Ratoon*; in Belize, *Amandla*, and later on the Yulimo group in St Vincent, and the New Jewel Movement in Grenada.

In the eyes of the local political elites in the Caribbean Rodney became a symbol of subversion. But to the generation of 1968 he was a symbol of the need for change. Rodney's thinking about his own life at the end of 1968 was reflected in a letter written to his good friend 'Bosco' Gordon Rohlehr who became involved with the *Moko* newspaper in Trinidad.

> About the recent past, I need say nothing. You understand it as well as I do. This is a brief statement of present and future perspectives. 'Stage one' requires dropping out of the public eye. A return to the West Indies is out of the question, because that phase for me is played out. I chose Jamaica to make my contribution to the region. Whatever little that has been accomplished in nine months there must stand as the sum total for some time to come – perhaps for a lifetime. People will always continue to struggle. There will be *Mokos* and there will be huge bunches of green plantain that require a lot of shifting.
>
> I left Canada on the 16th November, and from then I have been a fairly inconspicuous citizen of the world. In London, I avoided the public lectures that were a feature of my stay in Canada, and I saw Pat and Shaka for a few days. Whether or not Pat may shift from England before she has the baby is uncertain. What is certain is that she has been very courageous and is with me in the hope of carrying the struggle to a higher stage (and not just to a different arena). After all, even more so than when the old Shakes wrote 'all the world's a stage' is an observation of fact (Rodney 1968c).

Rodney stayed in London for some time and is said to have visited Cuba, spending a few months there before returning to Tanzania in mid 1969. Pat Rodney said that he wrote a manuscript entitled *Black Struggles* on his Jamaican experience but it got lost in Cuba. He wrote long letters to her about his impressions of Cuba. He was very impressed with the gains in health and education and did a lot of reflection on his own future (Pat Rodney 1989).

He was not to revisit Jamaica till 1976 during Carifesta.[59] Later, he was a guest of the Workers' Party of Jamaica at its launching in December 1978 and visited his wife when she was pursuing a degree in Social Work at UWI in the late 1970s. But in the post 1968 phase it was back to Tanzania from 1969–1974 and then the return to Guyana, 1974–1980.

Conclusion

Nationalist politics of the mid twentieth century in the Caribbean grew out of the activism of the anticolonial, especially labour, movement of the 1930s. Activism in the 1960s and 1970s reflected the disillusionment among sectors of the population with what had been achieved by the nationalist movements in political independence and the performance of the first postindependence governments. And out of these experiences fundamental questions were being asked about the character of political and economic development and about national identity in the English-speaking Caribbean not only among the intelligentsia but among Rastafarians at the grassroots. Rodney's political activism grew out of this period of the transition from nationalist anticolonialism to political sovereignty in which the middle classes now dominated Parliament and the cabinets in a context where there had been no fundamental change in economic relations. Rodney's early Guyanese politics had witnessed his involvement with radical anticolonial activism that would have been influenced by his father's involvement with Cheddi Jagan's People's Progressive Party. How the different ethnic groups would live together and shape a postcolonial society was a divisive one, especially so in Guyana where the political parties had become ethnically divided ever since the nationalist movement founded on a nonracial anticolonial platform had by the 1950s fractured along racial lines.

Yet the decolonisation process in the Caribbean had been relatively peaceful, but was paralleled by violent struggles elsewhere. Colonial wars had taken a heavy toll in Algeria's struggle against France in which a million people had been killed; more wars in Southern Africa were in the making against Portuguese rule in Angola, Mozambique and Guinea Bissau; and the political elite of South African apartheid was accelerating its brutality within Southern Africa as a whole. Moreover, the civil rights struggles in the United States in the 1960s had had a considerable impact on the Caribbean. Thus issues of class control, racial discrimination, economic underdevelopment and the attitude of the United States to the region were uppermost in the minds of Rodney's generation of political activists. It is within this general context that one must consider Rodney's intellectual and political activities in Jamaica in 1968.

Rodney's expulsion from Jamaica in 1968 had repercussions which spread to Trinidad, Guyana and other Caribbean territories as well as to the Caribbean populations in North America and England. It marked a new phase of regional radicalism influenced by the civil rights movement and Black Power rhetoric from the United States adapted to the Caribbean. Some of the young people influenced by this movement later on adopted Marxism. Maurice Bishop and Bernard Coard, leaders of the New Jewel Movement in Grenada, were the most prominent examples of the transition in the English-speaking Caribbean from Black Power to Marxism. But the impulse towards political involvement by Rodney's generation was primarily a response to the perception of neocolonialism within the Caribbean and Africa.

Rodney's expulsion from Jamaica gave him publicity in the Caribbean, North America, England and Africa. Bogle L'Ouverture's publication of his Jamaican lectures and speeches under the title *The Groundings With My Brothers* helped to shape his political reputation as the region's premiere radical-intellectual-activist. Many young Caribbean intellectuals followed in Rodney's mould in the 1970s but few were to have his intellectual depth, probity and Pan-African experience. Among the major Caribbean left personalities of Rodney's generation in the 1970s were D.K. Duncan and Trevor Munroe (Jamaica), Raffique Shah and Makandal Daaga (Trinidad and Tobago), Tim Hector (Antigua), Maurice Bishop and Bernard Coard (Grenada). They had all dialogued with him but none had his experience and knowledge of the African continent and few could rival his commitment to the working people. Moreover, this commitment was linked to an overriding concern to avoid manipulation of the working people which characterised the politics of the mass parties in the Caribbean and the centralism of the left wing organisations which facilitated middle class hegemony.

NOTES

1. I first saw Walter outside the television room in Chancellor Hall of the UWI, Jamaica campus one night after dinner early in the 1968. I was then in the final year of my undergraduate degree. Winston Davis, who had travelled to Cuba, was walking towards his subwarden flat in Chancellor Hall when Walter accosted him, "Winston, what's happening man? What's going on in this place?" They greeted each other warmly and as I was then passing on the way to my room Winston introduced me to Walter and was somewhat surprised that I had never heard of him. Winston Davis had

a reputation as an outstanding Spanish teacher and had taught me at Calabar High School. He was also doing research on Cuban literature under the distinguished Latin-American scholar at UWI, Professor Gabriel Coulthard. Because of his visit to Cuba and his activities in the Young Socialist League of PNP left wingers, he was under surveillance by the Special Branch of the Jamaican police.

2. At a party at his home which I attended, in the newly built middle class neighbourhood of Trafalgar Park, in March 1968 there were more Rastafarians and ghetto youth than students from campus.
3. Patterson used the common Jamaican terminology 'dungles' in his novel *Children of Sisyphus*. 'Dungles' combines 'dung (heap)' and 'ungle' and can be used interchangeably with 'slums' or 'ghettoes'.
4. Dr Peter Phillips, a UWI-trained political scientist, became in the 1990s a parliamentarian and a member of the cabinet of Prime Minister P.J. Patterson.
5. Michael Morgan later worked with UN international agencies in Tanzania in the 1980s.
6. Garth White is a talented musicologist who is an expert on Jamaican popular music.
7. A grouping within the Rastafarian movement that was influential in the 1970s and developed its own organisational form and rituals and attracted the adherence of popular reggae singers such as Bob Marley.
8. Millard Johnson was a Garveyite who tried to build a party supporting the principles of Garvey's People's Political Party in the period 1929–1930. Johnson's attempt in the early 1960s to resurrect the PPP was not successful but he reflected the sentiment among sections of the African-Jamaican population that the Jamaican white and mulatto elite wanted an independence that did not disturb their privileged positions so that racial discrimination in public and private institutions as well as in social life would be swept under the carpet. While sympathetic to the Rastafarians, Johnson was not an adherent. A businessman himself, he reflected the aspirations of the black middle class and entrepreneurs. After leaving Jamaica he lived for many years in the United States and Tanzania. See comment on Millard Johnson in Gray (1991: 60).
9. The strike at the government-owned Jamaica Broadcasting Corporation is discussed at length by Manley (1975). It was an important milestone in the development of the struggle for workers' rights, particularly middle strata workers, and in Michael Manley's trade union and political life.
10. In his book *Violence and Politics in Jamaica 1960–1970* Terry Lacey recounted that early April 1960, when the first members of a First Africa Corps commando group had already flown into Jamaica to join ARC militants in a guerrilla training camp in the Red Hills, the police carried out a pre-emptive raid against Claudius Henry, arresting him and some thirty of his followers over the next few days. Subsequently Claudius Henry and some of his group were charged with treason felony. The pre-emptive raid did not prevent the outbreak of the attempted rebellion. Despite the head of Kingston CID maintaining close touch with the New York police, even visiting the First Africa Corps headquarters in the Bronx, the Corps under the leadership of Reynold Henry . . . managed to infiltrate at least seven militants into Jamaica, along with automatic weapons. During April and May there was a series of civil disturbances and extensive arson in rural areas where there were Rastafarian camps. The First Africa Corps weapons were modern, purchased from the proceeds of a series of bank robberies which had been well organised by a black New York policeman. On 21 June a combined security sweep of police and military forces, including the West Indian Regiment and the Royal Hampshires, found the guerrilla

camp. Five men with automatic weapons shot their way out of the encirclement and through road blocks, killing two British soldiers and critically wounding three other members of the security forces. The subsequent combined police and army security operation lasted until 27 June, when First Africa Corp ARC fugitives were arrested. It involved over five hundred police and soldiers, and more than one hundred Rastafarians were arrested between April and June.

The Henry rebellion was an ill-conceived and poorly executed attempt at organising an armed rebellion against the Jamaican government and security forces. It ended in failure and the shooting or hanging of its principal participants (Lacey 1977: 82–83).

When Rodney went to visit Claudius Henry the security forces and the Jamaican government would have been alerted to danger in the link between a radical intellectual and a radical religious leader.

One of the documents that received considerable attention during the court case was a letter to Fidel Castro signed by followers of Henry, including his wife. It said in part:

We wish to draw your attention to the conditions which confronts [sic] us today as poor, underprivileged people which were brought here from Africa by the British slave traders over 400 years ago to serve as slaves. We now desire to return home in peace, to live under our own vine and fig tree, otherwise a government like yours that give justice to the poor. All our efforts to have a peaceful repatriation has proven a total failure.

Hence we must fight a war for what is ours by right. Therefore, we want to assure you Sir, and your government that Jamaica and the rest of the British West Indies will be turned over to you and your Government, after this war which we are preparing to start for Africa's freedom is completed; and we her scattered children are restored. We are getting ready for Invasion on the Jamaican Government therefore we need your help and personal advice.

We have the necessary men for the job. Since you cannot know sir without our information, the Black people of Jamaica are with you and your Government one hundred percent and desire to see Jamaica [that] gets into your hands before we leave for Africa (Chevannes 1976: 277).

11. Norman Manley won the election in 1955 and became Premier of colonial Jamaica, but he lost the referendum on whether Jamaica should stay in the West Indies Federation in 1961 when most of the Jamaican electorate voted no.
12. Michael Manley became Prime Minister in 1972 when his People's National Party defeated Hugh Shearer's Jamaica Labour Party. Manley was re-elected in 1976 but was defeated in 1980 by Edward Seaga who had replaced Hugh Shearer as leader of the Jamaica Labour Party.
13. The Workers' Party of Jamaica was founded as a Marxist-Leninist organisation in 1978 and was dissolved in 1992.
14. See report in *Daily Gleaner*, 13 April 1963.
15. It was a very dangerous situation for Haile Selassie as Rastafarians were smoking spliffs in the no-smoking and highly inflammable area outside the aircraft. By his intervention in clearing the way for the Emperor to disembark, Mortimo Planno saved the day for Jamaican protocol officers who had been pushed aside by the throng of Rastafarian men. Planno was one of the best informed and articulate Rastafarian intellectuals of the 1960s and was a spokesman for the movement. He had a big influence on Bob Marley. He is interviewed in the film *Stepping Razor* which portrays the life of Peter Tosh. Planno is referenced in Mulvaney (1990).

16. The visit radicalised middle class youth at high schools such as Jamaica College, Kingston College, Calabar High School and other institutions. Michael Manley's People's National Party cashed in on black consciousness in the 1972 election when he used the rod that was said to have been given him by Selassie as an electoral mobilisation symbol.
17. The Rastafarians exercised a positive influence on the youth in the 1960s in a social and religious sense. The pride of place they occupied in the ghettoes was usurped in the late 1970s by political henchmen and in the 1980s by 'dons' or gang leaders dealing in drugs.
18. 'Garrison' constituencies refer to those political constituencies where either the Jamaica Labour Party or the People's National Party have hard-core support. The party leader in the area maintains political dominance by harassing and intimidating the supporters of the opposition party through the use of violence, intimidation and the denial of scarce economic benefits. Partisan differences can easily escalate into armed conflict and bloodshed. These constituencies are mainly located in poor or working class areas in the capital of Kingston but have spread since the 1980s to other parishes such as St Catherine and Clarendon. Partisan allocation of low cost housing in the 1960s and 1970s contributed to the development of these garrison constituencies.
19. Prime Minister Hugh Shearer had successfully sponsored a resolution in the United Nations for 1968 to be declared an International Year for Human Rights.
20. Reference to the 1989 interviews conducted with the author.
21. He was a regular attender at Kingston's dance halls and a 'limer' in the homes of many friends. Outside of Kingston he used to 'lime' with Dr D.K. Duncan, a young dentist who had recently returned to practise in Brown's Town, and Arnold Bertram, a history student, both of whom were to become cabinet members in Michael Manley's administration as organiser and theoretician respectively of a radical democratic socialist PNP in the 1970s. ('Liming' is a Trinidadian term meaning "passing time, chatting and joking around". It was in popular usage on the Mona campus at the time.)
22. 'Groundings' refers to an informal gathering for social, cultural or political 'reasoning' or discussion in a yard or any other social space such as a football field, a dance hall or a street corner. Rodney met young people in circumstances which facilitated dialogue and helped to temporarily erode the hierarchical differences between himself as a university person and the unemployed youth.
23. Renamed National Heroes Park.
24. Derogatory reference to the police and special branch.
25. It was clear from the meeting that Henry and Rodney had met before, but the circumstances of their first meeting are not known. For an excellent article on Claudius Henry, see Chevannes (1976).
26. Brother Single became the husband of Lucille Edwards, a Barbadian student at the University of the West Indies in Kingston. Princess Alice was Chancellor of the University of the West Indies. As secretary of the Guild of Undergraduates, Lucille Edwards was required to carry the train of Princess Alice's gown at the annual graduation and she refused to do so in 1968 in protest at the continued symbolic and institutional importance of British royalty in West Indian societies coupled with the continued denigration of people of African descent.
27. See Anne Walmsley for comments on King's work (1992: 262–63, 268, 282, 296, 317).

28. Reference either to Garvey's Jamaican newspaper *Blackman* (1929–1931) or his London magazine *Black Man* which appeared from 1935–1939.
29. Abraham was his Twelve Tribes' name.
30. Frank Hasfal contributed to the collection *One Love*. He founded the Harambee Theatre in Eastern Kingston, near Bull Bay, in 1972. See Anne Walmsley (1992: 268–69, 296).
31. Sam Brown is said to be the first Rasta to run for public office in Jamaica. In the 1960s he was an unsuccessful candidate of the Black Man's Party in a West Kingston constituency.
32. The *Abeng* appeared as a weekly newspaper from January to October 1969 and was a result of the radical politicisation following the ban on Rodney in 1968. Among the editors were George Beckford, Robert Hill, Rupert Lewis and Trevor Munroe. The *Abeng* group, which met weekly to discuss national politics, included Ronald Thwaites, Vin Bennett, Dennis Daley, Richard Small and many others. Among contributors were the English political scientist Ken Post, who was declared persona non grata by the Jamaican government, Robin Small and Wilmot Perkins. In a comment on Lewis (1994) Girvan noted that

    the short history of *Abeng* contained all the seeds of the subsequent schisms in the radical movement. This needs to be the subject of a separate study, but I remember clearly that there was a clear split between people like Trevor Munroe and Bobby Hill who wanted *Abeng* to take a certain 'line', and people like George Beckford and myself who had a more populist, Jamesian, view of the paper, *ie* that it was to be a vehicle for the expression of the views and experiences of the 'masses' (Girvan 1995).

33. Other middle class people were also involved with working class and poor communities. Cultural activist, Marina Maxwell, had a session of her Yard Theatre at the home of Mortimo Planno on 31 May 1969 to remember Denis Sloley, a lawyer and *Abeng* activist who had been killed in a car accident. The occasion was also used to remember the "deaths of other conscious brothers – Che, Marcus Garvey, Fanon, Malcolm X, those who fell in the struggle in the USA, in Vietnam, in Africa, across the Third World" (Anne Walmsley 1992: 199).
34. A very useful source book on Rastafarian creativity, especially as it relates to Reggae music, is Mulvaney (1990).
35. Rodney is here referring to Janheinz Jahn's *Muntu – The New African Culture* which was published in English in 1961 and which was originally published in German in 1958. It was popular in academic and intellectual circles of the time and was a reference point for a revalidation of African and neo-African culture.
36. Pun on 'papacy' and the Church of Rome. For an analysis of Rastafarian speech see Owens (1976); Pollard (1980); and Warner-Lewis (1993). For treatment of Jamaican Rastafarianism see Chevannes (1994, 1995).
37. Reggae evolved from Ska music. Bob Marley's early recordings were in the Ska idiom.
38. McIntosh, Winston Herbert (Peter Tosh), 19 October 1944 – 9 September 1987, internationally acclaimed reggae singer, who sang with Bob Marley and Bunny Wailer. He was a sharp sociopolitical critic.
39. See report on this incident in *Public Opinion*, 25 October 1968.
40. *Bongo-man* was published and edited by Rupert Lewis from 1968–1972 and some of Rodney's writings appeared in it.

41. Edward Said's description of Fanon's *The Wretched of the Earth* is apt. "*The Wretched of the Earth* is a hybrid work – part essay, part imaginative story, part philosophical analysis, part psychological case history, part nationalist allegory, part visionary transcendence of history" (Said 1993: 269–70).
42. Michael Manley's success in the 1972 general elections in getting some Rastafarians to vote had a lot to do with his visit to Ethiopia and his manipulation of the rod which he reputedly received from the Emperor Haile Selassie. That experience bears testimony to the strength of African-Jamaican consciousness.
43. John Hatch was an English journalist who wrote on African politics. Sometime in 1968 he addressed a meeting sponsored by the African Studies Association of West Indies and was engaged by Rodney in discussion. Hatch was unaware of Rodney's own expertise on Africa and tended to be dismissive of some of what Rodney was saying. The intellectual engagement left Hatch red in the face.
44. 'ST' means literally "shit-talk". This is what limers do.
45. Reference here to Dr Aggrey Burke, a Jamaican psychiatrist.
46. For a useful discussion of the relationship between Caribbean governments and intellectuals at the University of the West Indies in the period 1968–1984, see Payne n.d.
47. See *Jamaica Gazette* (publication of the Government of Jamaica) Supplement, 18 July 1968.
48. Winston Davis was active in the Young Socialist League of the People's National Party in the 1960s and in the People's National Party in the 1970s.
49. Jamaican economist at the University of the West Indies who was an active member of the Young Socialist League in 1963–1964.
50. Professor George Beckford was a Jamaican economist who is best known for his book *Persistent Poverty*. In the 1960s he was active in the New World group and was one of the editors of its journal. He was very active in educational work among farmers of the Jamaica Agricultural Society and had visited Cuba. He was an influential scholar in the Department of Economics at the University of the West Indies.
51. Kathleen and Harry Drayton were active in Guyanese politics in the 1950s during the early Cheddi Jagan years. While in Jamaica Harry Drayton had connections with Richard Hart and the left wing of the People's National Party. He was prohibited from entering Jamaica in the 1960s. Rodney and the Draytons became personal friends and during the late 1970s he spent time with them in Barbados and corresponded with them. Kathleen Drayton taught at the University of the West Indies in Barbados and Harry Drayton worked as a representative of the Pan-American Health Organisation in Barbados.
52. Guyanese economist and prolific scholar who was a close friend and political associate of Rodney in the leadership of the WPA. He is a Professor in Economics at the University of Guyana and in 1992–97 was also a parliamentarian representing the WPA.
53. American Marxist political philosopher.
54. Expert on the Caribbean who is a Professor at Colgate University in New York state.
55. See *Jamaica Hansard* 1968–1969: 394.
56. The Black Writers Conference of 1968 was organised by a small group including the

Antiguan publicist, Tim Hector, on whom C.L.R. James had had a considerable impact. Hector's journalism in the *Outlet* newspaper is very Jamesian particularly his writings on cricket. Hector was founder of the Caribbean Conference Committee that organised the Black Writers Conference in Montreal at Sir George Williams University. See Walters (1993: 296–317) for discussion of this period and its implications for Afro-Caribbean Pan-Africanism.

57. For a very useful analysis of the implications of the 1968 events for the University of the West Indies see Girvan (1968).

58. In an interview in 1983, Sir Philip Sherlock who was Vice Chancellor at the time, expressed the opinion that

    Rodney was a very fine scholar, perhaps the finest scholar, historian, that U.W.I. has produced . . . I think that apart from his standing as a historian was his standing as a member of a society in which he felt that there was still hostility, an inner hostility, toward people who were black. And I think that he compelled the university, and the society, to consider the implications of blackness (Baugh 1983: 30).

59. Carifesta is a regional cultural festival initiated by the English-speaking islands. Guyana first staged Carifesta in 1970.

Rodney as a student at UWI, Mona.

Walter Rodney, lecturer at UWI, Mona.

Walter Rodney in Georgetown, Guyana, a few months before his death.

Walter Rodney and Cheggi Jagan in Georgetown in the late 1970s.

CHAPTER 6

Rodney's Academic and Political Agenda in Tanzania

This chapter is concerned with Rodney's political and academic life in Dar es Salaam. Tanzania's evolution[1] to constitutional independence had been overshadowed by Kenya's violent transition, but Tanzania's policies and Nyerere's leadership in the 1960s attracted expatriate intellectuals to the University. Tanganyika had been a German colony from 1891 to 1919 and for this reason had been occupied by Britain during the First World War. Tanganyika was formally mandated to Britain by the League of Nations in 1920, and then administered as a United Nations Trusteeship territory by Britain from 1946 to 1961. Tanganyika gained independence on 9 December 1961 and Zanzibar on 10 December 1963. Both territories were united under the name Tanzania in 1964.[2] The central figure in Tanganyika's struggle for independence was Julius Nyerere. In 1953 he was elected President of the Tanganyika African Association, and on 7 July 1954 he formed the Tanganyika African National Union (TANU) to replace it. Julius Nyerere, who came to be known as Mwalimu ('teacher'), was a very popular leader. In the election of November 1962 he received 97 percent of the votes and in the following month Tanganyika became a republic, remaining within the British Commonwealth.[3]

Tanzania had expected substantial flows of Western aid to fuel her first five year economic plan, but these were not forthcoming. The reasons for this have to do with the response of Germany, Britain and the United States to Nyerere's politics. In 1965 West Germany cut off aid because an East German mission, established in Zanzibar immediately after the 1964 revolution, was allowed to stay.[4] Moreover, in 1964 Nyerere was faced with an army mutiny over pay and demands for a faster replacement of British officers (Coulson 1978: 1). The army mutiny had been put down with British military assistance. These close ties with Britain changed when Nyerere broke off diplomatic relations with Britain in 1965 for her failure to take any action against Ian Smith's white minority government in Rhodesia that had unilaterally declared independence. Britain, in turn, suspended aid and froze a loan of £7.5 million and Tanzania had to do without British aid and experts (Coulson 1982: 143).

Tanzania had become the headquarters of the Organization of African Unity's (OAU) liberation committee and it gave considerable support to movements such as Zimbabwe African National Union (ZANU) and Zimbabwe African People's Union (ZAPU), the African National Congress (ANC) and the Pan-African Congress (PAC), Popular Movement for the Liberation of Angola (MPLA), South West Africa People's Organisation (SWAPO), African Party for the Independence of Guinea and Cape Verde (PAIGC) and Front for the Liberation of Mozambique. (FRELIMO). All these movements had active political representatives in Dar es Salaam and from 1964 FRELIMO used Tanzania as a rear military and political base.[5] There was bureaucratic resistance to this decision within Tanzania as some officials felt that Tanzania would be flooded by refugees and the economy could not sustain the cost involved in hosting these liberation movements (Bagoya 1990). Meanwhile, West Germany was opposed to the establishment by Tanzania of diplomatic relations with East Germany, and the United States was concerned about the implications of Nyerere's politics for East and Central Africa. Relations between Tanzania and the United States were "marked by such recurring mistrust as to make any major dependency on American aid most improbable" (Coulson 1982: 143). Kenya was the preferred location for Western transnationals.

Nyerere broadened Tanzania's diplomatic relations to include the socialist countries. Of the latter group, China had the biggest impact on Tanzania as Nyerere was impressed by what he saw of China's programmes for rural development on a 1964 state visit to that country. In return, Chou En-lai, the Chinese Prime Minister, visited Tanzania in 1965. China provided aid, first for the training of the Tanzanian People's Defence Force, a new army, closely tied to TANU to replace the army hit by the 1964 mutiny; and then for the Tanzania-Zambia Railway eventually built from Dar es Salaam to Kapiri Mposhi in central Zambia.

This was the political context in which Nyerere made public the Arusha Declaration in February, 1967 to an audience of 50,000 people (TANU 1967; Cliffe and Saul 1973: 40). The Arusha Declaration involved land reform and nationalisation of "nine foreign banks, eight export and import companies, eight of the biggest flour mills, and seven industrial enterprises, including a cement mill and a Bata shoe factory ... A state commercial bank and an insurance corporation was established" (Africa Books 1991: 1,826).

There was a code of conduct for the country's political leadership which prohibited government ministers and party leaders from receiving two or more salaries, owning shares in any company or owning houses for purposes of receiving rent. The code was necessary to try to reduce corruption and set a moral example to the population among the political leaders who through a one-party state dominated political and economic life.

Nyerere, who was a strong idealist, sought to invent a brand of socialism that was critical of both Soviet Marxism-Leninism, on the one hand, and capitalism, on the other. A practising Roman Catholic, Nyerere was opposed to atheistic Marxism. His ideas were eclectic, deriving from Africa's experience, Chinese Marxism and European social democracy, particularly British Fabianism and Scandinavian socialism.[6] Political scientists have described Nyerere's socialism as being "qualified by African nationalism and personal pragmatism" (Tordoff and Mazrui 1972: 445). Symbolically following in the tradition of Mao's long march, Nyerere walked 135 miles to a party congress to mark the Arusha Declaration (Rodney 1969a: 6). Nyerere's reputation[7] rested on his character and style of leadership which enabled him to mould national unity in Tanzania and later in 1985 to leave office peacefully.

The Indo-Trinidadian writer, Shiva Naipaul, no friend of African politicians, captured the esteem with which Nyerere was held in the 1970s when he wrote:

> with the possible exception of Kenneth Kaunda of Zambia, he is just about the only African head of state one can contemplate without immediate sensations of outrage or embarrassment. After Field Marshall Idi Amin, Emperor Bokassa, Mobutu Sese Seko and Dr Hastings Banda, after the gross corruptions of Nigeria and Kenya, after the genocidal manias of Rwanda and Burundi and Equatorial Guinea, one turns with relief to Julius Nyerere ... Even confirmed Tanzanophobes will pause at his name and dole out the ritual praise. Nyerere is a good man. Nyerere is a sincere man. Nyerere does not feather his nest. See how simply he dresses. See how simply he lives. The 'Mwalimu' (Teacher) reinforces faltering faith; he makes it possible to believe – if only for a little while – that Africa can be taken seriously, that Africa really wants to 'liberate' itself (Naipaul 1979: 197–98).[8]

Dar es Salaam: Defining an intellectual role

Walter Rodney worked at the University in Dar es Salaam in two phases, first in 1966–1967 in his capacity as Lecturer in History and then from 1969 to 1974.[9] From 1969 to 1972, he was Senior Lecturer and in 1972 to 1974, he was Associate Professor of History. He was Visiting Professor at the Center for Afro-American and African Studies, University of Michigan, in February to June 1972.[10] The Tanzanian years were important in Rodney's development, not only as a historian of Africa, but as a father. He travelled from London to Tanzania a few days after the birth of his son, Shaka, on 5 July 1966 and Pat, his wife, followed. Two girls, Kanini and Asha, were born in Tanzania on 28 March 1969 and 22 March 1971. Pat and Walter built many close relationships with Tanzanians and other Africans and seemed to be constantly expanding their extended family. Rodney's book, *How Europe Underdeveloped Africa*, is dedicated to "Pat, Muthoni and Mashaka and the extended family". Muthoni was a Kenyan woman who worked in administration at the University of Dar es Salaam dealing with student matters and Mashaka was a Tanzanian who worked with them in the home and also went to school. Together with his children this was the nucleus of a close personal network that Pat and Walter built during their Tanzanian years. Pat was one of his links to the lives of the ordinary Tanzanians outside of the university and political circles in Dar es Salaam since she worked as a public health nurse and this led to her picking up Kiswahili in her interaction with Tanzanians.[11]

Rodney arrived in Tanzania to a familiar university setting. His alma mater, the University of the West Indies, was only 13 years older than the University of Dar es Salaam. Both had been influenced by the British university system, and both had experienced a similar transition from the tutelage of the British university system to an independent regional institution. The University College of Dar es Salaam was opened in October 1961, a few weeks before Tanzania got independence. The 1961 opening saw the establishment of East Africa's first Law Faculty which had 14 students and was located in downtown Dar es Salaam. In 1964 "the University moved to the hill, six miles from the city centre and the Faculty of Arts and Social Science enrolled its first ninety-four students" (Coulson 1982: 224). The newly built University of Dar es Salaam was a few miles from the centre of town and was located on a hill which gave it an air of privileged isolation.[12] The Science Faculty was opened in 1965, Medicine in 1968, Agriculture in 1969 and Engineering in 1973. From 1963 to 1970 the University in Dar es Salaam was part of the University of East Africa, which included campuses in Kenya and Uganda. But in 1970 the "three constituent colleges of the

University of East Africa became three autonomous national universities" (Mazrui 1978: 240).

Dar es Salaam attracted a number of radical expatriate scholars.[13] According to Coulson:

> from the start the university attracted staff interested in socialism, especially in the Faculty of Arts and Social Sciences. The historian Walter Rodney, from Guyana, was probably the most well known. In political science, John Saul and Lionel Cliffe formed a powerful team. Economics professors at Dar es Salaam all had, or gained, international reputations. Many expatriate staff were liberals, attracted to Tanzania by Nyerere's rhetoric and who expected to see the fruits of socialist policies, whether in government planning, education, or merely in the way history or politics was studied and used. Their work could be seen in the numbers of papers published by the research bureaux in the early years, and in the establishment of a 'Dar es Salaam view of history', with its slogan of 'putting the African back into African history' popularized by the first professor of history, Terence Ranger, and carried through in the collection of articles *A History of Tanzania* edited by two Tanzanian lecturers in the Department (I. Kimambo and A. Temu) and published in 1969 (Coulson 1982: 226).

Fred Kaijage, a Tanzanian historian who was recruited by Terence Ranger, said that Ranger

> deserves a lot of credit for what he did at the University of Dar es Salaam and it is no wonder that the Department of History is still one of the best departments in the Faculty of Arts and Social Sciences in many ways. We may in part attribute some of these achievements to Ranger. He recruited some of the best minds wherever he could get them . . . I think he must have encouraged some team spirit (Kaijage 1991).

Ranger supported Rodney's rehiring by the University of Dar es Salaam in 1969 after he was declared persona non grata by the Jamaican government in 1968.[14]

Apart from the collection *A History of Tanzania*, another text that came out of the department in the 1960s was *Aspects of Central African History* to which Rodney contributed an essay entitled "European Activity and African Reaction in Angola". The volume, which was made available to an international audience by Northwestern University Press in Illinois, arose from a conference put on by the history department in response to a request by the Ministry of Education in Dar es Salaam "to help teachers prepare for the Central African section of the second paper of the new School Certificate Syllabus in History" (Ranger 1968a: v).

However, the relationship between state and the University was not always an easy one. Yet University faculty and students did have much more licence to criticise than elsewhere in Africa. Haroub Othman, a Dar es Salaam law and development studies professor and close colleague of Rodney, described the campus in the 1960s, somewhat nostalgically, as the "epicentre of radicalism in the African continent . . . situated 20 kilometres away from the city". He continued:

> the university is on a hill which used to be the location of the Observatory Station . . . In the ten year period 1967–1977, the University was a major cooking pot of ideas, and provided a splendid platform for debates and discussions. No African scholar, statesman or freedom fighter could ignore its environs (Othman 1987: 40).

Among the visitors were Rev U. Simango; Eduardo Mondlane and Marcelino dos Santos from FRELIMO, the leading liberation organisation in Mozambique; Agostinho Neto, leader of the People's Movement for the Liberation of Angola (MPLA), who became Angola's first President; the Tanzanian President, Julius Nyerere; Adbulrahman Babu, who was Minister of Planning and was later imprisoned during Nyerere's regime, and Ben Mkapa, then editor of the *Nationalist* and later Tanzania's Foreign Minister. Among African exiles were the Marxist theoreticians Dan Nabudere and Yash Tandon from Uganda. Among the visitors from South Africa were the poets Dennis Brutus and Keorapetse Kgositsile and from Ghana the scholars Aki Sawyer and Kwesi Botchwey, who later became Minister of Finance. On staff there was Nathan Shamuyarira, who became Zimbabwe's Foreign Minister, and prominent among the foreign students was Yoweri Museveni later to become President of Uganda with whom Walter had a personal relationship and on whom he had a significant intellectual and political impact. Interesting and controversial debates also took place between Professor Ali Mazrui, Kenya's distinguished political scientist and writer, and Rodney.

This was a period of political and intellectual ferment when fundamental issues were being debated, important decisions taken, and a new elite created in postcolonial Africa. The University's role was also affected by the fact that Tanzania was the headquarters for a number of liberation movements in Southern Africa and this together with Nyerere's own radical positions and liberal-mindedness gave some staff members a sense of a wider Pan-African mission. Horace Campbell pointed out that "The University had to grapple with a whole host of contradictory demands: the demand for skilled manpower, the anti-colonial thrust of the freedom fighters and the thirst for knowledge by the producing masses" (Campbell 1986: 14).

For Rodney it was an intellectually and politically stimulating period and he developed a network in Africa among intellectuals, academics, political activists and ordinary people. But he was aware of the fact that however much he felt at home, he was not a Tanzanian. He was critical of those expatriates on the left who wanted to tell Tanzanians what to do as he felt the paternalist mentality affected expatriates of whatever ideological persuasion. In reflecting on his Tanzanian years in 1975, Rodney said:

> My political role in that situation was fairly well-defined: to stay within the university walls, first and foremost, to develop and struggle at the level of ideas, to relate to the student population. For me, being a non-Tanzanian, it meant that I had to relate to the indigenous Tanzanians, indigenous intellectuals and students within the university, and only secondarily to Tanzanians outside the walls of the university. I draw that distinction. Many people may say, well, it's a spurious distinction and it's part of the elitism of the university, or something of that sort. I don't think so. One must recognize certain limits in any given political situation: limits of culture, limits of one's legal and citizenship status, limits that come from the fact that we were speaking in the university in one language, which is English, and the people of Tanzania were speaking Kiswahili. And one must take all these things into account, along with the historical record – the Tanzanian people, like other African peoples, had constantly been subjected to harangues from outside as part of cultural imperialism. It was necessary, therefore for these historical reasons, that we as progressive individuals (the majority of whom, indeed, initially were non-Tanzanians in the university), play our role mainly within the university (Rodney 1990: 39).

While Rodney observed these limits it did not prevent him from being involved in political activities outside the campus. This statement has to be examined in the light of his criticisms of expatriates who trotted out superficial solutions to Tanzania's problems and his feeling that Tanzanians were ultimately responsible for the future of their country. It is difficult to maintain a Chinese wall between the society and the campus given the fact that the University was a vital recruiting base for the postcolonial Tanzanian elite. Teaching, research, study group activity as well as public speaking within the environs of the country's only university had a profound impact on the debates that were taking place about the nature of political and economic development. The debates around the Arusha Declaration showed the integral connection between campus academic activity and the society. Central to Rodney's work on the Dar es Salaam campus was his political involvement with the students.

African students

Rodney had a significant impact on university students on African and Caribbean campuses during the 1960s and 1970s. His popularity was seen in the many invitations he received to lecture and the large turnout when he spoke. The gap in age between himself and his students was not great as he was most active as a lecturer and study guide in Dar es Salaam from his mid twenties until age 32 when he left Tanzania for Guyana. The forms of this involvement varied within and outside university campuses. It involved the teaching of African history at the graduate and postgraduate levels and also included courses on the Russian Revolution, blacks in the new world, European, Latin American and Caribbean history, and development issues. A high level of preparation and much creative thought were characteristic features of Rodney's preliminary work for his lecturing on and off the campus. His involvement with Marxist study groups in Tanzania and the Caribbean bore out his belief in the importance of defining the intellectual substance of the problems under discussion. He took public positions on a number of issues and was equally popular as a public speaker and as a lecturer at the University.

According to Issa Shivji, Professor of Law at the University of Dar es Salaam, Rodney was among the organisers of the Socialist Club which was

> founded by a few radical students from Zimbabwe, Kenya, Uganda, Malawi, Sudan, Ethiopia and Tanzania . . . the initiators of the Club soon realised the organisational limitations of the club. It could organise discussions. But the militant students did not want to stop there. They wanted to translate these discussions into action. Hence in November 1967 they formed the first fully-fledged student organisation called the University Students African Revolutionary Front (USARF) which lasted for three years (Shivji 1980: 30–31).

Rodney was an associate member of USARF which issued statements on international events, among which was the condemnation of the Russian invasion of Czechoslovakia in 1968. Shivji said: "Rodney was among the most active. But he was like others, a comrade among comrades. Self-elevation and arrogance were foreign to him. He was never a father-figure and there was no student-lecturer relationship" (Shivji 1980: 31). One of his colleagues recalls that in 1969 when a Visitation Committee was appointed

> to prepare for the inauguration of the University of Dar es Salaam and sought views from the members of the then Dar es Salaam University College community, Walter and a few of us academic staff members met with the militant wing of the student body organised under the University Students African Revolutionary Front and the TANU Youth League, University College of Dar es Salaam branch. Together we prepared a joint memorandum which we presented to the Visitation Committee (Kanywanyi 1990: 1).

In 1975 while recalling his association with USARF on a visit to speak to university students in Trinidad, Walter said:

> Years now people don't address me as Dr Rodney and Professor Rodney; it is only since I've come back to these parts. I'm accustomed to relating to students and the common title is Comrade; that's all. It doesn't matter whether one is a student or staff. Now, if a Comrade is afraid of victimisation, part of my duty is to ensure that he doesn't get victimised because I would have some access to things like the examination meetings and the like. I have the right if necessary to say, 'I would like to see the script of candidate No. 2743' because I have already been warned by one of the students or I have reason to believe (sometimes even, we know) sometimes we have overheard other staff members who say they are going to fix up certain students. We know it before the student in fact, and we are on the lookout to see that the student doesn't get victimised (Rodney 1975a: 2).

Rodney was active off campus in his capacity as an honorary member of the TANU Youth League and appeared on many of their platforms in Dar es Salaam and the rural areas. Intellectual ferment went hand in hand with political discussion and student activism. He lived in Tanzania during a high point of national debate about development strategy as well as the character of democratic processes. University students were an integral part of this process but not necessarily in ways that suited the government. On the other hand, a protest of 400 students against compulsory National Service in October 1966 had some impact on Nyerere and the government's adoption of the 'Arusha Declaration' in February 1967. Conscious of their position as an elite group and aware of the fact that politicians and other sectors were feathering their nests through their government positions, they were critical of rendering national service. Fred Kaijage, who was one of the students involved in the protests and among those suspended for a year, pointed out that they were not in principle opposed to national service but found the terms too harsh. Students were expected to serve two years. They started out five months in camp with 20 shillings pocket money, the other eighteen months they worked in their field at 40 percent of salary and then spent the final month in camp before passing out. They felt the pocket money should be increased and that instead of receiving 40 percent of salary they should receive 60 percent. The government had imposed the policy and had had no dialogue with the students to iron out problems such as these. During the demonstrations one student had a placard which said "TERMS HARSH – COLONIALISM WAS BETTER" (Coulson 1982: 225). The students also claimed that the politicians were not making any sacrifices in the nation's interest. Nyerere was jolted by this demonstration and the sentiments expressed on the placard. The majority of the Tanzanian student body were suspended and sent back to villages 'to rusticate'. But mindful of the students' political criticism of his colleagues, Nyerere ordered that all ministers and senior and middle grade civil servants accept a wage cut amounting, in some cases, to 15 percent (Nyerere 1972: 12).

Nyerere's angry impromptu speech in response to the students illustrated the political mood of those years as well as the development and politics of the postcolonial petty bourgeoisie.

> You are right when you talk about salaries. Our salaries are too high. You want me to cut them? (some applause) . . . Do you want me to start with my salary? Yes, I'll slash mine. (cries of 'No'.) I'll slash the damned salaries in this country. Mine I slash by twenty per cent as from this hour . . . Do you know what my salary is? Five thousand damned shillings a month. Five thousand damned shillings in a poor country. The poor man who gets two hundred shillings a month – do you know how long it's going to take him to earn my damned salary? Twenty-five years! It's going to take the poor man in this country, who earns two hundred shillings a month, twenty-five years to earn what I earn in a year. The damned salaries! These are the salaries which build this kind of attitude in the educated people, all of them. Me and you. We belong to a class of exploiters. I belong to your class . . . We belong to this damned exploiting class on top. Is this what the country fought for? (Coulson 1982: 181–82).

Rodney is said to have spoken out on the issue of the role of the university in the wake of the disciplinary action taken against the students. He argued that "neither the government nor the University College originally saw the need for special insistence on ideological conditioning. There seems to have been a facile assumption that a locally trained Tanzanian would identify his interests with that of the nation and the people" (Alpers 1982: 64). He went on to define the role of the students in Tanzania's postcolonial transformation:

> The fact is that the workers and peasants in most ex-colonial countries are largely unaccustomed to expressing themselves either in the idiom of power or in the terms of the scientific world of the mid-twentieth century. The students are being subsidised to acquire at least the second of these two attributes (and besides the two are not unrelated). Many of the students have the added advantage of coming straight from the homes of disprivileged workers and peasants. The task of the students (as members of the party) is essentially to aid in the mobilisation process and in the political dialogue which is the basis of that mobilisation. The party needs this help, the nation needs this help, and the students need this opportunity for their own self-realization in terms other than the profit motive (Alpers 1982: 64–65).

This class orientation towards the working people was the perspective which directed Rodney's politics and historical writing. And he was very harsh in his critique of middle class privilege at the expense of the masses from whence they had come. According to Shivji, the October protest brought into focus two fundamental questions – the role of the university in a backward country and the ideology of socialism (and therefore its converse, imperialism) (Shivji 1990: 51).

In the mid 1960s, the Dar es Salaam campus was typical of many of the campuses in Africa and the Caribbean that had been shaped by a relationship with the British university system. It was the cradle of the new middle class which by education was being prepared to run the state, the bureaucracy and the military. Having been educated in the Caribbean and England, Rodney understood the ideological processes at work in substituting African faces for British ones, without any change in the system of education. Work in critical socialist theory undertaken by some faculty and students at Dar represented the efforts of a minority that was committed to decolonisation and would draw on whatever that minority could lay their hands and minds on to restructure their countries. Nationalist literature as well as radical European socialist theory, particularly the writings of Marx and Lenin, and of Russian and Chinese political literature, played an important ideological role in the politics of the time, although too frequently dogma became a substitute for hard thinking.

Among this influential student minority was Yoweri Museveni who went on to become President of Uganda. He had come to Tanzania with high hopes.

> I expected a lot, probably too much, of the Tanzanian Revolution. At a distance, one gets an exaggerated image of Tanzania's anti-imperialist stance. You get the image of clearheadedness regarding socialism, anti-imperialism, Pan-Africanism etc . . . it was mainly because of this over-evaluation of Tanzania's achievements that while away home in Uganda, I was determined to come to Tanzania at any cost. I was so determined that I put University College, Dar es Salaam almost as my only choice on the University entrance forms. In fact, if, for any reason, I had failed to gain admission to University College, Dar es Salaam, I would not have gone to University at all. This is because I was not so much interested in going to a College as in coming to Dar es Salaam – to Tanzania. It is Dar es Salaam's atmosphere of freedom fighters, socialists, nationalisations, anti-imperialism that attracted me rather than the so called 'academicians' of the University College, Dar es Salaam. I considered my stay at the College as a means of staying in Dar es Salaam (Museveni 1970: 12).

But when Museveni arrived in July 1967 he was "almost immediately, disappointed" and claimed to have found the student body lacking in political consciousness and militancy. In support of this claim he recalled that when Chief Albert Luthuli of the ANC died not many students turned out although transport was provided (Museveni 1970: 13). Museveni was one of the students who formed the Socialist Club and USARF. Among the personalities who addressed the students on USARF's platform were Walter Rodney, C.L.R. James, Stokeley Carmichael, Cheddi Jagan, Eduardo Mondlane, among others.

USARF was opposed by the political leadership to the right of Julius Nyerere. According to Museveni, "the fears of the reactionaries were further heightened when we started holding ideological classes every Sunday, publishing a paper and generally solidifying our revolutionary theory" (Museveni 1970: 14). Five members of USARF including a Kenyan student, Simon Akivaga, had visited Mozambique with the FRELIMO forces and they returned "convinced that not enough was being done to help the liberation movement, and were struck by the ease of conditions for the 'revolutionaries' on 'the Hill' compared with the reality of what was going on across the frontier" (Legum 1972: 12).

USARF's opponents in the state tried to depict it as espousing an alien ideology and being opposed to Nyerere. The conflict between the state and the university administration on the one hand, and the radical students on the other, came to a head in the 'Akivaga crisis'. Student protests occurred in 20 African countries in 1971 so Tanzania was not unique as it too was touched by this wave of activism.[15]

The 'Akivaga crisis' of July 1971 demonstrated the contradictions between the left wing students and the administration on the issue of democratisation. It arose from a letter written by Symonds Akivaga, a Kenyan, who was President of the Dar es Salaam University Students Organisation (DUSO), to the Vice Chancellor "charging bureaucratic maladministration and lack of consultation of students on important decisions" (Shivji 1980: 36). The Vice Chancellor, Mr Pius Msekwa, had previously been Secretary General of TANU and one of his political tasks was obviously to discipline left wing students who fell outside the TANU Youth League framework. Mr Msekwa had two targets in mind: one was USARF and the second was its journal *Cheche* which had been named after Lenin's *Iskra* (Spark). In 1970, USARF was compelled to cease publishing its journal. The TANU Youth League and its journal *Maji Maji* and the Dar es Salaam Students Organisation were then able to assert hegemony over student politics.

Akivaga's sharp criticism of Vice Chancellor Msekwa in an open letter in 1971 for his failure to consult with the elected student leaders on important issues angered the authorities (Legum 1972: 12–14). It was perceived by the government as a political attack by radical students outside the framework of the TANU Youth League. But Akivaga was making the same claims for the involvement of students in University decision making that the government had made in the 1971 Mwongozo declaration for the workers and farmers in their relations with the party and the parastatals (Coulson 1978: 36–42). Akivaga was 'rusticated', as Tanzanians described those students who were expelled and had to return to their villages. In fact, he was taken away by the army and this incensed the students who initiated a boycott of classes. According to Shivji, "Walter Rodney was once again one of the prominent participants in staff and joint student/staff meetings during the crisis" (Shivji 1980: 36). Together with John Saul, Rodney "initiated a petition asking the Vice Chancellor and the chief administrative officer to attend a meeting to explain their actions in dealing with the students" (Legum 1972: 14).

Walter Rodney's practical involvement with the struggles of the students and his ideological/intellectual work reinforced each other, built bridges and cemented personal ties with East African students at Dar es Salaam. The dedication of a special issue of *Maji Maji* to his memory in August 1980 was but one small bit of evidence of this bond. He was held in high regard by the intellectual and political community in Dar es Salaam and by many scholars on the African continent. Fred Kaijage, who was taught by Rodney in the 1960s, said:

He had the most lasting impact on my own development. None of us had been exposed to a Marxist perspective so he was really the first person to open our eyes to a different way of looking at the world and looking at history. And he did it so well. He didn't just sloganeer, he involved us in an intellectual discourse and led us to sources that we otherwise would not have read. He was so lucid in his exposition that we were able to grasp very basic ideas on Marxism, the Marxist interpretation of history and to understand that history was written from different ideological points of view. Before that, most of us thought that history was just history. From that time on my perspective was changed (Kaijage: 1991).

It is in this intellectual climate at Dar es Salaam that Rodney entered the national debates in Tanzania on Ujamaa.

Rodney on Arusha

Rodney wrote several articles on Tanzania's social experiment and gave many public speeches on it in Africa, the Caribbean, Europe and the United States. In an article entitled the "Tanzanian Revolution", Rodney noted its relatively peaceful character but placed it in a broader context of British postwar colonial strategy. He argued that

in two areas of Africa, the level of violence in the '50s transcended the sporadic and the defensive, and constituted sustained armed attempts to overthrow the colonial order. Those two were Algeria and Kenya, the latter being more significant for Tanzania and for British colonialism in Africa. Mau Mau demonstrated to the British that when an African people took to arms, the maintenance of colonial rule became unprofitable. They, therefore, moved rapidly in their adjacent mandated territory of Tanganyika, and in December 1961 acquiesced to Tanganyikan demands for political independence. This meant that local political power was won by the petty bourgeois fraction, who were expected to guarantee the stability of the imperialist system. The offshore island of Zanzibar fared worse, for the Colonial Office engineered 'independence' in such a way that the government fell into the hands of a quasi-feudal elite and the former slave-owning Arab dynasty. Zanzibar took a step forward, when popular forces gunned down the Sultan's henchmen and declared a Republic of workers and peasants. With the union of Tanganyika and Zanzibar a few months later, the new nation of Tanzania assumed this heritage of revolutionary violence and justice (Rodney 1969a: 5).

This is typical of Rodney's political analysis which zeroes in on the nexus between the external and internal relations of power and the petty bourgeoisie who succeeded to power. Given the class characteristics of the local power holders, he advanced that

> in some respects the Arusha Declaration was an act of self-abnegation on the part of top party and Government personnel who were typical of the acquisitive new African elites, but who found themselves caught in the contradictions of neo-colonialism, and could no longer deny the masses in exchange for imperialist bribes. All party and government leaders were forced by the Arusha Declaration to rid themselves of their second, third and fourth house, to return their government-purchased Mercedes-benz, to agree not to engage in entrepreneurial activity or to hold directorships in capitalist countries. Simple as these things may seem, they served a crippling blow to the corruption which highlights all colonial elites, to the equally common transformation of a 'political class' into a propertied class, and to the already existing comprador group of merchants and manufacturers, who are now isolated from the political machinery in Tanzania (Rodney 1969a: 5).

Given the corruption of the political class, the Arusha Declaration was an important corrective. However, the state economic enterprises arising from the programme of nationalisation were run by bureaucrats appointed by the politicians. One of the problems with the Arusha declaration and Rodney's analysis of it is that both talked about a state of workers and peasants, and ignored the issue of the development of an entrepreneurial class. For Nyerere and Rodney this entrepreneurial function was subsumed in the bureaucratic role of the state and the parastatals and was never fully articulated because of the strong anticapitalist ethos of the period. The Arusha declaration, though well intentioned, was naive on economic questions but its main strength lay in its strong sense of public responsibility and morality.[16] But that is not enough to build an economy.

At a teach-in held at the University College, Dar es Salaam in 1967 which was opened by President Nyerere, Rodney addressed the issues of leadership, party organisation, socialist planning and rural reform in the context of the gap between the rhetoric of change and actual change and problems of implementation. A big obstacle to reform was those political elites who used the state for enrichment. This was also the situation in Tanzania inside the ruling party. Rodney pointed out that

> owing to stresses of neo-colonialism, President Nyerere, articulating the interests of workers and peasants and supported by a section of the leadership

pushed ahead and framed this document in face of opposition footdragging on the part of another section of the leadership. The contradiction between these two groups has not ended, and will now take the form of varying interpretations of the Arusha Declaration so that the socialist fraction needs to be strengthened for the struggle (Rodney 1969b: 3).

He recommended the revitalisation of the post of Secretary General of the party and that two or three agrarian models should be taken to the people. He pointed to the fact that owing to the different social structures in the countryside, the Arusha Declaration could mean something vastly different in one area as opposed to another. The issue of democracy was a central point of departure in Rodney's critique of Nyerere's programmes. He stressed that there was a "need for local and regional mobilisation to help formulate and implement programmes" (Rodney 1969b: 3).

Rodney noted the cultural significance of Nyerere's decision to introduce Kiswahili as the language of instruction in all primary schools and in the conduct of government business. Kiswahili, he wrote:

> was spoken as a second language by nearly all of the numerous ethnic groups in the country, and is the mother tongue in Zanzibar and along the coast ... Kiswahili is widely spoken in Kenya, Tanzania and Uganda and to a lesser extent in Congo, Burundi, Mozambique and Zambia (Rodney 1969b: 3).

Much of the campaign for Arusha was conducted in Kiswahili and the ensuing political debate among the population gave rise to the political language, Kiujamaa.[17] His discussion concluded with the role of Tanzania and its uncompromising position on white domination in Mozambique, Angola, Zimbabwe, South Africa and South-West Africa. Thus in 1967, at age 25, Rodney was involved in important public debates in Dar es Salaam which had implications for national policy.

One of his controversial pieces on Tanzania is the theoretical article "Tanzanian Ujamaa and Scientific Socialism" which was published in *The African Review*, a Dar es Salaam academic journal. According to Issa Shivji, this article was discussed with his colleagues and they were critical of Rodney's tendency to give Nyerere's Ujamaa a 'scientific' designation which meant left wing ideological validation. Joe Kanywanyi, a very close friend and colleague of Walter's, has argued that

> Walter's response to Nyerere's programmes was generally supportive though also critical. He supported the policies of socialism and self-reliance, ujamaa villages, nationalisation of the commanding heights etc. but he was critical

when it came to the approaches of the state towards implementation. He saw them (policies) as progressive and even 'revolutionary'. At one point, indeed, in sharp difference with most of us, he even regarded them as 'scientific' and wrote an article to that effect (Kanywanyi 1990).

A re-reading of this article from the standpoint of Marxist theorising shows Rodney's ability to depart from the excessively abstract theorising and banal thinking that characterised dogmatic Marxist-Leninist analysis of the 1970s. The article was a critique of those who looked condescendingly on Nyerere and Ujamaa as having very little to do with Marxism and scientific socialism. Nyerere was dismissed by some on the European left as a utopian socialist. After all, he had not declared himself a Marxist or adhered to any faction within the international communist movement, the basic division being between the Chinese Communist Party and Communist Party of the Soviet Union. An important theme in his critique was his emphasis on the importance of understanding Tanzanian conditions. Rodney tried to "identify Tanzanian Ujamaa with scientific socialism in certain ideological essentials" (Rodney 1972a: 61). He went on to differentiate between Ujamaa and African socialism and argued that

> a necessary piece of ground-clearing must be performed by advancing the negative proposition that Tanzanian UJAMAA is not 'African socialism'. Such a disclaimer may appear curious and even presumptuous in view of the fact that in 1962 Mwalimu Nyerere referred to ujamaa as 'the basis of African socialism'. But there are several reasons for keeping the two concepts widely apart. When 'African socialism' was in vogue early in the 1960's, it comprised a variety of interpretations ranging from a wish to see a socialist society in Africa to a desire to maintain the status quo of neo-colonialism. Since then the term has come to be identified with its most consistent and least revolutionary ideologue, Leopold Senghor,[18] and with the late Tom Mboya.[19] As such, 'African Socialism' is generally taken to mean a set of relations which leave capitalism and imperialism unchallenged. It is therefore essential to disassociate the anti-capitalist and anti-imperialist stance in Tanzania from a caption that has been pre-empted by non-revolutionary African leaders. Furthermore, when UJAMAA was presented as an option shortly after the independence of Tanganyika, it was (knowingly) defined as an abstract set of values without reference to the social forms necessary for their realisation. Much has now been done in the way of policy decisions to indicate and build the relevant social structures, therefore further differentiating UJAMAA from its erstwhile counterparts of 'African socialism' insofar as the latter never advanced from the ideal to the real. Above all, one must take note of the

progressive evolution of Tanzanian theory and practice over the period of nearly a decade, as a positive response to national, African and international developments (Rodney 1972a: 61–62).

Rodney can be criticised for overstating the extent to which the relevant social structures were being built; moreover, Ujamaa was an economic failure. Its politics, however, certainly contributed to the development of a Tanzanian nationality in a continent where ethnic rivalries have bedevilled many nation-states. Dysfunctionality of the political order arising from ethnic conflict has affected Africa as well as many parts of the world. The conceptual and empirical bases on which he distinguished Ujamaa from "African socialism" were, nevertheless, interesting. He pointed out that

> for Marx, 'scientific socialism' is quite simply socialism that is scientific . . . 'African Socialism' is utopian in its refusal to come to grips with the class relations in which Africans are enmeshed and in its romanticised ignorance of the stages of African historical development. It is the contention of the author that in contrast, Tanzanian UJAMAA is correct in its perception of the principal motion of its own society (Rodney 1972a: 63).

For Rodney, therefore, to the extent to which Ujamaa was based on the working out of its own internal dynamism or social motion, that was the extent to which it approximated scientific social analysis. Whether this amounted to scientific socialism was another matter, given the inherent ideological biases of the term in twentieth century usage. These observations are important because the idea of socialism that came from Marx was one that assumed an industrial capitalist base. Applying the idea of socialism to a peasant-agrarian society demanded a revision of the notion of socialism and the role of the working class given its small size in most postcolonial countries. Marxism privileged the role of the working class as the leading force in bringing about socialist transformation. One of the concerns of Frantz Fanon in his *The Wretched of the Earth* was to critique the dogmatic application of this idea to the African continent. Rodney's work followed in this vein but it certainly did not resolve the issue of whether the validity of the questions Marx posed for his day and time, or for that matter what Lenin posed for late nineteenth century Russia, could be applied to the complex realities of twentieth century Africa. The issue with which Rodney was concerned was that of methodology and this is why he assessed Nyerere's ideas on the basis of the extent to which they reflected a coming to terms with the internal laws of motion of Tanzanian society. In order to tackle this problem of methodology, Rodney had to research the history and political economy of the country.

To approach the problem from the standpoint of the applicability of Leninist theory would have meant starting with the fact that Tanzania had a most underdeveloped working class, that for economic, social and political reasons could not play the role that the Russian working class had played. The appeal of socialism can best be understood not so much as an effort to understand the laws of motion of particular societies in Africa, which was Rodney's concern, but as a response to the politics of decolonisation in the 1960s and 1970s. Socialism was a mobilising ideology to rally support of the population behind the centralisation of economic and political power within the ruling party that had successfully won the anticolonial struggle. Socialist ideology was also a function of the Cold War competition between Eastern and Western powers over the ex-colonial world as well as between the Soviet Union and China. In the case of both Tanzania and Mozambique, China's influence was significant (Mazrui 1978: 176). The ideological struggles that ensued around the idea of socialism involved arguments among the educated political and intellectual elites about the possibilities of postcolonial realignments and this is why Dar es Salaam was the base for embassies from both the Western capitalist and Eastern socialist blocs.

Rodney's intellectual work is not so much concerned with those issues of contemporary politics provoked by the Cold War, but with understanding and reconstructing the longer-term processes that had shaped the African continent in national and global terms. Rodney was cognizant of the material conditions of Tanzania. He was of the opinion that

> Tanzania is exceptional in that even at the end of the colonial period the communal forms were still recognisable. This is a consequence of its people having been relatively little involved in the capitalist money economy of mining, settler plantations and cash-crop production. The low degree of internal stratification at the time of constitutional independence was reflected in national cohesion and the solidarity of a single mass party. Between 1961 and 1967 there was increasing differentiation, so that 'Socialism and Rural Development' dealt with the core of the problem by determining that socialism could only be built in Tanzania by halting stratification and the creation of a rural proletariat. This was the first of the conditions which Marx and Engels laid down when discussing how socialism might have been built on the basis of the Russian commune (Rodney 1972a: 69).

Rodney did not have much in classical Marxism to help him here but he was trying to link Nyerere's experiment to that tradition. The fact of the matter was that Tanzania had a poorly developed economy and neither in Rodney's article nor in Nyerere's paper "Socialism and Rural Development" which tried to set out an alternative economic policy, did they sufficiently focus their thinking on this fact. Economic policy and thinking were driven by ideological considerations.

It was therefore unpopular and virtual heresy for anyone to argue in the radical camp that the problem with applying socialist theory to Tanzania was insufficient capitalist development. Rodney had observed that

> Africa has experienced almost as many years of capitalist development as Europe, but in our case the unfolding of capitalism has meant historical arrest and backwardness. The accompanying stratification never approximated to the dynamic of capitalism in the metropoles. Thus, one could never expect capitalism to perform in Africa the historically progressive role it played in Western Europe (Rodney 1972a: 70).

Capitalism via the slave trade and colonialism did arrest the development of internal capitalism in Africa. While this is so, insufficient attention was paid to encouraging its internal capitalist development in both private and state forms in the postindependence years as part of a development strategy. The ideas of Arthur Lewis concerning capitalist development in postcolonial Africa and the Caribbean were not adequately explored. They were treated ideologically and dismissed largely on the basis of the neocolonial experience of Puerto Rico without reference to other experiences such as Singapore's. This is certainly the case with Rodney's critiques of Arthur Lewis in his speeches in the 1970s which were similar to the views expressed by a younger generation of social scientists in the New World Group at the University of the West Indies.[20]

Rodney pointed to the backwardness of Tanzania in capitalist terms when he suggested that "Socialism is inconceivable prior to the emancipation of man from such elementary forces as drought, flood and disease" (Rodney 1972a: 68). These natural forces plus the elemental force of the world economic system, and poor state management of the economy by Nyerere and his successors turned the dreams of the early postcolonial years into an economic nightmare for many Tanzanians but it allowed for a less authoritarian political culture than other one-party regimes in Africa as well as helped to create the conditions for national unity.

On the question of the relations with socialist countries, Rodney felt that

> the unstinted aid supposedly from the Soviet Union would be regarded as illusory by most progressive Africans who are learning that self-reliance is definitely a superior alternative to any 'Big Brother'. However, it is true that the socialist sector of the world (divisions notwithstanding) offers a set of models, a set of alternative partners for trade and a more accessible source of

technical aid. Tanzanian external political and economic relations have already gone a long way towards maximising the advantage created by the existence of socialism in various parts of the world (Rodney 1972a: 70).

Rodney's comments were very important since many dogmatic Marxists of the 1970s looked at self-reliance as belonging to the nationalist vocabulary and not to the lexicon of the more favoured Marxist class terminology. Rodney tried to combine notions of self-reliance with foreign policy choices that were in the nation's interest rather than advocate an adherence to one political bloc or another in the wider East-West global polarisation.

Rodney was critical of the textbook Marxists who thought that 'scientific socialism' was found exclusively within the pages of Marx's writings.[21] He advocated that Ujamaa needed to be judged on its own terms as a Tanzanian attempt at a transition to socialism. He sharpened the distinction between 'African Socialism' and Ujamaa by positing that the former is

> the inflection which the African petty bourgeoisie have given to bourgeois ideology in an attempt to camouflage from the masses the deepening capitalist exploitation of the neo-colonial era. In sharp contrast, Tanzanian ujamaa has begun to make the decisive break with capitalism. The evidence lies in the Arusha Declaration, in the MWONGOZO, in the TANZAM railway, in the nationalisation of certain buildings and in virtually every act of Tanzanian foreign policy (Rodney 1972a: 73).

This was to be Rodney's strongest identification with Nyerere's programme. It was one and the same time a critique of an abstract Marxist opposition to Ujamaa and a plea to the left to widen its framework of Marxist thinking and judge the process in terms of Tanzanian conditions.[22] In the camp of abstract Marxists, Rodney placed his progressive European friends who he said, "often display a penchant for armchair Marxist perfection, so that for them Nyerere and Senghor are indeed in the same bag, because the former has not come forward to declare for Marxism" (Rodney 1972a: 74). And again he emphasised that "progressive Europeans are the ones who display the hegemonistic tendencies characteristic of the imperialist metropoles, in so far as they have no time for insights that seem in any way to depart from models originating in Western Europe" (Rodney 1972a: 75). But it still begged the question as to what was socialist about Ujamaa. He repeated what he considered the substance of Ujamaa:

> its stand against capitalism, against imperialism, against racism and against exploitation of all kinds; and (to put it affirmatively) its stand for the

emancipation of the working population of Africa and for the remodelling of the society along lines of socialist equality and socialist democracy (Rodney 1972a: 74–75).

The question could have been asked however: wasn't there a need to judge this development strategy that was conceived by the Tanzanian elite of the 1960s less ideologically and more empirically on the basis of precise and realistic goals? In other words, why was ideology so important? Ideology became important because of two principal conjunctures of the mid twentieth century. First, was the dissolution of the British, French and later Portuguese colonial empires. The dissolution of empires and the aspirations of former colonial peoples required of the latter new definitions of themselves, their nations and their relations with their neighbours and the rest of the world. Nationalism as well as Marxism provided the political rhetoric for this exercise. Secondly, the expansion of communist power and influence in the Third World, particularly China, Vietnam and Cuba, and the links with Moscow and Eastern Europe gave some postcolonial governments the option of negotiating complex Cold War politics through the adoption of non-aligned politics or support for one side or the other in international politics. Marxist political rhetoric, on the one hand, or modernisation political rhetoric associated with American social science scholarship and the US State Department, on the other hand, were a necessary part of the discourse which defined the intellectual standpoint of the political elite. Ideology therefore offered a guide to the politics and the social commitments of the early years in the life of new nations. But ideology had a cost that had to be weighed against other pragmatic goals and policy options. The shifts in global politics since the late 1980s have forced the political elite in many African and Caribbean countries to reassess more carefully the relationship between ideology and economic imperatives.

Shivji's intervention

Postcolonial political leaders had a formidable agenda which included nation building, state and institutional formation and economic development. The postindependence leaders underestimated the enormity of the task that faced them in a world where the former colonial powers had not disappeared and their influence in Africa remained strong, being exercised through bilateral relations as well as through a number of multilateral institutions. Internally, some politicians exploited ethnicity and many cynically plundered the treasuries of their new states. Moreover, these fragile new states had to contend with the East-West Cold War competition for political influence in Africa as well as with powerful international financial interests.

The attempts to develop the non-aligned movement were bedevilled by the overarching politics of the Great Powers. Nyerere certainly provided a vision for Tanzania although it was not the one shared by left wing Marxists. Scholars at the University, some of them non-Tanzanians, played a part in critically responding to the alternatives that were being posed. According to Shivji: "The University has been a crucible of different theoretical premises which have underlined major policy decisions in the country. Indeed, the Dar es Salaam campus has been one of the few in Africa where debates and discussion have been a hallmark of academic life" (Shivji 1990: 49).

Many attempts were made to apply Marxism to Tanzania. Some of them were crude and dogmatic and they betrayed the authors' own obtuseness and threw absolutely no light on Tanzanian reality. Others were innovative in setting out the terms of the debate and the role of class in national development. The role of class was important in postcolonial analyses because nationalism as an ideology sought to suppress divisions based on either ethnicity or class on the grounds of national unity against the colonial power. After political independence the issue was always posed as to the social and class orientation of the emergent political elite. Among the most influential pieces was Shivji's long essay entitled "Tanzania – the Silent Class Struggle" which was published in *Cheche*, September 1970. Shivji said that he set out to

> do a scientific analysis of the socioeconomic formation in Tanzania. The vacuum resulting from the lack of a theoretical analysis of the total situation has given rise to the dangerous phenomena of finding a substitute in platitudes, phrase-mongering or chanting of hollow slogans . . . Appearances pass as reality while proper analysis of reality is met with ignorant contempt or condemned as 'doctrinaire'. Subjectivism is on the verge of triumph! . . . without a clear class analysis, it is impossible to chart out a correct strategy and formulate appropriate tactics . . . How can we talk about a 'Tanzanian Revolution' without even knowing the friends and the enemies of such a revolution? An analysis of the socioeconomic formation of Tanzania is therefore urgently needed (Shivji 1973: 304).

Shivji, a law student, tried to understand the material basis of Tanzanian politics and therefore to provide a foundation for understanding the changes, reversals and advances that were taking place. His objectives were ambitious and he could not have fulfilled them in his pamphlet. But he did point to the role of Tanzania within the context of the world capitalist system, developing ideas about the neocolonial mode of production, bureaucratic capitalism, and state capitalism. His study drew on research on Tanzania's political economy and it showed that although Tanzania was not fighting a military war of liberation there was "a silent class struggle" going on with international capital. This work fell within the dependency and structuralist school of analysis and started an interesting debate with critical essays by Tamas Szentes,[23] Walter Rodney and John Saul in the journal *Maji Maji* (Cliffe and Saul 1973).

In his response, entitled "Some Implications of the Question of Disengagement from Imperialism", Rodney noted that the editors of *Cheche* had argued that disengagement did not mean total isolation, but "reduction of economic dependency, elimination of surplus outflow, utilization of this surplus for construction of nationally integrated economies, equitable cooperation with friendly socialist countries and mobilization of the masses for rapid development and defence" (Rodney 1974a: 62).

The politics of disengagement was based on a radical interpretation of economic decolonisation which saw links with socialist countries, greater cooperation between developing countries, development of the national economy, and less dependence on foreign capital as ways to rupture the legacy of colonial economic dependency. The concept of disengagement was a vague one that could be interpreted either in the barren and dead-end sense as meaning autarky or in a more pragmatic way as a series of policy measures geared to strengthening national capital. The best known defender of the notion of disengagement, which later became known as delinking, was Samir Amin.[24]

One of the popular mechanisms of the time was nationalisation of key foreign owned companies in critical areas of the economy. Together with disengagement, there was the idea that capitalism was declining. Rodney contended that

> before 1917 capitalist power encircled the whole globe. Today it has been pushed out of huge areas of the world and it is receding. When a mode of production is dying, its ideological superstructure is also destined for extinction, so that the characteristic modes of bourgeois thought are on the wane. But their disappearance cannot take place without intense intellectual battle. That is very much part of the *silent class struggle* (Rodney 1974a: 67–68).

This type of assessment dominated left wing circles and deduced the decline of capitalism from the Russian and Chinese revolutions, the Vietnam war, and the decolonisation movement that involved a majority of the world's population. But the end of modern empires has seen the growth of what Samir Amin has called a new capitalist globalisation (Amin 1992).

Tamas Szentes, the Hungarian economist, was more realistic in his comments on Shivji's work when he pointed to the need to look at the processes at work in the development of capitalism and the changes that were underway within it. He was also positive in his attitude towards state capitalism and national private capitalism insofar as they served to develop the productive forces. Among many African Marxists, there was a visceral hatred of capitalism because of its identification with colonialism and it was hard to see it in a positive light. Moreover, the symbols of capitalism in Africa were the extravagant spending of politicians and their cronies who used state resources for personal enrichment. In East Africa they were known as the Wabenzi.[25] They had a lot of land, many houses, their wives travelled abroad frequently on shopping sprees and their children were educated in foreign schools.[26]

Rodney's response

While praising Shivji for dealing well with the international class dimensions of the Tanzanian situation, Rodney was critical of Shivji's neglect of the internal class structure. Rodney deduced that

> Shivji's generalisations are rather loose. He holds that 'the fundamental contradictions in Tanzanian society are to be found in the content and nature of the relationship of Tanzania's economy with international capital.' It would be more accurate to say that the content and nature of the relationship of Tanzania's economy with international capital both in the past and at present has given rise to the most decisive contradictions within Tanzanian society. That refinement is not a mere ideological nicety. It is absolutely necessary so that one proceeds to discern which are the decisive contradictions internally, and how their resolution would in turn break the stranglehold of external capital. Because it is clear that the slow rate of disengagement of the Tanzanian economy from the imperialist world economy is partly due to internal blockages of a politico-ideological nature – apart from whatever manipulations the imperialists are up to (Rodney 1974a: 64–65).

This exchange revealed some of the issues of concern to Rodney in his efforts to grasp the workings of African and Caribbean societies. To a certain extent it differentiated him from the theorists of structuralism and dependency in that while recognising the imperial dimension of exploitation he always sought to look at its connections to the internal class dynamics. This was true of his study of history as well as contemporary politics. It certainly put him in a different camp from Arthur Lewis who reasoned in *Politics in West Africa* that

> most of the political philosophy of Europe and the Americas, stretching back long before Marx, derives from the clash between haves and have-nots; as we shall see later, when transported to West Africa much of this philosophy is irrelevant. Now to say that this is not a class society is not to say that society is undifferentiated . . . the society is divided both vertically and horizontally; vertically in the sense that some people rank higher than others; and horizontally in the sense that some groups are marked off from each other by tribe, language, habitation or other division which causes group solidarity. These vertical and horizontal divisions play their part in the political structure (Lewis 1965: 18–19).

Lewis recognised class differentiation but this is not the same thing as seeing class struggle as a dynamic historical force and privileging particular social classes as leading groupings in the revolutionary process. The difference between Lewis, on the one hand, and Rodney's generation of radical West Indian academics, had implications not only for differences in approaches to scholarly issues but also to politics. Class struggle was a key theme in Rodney's analysis of the national and international circumstances and within that context race interpenetrated it as part of the process of exploitation. He stressed the fact that given the global strength of capital and the strategic location of the European colonial powers in global power relations, the decolonising nations were at a severe disadvantage. This fact was a key determinant in the foreign relations of the new states. In the transition to independence, the colonising power tried to ensure that the political leaders and parties most favourable to what Nkrumah called neocolonialism, would succeed to power. Moreover, their own domestic polities were marked by internal class and ethnic power struggles.

Shivji went on to write *Class Struggles in Tanzania* in response to Rodney and other critics. This text was the first to discuss class relations in Tanzania. In his comments on Shivji's book, Rodney focused his attention on the petty bourgeoisie, the class that was leading the country. He pointed out that he was not using the term in a pejorative and abusive sense. He was concerned more with exploring the political and ethical possibilities of petty bourgeois leadership. His critique of the petty bourgeoisie in Africa and the Caribbean had a very strong moral dimension which is very much influenced by Amilcar Cabral's notion of the revolutionary petty bourgeoisie committing class suicide in order to be able to be faithful to the struggle for genuine liberation. Cabral had proposed in a conference in Cuba in 1966 that

> in order to play completely the part that falls to it in the national liberation struggle, the revolutionary petty bourgeoisie must be capable of committing suicide as a class, to be restored to life in the condition of a revolutionary worker completely identified with the deepest aspirations of the people to which he belongs. This alternative – to betray the revolution or to commit suicide as a class – constitutes the dilemma of the petty bourgeoisie in the general framework of the national liberation struggle (Cabral 1980: 136).

Given the conditions of Guinea-Bissau in the struggle against Portuguese colonialism, this was a valid approach to the petty bourgeoisie that had been adopted in circumstances where the revolutionary overthrow of colonialism was underway (Davidson 1994: 220–26). This idea could therefore be validated in the context of many armed struggles in the Third World against colonialism, or in acute political struggles within a national context when a qualitative shift in the balance of social and political forces between adversaries was possible. It is not meaningful in a theoretical and political sense when one comes to deal with long-term postcolonial socioeconomic developments and processes given the peripheral character of postcolonial economies. The conditions for economic growth are very different from the requirements of political mobilisation.

So Rodney tried to come to grips with the role of the petty bourgeoisie in Africa and the Caribbean and was influenced by Cabral's thinking. Apart from this, a striking feature of Rodney's thought was his emphasis on the role of the subjective factor in effecting fundamental changes in social, political and economic systems in the process of decolonisation. His focus on the different trends within the politically dominant petty bourgeoisie and efforts to create a radical intelligentsia can be seen as an extraordinary effort to take advantage of a moment in time when the possibility of shaping society and changing history offered itself to the first postcolonial generation. But these circumstances did not allow the actors a free hand to do what they wanted. They had to act in accordance with the conditions determined by the strength of the international capitalist system, the legacies of colonialism, the disadvantageous material conditions of the ex-colonial country, and the strengths and weaknesses of the nationalist movement that was now politically at the helm. The process of transformation could not be measured in five-year plans but required a much longer view of history which politicians seldom have time for, given the exigencies of political life. Rodney, at times, overstated the ability of the subjective factor, of what was possible, but the main merit of his political contribution lay, not so much in the answers he sometimes put forward on specific courses of action or policies but in his ability to pose fundamental questions and in so doing to draw on a strong sense of the historical processes underlying contemporary politics.

Rodney continued the discussion of class relations in Africa in an essay on "Class Contradictions in Tanzania" which was published in 1980 and was based on a lecture given at Northwestern University on 21 April 1975, while on a visit to the United States. The article presented important theoretical observations about class formation and politics in Tanzania. Rodney notes that in the postindependence years in the 1960s it was quite common to hear that African societies had no classes and that those who were trying to conduct analyses along those lines were intent on sowing the seeds of division. That was changing both at the academic and popular levels of perception. He pointed out that Tanzania was probably one of the territories where class formation was least developed on the African continent and that classes in Africa were embryonic, and were still very much in the process of formation. But his main point of departure was that class formation in the years since independence in 1961 was "as important if not more important than class formation before independence . . . Attempts to get conservative African nationalists to organize a political party to oppose the TANU had far less success than similar attempts in Ghana to oppose the Convention People's Party" (Rodney 1980c: 20).[27]

This was because Ghana had a larger and more developed petty bourgeoisie than Tanzania and the state apparatus through the executive, judicial and legislative, administrative and economic sectors of the state had ample room for expansion. Political struggles within the elite were largely a result of struggles to access these fruits of power. In Tanzania the Arusha Declaration and other policies acted as a brake on the more negative features of this type of development among the petty bourgeoisie.

Moreover, Nyerere's management of the state sought to secure national unity across ethnic divisions. Rodney was sharply critical of those African politicians who exploited ethnic differences in their search for political power. He recognised that

> ethnic differences exist . . . they are not necessarily political differences however. They don't necessarily cause people to kill each other. They become so-called 'tribalism' when they are politicized in a particular framework. And in post-independence Africa they have been politicized largely by sections of the so-called African elite . . . if we broke Tanzania down, we could pick out two or three very dominant ethnic groups. The pattern in Tanzania is not all

that dissimilar from, say, the pattern in what is now Zaire, where ethnic politics have become important. So the lack of politicization is . . . due to the rather weak development of the petty bourgeoisie as a class (Rodney 1980c: 21).

The politicisation of ethnic relations and the role of petty bourgeois politicians in this area have been a central theme of postindependence politics in Africa and the Caribbean. However, some scholars have taken ethnic antagonisms as given or have examined them primarily with respect to colonial distortions without due regard to their exacerbation by neocolonial politicians. On the other hand, Nyerere's approach towards building national unity and his appeals to the Tanzanian population across ethnic and class lines, the emergence of Kiswahili as the national language and his own retirement from national political leadership were among his major contributions to nation building in Africa.

Rodney links the weakness of the petty bourgeoisie to Tanzania's decision to implement a radical socioeconomic programme.

In other parts of Africa where the petty bourgeoisie or some of its elements were already sufficiently entrenched, it would have been difficult to envisage an Arusha Declaration. I was fortunate to have been in Tanzania at that particular time; in seeing members of the leadership of TANU then, in 1967, one got a distinct impression of the discomfort on their part. Many elements, people that you could look up to as individuals – ministers, members of the hierarchy and the civil service, were applauding the Arusha Declaration very painfully. One could see that it did not exactly fall in line with their conception of where the country should have been going. And one must therefore say that in a certain sense they were coerced, or at least constrained to move in that direction . . . the constraint was a class struggle, it was between themselves and the mass of the people. The mass of the people, workers and peasantry, came out in such tremendous force behind that document that I don't think that the small fragile petty bourgeoisie could ever have had the confidence, or that anyone in that class could get up and say, 'we stand opposed to this option'. It would almost have been equivalent to committing suicide (Rodney 1980c: 21).

Here Rodney looks at the weak Tanzania petty bourgeoisie in relation to the correlation of class forces from below that were in support of the radical Arusha programme. However, the petty bourgeoisie with its Western education and skills would effectively, through the bureaucracy, use its technical and administrative power to frustrate the democratic intentions of Arusha. For all that, not only was the petty bourgeoisie in Tanzania small, but it was located in the civil service, the army, and police and had no roots in trade, manufacture or in commercial agriculture and was totally lacking in modern entrepreneurial skills. Indeed, these formed major handicaps in its ability to lead the state on issues of economic development.

For its part, the working class, which had been privileged in Marxist class analysis, was very weak given the low level of development of the Tanzanian economy. In evaluating the working class, Rodney distinguished the following features: its small size, the high proportion of migrant labour, the rural character of the working class and its low levels of skill and organisation. The trade union movement in Tanzania was frustrated in its efforts towards independent organisation and the workers had to function through the ruling party after the 1964 army mutiny in which some trade union leaders were implicated. In light of this history, Rodney posed the question as to the relationship between these two social forces in the party and the state. In the mid 1960s the "Tanzanian economy was definitely stagnant in the face of declining world prices for major products (like sisal and cotton). The option (Arusha)... was taken by the petty bourgeoisie under pressure from the working masses" (Rodney 1980c: 26). But neither the rural producers nor the working class in Tanzania were able to challenge the hegemony of the petty bourgeoisie over the state. Rodney did not pay sufficient attention to the problems of the peasantry. Their problems were seen as being dependent on the resolution of the conflict between the state and the proletariat. But this held out little prospect for real change because the proletariat was so economically puny and organisationally weak and lacking in class consciousness that with the exception of the trade union movement in South Africa it has not played an important role in either Tanzania or in Southern Africa.

In looking at the Indian mercantile sector in Tanzania, Rodney saw it in economic terms and analysed it in relation to the struggle between the (African) bureaucratic petty bourgeoisie and the commercial petty bourgeoisie (Asian). He saw the development of such instruments as the State Trading Corporation as mechanisms for undercutting the Asian entrepreneurs. The issue of strengthening the petty bourgeoisie through private enterprise was not a position that was compatible with the anticapitalist thrust of Arusha. Thus Rodney could argue in the 1970s that "the Asians are completely finished as a class – that there is no longer any future for them in the old roles which they had in East Africa and Tanzania" (Rodney 1980c: 29). Yet on the basis of disastrous domestic economic policies, adverse terms of trade, and the pressures of international capital through the IMF, Tanzania's economy has opened up and by the 1980s some Asian businessmen had returned.

Revolutionary pedagogy

There is a revolutionary pedagogy in Rodney's writings and practice that is related to the agenda of decolonisation. In his essay "Education in Africa and Contemporary Tanzania", he critiqued colonial education and wrote that

> it was doled out to a minority. Colonial education was elitist, because it was based upon elitist philosophical and ideological assumptions derived from European class society, as distinct from African society which was communal and relatively unstratified. In a stratified social system, education serves the interest of the dominant class, caste, race, or geographical unit, irrespective of pretensions to the contrary. Such an education is for the few, whether they be the actual children of the ruling class, or children of the exploited and oppressed classes who are coopted into the services of the system (Rodney 1972b: 83).

Rodney was very positive concerning the advances made by Tanzania in education during the ten years following independence and was supportive of Nyerere's "Education for Self-Reliance".[28] But he visualised the relationship between education and social liberation in much broader terms and was convinced that although education was a

> critically important aspect, educational transformation alone will never lead to the total liberation of the society. Indeed, it is dialectically impossible for profound change to take place in the old educational system without antecedent and concomitant transformations in all aspects of the political economy (Rodney 1972b: 98).

This challenge presents a radical vision with multiple problems and is easily open to the charge of the politicisation and ideologisation of education. While all educational systems do have ideological and political underpinnings, one of the critical questions involves the extent to which the guardians of order, in any given polity, can frustrate and undermine intellectual creativity when intellectuals or scholars do not toe the line ideologically. In the context of Nyerere's radical project, Rodney advocated a more politically committed higher education system where

> the object must be to challenge the minds of the students to recognise the superiority of the socialist world-view as it is applied to their particular fields of academic study. Courses on Socialism, per se, are marginal to the achievement of victory in the realm of ideas. The two prerequisites for a

successful socialist orientation of students of the university and institutions of higher learning are, first, the need for committed socialist staff (especially within certain strategic social disciplines); and second, the need for a concerted effort to illumine the social realities of Tanzania and Africa, in a perspective that is hostile to imperialism and class domination (Rodney 1968b: 83–84).

But what were the criteria to be used to determine who was a "committed socialist academic"? And what if they were neither members nor supporters of the ruling party? What about the independence of the socialist and nonsocialist staff? While some could trust an academic like Rodney, what would happen when someone who was committed but a political hack and academic lightweight was placed in power? Rodney's agenda poses substantial theoretical and practical issues which have no short-term answers. Ranger's observation with respect to the Tanzanian state and the university is apt.

> One does not have to agree with everything in the left critique of Tanzania to be aware that the structures of party, trade union, etc. harden all too easily into privilege; if an academic wants to speak for or to the 'people' he is not readily going to be able to do so if he is subject to the instant correction of members of this new 'establishment' (Ranger 1981: 19).

Rodney's approach to education, conceptualised in terms of support for a national project of socioeconomic and political reform, stood in contrast to Arthur Lewis' prescriptions for education and development in Africa regarding options for resource allocation in the context of poor economies and a gradualist path to changes in socioeconomic relations (Lewis 1983: 483–97). Lewis was a liberal West Indian Pan-Africanist who had stated:

> to me, of African descent, a visit to Africa is always exciting emotionally and intellectually. Besides, I have known the chief Pan-African leaders personally for thirty years, sharing their anti-imperialism, and their goal of an Africa united in stages. I also share their goal of a free Africa, and it is only the defection of some from this goal that has wrung this pamphlet from me (Lewis 1965: i).

Lewis had served as adviser to Kwame Nkrumah's government in Ghana and his book on the *Politics of West Africa* showed his valuable insights into postcolonial politics and economic development. Lewis' approach stressed economic calculations as to how much should be allocated to primary vs secondary vs university and adult education and how many people should be sent abroad for study. On a technical-economic level as well as on an ideological level Lewis' analyses are important. Firstly, resource allocation is a universal problem and especially so in postcolonial countries. Secondly, the best Marxist thinkers are those who have mastered so-called bourgeois knowledge such as Marx himself or for that matter Rodney, who had mastered the tools of 'bourgeois' scholarship in history. Lewis in his article on "The University in Less Developed Countries" clearly saw the development of capitalist society in the postcolonial countries and was involved in discussing the educational philosophy from the dominant Western system that could best be transplanted. Lewis was firm in his view that "one of the principal functions of the university is to train the middle class for the jobs it has to do" (Lewis 1983: 551). On the question of the political activities of professors, Lewis felt that they should not be party affiliated as

> it is inappropriate for your one and only heart surgeon to be a prominent member of some political party, since members of other parties may fear that his knife may inadvertently slip when he performs on them. It is equally inappropriate for your one and only professor of economics, whose salary is paid by all, so to conduct himself that he has only the confidence of and is consulted only by the Chamber of Commerce, or the trade unions, or the government or the opposition. Such conduct does not matter in a developed country where professors are two a penny and available in every hue. But in our countries, with one university only, or only one per province, the political professor fails in his duty as a public servant (Lewis 1983: 556–57).

Lewis felt that in Third World countries the right of academics to participate in party politics ought to be curtailed at the same time as their right to participate in public discussion in a nonpartisan way was enhanced and of course their right "to publish the considered results of research, study or reflection without regard to their effect on existing interests or opinions" was held to be sacrosanct (Lewis 1983: 558).

The Lewis model was centred on the rights of the middle class intelligentsia who were in his view the guardians of the postcolonial era and it assumed a level of development in civil society that was tolerant of political pluralism and where political, religious, ethnic and cultural differences were respected. Lewis felt that the academic in a state-funded university was akin to a civil servant and that the lesser part of academic freedom that he would forego was the "right to participate in party politics. This limitation would put professors into the same category as civil servants, which is what they essentially are in these circumstances" (Lewis 1983: 558).

Rodney was opposed to this conception and its assumptions, as he argued that he owed his education to the taxpayers and especially the mass of working people and his intellectual work and activism were dedicated to them. The Lewis formula was too great a concession to the postcolonial political elite. Lewis' conception of the role of the academic was stated in the context of poverty and scarce resources of postcolonial countries.

> A poor country has very few educated people. To have in its midst a body of one or two hundred first-class intellects can make an enormous difference to the quality of its cultural, social, political and business life. This, however, depends on participation. If the university is built in the bush, and isolates itself as a self-contained community, it misses a tremendous opportunity of service. Countries rich in income and talent can afford to have their universities in the countryside. But the universities of poor countries should be in the heart of the urban centres, where they can do most good. The opportunities for participation are immense: membership of public boards and committees; guidance of teacher-training colleges; availability for consultation by administrators and business people; membership of musical, dramatic, artistic and other groups; journalism and radio work; adult education classes. If the staff of the university is not giving active leadership in all these fields, it would be cheaper to close the place down, unless it is also doing excellent research (Lewis 1983: 696–97).

Even this liberal agenda of public involvement can be and has been problematic in postcolonial societies. Raising questions and making criticisms have, in too many Third World countries, partisan political significance. So the role of the so-called bourgeois intellectual should not be seen as a bed of roses. Ali Mazrui's role in East Africa in the 1960s and 1970s could be taken as a case in point of the liberal scholar who was not partisan but who invariably fell foul of the political leadership who wanted to manipulate the academic.

The political risks of scholarship facing the liberal scholar emerged in Mazrui's experience. In 1968 while at Makerere, Mazrui was summoned by the Principal of Makerere University College, who asked him if he had written an article comparing President Obote of Uganda with Thomas Hobbes' sovereign, Leviathan. Mazrui noted:

> Obote was then in power. It will be remembered that Hobbes, the English political philosopher of the seventeenth century, was a champion of absolute government. He favoured strong centralized authority, and has been interpreted as an advocate and defender of political dictatorship. If I was comparing Obote with Thomas Hobbes' concept of sovereign, I could be

interpreted as implying that Obote was an absolute dictator . . . Some months later I was in the Presidential Lounge of Parliament Building in Kampala engaged in a discussion with President Obote and some of his Ministers. In the course of the conversation President Obote referred to a diagram I had drawn on the blackboard in my first-year class at Makerere. In that lecture I had been discussing the relationship between class formation and the ethnic structure of African societies . . . To illustrate this idea of criss-crossing loyalties I must have drawn a diagram on the blackboard for the first-year undergraduates. That was supposed to be in the privacy of my own class at Makerere. And yet here was the Head of State of Uganda complaining to me in the calmness of his Presidential Lounge that he had not been able to understand the diagram I had drawn on the blackboard in my class at Makerere! It then dawned upon me that the President was taking a special interest in what I said to my students in my classes, and that he had informers in my classroom (Mazrui 1978: ix–x).[29]

East Africa needed both Mazrui and Rodney but civil society in postcolonial societies had not yet coalesced in ways that allowed political differences to be sorted out in open competition and through democratic forms. Lewis' doctrine was challenged at the University of the West Indies in the late 1960s and 1970s by some academics who were politically active and were able to function as both politicians and teachers. But a price was paid in that academic research and publications suffered and teaching had a tendency to be warped by political and ideological preferences. In addition, cabinet ministers were recruited from university departments. This was an inevitable development given the fact that the university is a pool of skilled personnel. But recruitment only affected a small number and the general question posed by Lewis about university academics being available to render public service to a community organisation, trade union or the Chamber of Commerce, remains valid and underlines the need for not confusing the academic who chooses to be politically active with the majority who will not be so involved. How this is worked out depends on the stage of development the society finds itself in, the nature of the problems and how the relationship between the university and the government has been built up over time.

The strength of this period – the 1960s and 1970s – for radical scholars at the University of the West Indies was their connection and involvement with the issues that were central to the majority of the population whether they took place under Michael Manley's tenure during the 1970s or under Maurice Bishop's Grenada of 1979–1983. All the fundamental issues of postcolonial politics and economic transformation were raised. Moreover, that experience formed part of a wider international struggle that marked the fall of communism and the end of the Cold War. As such, in twentieth century West Indian politics, the 1970s and 1980s have a political significance that can be approximated to the anticolonial impact of the 1930s Depression and the decolonisation movement following the Second World War of 1939–1945. These historical turning points have had a dramatic impact on the way intellectuals and academics see themselves and how they function.

In the context of the decolonisation that took place, Arthur Lewis saw himself as an institution builder.[30] His record of consultancies in Africa, Asia, and the Caribbean did have class as well as political implications but he could argue that this was inherent in any social-intellectual project and was not the same thing as the advocacy of a particular party line. The relationship between the intelligentsia, the university, the state and diverse political interests has to be dealt with concretely and on principles which are based on notions of academic freedom and democratic political values.

On the other hand, in his intellectual and political work Rodney took what he considered to be the position of the poorer classes, was critical of middle class leadership and determined an intellectual agenda around issues of development and social liberation. Lewis, by contrast, placed a lot of hope on the educated West Indian enhancing socioeconomic and cultural development and not only his or her class position. But both intellectuals shared a certain optimism about the abilities of postcolonial peoples to transform their societies. How this should be done and what social forces are able to effect this transformation remain unresolved questions. The issue for postcolonial societies cannot be between a Lewis, on the one hand, or a Rodney on the other. We have to examine both critically as part of the unfolding West Indian intellectual legacy.

Teaching and research

In his passport under the title 'profession' Rodney put 'historian' not simply the general title professor or lecturer. He devoted much of his time in Dar es Salaam to researching and writing on Tanzanian history, in devising courses for undergraduate study, in developing the graduate programme, in preparing for a journal to be published by his Faculty, in developing the History Teachers Association, and making himself available for talks in whatever part of Tanzania and Africa he was invited to speak.

Kaijage points out that Rodney was as influential inside the history department as he was in teaching University-wide courses, especially what was first called the Common Course. The Common Course was a precursor to Development Studies.

The course was optional but as many students as possible were encouraged to attend. The idea was to launch an assault upon the students' presumed reactionary ideas and expose them instead to progressive ideas and inculcate in them a sense of public spirit. It was also meant to discuss ideas on development. Common Course lectures were organized on an ad hoc basis but they were fairly frequent. Walter was one of those who participated quite frequently in this course. So students from law (e.g. Shivji), political science, economics, the languages, etc. had the opportunity to listen to Rodney. He also spoke at special events, for example debates and teach-ins and always drew large crowds thereby influencing many young minds. Most probably, he is partly responsible for inspiring the creativity of the young Tanzanians (Kaijage 1991).

Rodney's ability to draw a large following among young people of different social and ethnic backgrounds made him a political target in the Caribbean and Africa. Kaijage offers this explanation of his appeal in Tanzania.

Rodney's power to draw a large following and to command respect from a wide spectrum of the Tanzanian intelligentsia on and outside the Dar campus, cannot be adequately explained only in terms of his intellect or, indeed, his oratorical skills. It was the combination of these gifts together with his character, his humanity, his modesty and his unassuming manner of conducting himself that rendered Rodney such a charismatic figure with power to influence so many minds and draw a large following, even from among those who disagreed with his position. At the time when I was an undergraduate at Dar, he was the only Marxist historian in the department. Yet he evoked so much affection and respect among his departmental colleagues. His contributions to the richness of the discourse and to the intellectual development of the students was widely acknowledged. This is how come he was invited back to the department immediately after he was declared persona non grata in Jamaica (Kaijage 1991).

The Caribbean's loss was Tanzania's gain as this was the most creative period of his life, when he developed the graduate programmes in history and wrote *How Europe Underdeveloped Africa*. Many important works were emerging from the Dar es Salaam campus. Among them were Justinian Rweyemamu's *Underdevelopment and Industrialization* (1973), Clive Thomas' *Dependence and Transformation* (1973), Lionel Cliffe's and John Saul's two volume collection *Socialism in Tanzania* (1972–1973) which brought together many of the texts in the debate on Tanzania and Issa Shivji's *The Silent Class Struggle* (1973) and *Class Struggles in Tanzania* (1975).

Dar es Salaam historiography

Henry Slater in his essay, "Dar es Salaam and the Postnationalist Historiography of Africa", identified Walter Rodney as one of the movers in shaping postnationalist African historiography (Slater 1986: 256–57). Terence Ranger, along with the Tanzanian historians, Isaria Kimambo and Arnold Temu, represented the nationalist phase; Rodney occupied a transitional phase characterised as transitional "petty bourgeois" history where development theory predominated. This was succeeded by Jacques Depelchin and others who were more class oriented. Rodney was seen as being somewhat nationalistic because the "analytic concepts deployed are those of 'Europe' and 'Europeans' or 'Britain' and the 'British', on the one hand, and 'Africa' and 'Africans' or 'Tanzania and Tanzanians'"(Slater 1986: 257).

Slater's approach is somewhat schematic but it does attempt to relate the production of historical texts to the post-Arusha period. Slater argued that "within the post-Arusha context of the production of historical knowledge, the 'development of underdevelopment' replaced the 'growth of nationalism' as the central motif, and the focus therefore shifted from the political superstructure to the economic" (Slater 1986: 255).

Yet Rodney had a deep interest in political economy and this was reflected in his research on Tanzania. Among the substantial articles of importance on Tanzania's political economy were "The Political Economy of Colonial Tanganyika, 1890–1930" (1980b), "World War II and the Tanzanian Economy" (1976a) and "Migrant Labour and the Colonial Economy" (1983).[31] He also examined the role of coercion in the labour process in papers such as "Policing the Countryside in Colonial Tanganyika" (1973b) and "Recruitment of Askari in Colonial Tanganyika 1920–1961" (1973a).

On a draft curriculum vitae Rodney listed the courses he taught, most of them at Dar es Salaam, and these included: Surveys of African History (precolonial and colonial), Economic History of Tanzania, the History of Revolutions – the English Civil War, the French Revolution and the Russian Revolution, History of Black People in the Americas, International Political Economy. He also assisted in the drafting and teaching of an important 'Common Course' which was the basis for what later evolved as the interdisciplinary course of Development Studies.

In a report on the MA History 1973/74 programme in which he had six students doing field work, the topics covered were as follows: Mr Bakengesa – "Evolution of the Bukoba coffee industry"; Mr Magoti – "Rise and spread of the money economy in Musoma district"; Mr Manyanda – "Historical development of cotton growing in Kwimba District, Mwanza Region"; Mr

Mlahagwa – "Agricultural change in Uluguru"; Mr Sago – "Labour migration and the economy of Kasulu district, Kigoma Region"; Mr Tambila – "A History of the Tanga sisal labour force"[The Rodney Papers (a)]. In 1983 a book entitled *Migrant Labour in Tanzania During the Colonial Period: Case Studies of Recruitment and Conditions of Labour in the Sisal Industry* (1983) which he co-edited along with Sago and Tambila was published in Hamburg, Germany. And in 1984 Rodney's German colleagues published his lectures *One Hundred Years of Development in Africa* (1984) which had been given at the University of Hamburg in the summer of 1978.

Rodney's 1973/74 MA programme indicates the thoroughness of his approach in building the research capabilities of his graduate students and equipping them to lay the foundation for the development of the discipline of history within the Tanzanian and the East African educational system. Rodney wrote:

> before leaving for their respective areas of field research, each student completed two written assignments. The first was an assessment of different aspects of the History curriculum in secondary schools – a paper undertaken with the understanding that most of these graduates will return to teaching and need to give thought to improvements in their schools. The second assignment was an extended review of several books covering a given aspect of Tanzanian history – e.g. in the spheres of education, agriculture and social change. Teaching has partly been geared to the written assignments and the thesis. That is to say, some insights have been offered on the nature of curricula, the process of selecting books for teaching purposes, the methodology of book reviewing and assessment, and the techniques of oral and archival research. A second segment of teaching comprised lectures on various aspects of the political economy of Tanganyika during both German and British colonial rule [The Rodney Papers (a)].

In evaluating the students he noted that

> the emphasis on research and on maximum student participation in seminars has given greater confidence to students and has brought out their initiative in a way that both teachers and students feel would have been impossible if the course were to be structured more along the lines of formal lectures followed by written examinations. On the other hand, the written work so far has not been outstanding, indicating the need for considerable coaching with respect to writing skills and expression. The subsidiary role of English as a medium of expression as far as most students are concerned complicates this problem [The Rodney Papers (a)].

Fred Kaijage, in commenting on Rodney's impact on the academy said:

because Walter's position was unabashedly revolutionary, we went along with him. We did so not as sycophants but as converts after a refreshing intellectual encounter. No teacher could match his 'proselytising' powers and his inspiring oratory; no literature was as intellectually engaging as that which he put at our disposal. One point that operated very much in his favour is that this moment was propitious for a socialist point of view in Tanzania. Socialism was in vogue and the youth, in particular, was enchanted by the concept. It was therefore not surprising that Rodney's students rose to the occasion (Kaijage 1991).

Conclusion

Tanzania's radical programmes starting with the Arusha Declaration and its involvement with the Southern African liberation movements provided the impetus for Rodney to embark on an academic career as a historian and to develop as a political activist. The Tanzanian years saw him grappling with the problems of postcolonial development and the role of social classes in that process as well as in the rewriting of African history. His teaching, writing and public involvement had a significant impact on African intellectuals who embarked on academic as well as political careers. He was able to introduce innovative curricula and to initiate graduate programmes in the Department of History, while taking part in the political debates of the day. Not many intellectuals were able to combine intense political involvement with serious academic work. Political activism and scholarship were inseparable in Rodney's case and stimulated others to connect their academic agenda to the central issues of social liberation. This connection was to be severely tested in the years 1974–1980 when he returned to Guyana.

NOTES

1. For some of the information on Tanzania's historical background I have relied on the encyclopaedic *Africa Today*. London: Africa Books, 1991.
2. *Africa Today* 1991: 815.
3. *Africa Today* 1991: 1,824.
4. The Zanzibar Revolution brought key political leftists such as Abdulrahman Mohamed Babu to Nyerere's cabinet where he served as Minister for Economic Affairs and Development Planning. Political events in the early 1970s contributed to the marginalisation of the left. Five hundred people were arrested after the assassination in April 1972 of Sheikh Abeid Karume who was replaced by Aboud Jumbe. Among those arrested on the mainland were Abdulrahman Mohamed Babu, founder of the

defunct Umma Party. Rodney was a close associate of Babu who wrote the postscript to the 1972 edition of *How Europe Underdeveloped Africa*.

5. An interesting footnote which emerged in the interviews done by me in Dar es Salaam in 1990 was the activity of the Jamaican architect, John Holness and his English wife. Holness was described as an orthodox Marxist-Leninist adhering to Moscow. His wife, Marga Holness, was very close to the MPLA and she became Agostinho Neto's secretary (Bagoya 1990).

6. According to Haroub Othman, social democrats in Scandinavia chose Tanzania as the example of a country "following a peaceful road to socialism, a prototype of reformist ideology in the third world, and to the Afro-American liberation movement in the Western hemisphere, we were a symbol of all their hopes and dreams associated with the concept of Black Power" (Othman 1977: 2).

7. Ten years after his retirement Nyerere remained an influential patriarchal figure in Tanzania and his reputation as a statesman and political guru has remained strong. See Legum and Mmari (1995).

8. Shiva Naipaul's *North of South – An African Journey* is written with nineteenth century English colonial narratives in mind. The book utilises racial cliches and stereotypes such as "The African soul is a blank slate on which anything can be written; onto which any fantasy can be transposed . . . " (p. 199). When he gets down to reporting what people were saying and how they lived he does provide useful insights into Tanzanian life.

9. His curriculum vitae of 1978 states that he was Senior Lecturer from 1968. But one of the letters in his papers, dated January 1971, suggests he was promoted from Lecturer to Senior Lecturer in History a year later. See appointment letter from V.B. Mtabi, secretary to the University Council, 14 January 1971.

At a certain point it seemed as if Rodney was going to settle in Tanzania. In November 1970 he received a letter from the Regional Land Officer of the Coast Region which referred to his "application for the piece of land at Ubungo, Dar es Salaam, which you wish to develop as a residential and a poultry farm". See letter from Regional Land Officer, Coast Region 16 November 1970 [Letters in The Rodney Papers (a)].

10. "Curriculum Vitae, Walter Anthony Rodney, 1978" [The Rodney Papers (a)].

11. Running a Health Centre in Dar es Salaam was a major experience for this young Guyanese woman especially because she had to be able to communicate with patients who had a very different cultural background from her own and who spoke Kiswahili. Pat looked like many of the women around Dar es Salaam so she was frequently spoken to in Kiswahili. Once when going to the market she met an old man.

> I greeted this elderly man and he greeted me and after exchanging these pleasantries he wanted to know how my mother was . . . Somebody was translating for me what he was saying . . . He was saying that he doesn't understand these young people, when they go abroad they come back and behave like Mzungu, which is white people, that I didn't want to speak Kiswahili any more and I felt ashamed of my language. And he knew my mother, my mother was Zanzibari. People always said I looked very Zanzibari, and that's before I had my hair cut . . . that I have very kind of Arabic features and he was certain my mother was in Zanzibar. And then when the person said, no, she is not, you know, he wouldn't believe it. Then somebody came and said no, I wasn't from Tanzania, and his reply was that even if she is not from Tanzania she is supposed to speak Kiswahili because all black people supposed to know how to speak Kiswahili (Pat Rodney 1989).

Many West Indians who travelled to Africa to work in the postindependence years could recall similar experiences.

12. Pat Rodney's view of their Tanzanian years fills out the personal context in which Rodney operated. The Rodney family included Ann, seven-year-old daughter of Virgil Duncan, their friend from London.

    It is a very beautiful campus, the housing was very elaborate, the lifestyle, certainly for us, was very different. I did not have to do any housework myself because everybody had house help. It was a big responsibility having a young child and a seven-year-old to bring up. While Ann was at school, I had some help with Shaka so I found life a bit boring because I was used to working. So one night at a party we met the Medical Officer of Health who was a World Health Organisation consultant and he said they badly needed nurses to work in public health and was I interested. And I said yes . . . I decided I would just work part-time to begin with, because Shaka was still very young. So I worked from 7 a.m.–12 p.m. every day . . ." (Pat Rodney 1989).

13. One of the most prominent expatriate economists was the Hungarian, Tamas Szentes, whose work on development economics influenced Rodney. Rodney also arranged for the Guyanese economist, C.Y. Thomas, to visit and he spent a year at Dar es Salaam in the early 1970s.

14. See Ranger (1981) for a discussion of academic freedom in East and Central Africa, especially his Dar es Salaam years.

15. In 1971 there were student protests throughout the African continent. Among the countries affected were Madagascar, Senegal, Dahomey, Congo People's Republic, Ivory Coast, Upper Volta, Gabon, Zaire, Zambia, Tanzania, Uganda, Ethiopia, the Sudan, Algeria, Nigeria, Ghana, Libya, Egypt, Rhodesia, South Africa.

16. See especially the Arusha resolution of the National Executive Committee on Leadership which set guidelines limiting the acquisition of private property by party and government leaders.

17. I am grateful to Dr Hubert Devonish for showing me Magdalena Hauner's (1981) article.

18. Léopold Sédar Senghor, Senegalese statesman and distinguished poet, was President of Senegal from 1960–1980. He is also one of the apostles of Négritude along with the Martinican poet, Aimé Césaire.

19. Tom Mboya (1930–1969) was a brilliant trade union leader and politician and one of the founding members of the now ruling Kenya African National Union (KANU). A close associate of Jomo Kenyatta, Mboya was elected KANU's Secretary General in 1966. He was assassinated in 1969. The reasons for his assassination are not clear but commentators suggest that this may have been due to ethnic tensions and political rivalry.

20. The reassessment of the intellectual legacy of Arthur Lewis rejects this representation of his economic ideas (Ralph Premdas and Eric St Cyr 1991; Mark Figueroa 1993).

21. Some examples of this kind of writing are to be found in polemical essays written in the 1970s by Dan Nabudere and Yash Tandon who were leading East African Marxists.

22. In an interview with Babu in London in 1990 he was very critical of Nyerere, feeling that the latter made the state sector too big. The rural collectivisation only created more state bureaucracy and did not sufficiently involve the rural population. What was needed was some kind of partnership between the state and the private sector.

To what extent this position benefits from hindsight on Babu's part or whether those were his criticisms in Tanzania during the late 1960s is a matter for those interested in these issues to pursue.

23. See Tamas Szentes (1985) whose writings were influenced by the Tanzanian debates of the 1960s and 1970s.
24. He defined delinking as the "pursuit of a system of rational criteria for economic options founded on a law of value on a national basis with popular relevance, independent of such criteria of economic rationality as flow from the dominance of the capitalist law of value operating on a wide scale" (Amin 1990: 62).
25. Wabenzi refers to the owners of Mercedes Benz and in the case of Nigeria as a result of its oil wealth the wabenzi could own airplanes and other prestige symbols.
26. The novels of the Kenyan writer Ngugi Wa'Thiongo satirise and expose this postcolonial elite with evangelical fury. See especially *Petals of Blood* and *Devil on the Cross*.
27. Kwame Nkrumah's party.
28. See Nyerere (1967).
29. See Karioki (1974) for a critique of Mazrui.
30. See Dwight Venner (1993). This tribute to Sir Arthur Lewis focuses on his role not only as an economic thinker but as UWI's Vice Chancellor, UN Consultant to Third World countries and as the first President of the Caribbean Development Bank.
31. Rodney, Tambila and Sago (1983) includes research papers by his students Kapepwa Tambila, "A Plantation Labour Magnet: The Tanga Case" and Laurent Sago, "Labour Reservoir: the Kigoma Case".

CHAPTER 7

Rodney's Pan-Africanism

Rodney's positions on Pan-Africanism[1] reflected his Marxist outlook and in this regard he belonged to the group of Caribbean Pan-Africanists such as George Padmore, C.L.R. James and Frantz Fanon. They had been influenced by Marxist methodology and communist parties in Europe and the United States but within that ideological framework had developed independent positions on the anticolonial revolution in Africa and the struggles of peoples of African descent in the diaspora. They thus expanded Marxist terms of reference. Padmore had worked with the Comintern and with Stalin, James had worked with Leon Trotsky, and Fanon had been influenced by and become critical of the French Communist Party and the French left during the Algerian war of independence.[2]

Rodney belonged to a different political generation. He benefited from the legacies of Padmore, James and Fanon and their considerable political experience with the European communist left. But like them he insisted on his ideological independence. In his lecture notes on the Russian Revolution at the University of Dar es Salaam[3] he said, "there are many Popes in the Marxist world who ordain and excommunicate this or that person or organisation as true or false Marxists. Hopefully, that attitude will be avoided in this study" [The Rodney Papers (b)].

Rodney, as was the case with the Latin American and Caribbean left, used the theoretical and ideological debates of the Russian Revolution as a point of departure in thinking about contemporary revolutions. The extent of his reading and lecturing on the Russian Revolution is evident in an undated letter to his friend Ewart Thomas at Stanford University. Written in 1971 he pointed out:

> I've given the occasional seminar on Cuba and I've helped with seminars on China, but my main teaching field has been Russia. My publications obviously do not provide evidence of expertise in European History, but I really have done a great deal of work on the Russian Revolution. This year I was about to start on a monograph covering the 1917 Revolution and the period up to World War 2 and I put it aside only because the African material had to be given higher priority [The Rodney Papers (a)].

In a Jamesian way Rodney had identified with the Russian revolutionaries, and tried to show the interplay of social forces and the way important historical figures mirrored social contradictions and movements. In the course of his lectures Rodney was sympathetic to Lenin, without being Leninist in the theological sense of the term, again very much in the way that James used Lenin's writings as a point of departure in thinking about politics. This is because there was nothing that Rodney had to learn from Lenin on Africa. In looking at what little Lenin had to say on Africa Rodney had observed:

> it must be reiterated that Lenin had little to say that was explicitly concerned with Africa. From that it follows that while his insights provide an immediate point of departure for an analysis of the imperialist partition of Africa, one should not expect to find all the answers in his writings. For that matter, Lenin did not pose a very significant question: why did imperialism appear in Africa in the form of political partition? This omission is one reason why bourgeois writers have got away with blurring of the distinction between imperialism and the political partition of Africa. The two things are not interchangeable. Imperialism derived from the expansion of the capitalist economy, while partition was determined by a) the nature of African social formations b) the element of racism within the capitalist superstructure and c) the opposition of Africans to European incursion (Rodney 1971b: 3).

Although Lenin did not help much on Africa, the Russian Revolution was the European revolution most used by Third World Marxists as the laboratory for their political theories, strategies and tactics. It was the most accessible of modern Revolutions through literature and through direct contact between the Communist Party of the Soviet Union and Third World left wing and communist parties.[4] This ideological and theoretical influence had a considerable impact on James' as well as Rodney's thinking. While James was very neo-Hegelian in his thinking, Rodney was less influenced by Hegel and had more in common with thinkers like the British historian E.P. Thompson who, like Rodney, was a Marxist historian and activist.[5]

Reading Rodney's lecture notes on the Russian Revolution one is reminded that many Third World academics and political radicals had paid intellectual attention to this topic. Rodney had the benefit of having studied it with C.L.R. James who had had a political relationship with Leon Trotsky and who had been a close observer and analyst of the post-Lenin era of the Russian Revolution. Moreover, Rodney had been thorough in his reading of Western scholarship on the Russian Revolution. His critical comments on a wide variety of scholars ranging from émigré writers to Soviet historians, American political scientists and British historians, showed a command of the material. Rodney was concerned with interpreting the Russian Revolution from an African perspective as distinct from the dominant European and American bourgeois interpretations. He was speaking about the Russian Revolution in the context of African decolonisation and the radical prospects in Tanzania and Southern Africa. The topic had more than a narrow academic significance and was connected to tasks of revolutionary transformation as he saw it in Africa. His analysis showed an understanding of the policy and ideological differences that emerged in the course of socialist construction in the Soviet Union and he was able to guide his students through the available literature with a sharp and incisive analysis. He got very quickly to the heart of a book and to an author's main analytical point of departure. His historiographical method can best be described as radical demystification. However, in focusing on the class premises of scholarship and the social orientation of the Russian Revolution, Rodney paid little attention to the national and ethnic questions in the Soviet Union. This is somewhat surprising as much of his research and writing had a bearing on ethnic and racial issues, and an African revolutionary perspective required treatment of the class and national/ethnic dimensions of political processes.

Rodney's lectures on the Russian Revolution showed his efforts in linking scholarship with issues of contemporary change in Africa. He brought his critical vision to bear on analysing its development, thus avoiding the pitfalls of left wing ideological dogmatism which gave either uncritical support or saw it as a revolution betrayed. The most important aspect of Rodney's approach to the Russian Revolution was that its experience and lessons could not be mechanically applied to the African continent. In looking at Africa, Rodney realised how much intellectual work needed to be done to rewrite and reinterpret the social, economic, cultural and political characteristics of the continent and its place in world history. Moreover, there was a small but growing body of thinkers and activists who were involved in the movement not only to end colonial rule but to reconstruct new social orders. It is to these thinkers that Rodney belonged.

In 1960, Frantz Fanon had written, "to put Africa in motion, to cooperate in its organisation, in its regrouping, behind revolutionary principles, to participate in the ordered movement of a continent – this was really the work I had chosen" (Fanon 1970: 187–88). This was very applicable to Rodney and reflected the tradition in which he saw himself as he combined academic research and teaching with political activity. Shivji has pointed out that Rodney "believed his main role was to participate in ideological struggles and in the process clarify the character of the African Revolution" (Shivji 1980: 29).

Rodney was ill when the Sixth Pan-African Congress took place from 19 to 27 June 1974 in Dar es Salaam, Tanzania.[6] His paper entitled "Aspects of the International Class Struggle in Africa, the Caribbean and America" was widely circulated and had an impact on the ideological debates that took place among the delegates.[7] That year saw a growth in radicalism in Africa with the overthrow of fascism in Portugal for which the liberation movements in Angola, Mozambique and Guinea-Bissau could take some credit.

Rodney's paper was a sharp critique of postindependence regimes and he was especially critical of the exclusion of nongovernmental radical parties by ruling parties. The planning of the Sixth Pan-African Congress saw a conflict between these two groups with the official delegations in the case of Guyana not wanting to give space to organisations that were not connected to the ruling party led by President Forbes Burnham.[8] According to Wole Soyinka:

> the Congress had been taken over by governments who had proceeded to place the Order of the Leper, as usual, on representatives of progressive groups. For example, the then government of Mr Eric Gairy had proscribed the New Jewel Movement, though he proved incapable of preventing the distribution of their statements by sympathisers at the Conference. And yet another government of the Caribbean had somehow rendered another revolutionary, who was actually present in Tanzania, invisible. That man was Walter Rodney. Indeed if my memory serves me correctly, more than one Caribbean government had, through their representatives, indicated that their delegations would quit the Congress if Walter Rodney participated in any capacity (Soyinka 1980: 7).

Soyinka's observations and Rodney's paper underscored an important point about postcolonial politics, and that was the coming to the fore of class issues in national politics. In this context racial solidarity of the kind characteristic of the anticolonial period was giving way to hard social and political analysis of the class realignments in the postcolonial world. Rodney's paper placed the Sixth Pan-African Congress within the context of previous Pan-African congresses, noting that since the Fifth Congress held in Manchester in 1945:

the political geography of Africa has been transformed by the rise of some forty two constitutionally independent political units presided over by Africans ... Yet, following in the wake of the great pageant of the regaining of political independence, there has come the recognition on the part of many that the struggle of the African people has intensified rather than abated, and that it is being expressed not merely as a contradiction between African producers and European capitalists but also as a conflict between the majority of the black working masses and a small African possessing class (Rodney 1976b: 21).

The questions Rodney wanted placed on the agenda of the Pan-African Congress concerned the class character of the national movements. These were: Which class leads the national movements? How capable is this class of carrying out the historical tasks of national liberation? Which are the silent classes on whose behalf 'national' claims are being articulated?

In this 1974 document Rodney criticised both Padmore directly and James indirectly through his critique of the call for the conference. Rodney accused some African leaders of propagating "the false antithesis between Pan Africanism and Communism, an intellectual activity spearheaded by no less a person than George Padmore" (Rodney 1976b: 27). In articulating this position, Rodney differentiated between his Marxist Pan-Africanism and what he perceived as Padmore's legacy of anticommunist Pan-Africanism. For those who were unaware of Padmore's passage from Stalinism to Pan-Africanism and the important political experience this represented for the relationship between anticolonial and communist movements Padmore's position could easily be interpreted exclusively with reference to Cold War anticommunism. That would certainly lead to a misinterpretation of Padmore's legacy which was his advocacy of the ideological independence of nationalist movements in Africa and the forging of their own path in a bipolar world.

In a tactful letter C.L.R. James wrote Rodney about the politics of his paper arguing:

It is a splendid document. But what do you intend to do with it? In it you make some criticisms of the call. I had a long share in fact, a substantial share in its preparation. Whatever its deficiencies it offers a base ... Do write to me, not about political ideas, we have no quarrel about that. What I am concerned with is who, what, where and when we can get some of these ideas across ... We of the Caribbean cannot go to the Pan-African Congress and be the leading ones in putting forward these ideas. That would be a political blunder of the most primitive type (James 1974).

This letter showed there was a fundamental difference in approach between C.L.R. James and Walter Rodney in 1974. James' call was anti-imperialist and sufficiently general on issues of economic independence not to have offended ruling political circles in Africa (TPH 1976: 219–22). The call was DuBoisian in character with a Jamesian touch. It started out by asserting "The 20th century is the century of Black Power" which was reminiscent of DuBois' statement, "The problem of the twentieth century is the problem of the colour-line – the relation of the darker to the lighter races of men in Asia and Africa, in America and the islands of the sea" (DuBois 1986: 372). The Jamesian input was seen in the formulation which went:

> white power, which ruled unchallenged for so long during this very century, is marked by unparalleled degeneration, first by two savage and global wars such as the world had never before seen. The same mentality prepares for a third war. Its barbarism unpurged, European power strives at all costs to maintain that domination from which the formerly colonial peoples are breaking (TPH 1976: 219).

James' call avoided any critique of African political leadership. He sought a way to work with the most progressive regimes, particularly with Julius Nyerere for whom he had a great deal of political respect. Moreover, he felt that the initiative on Pan-Africanism belonged to continental Africans, and the diasporan activists like himself and Rodney had no political base to up-front in the way Rodney had. In short, James seemed to have felt that Rodney's paper was politically immature and could be self-defeating. Rodney, on the other hand, worked from the standpoint that there was a radical faction within some of the liberation movements and ruling parties to which his ideological positions spoke and he obviously felt very strongly that African and black political leadership in the diaspora could not be let off the hook.

The differences between Rodney and C.L.R. James rested not simply on tactical differences concerning the 1974 Pan-African Congress but on two factors. First, there was a different assessment of the political role of the African and Caribbean petty bourgeoisie and what it could do. James was more optimistic about the possibilities for a postcolonial Pan-Africanism. Rodney was not. Secondly, James had a tendency to overstate the role of political personalities and this is seen in his fulsome endorsement of Julius Nyerere and Michael Manley. Rodney was more critical of them and always focused on the social forces they represented.

This critical attitude towards African political leadership had brought him into the centre of political debate in Dar es Salaam. One such debate arose from his presentation entitled "The Ideology of the African Revolution" to a seminar of East and Central African Youth held in Dar es Salaam in November 1969. The seminar had been organised by TANU's Youth League and participants included the National Union of Kenyan Students, National Union of the Students of Uganda, the Pan-African Youth Movement, the FRELIMO Youth League, the University Students Association of East Africa, MPLA, ZAPU and ZANU. So the gathering was an important Pan-African event. Rodney spoke in terms of seeing African realities from the standpoint of its working people. But he was pointed in his criticisms of African leaders. The *Nationalist* newspaper reported him on 10 December 1969 as having said it was a pity that most African leaders who had been spokesmen for their people during pre-independence days had been turned into servants of imperialists and capitalists of North America and Western Europe. Rodney's comments were interpreted by ruling circles in Tanzania as being critical of their policies and a critique of his speech was published in the *Nationalist* of 13 December 1969.[9]

Rodney defended himself in a letter published on 17 December 1969 in the *Nationalist* newspaper in which he wrote:

> I trust that my use of words such as 'capitalism', 'imperialism,' and 'neo-colonialism' will not be deemed as a cover for sinister intent. My indulgence in those terms is aimed at opposing a system which is barbarous and dehumanising – the one which snatched me from Africa in chains and deposited me in far-off lands to be a slave beast, then a sub-human colonial subject, and finally an outlaw in those lands. Under these circumstances, one asks nothing more but to be allowed to learn from, participate in and be guided by the African Revolution in this part of the continent; for this Revolution here is aimed at destroying that monstrous system and replacing it with a just socialist society (Shivji 1980: 29).

While it was alright to criticise imperialism, criticism of political leadership in Africa could bring swift political reprisals. Rodney's defense of himself was the appeal of a diasporan black intellectual to African authorities and revealed an awareness of the "outsider" status that could be invoked against him on grounds that he was not a citizen and he therefore could be treated like any other foreigner, black or white.

But when the Sixth Pan-African conference took place he was preparing to return to Guyana and certainly felt less compelled to self-censor his views. He was not prepared to invoke anti-imperialist rhetoric while remaining silent on African political stewardship. Rodney was therefore sharply critical of African political leadership and he focused his criticisms on the gross inadequacies of their stewardship. He saw Pan-Africanism as one of these progressive sentiments, which served as a platform for that sector of the African or black petty bourgeois leadership which was most uncompromising in its struggle against colonialism... It would be unhistorical to deny the progressive character of the African petty bourgeoisie at a particular moment in time. Owing to the low level of development of the productive forces in colonised Africa, it fell to the lot of the small, privileged, educated group to give expression to a mass of grievances against racial discrimination, low wages, low prices for cash crops, colonial bureaucratic commandism, and the indignity of alien rule. But the petty bourgeoisie were reformers and not revolutionaries. Their class limitations were stamped upon the character of the independence which they negotiated with the colonial masters. In the very process of demanding constitutional independence, they reneged on a cardinal principle of Pan-Africanism: namely, the unity and indivisibility of the African continent (Rodney 1976b: 22–23).

In making such a challenge, Rodney took an adversarial approach to the African elite and its nationalism, challenging their narrow nationalistic outlook. He pointed out that the bourgeoisie had spearheaded national unity in Western Europe but the

African petty bourgeoisie is not directly involved in economic enterprises, their real sphere being the professions, the administration and the military/police hierarchy. They lack both the vision and the objective base to essay the leap towards continental unity (Rodney 1976b: 24).

Rodney's line of reasoning suggested that if the petty bourgeoisie was able to become directly involved in the economy it would be more capable of creating the necessary vision for continental unity in its quests for wider markets. This, of course, did not necessarily follow. However, it provided a contrast between the potential long-range needs of an African petty bourgeoisie rooted in local economic activity capable of transforming itself into a bourgeoisie with wide economic horizons as against a bureaucratic group rooted in the state administrative machinery and limited by their tenure of power. Given the latter's poor performance at national levels, it was therefore not surprising that postcolonial governments led by this petty bourgeoisie faltered when it came to taking the steps necessary for continental unity. The Organisation of African Unity was described as having done "far more to frustrate than to realise the concept of African unity" (Rodney 1976b: 26). Rodney launched a parallel assault against Négritude. While speaking positively of Négritude as anticolonialist and antiracist, he analysed that like Pan-Africanism, Négritude in the hands of petty bourgeois black states became a sterile formulation of black chauvinism, incapable of challenging capitalism and imperialism. Négritude in Senegal buttresses neocolonialism, while in Haiti it is used to gloss over an even more desperate situation of exploitation and suppression of the black masses (Rodney 1976b: 30).

These critiques of the African petty bourgeoisie were consistently made by Rodney during his sojourn in Africa and were reiterated in a wide-ranging speech in Kenya on African politics in March 1974 (Rodney 1974b). Yet he did not lump all African politicians together but differentiated between individuals such as Lumumba, Nkrumah and Nyerere and others such as Mobutu, Houphet-Boigny and militarists like Idi Amin. Rodney showed how the assassination in 1961 of Patrice Lumumba, the Prime Minister of the Congo, exposed the weakness of African nations. On the Congolese crisis in the early 1960s, Rodney said:

It was a trial of strength in which the whites of the south sent up their mercenaries and a few African states (Nkrumah and the Nigerians) attempted to send a few troops. A few Africans sent resolutions and as you are well aware the mercenaries defeated the resolutions and in fact defeated the few troops we could muster because those few troops were not under our control as you would find by reading some of Nkrumah's literature. You would find that the few troops which he sent were not under the control of Africans, they were not fighting for Africa but were the same forces that helped in the demise of Lumumba (Rodney 1974b: 4).

Another of his criticisms was that African governments had not done enough to inform themselves and their populations about the struggles in Southern Africa – a basic requirement for solidarity. He said:

Our governments and our people do not even have at their disposal the requisite information concerning the structure and nature of the problems in Southern Africa, to this date. I find, for instance, that if I want to find specific information about Southern Africa, if I cannot get it from the liberation movement itself who are often very busy, they are concerned essentially with the struggle underground; they do not have the time to document and get certain background information. To whom does one turn? One cannot turn to any African government, you cannot turn to the OAU. You will have to turn to a liberation support movement based in Sweden or Holland or Britain. Our governments do not even have the information (Rodney 1976b: 4).

Rodney's paper sought to redefine Pan-Africanism in the postindependence period. While giving priority to the colonised parts of Southern Africa, Rodney insisted on a platform directed at the nongovernmental left wing constituency. He concluded the paper with the following points. These were:

1) The principal enemies of the African people are the capitalist class in the USA, Western Europe and Japan.
2) African liberation and unity will be realised only through struggle against the African allies of international capital.
3) African freedom and development require disengagement from international monopoly capital.
4) Exploitation of Africans can be terminated only through the construction of a socialist society, and technology must be related to this goal.
5) Contemporary African state boundaries must be removed to make way for genuine politico-economic unity of the continent.
6) The Liberation Movements of Southern Africa are revolutionary and anti-imperialist and must therefore be defended against petty bourgeois state hegemony.
7) The unity of Africa requires the unity of progressive groups, organisations and institutions rather than merely being the preserve of states.
8) Pan-Africanism must be an internationalist, anti-imperialist and socialist weapon (Rodney 1976: 33–34).

By these prescriptions Rodney attempted to reorient the Pan-Africanist movement along revolutionary class lines. On the other hand, James' call was anticolonialist: it avoided engaging the issues Rodney raised. Thus Rodney and James had different readings of the politics of Pan-Africanism in the 1970s. At that moment, James felt that it was tactically necessary to avoid any remarks critical of contemporary African or black governments. Rodney, on the other hand, put forward positions that assumed that Pan-Africanism could become an anticapitalist platform and did not have much political realism particularly on issues dealing with economic development. It was a starting point for discussion, not the basis for a programme of action that could be taken to conference for discussion and ratification. The late 1980s and early 1990s have witnessed the end of socialism in Eastern Europe and altered the balance of forces in such a way that Rodney's ideological agenda is certainly not realisable in the twentieth century. More fundamentally, the way he conceptualised African unity would be more sharply debated today given the anticapitalist direction of his thinking.

The key assumption in Rodney's thinking was that Pan-Africanist rhetoric that inveighed against external forces while being silent on internal forces served to maintain the system intact. Moreover, the key concern for him was the conditions necessary for the emancipation of the working people of the African continent. Pan-Africanist thinking that failed to look at the class basis of power within Africa would remain stuck at the nationalist phase which suited the contemporary African political elite.

It was this focus on the class characteristics of nationalism that gave Rodney's statements on Black Power in the United States and the Caribbean its critical edge. Many of the lectures he gave in the United States in the 1970s were concerned with the relevance of Marxism to Africa and the Third World.[10] In his essay on George Jackson written in Dar es Salaam he demonstrated the merits of his approach which grasped both the class and race dynamics of the black experience in the United States. Rodney's essay which appeared in *Maji Maji*, journal of the TANU Youth League, is a tribute both to George Jackson, who had been killed in prison in August 1971, and the African-American struggle at the start of the 1970s. Rodney saw Jackson's politicisation in prison as an example of the possibility of change in 'lumpen' elements and compared it to that of Malcolm X. Like Fanon, he did not particularly like the ideological death sentence that Marxists had passed on the 'lumpen proletariat' arguing that it "was originally intended to convey the inferiority of this sector as compared with the authentic working class" (Rodney 1971d: 4). For them, as with the petty bourgeoisie with whom he engaged so frequently, political conversion was possible and it was necessary to seek them out.[11]

Commenting on the processes of lumpenisation which creates the conditions for criminality, Rodney contended that

> under capitalism, the worker is exploited through the alienation of part of the product of his labour. For the African peasant, the exploitation is effected through manipulation of the price of the crops which he laboured to produce. Yet, work has always been rated higher than unemployment, for the obvious reason that survival depends upon the ability to obtain work. Thus, early in the history of industrialisation, workers coined the slogan 'the right to work'. Masses of black people in the USA are deprived of this basic right. At best they live in a limbo of uncertainty as casual workers, last to be hired and first to be fired. The line between the unemployed and the stable black portion of the proletariat is difficult to draw, and ever since 'reconstruction' a century ago, white racist policies have tended in the direction of transforming the whole

of the black population into lumpen. Under these circumstances, black people in the USA who are unemployed or 'criminals' cannot be dismissed as white lumpen in capitalist Europe were usually dismissed (Rodney 1971d: 5).

Rodney's position was that the lumpen proletariat should not be ruled out of the movement for change. Moreover, Rodney observed that "Jackson knew well what it meant to seek for heightened socialist and humanist consciousness" and was conceptualising the African-American struggle in international terms. Elaborating on this, Rodney argued that "For more than a decade now, people's liberation movements in Vietnam, Cuba, Southern Africa, etc. have held conversations with militants and progressives in the USA" (Rodney 1971d: 6). Rodney felt that these connections were very important as the white working class in the USA was historically incapable of participating as a class in anti-imperialist struggle. White racism and America's leading role in world imperialism had transformed organised labour in the USA into a reactionary force (Rodney 1971d: 6).

With this position Rodney differentiated himself from the political conclusions of black communists in Europe, the United States, the Caribbean and Africa who tended to be uncritical of the communist parties and working class movements in the developed countries. In articulating his views Rodney was repeating positions held by Fanon when he criticised the role of the French left in the Algerian war of independence and these views were consistent with the thinking of James and Padmore on these issues.

When he returned to the Caribbean, Rodney continued in the role of link between the liberation struggles in Africa and the Caribbean and was very vigorous in his support of the Cuban efforts in Southern Africa in the 1970s. The ruling parties of Guyana and Jamaica also established relations with the liberation movements in Southern Africa. While being supportive of this development, Rodney viewed their positions as a function of internal class struggle, in other words there were strong social and political forces which had called for and sustained these policy positions of solidarity. While this may have been the case in the region in the 1970s it nevertheless risked giving no credence to both Manley's and Burnham's position on African solidarity. The destabilisation of Jamaica in the late 1970s is connected to Manley's support of the Cuban presence in Angola. For Kissinger this was no question of Caribbean-Angola ethnic and nationalistic solidarity; rather, it was a matter of a small state intervening in global issues against the United States at a time when Vietnam had been lost and the Soviet Union was seen as being at its most expansionist in the Third World.[12] The governments of Barbados and Trinidad and Tobago were more cautious. For example Rodney noted:

As soon as the Americans made a noise, and reproached the Barbadian government for allowing Cuban planes to land, the Barbadian government promptly rescinded the facilities. The Trinidad government was not any better: they were not offering any facilities and declared that if asked they would not offer any landing permits (Rodney 1987: 10).

So although Manley and Burnham took positions that were to the left of their region they were to the right of Rodney. How much further these regimes could have gone on this issue is certainly up for discussion. The fact is that the late 1970s marked a high point in Caribbean solidarity with Southern African struggles particularly the war in Angola and this was partly expressed through governments that did take risks and did disagree with the United States when it came to the Cuban presence in Angola. It may be that Rodney underestimated the significance of these actions.

Those qualifications notwithstanding, Rodney was best placed to continue that "communication between the Caribbean and Africa and the United States to bind the people together, that we have lost. That's what we have lost in Walter Rodney" (James 1980: 30). C.L.R. James saw Rodney as a loss to the African Revolution and Ali Mazrui has assessed Rodney as being the link between global Africa and socialism (Mazrui 1990a). Pan-Africanism, from Rodney's standpoint, rested not only on notions of black solidarity and nationalism but on the injection of social analysis that borrowed from Marxism. In this way Rodney sought to develop and reshape tools of critical theory on the African and Caribbean experiences with a sharper focus on the internal dynamics of the political processes within Africa.

NOTES

1. For other commentary on Rodney's Pan-Africanism see Hill (1982) and Walters (1993).
2. In her memoirs Simone de Beauvoir (1968) speaks very affectionately of the relationship between Frantz Fanon and Jean-Paul Sartre. Sartre wrote the introduction to Fanon's posthumously published *The Wretched of the Earth – a Negro Psychoanalyst's Study of the Problems of Racism and Colonialism in the World Today*.
3. Fred Kaijage, who heard Rodney's early lectures on the Russian Revolution, offered a critique when he said:

    I suspect that the notes that you examined constituted a refined product, achieved after some years of teaching and additional reading. Although I would still characterize Walter's approach as sophisticated and scholarly, his earlier approach in the first two years of teaching is likely to have been more sympathetic to the Stalinist tradition than the notes, you have seen do suggest. If he was critical of Stalin, he was damning to the bourgeois historical tradition. It is also possible that as students we missed some of the nuances in his analysis. Certainly for us, the bourgeois historians of the Revolution were demons and Stalin, despite Rodney's reservations about the official interpretation, had hardly any case to answer. This may have represented on our part what one may term as the vulgar Marxism of the newly converted.

One must credit Walter for his nuanced analysis of the Revolution's historians from those who predicted the Revolution through the contemporaries to such subsequent historians as E.H. Carr and I. Deutscher. We were able to distinguish between émigré historians voicing the views of the fallen Czarist social order and bourgeois historians whose hostility to the Revolution had a different basis. We were cautioned that we could not take Trotsky's *Revolution Betrayed* at its face value because Trotsky was a protagonist of the Revolution. Our attention was drawn to sympathetic western writers like John Reed's *Ten Days that Shook the World*. We dealt with the historians' handling of specific issues and their relationship to the Revolution. Examples include, for example, the question of nationalities and Stalin's collectivization of agriculture.

It is difficult to do justice to a course taught twenty-four years ago. I can only reiterate my point that Walter's lectures along with the kind of literature he exposed us to had a lasting effect on most, if not all of us. History could not be the same again. In every historian we began to discern ideological commitments and class alliances. Even the whole notion of objective history was no longer credible (Kaijage 1991).

4. The considerable ideological influence of the Russian Revolution on the Cuban Revolution can be studied through the impact of the communist intellectuals organised in the Partido Socialista Popular (PSP) and their impact on Fidel Castro's 26 July movement. Cuba's Vice President, Carlos Rafael Rodriquez, is the best-known survivor of the PSP in Castro's government.

5. For an interesting essay on E.P. Thompson which discusses him as a historian and activist see Bess (1993).

6. According to his colleague, Horace Campell, Rodney became ill because he had been working on too many fronts. Rodney's absence from the conference was a blow to those who wanted a more radical outcome that would allow for nongovernmental organisations and liberation movements to determine the character of modern Pan-Africanism. June Ward, a Guyanese activist, and Marcelino dos Santos helped to draft the final communique (Interview with Horace Campbell 1990).

7. Rodney's paper was published in the proceedings of the conference (Tanzania Publishing House 1976). There were many positive developments that made the Conference worthwhile. President Julius Nyerere had stated that

> We now have to recognise that an end to colonialism is not an end to the oppression of man, even if it means an end to oppression based solely on color. And we now have to work against oppression by the leaders of those countries which have recently attained freedom, whether this is directed against other black men and women, or against people of different races (TPH 1976: 7).

All the Southern African liberation movements were present. Among them the ANC, PAC, SWAPO, ZANU, and ZAPU. The Palestine Liberation Organisation (PLO) was represented and a resolution supporting their struggle was passed. Abdias do Nascimento of Brazil spoke on "Cultural Revolution and Future of Pan-African Culture" with the black experience of his country in mind and Imamu Baraka, the African-American writer, spoke on "Revolutionary Culture and Future of Pan-African Culture" with the situation in the United States as a background. There were resolutions on black women as well as on science and technology in Africa's development. The problem with conferences like these is that there is no institutional follow-up, no small step taken that could lead to the building of a resource centre that would provide information on critical issues in Africa and the diaspora.

8. See Horace Campbell (1990) and June Ward (1990).
9. The editorial in the *Nationalist* of 13 December 1969 was torn out of that edition of the paper, which I consulted in the library of the University of Dar es Salaam in August 1990. Other issues, such as the one for 10 December 1969, which reported Rodney's speech had not been tampered with and were in good condition.
10. See for example his lecture "Marxism as a Third World Ideology", which was given along with other talks at the University of Waterloo, University of Western Ontario, Carleton University, the University of Guelph, the University of Toronto, York University and McMaster University in November 1975 [The Rodney Papers (a)]. See also "Marx in the Liberation of Africa" which he gave at Queen's College, New York in 1975. The introductory note to the transcript of this talk stated:

   > His audience was a huge crowd of white, Puerto Rican but mainly Afro-Amerian students – the vast majority of whom were uninformed about Marxism but insistently 'anti-marxist'. For the Afro-American students, their insistent rejection of Marxism had partly to do with the fact that Marx was European, that Europe had oppressed nonwhite peoples for centuries, and that no European, therefore, could contribute to a way of understanding the world that could advance any nonwhite people (Rodney 1981a: i).

11. Andaiye, his close political associate in the WPA in Guyana, contends that Rodney made himself vulnerable to such elements by his openness to them and spent much time drawing such people, who were at the bottom of society and who had fallen foul of the law, into radical politics (Andaiye 1989).
12. In a public address in 1995 Manley admitted that he came under considerable pressure from Henry Kissinger who tried to persuade him to denounce the presence of Cuban troops in Angola. Manley claimed that Jamaica lost a $100 million line of credit in the 1970s because of the then Government's support of Cuba's military assistance to Angola. Manley told Kissinger that it was a matter of conscience that Jamaica had to support Cuba's presence in Angola. Manley said that soon after the US Central Intelligence Agency (CIA) in Jamaica was trebled and the *New York Times* described him as "the surrogate of Fidel Castro". (See *Gleaner,* 25 November 1995). The increased levels of destabilisation of the Manley regime is linked to this event. Kissinger viewed the Cuban developments in broad global terms from the standpoint of American interests and saw Caribbean leaders as interfering in the struggles between East and West. He wrote:

    > The collapse of Indochina in 1975 had been followed in America by a retreat from Angola and a deepening of domestic divisions, and by an extraordinary surge in expansionism on the part of the Soviet Union. Cuban military forces had spread from Angola to Ethiopia in tandem with thousands of Soviet combat advisers. In Cambodia, Vietnamese troops backed and supplied by the Soviet Union were subjugating that tormented country. Afghanistan was occupied by over 100,000 Soviet troops. The government of the pro-Western Shah of Iran collapsed and was replaced by a radically anti-American fundamentalist regime which seized fifty-two Americans, almost all of whom were officials, as hostages. Whatever the causes, the dominoes indeed appeared to be falling (Kissinger 1994).

CHAPTER 8

Caribbean Historian at Work

Pat Rodney returned to Guyana in May 1974, three months before Walter, and by the time he returned she had put the children in school, found a job running a day care centre and had bought a house (Pat Rodney 1989). She described the impact of returning to the Caribbean from Tanzania with the children and the psychological adjustments that had to be made.

> Going back to Guyana was like a culture shock to them. First, people didn't greet each other; in Tanzania everybody greets you in the morning. They were going into a culture they did not understand. They knew this is where their Mummy and Daddy came from; even though they had gone on vacation they were too young to understand. So they didn't like it; they missed Tanzania. To begin with, Shaka had a lot of problems in school because he was already 9, and his first language was Kiswahili. He had to relearn English, the children felt he spoke differently, he had an African name which was still not the thing; they all had African names. But they were confident. I remember Kanini insisted that they were Africans but their father and mother were Guyanese, so they were always proud of their heritage. When children said to Asha, 'you all hair braid like snakes'. Kanini would say, 'because we are Africans we are different, you know', and always took positions about their father's work and what he was doing. But initially I would say they didn't like it (Pat Rodney 1989).

Self-hate and ambivalence among Caribbean people of African descent showed itself in many ways. Social movements such as those associated with

Garvey and Rastafarianism, the music of reggae, and black conscious groupings that have functioned in the Caribbean in the twentieth century have engaged the difficult problem of the black self. Throughout his life Rodney engaged the problem of the black self in his lectures, groundings and books.

Rodney had no job or regular income in Guyana from 1974 to 1980 and had to do a lot of lecturing in North America and Germany in order to make ends meet. Moreover, he was fully involved with Guyanese politics as one of the leaders of the Working People's Alliance and in the 1979–80 period his political involvement was at its peak.

In the 1970s some West Indian left wing academics abandoned scholarship for political struggle. This was not Rodney's approach as he realised that one of his main contributions to decolonisation lay in his role as a historian. George Lamming, the Barbadian novelist, said Rodney "believed that history was a way of ordering knowledge which could become an active part of the consciousness of an uncertified mass of ordinary people and which could be used by all as an instrument of social change" (Lamming 1981: xvii) He therefore made time to do historical research and sought out funds to pursue work in the archives in England and Guyana.

Reflecting on the late 1970s not long before he was killed Rodney said:

> It seems to me that there are tensions that do arise between one's domestic concerns and one's political concerns, between one's political concerns and one's work as an academic; but they are not contradictions, and, indeed, the extent to which one can streamline it so that the various streams march together is a measure of some achievement at a personal level (Rodney 1980d: 3).

Indeed, the yoking of one's domestic, political and academic pursuits is no easy issue especially when one is being hounded politically and cannot function normally in one's own country. Moreover, Rodney had political and intellectual responsibilities outside of Guyana which he did his best to carry out. The domestic responsibilities fell on his wife, Pat, although he was supportive in this domain, but the political and academic agenda still had to be blended and this he did superbly despite the formidable obstacles to inquiry:

> Right now in Guyana, the past few years, it has not been possible to do a great deal of academic work, and yet, at the same time, I feel fairly satisfied that I've done as much as could possibly be done under the circumstances, the circumstances being very backward material conditions for carrying out any research and scholarly activity. For example, I've done historical research in the archives of Guyana; but I'm sure they must rate as the most poorly kept

archives in the world. This is no exaggeration and I'm not blaming any government. I'm just reflecting on a fact that they're pretty bad. And the conditions are also hostile to creative work because of the general philistine atmosphere which exists, the way in which the government has moved against the university. The whole spirit of mendacity which prevails in the society could hardly be compatible with the search for truth and producing serious scholarship, although I will concede that historically there are times in the depths of the most backward systems that great literature has been produced (Rodney 1980d: 3).

Elsewhere he was more specific regarding the nature of the archival and bureaucratic obstacles he faced:

The research into Guyanese history . . . has . . . been proceeding well. As suspected, there is a great deal of data lying about which can be uncovered. The Sugar Producers' Association were not cooperative when I approached them, but Bookers Sugar Estates have been most helpful. I was able to consult a number of old minute books in their possession, and the head office has also facilitated my visits to the individual estates. The interviews with old sugar workers have been stimulating, and I have already met a number of Indians who came from India as indentured labourers. Needless to say, they are fast dying out (Rodney 1975e).

These difficult circumstances, notwithstanding, few West Indian academics who were also political activists in the 1960s and 1970s were able to produce as much as Rodney did and this capacity for concentration resulted from his self-discipline and sense of vocation as a historian and the relationship between that sense of vocation and politics.

Politics and professorship

Rodney's return to Guyana had long been his priority. His efforts at resettling in the Caribbean had been frustrated after his expulsion from Jamaica in 1968. On 31 October 1972 Rodney wrote the Registrar of the University of Guyana applying for an appointment as Professor of History or its equivalent. There was a position as a Director of Caribbean Studies for which he also applied. He indicated that he was prepared to leave Tanzania in December 1973 (1972d). Peter Ramkissoon, an assistant registrar at the University of Guyana, replied on 29 December 1972 that there was no suitable vacancy in the Dept of History for someone with your qualifications and experience. Your letter is on file and as soon as there is a suitable opening it will be given due consideration. The post, Director of Caribbean Studies, was offered to another candidate (Ramkissoon 1972).

However a position in the history department was to be offered to him not long after. In 1974 Rodney recalled:

My application to join the staff was first dispatched from Tanzania in 1972 at a time when I had already taken the decision to return to Guyana. No vacancy existed. I reapplied recently when the post of Professor of History was advertised. This second application was acknowledged, but no further official communication was received from the University until a letter dated 23rd August which simply advised me that I had not been selected. It was a standard stencilled form which made no reference to the process by which the decision was reached.

It is now well known that my appointment was approved through the regular academic channels and that it was disallowed for supposedly political reasons. In this connection, it is necessary for me to draw attention to the fact that I have been absent from Guyana for fourteen years (for all practical purposes), and I have never actively participated in national political life. It is not for me or any other private citizen to provide answers by way of speculation as to what was the Government's motivation. It is the duty of the Government to explain its reasoning to all citizens – myself included.

My professional training was carried out at the expense of the people of Guyana and the British Caribbean. To be denied the opportunity to pursue my profession at home is tantamount to being condemned to exile and hence to be cut off from direct access to the community which was my sponsor. I shall not be intimidated. But, once more it is necessary to emphasise that it is not a matter of mere personal predicament or personal resolve. The University as a national institution, and Guyanese of a variety of ideological and political beliefs must confront the principle of whether an individual's service to the nation is to be exclusively and arbitrarily determined by mysterious political evaluations made by the Government in power. This would represent at least the basis of national political responsibility (Rodney 1974d).

The Burnhamites on the Board of Governors of the University of Guyana had overturned the decision of the academic appointment committee. But Rodney was determined to live and work in Guyana. It was both a political and personal matter. Rodney felt that politically he could not do much more as a foreigner in Africa or anywhere else in the Third World.

> I would say that there is a development which needs to be stressed – a certain localization of the revolution . . . because for many, many years citizens of the Caribbean have become engaged in one revolutionary process or another. We have tended, through force of circumstance, to become involved in what we may broadly call the international revolution, or Pan-Africanism, or something that seeks to hasten the total dialectical change from a capitalist, eurocentric society to one in which our peoples as a whole – whether as working peoples, as African peoples or Third World peoples – will participate more fully. However, the present generation recognizes much more that it is extremely difficult to make any of these ideas come to fruition except in a Caribbean context itself. This is partly due to an increase in the sorts of pressures, exclusivist pressures, and partly due (even in the Third World) to the development of relatively narrow nationalisms and chauvinisms, so that one is not likely to go to some other part of the Third World and fully and firmly engage in political transformation. Therefore the need to engage in a local struggle becomes greater (Rodney 1976d: 127).

On a personal level he wanted to return home. According to Pat Rodney (1989), Walter said he would "drive a taxi if it took that" to stay in Guyana. He was determined to live in Guyana and even applied to some high schools for employment. At age 32, having spent all his adult life outside of Guyana, he wanted to make his contribution at home. The longer he remained outside of Guyana the more difficult it would be to return. Having been denied a job, he felt morally compelled to stay and fight. His moral position was unambiguous.

> When political forces like the WPA (Working People's Alliance) say to people, you have to stand up, to organise and defend your rights in spite of the threat of economic victimization', then the least we can do, who ourselves have suffered such victimization but who can somehow make a living here, is to remain in the political situation. Otherwise our actions would show that it's impossible to take a political stand, because to do so is either to be jobless or to be forced to move abroad in order to exist (Rodney 1976c).[1]

The moral imperative of Rodney's politics functions throughout his brief life as a determining factor whether it is in popular education in the ghettoes of Kingston at the risk of political victimisation or confronting Burnham's dictatorial regime at home. During the 1979–80 period when supporters of the WPA were being arrested and killed and he was advised to "cool out" he still felt that he could not be calling on the working class cadres to undertake risky political tasks and to remain in Guyana while he went into exile.

Moreover, he had been influential in encouraging a number of his friends such as Andaiye and Rupert Roopnaraine to return home from the United States and contribute to the struggle. Andaiye, whose father was Burnham's doctor, had been fired from her job as a teacher in 1971 and had gone to New York to work. She returned to Guyana in January 1978 to participate in the political struggle at home. Andaiye played an important role in the WPA executive as party coordinator, editor of *Dayclean*, International Secretary and Women's Secretary. She also worked with Rodney on his book *A History of the Guyanese Working People*. Rupert Roopnarine, who made the film *Terror and the Time*, about Guyana's political history, was also encouraged to return home by Walter. Moreover, the enormous moral example of Eusi Kwayana's humble and even ascetic life showed that it was possible to live and struggle against economic and political victimisation in Guyana. These were some of the key personalities in Walter's years at home but there were many other working people of African and Indian ancestry in whose homes he ate and slept and from whom he drew energy in the struggle against the dictatorial Burnham regime. He was the most celebrated victim of the Burnham regime but they too had been victims of political discrimination. His decision to stay was therefore both a moral and political one.

Rodney's applications at other levels of the educational system such as the high schools did not prove successful. So he had to take up offers to do guest lectures in North America and Europe as a means of earning an income so as to be able to survive in Burnham's Guyana. He also secured a research grant from the International Development Research Centre in Canada for a study of the political economy of Guyana, 1880–1939.[2] He refrained from considering any deal with the Burnham regime and his commitment to his country meant that he did not take up full-time employment abroad. In his last six years he pursued politics, historical research, and travelled regularly. It was a very difficult period which took a toll on his family life and cost him his life. What made the sacrifices worthwhile was the response of the Guyanese people and the possibilities of radical shifts in the region against authoritarian regimes as happened in Nicaragua with the overthrow of Somoza by the Sandinistas and the removal of Gairy by the New Jewel Movement in Grenada in 1979.

Writing Caribbean history

It was as an independent scholar that he lived for the last six years of his life. Researching and writing Caribbean history had been on Rodney's academic agenda since the early 1960s. In 1963 he had prepared a plan for researching Guyana's history but had put this work on the back burner in favour of African history. Evidence that he had been working on Guyana's history is seen in his article "Masses in Action" published in the 1966 Guyana Independence issue of *New World* where he surveyed Guyana's development from 1900 to 1928 (Rodney 1966c). It is a credit to his sense of vocation as a historian that he produced so much in the 1970s at the height of his political activism in both Tanzania and Guyana. He was prepared for this period psychologically, having been seasoned in Tanzania and Jamaica into making time for political activism and academic research. Moreover, he had been anxious to make a contribution to the writing of Caribbean history. Although this area of his work has been overshadowed by his sterling contribution to African historiography, it remains significant.

Rodney continued working on African history but focused on researching the development of Guyana's political economy. In 1975 his long essays, "The Guinea Coast" and "Africa in Europe and the Americas", appeared in *The Cambridge History of Africa*. Vol. 4. *How Europe Underdeveloped Africa* was published by Howard University Press in 1974 and there were translations into Portuguese and German in 1975 and a Japanese translation followed. This book was on its way to becoming a best seller and certainly the best-known text by a Caribbean scholar since Eric Williams' *Capitalism and Slavery* and C.L.R. James' *Black Jacobins*.

In May to June 1976 he presented three papers at the Institute of Commonwealth Studies, University of London (1976e, 1976f, 1976g). On 17 May his paper was entitled "Immigrants and Racial Attitudes in Guyanese History" and on 31 May he presented a paper entitled "Subject Races and Class Contradictions in Guyanese History". These themes were to be developed in his book on Guyana. On 14 June his paper was entitled "The Colonial Economy: Observations on British Guiana and Tanganyika".

While in Guyana he continued his work on Tanzanian history. One of his posthumously published works is in the collection *Migrant Labour in Tanzania during the Colonial Period*. This book includes an essay by Rodney entitled "Migrant Labour and the Colonial Economy" as well as "Case Studies of Recruitment and Conditions of Labour in the Sisal Industry" based on dissertations he had supervised by two of his former graduate students at the University of Dar es Salaam. Kapepwa Tambila, who went on to become head of Department of History at Dar es Salaam, wrote "A Plantation Labour Magnet: the Tanga Case" and Laurent Sago wrote "A Labour Reservoir: the Kigoma Case" (Rodney, Tambila, Sago 1983).

Forced and voluntary labour migration in African and Caribbean history were key themes in Rodney's writings. In 1977 he attended the Ninth Annual

Conference of Caribbean Historians at the University of the West Indies campus in Barbados where he presented a paper, "Barbadian Immigration into British Guiana 1863–1924". In March 1979 he presented a paper entitled "Slavery and Underdevelopment"[3] to a conference with the theme "Slave Studies: Directions in Current Scholarship", sponsored by the departments of History of the University of Waterloo and Wilfrid Laurier University.

In 1979 Rodney had edited and published a book entitled *Guyanese Sugar Plantations in the late Nineteenth Century – A Contemporary Description from the Argosy*. This arose from his research work for *A History of the Guyanese Working People* which was scheduled to have been a two-volume study taking the analysis well into the twentieth century. In the acknowledgments Rodney thanks Elsa Goveia, Professor of History at the University of the West Indies, "for all she contributed to my growth as a historian over twenty years". It was an appropriate acknowledgment from one first class Guyanese historian to another. Goveia had read the manuscript and Rodney had been able to make revisions based on her observations and comments. Both were to die within months of each other in 1980.[4]

Reading *A History of the Guyanese Working People, 1881–1905*, the majority of readers would have no idea of the circumstances under which this work was produced. It is unlike the polemical character of *How Europe Underdeveloped Africa* and has the pace of a work written by a comfortably placed tenured professor. In fact, Rodney submitted the manuscript to the Johns Hopkins Studies in Atlantic History and Culture and he later revised it while in jail in 1979 on charges of arson (Knight and Price 1981: xiii).[5] In *A History of the Guyanese Working People, 1881–1905* Rodney tried to understand how the political economy of modern Guyana had taken shape and this led him to examine what Guyana had been like at the beginning of the twentieth century and the circumstances shaping the lives of the African and Indian working people. It raises issues such as the impact of the environment on society; ethnic, class and social formation under colonialism; and early twentieth century anticolonialism. In this work Rodney was concerned not so much with general issues of Guyanese and Caribbean underdevelopment but with specific aspects of Guyana's social formation particularly the relationship between the two principal ethnic groups – the Africans and the Indians. The work is very empirical and showed his very careful use of historical evidence.

Issues of class and race are fairly commonplace in Caribbean history and social science literature but issues of the environment have only recently been part of the intellectual fare of Caribbean scholarship. It is to Rodney's credit that in his opening chapter entitled "Internal and External Constraints on the Development of the Working People" he discusses the impact of the environment on the production of sugar and on the lives of the managers and labourers on the sugar estates. This strong sense of the environment comes through in his examination of the coastal region but some discussion takes place on the hinterland and gold prospecting in the postemancipation years. Rodney pointed out that each plantation

> required a front dam along the sea front, or 'facade', together with a back dam of corresponding length and two connecting sideline dams, to complete the rectangular polder. The dams were meant to keep out the salt water at all times, while the fresh water from the swampy rear had to be let in and out in a calculated manner. An elaborate system of canals served to provide drainage, irrigation, and transportation – the volume of water in an estate's canals being regulated by a large koker, or sluice, in the front dam and smaller back dam koker (Rodney 1981c: 2).

The land was subject to drought and flood and the working people made a

> tremendous contribution to the humanization of the Guyanese coastal environment . . . there were many important respects in which the coastal environment played a determining role in limiting the activities of all sections of the population. It is certainly impossible to provide an intelligible narrative or analysis without an understanding of the peculiarities of the narrow strip of empoldered coastland to which the majority of the people were confined (Rodney 1981c: 3).

Flood and drought as well as the ravages of the sea did not follow set patterns and sometimes hit the planters unawares; this of course made the fortunes of planters and the livelihood of the workers precarious. Sea defence, drainage, and irrigation were constant costs incurred by the planters.

> The enormous influence of flood and drought was brought to bear on several facets of the lives of working people. They were unemployed in periods that were extremely dry because estates had to cut back on their allocation of task work. Any drought in November/December and a drop in the level of water in the canals meant that the punts could not operate to carry canes from the fields to the factories; cane cutting and grinding therefore ceased. When the rains were excessive the ultimate result was the same – namely, an increase in seasonal unemployment. In times of drought planters fumed and fretted, while workers had little to drink or even eat. The incidence of gastroenteric disease shot up, and such water as was available was imbibed along with the mud of the trenches. Floods took an even greater toll on health, on livestock, on crops,

on the roads and dams, and on the capacity of the villagers to pay rates and retain possession of their houses and provision lots (Rodney 1981c: 10).

Rodney estimated that this humanisation of the coastal landscape involved the slaves moving "100 million tons of heavy water-logged clay with shovel in hand, while enduring conditions of perpetual mud and water" (Rodney 1981c: xviii).

The detailed attention to the agricultural engineering problems of the sugar industry is characteristic of Rodney's approach to other areas of Guyana's social and ethnic structure and political economy. This book is really a micro-study of a single postemancipation Caribbean society. Rodney's reputation was as a scholar who had posed issues of development and underdevelopment for Africa which paralleled the 1960s and 1970s interest in the topic among Latin American and Caribbean scholars. Now he touched on Guyana's political economy in the context of the global economy but did so in terms of necessary background while demonstrating the international constraints on the economy. He pointed out that after slavery

> Caribbean economies lost their preeminence in the process of capital accumulation, but dependent integration into the world capitalist system remained a significant feature. The periods of prosperity and depression, as reflected in the 'business cycles' of the metropolitan capitalist countries, provided some of the circumstances which shaped the lives of Guyanese – irrespective of whether or not persons were aware of this external environment (Rodney 1981c: 19).

Rodney weaves the economic data into his historical narrative to show how these "business cycles" affected the planters and the workers. He explains that

> the rhythms of the business cycle were superimposed upon the colonial economies by way of price mechanisms. The onset of economic depression was usually felt somewhat later in British Guiana than in Europe, and correspondingly, recovery was manifested after it had already made its appearance in the principal capitalist economies. Thus, the results of the depression of the 1870s were still being felt in 1880; the boom in Europe of 1880–82 touched the colony briefly in 1882–83; the depression of the 1880s in British Guiana lasted from 1884 to 1888; while that of the late 1890s barely paused before it was part of another slump in the first years of this century (Rodney 1981c: 19).

However, his Marxism makes him suggest that the weak, fragmented and ethnically divided Guyanese working class was "in a position to recognize its affinities with labour elsewhere" because it was part of the international division of labour (Rodney 1981c: 165). But this type of solidarity was, of course, more the exception than the rule and was to be partially realised among a minority of the more politicised workers in the twentieth century with the development of the modern trade union movement and nationalist politics.

Rodney discussed the changing character of the labour force after the postemancipation years. The major change was Indian immigration which led to 228,743 Indians being introduced between 1851 and 1917 (Rodney 1981c: 33). The other major issue was the free village movement of the middle years of the nineteenth century which

> gave to the African estate worker a partial independence deriving from residence outside the plantation 'nigger yards' as well as from alternative subsistence activities. Village laborers could bargain, they could specialize in certain tasks, and they could influence the weekly and seasonal deployment of their own labor power on the estate (Rodney 1981c: 42–43).

He is very careful in noting that the movement of African creole labour away from the estate and the movement from the plantation of Indians later on reflected only partial independence as "it did not prevent the persons concerned from continuing as estate labor. It did mean that this labor behaved differently from residents – both bonded and free" (Rodney 1981c: 53).

Rodney identified three occupational divisions within the labour force. These were: a minority who remained on the estates and secondly

> there were those who obtained a material base on the land, sufficient to exempt them from wage labor. Thirdly, and most importantly, there was a large number who fell into an area of overlap between the wage workers and the provision-growing peasantry. Wage workers and their families lived in the villages and practiced small-farming away from the plantation. The incomplete crystallization of an independent peasantry was reflected in the incomplete separation of workers from peasants. This proved to be a long-term rather than a temporary feature of class delineation in Guyana (Rodney 1981c: 61–62).

This was the case not only in Guyana but was so for the rest of the Caribbean especially where agricultural exports predominated in the plantation/economic system. One cannot really speak of a fully developed working class or peasantry in the region given the overlap between both groups hence the merit in using the loose category of "working people".

Rodney discussed the economic differentiation that took place with the development of peasant farming and exploration of the hinterland. He noted that

> the gold and balata industries were structurally no better than the sugar industry in terms of domestic linkages; but village labor had laid the groundwork for the economic exploration of the hinterland, and this ranks as a decisive and lasting contribution to the political economy of Guyana in modern times (Rodney 1981c: 102).

Social stratification among Africans and Indians was very evident by the end of the nineteenth century. Among the Indians, he notes:

> the highest remittances to India were sent by cattle-keepers, shopkeepers, drivers and cart owners. The most likely bases for differentiation of the Indian immigrant community were cattle ranching, rural landlordship, retail shop keeping and commercial rice farming (Rodney 1981c: 110).

Among the African creoles, in addition to small farmers, there was the growth of a black educated middle class and by the 1880s "creole clerks were to be found in every place of business in Georgetown" (Rodney 1981c: 112). As elsewhere in the Caribbean, education was important in shaping the West Indian middle classes. Queen's College which was founded in 1844 became an important institution in this regard and was "the fulcrum of the Guyanese intelligentsia" (Rodney 1981c: 116). It was the alma mater of Forbes Burnham as well as Walter Rodney and had nurtured the debating skills of both these political gladiators.

The development of this class is important because it dominated anticolonial politics with its skills of public speaking and advocacy and its capacity for mass mobilisation. It was adroit at using the newspapers to criticise colonial policies and officials. In the ideological space it created for itself, it claimed to serve the people. This was partially because at the start of the twentieth century the middle class had not yet disconnected itself from the masses. Rodney puts it this way:

> Life in the villages and on the estates cannot be chronicled without reference to the activities of these well-to-do elements who joined their fellows in the search for better schooling, improved conditions for land husbandry, additional sanitary and medical facilities, and so on. The energies of working class and peasant families, the moral force of large masses of people, and the actual political mobilization of the working people were required to help create

for the middle classes the conditions of accelerated development. The middle layers had not yet been brought into fundamental conflict with the base from which they had emerged (Rodney 1981c: 119).

This conclusion is examined in relation to the 1905 riots. He notes the aversion of the middle class to the lumpen proletariat and how even "A.A. Thorne, who stood most firmly on the side of the wage earners, explicitly disassociated himself from the 'rabble' and the 'centipedes', who supposedly did the looting and the stoning" (Rodney 1981c: 205).

Rodney's portrayal of the role of the middle class shows that what was taking place in Guyana at the end of the nineteenth century was very similar to what was happening elsewhere in the Caribbean. The middle class organised reform associations and political clubs that were critical of planter domination and sought to widen the franchise and to call for social and economic reform.[6] The "backbone of the reform constituency would have included sanitary inspectors, clerks, bookbinders, tailors, shopkeepers, cabinetmakers, wharfingers, printer-compositors, druggists, and school-masters" (Rodney 1981c: 148).

In his chapter entitled "Resistance and Accommodation" he theorises on the responses of the working population to the labour regime of the plantation system, contending that struggle

> was implicit in the application of labor power to earn wages or to grow crops, while accommodation was a necessary aspect of survival within a system in which power was so comprehensively monopolized by the planter class. Some persons resisted more tenaciously and consistently than others; but there was no simple distinction between those who resisted and those who accommodated. Moments of struggle and moments of compromise appeared within the same historical conjuncture, but ultimately, resistance rather than accommodation asserted itself as the principal aspect of this contradiction (Rodney 1981c: 151).

Rodney discussed the struggles of the Indian immigrant work force and exploded the myth of their docility. He also undertook a parallel discussion on the struggles of the African-creole working people. The ethnic division within the working people made this division necessary in his reconstruction of this period of history and the significance of this ethnicity was highly controversial. The sense in which Rodney uses the term 'working people' takes into account the complexities of occupation and ethnic divisions but underlying it is his view of the homogenisation of the labour process and the hope that new weapons of struggle could be formed by a more class conscious proletariat. But Rodney is fully aware of the factors that delay or arrest this development. It is this understanding of the historical process which leads him to be critical of the racial character of Guyanese politics in the years after the 1960s when Jagan's public discourse is Marxist but he is de facto head of a predominantly Indian party and Burnham uses socialist and Marxist rhetoric and heads a predominantly African party and government.

Rodney adopts a class approach to social development but is fully aware of the relative autonomy of ethnicity and race. All the same, he avoids the error of reading back the communal-type conflicts of the mid twentieth century into an earlier historical period. Instead he traces the development of postemancipation African-creole labour on the estates and in the villages as well as the fortunes or misfortunes of indentured Indian labour. In chapter 7, entitled "Race as a Contradiction among the Working People", he explores some of his findings on this issue. He finds that

> evidence of this early period does not sustain the picture of acute and absolute cultural differences coincident with race. It would be more accurate to contend that the existing aspects of cultural convergence were insufficiently developed to contribute decisively to solidarity among the working people of the two major race groups. The obverse of this race-class conjuncture is that the development of class forces and class consciousness was inadequate to sustain unity of the working people across the barriers created by legal distinctions, racial exclusiveness, and the separate trajectories of important aspects of culture. There were in effect two semiautonomous sets of working class struggles against the domination of capital – the one conducted by the descendants of ex-slaves and the other by indentured laborers and their fellow Indians. Pursuing their legitimate aspirations, these two ethnically defined sectors of the laboring people could and did come into conflict with each other (Rodney 1981c: 179).

As such he recognised the tensions that existed between the two ethnic groups and showed how the planters manipulated this issue but he essentially came down strongly on the side of the creolisation[7] thesis against the cultural pluralist interpretation.[8] Rodney recognised that the

> Creole-Indian immigrant antithesis took the form of an African racial confrontation. Differences in culture constituted obstacles in the way of working class unity across racial lines. Indians lived mainly on the estates. As they became more concentrated in the 1890s, their residences were often set apart from the African villages founded after Emancipation. This partial separation undoubtedly contributed to perpetuating differences in religion,

language, and customs. Nevertheless, the process of 'creolisation' was already evident among Indians in the final quarter of the nineteenth century. Their food, dress, speech, and funeral customs were undergoing transformation under creole influence (Rodney 1981c: 178).

He therefore concluded that

> racial conflict was far less pronounced than might have been expected from the manner in which the two main races were thrown into economic competition; but I'm not seeking to minimise a crucial aspect of the historical reality. Indentureship and racial competition held back the development of a plantation workers' movement until long after the period in question (Rodney 1981c: 219).

Rodney was equally careful in his approach to class formation, pointing out that

> care has been taken to avoid imparting to the various social classes greater precision than they had achieved within the evolving social formation of the nineteenth century and the early twentieth century. If classes are to be defined in their mutual opposition (as would seem logical) then the differentiation of working class, peasantry and middle class was incomplete (Rodney 1981c: 218).

This issue of class development was at the core of both academic and political enquiries into Caribbean social structure in the postindependence years.[9] With the rise of the Marxist parties and organisations in the 1970s assessments of the character of the Caribbean working class were seen as a matter of political urgency. It is to Rodney's intellectual credit that he did not get swept away by doctrinaire ideological positions but stuck to the examination of Guyanese reality and drew his conclusions very rigorously from his research. Rodney, however, did have a bias toward class explanations and his main critic Brian Moore, a fellow Guyanese historian, rewrote Guyanese nineteenth century history stressing ethnic and racial differentiation. Brian Moore in his study *Race, Power and Social Segmentation in Colonial Society: Guyana After Slavery, 1838–1891* argued that Rodney was evidently misled by the relative absence of communal conflict on a scale akin to that which occurred on several occasions between the Creoles and the Portuguese. But this did not mean an absence of serious conflict particularly at a localised and individual level. In Moore's view the "principal social effect of emancipation in Guyana was the ethnic diversification of the society . . . For most of the post-emancipation 19th century, the constituent social categories were sharply differentiated by race and culture" (Moore 1987: 213).[10] For Moore, therefore, race was "the primary factor of social segmentation in postemancipation Guyana" (Moore 1987: 214). Moore contends that Rodney emphasised

> the similarities in experiences and responses of the subordinate population to the exploitation of the planters. In stressing the shared work experience on the plantations and the process of 'creolisation' (defined as an 'indigenising experience'), he tended to minimise the degree of ethnic segmentation among these social sections (Moore 1987: 218).

Unfortunately Rodney did not live to see the publication of his work nor was he able to answer his critics. He recognised the difficulties inherent in the racial contradiction among the Guyanese and made a plea for more work to be done on the political culture of the working people in order to better understand how they behaved. Hubert Devonish (1991) has taken up this challenge in the sphere of language in a very useful paper entitled "Nature of African-East Indian Contact in 19th Century Guyana: the Linguistics Evidence" which studies the shifts in Creolese, used mainly by Africans, but also by Indians. Devonish concludes that the

> linguistic evidence suggests that Africans and Indians in 19th century Guyana did share a common language, Creolese. There were ethnic differences at the level of language. There was the consolidation of a koineised variety of Bhojpuri as an ethnic language. There was, as well, the emergence of a Bhojpuri influenced variety of Creolese. The former was restricted, however, by the importance of the workplace and the language of the workplace. The latter was purely a transitional point on the way to acquiring native-like competence in Creolese.
>
> The significance for the Rodney vs. Moore debate is this. Two groups which, from an objective point of view, share major common cultural features, may not consider that they do. They may choose to emphasise what are trivial differences in order to explain or rationalise conflict. On the other hand, two groups which share little in common may choose to emphasize that which they share in order to rationalise cooperation and unity between them. The fact of sharing or not sharing major cultural features does not determine or even explain conflict or the lack of it. Rather, cultural features provide symbols which are manipulated to explain or justify an existing state of relations between groups (Devonish 1991: 16–17).

Devonish's linguistic analyses and his approach are useful in this debate as he recognises the variability of the factors that could lead to ethnic conflict and the way ethnicity can be easily politicised. It is therefore possible to have creolisation at the same time as high levels of ethnic tension: shared cultural characteristics are no guarantee against ethnic conflict. When ethnicity is mixed with politics as was the case in Guyana the political situation can become inflammable.[11]

Rodney's article "Masses in Action" suggests some of the themes which he would have dealt with in a sequel to *A History of the Guyanese Working People*. Among these are the development of the bauxite industry; diamond and gold mining and the phenomenon of the Guyanese 'pork-knocker'; the development of rice farming and the movement of the Indians from the estates; the growth of race and class consciousness and their expression in a variety of political and social organisations. Rodney concludes this article with some observations on race and class in Guyana:

> In the decade after 1955 these two factors proved antagonistic, and consequently the anti-colonialist struggle of the Guyanese masses received a serious setback. However in 1900–1928 the situation was entirely different. Then, it was the awareness among both Indians and Negroes of the peculiar disadvantages under which their own race laboured which precipitated an attack on the colonial society (Rodney 1966c: 36).

Referring to the later antagonisms, Rodney had this to say:

> what occurred in the period after 1955 was that communal awareness was for various reasons turned inwards to exacerbate racial contradictions among the Guyanese workers and peasants. I say 'exacerbate', because racial conflict in Guyana was an inevitable concomitant of the fact that indentured labour (East Indian, Chinese and Portuguese) was conceived specifically to break the back of Negro opposition to the planter class. Throughout the decades after Indian immigration began in 1838, there were differences over wages between racial groups on the sugar estates, brought about by the deliberate policy of the planters of playing one group off against another. No doubt, racial conflict bred racialism, and vice versa; and indeed, there are a host of other such interconnections that one could make. What is certain is that simple and definitive explanations must give way to a more sober analysis of the complexities of the development of the Guyanese mass movement – of the relationship between racial consciousness and racial prejudice, between economic competition and racial conflict, between communal identification and class objectives (Rodney 1966c: 36–37).

His research into Caribbean history not only found its way into academic texts but into writing for children. His children's book *Kofi Baadu Out of Africa* was published posthumously. Rodney's objective was to tell the story of each migrant group in Guyana. Other titles were to have been *Lakshmi: Out of India*; *Fung-A-Fat: Out of China*; *Adriaan Hendriks: Out of Holland;* and *Joao Gomes: Out of Madeira*. Working with Rodney on this project were Andaiye who played an important role in researching, editing and typing the manuscript of *A History of the Guyanese Working People*, Colin Carto 'Abyssinian' who worked on the maps, and Brian Rodway who restored old photographs.[12]

In 1982 the American Historical Association posthumously awarded the Albert J. Beveridge prize to Walter Rodney for his *History of the Guyanese Working People, 1881-1905* and in 1983 the Association of Caribbean Historians followed suit with an award. This work was described by the Association of Caribbean Historians as being

> elegant in style, committed in tone, impeccable in research, profound in analyses and universal in its application. It represents an outstanding contribution to Guyanese historiography, to Caribbean historiography, to American historiography as well as a monumental achievement in the writing of social history.[13]

Rodney's role as a Caribbean historian went hand in hand with his role as a political activist and he tried through his historical research to understand more profoundly the problems faced by the Caribbean working people. Drawing on his historical research into Tanzanian and African history and his data on Guyana, Rodney advanced that

> Peasant history (with the rare exception of peasant revolts) proceeds not from one great turning point to another but through a series of cyclical patterns, reflecting the dominance of the environment, the stagnation in technology, and the slow rate of change in the overall social structure. These characteristics direct that historical reconstruction should accord due attention to the minutiae of difficulties in the peasant existence. Moreover, the awareness and discussion of these difficulties reached a high point during the 1880s and 1890s, even if the problems themselves were typical of those that went before and after (Rodney 1981c: 75-76).

No other work by Rodney is characterised by this attention to the minutiae of everyday life in recreating the history of the Guyanese working people. This provides a striking contrast to the way *How Europe Underdeveloped*

Africa was conceived and written. The latter dealt with broad themes and debates concerning the relationships between Africa and Europe from the fifteenth to the twentieth centuries. *A History of the Guyanese Working People* tackles the consequences of this relationship from the standpoint of the Africans and Indians who came to the Caribbean to labour on the British plantations.

NOTES

1. The last six years of his life took its toll on the relationship but Pat remained an anchor in organising the family.
   > Walter never knew how much he worked for. I was always in charge of the finances. I bought our house, the house was in my name . . . I think I took a lot of that stress off him, having to deal with the education of the children and just the general running of our home (Pat Rodney 1989).

2. See letter to Walter Rodney from Louise Rohonczy, Senior Program Officer, Social Science and Human Resources, dated 5 July 1978. The value of the award was Can $27,000 [The Rodney Papers (a)]. See also letter from Immanuel Wallerstein to Walter Rodney with a cheque for US $2,995.60 [The Rodney Papers (a)]. It was not clear what Rodney did to earn this sum. His international connections were vital to his economic survival and his scholarly and political work in Guyana.

3. See Orlando Patterson's response to Rodney in which he stated:
   > I sympathise with the basic thrust of his argument, and share many of his views on the problem of underdevelopment and the conception of slavery. However, we differ, first, over my inclination to take a rather broader view of underdevelopment, and not to identify it necessarily with what Wallerstein calls the modern world system, or with capitalism (Patterson 1979: 287).

4. Elsa Goveia died in Kingston, Jamaica. It has been said that more than anyone else at the University College of the West Indies in the 1950s, Elsa Goveia (1925–1980) "opened the eyes of her students and set them asking questions about their society and their identity" (Sherlock and Nettleford 1990: 79). The Departments of History, University of the West Indies, sponsor Elsa Goveia Memorial Lectures each year. Among her major published works are *A Study of the Historiography of the British West Indies to the End of the Nineteenth Century* (1957) and *Slave Society in the British Leeward Islands at the End of the Eighteenth Century* (1965).

5. Arising from the government's accusation that he was involved in the burning down of the headquarters of the ruling People's National Congress.

6. For a study of Jamaica at the turn of the nineteenth century with similar conclusions about the emergence of a creole middle class, see Bryan (1991b).

7. This interpretation would apply to Trinidad and Suriname. See Braithwaite (1971, 1985) for the development of creole society in Jamaica and the Caribbean region.

8. For discussion of cultural pluralism in the Caribbean, see M.G. Smith (1974, 1984) and for criticisms of Smith see Don Robotham (1980). See La Guerre's (1987) criticism of Walter Rodney's approach to relations between Africans and Indians in Guyana.

9. For an assessment of Caribbean social science scholarship on this and other issues, see Sankatsingh (1989).
10. Moore (1995) develops his claims on the role of culture in postemancipation Guyana.
11. Perry Mars (1990) is very useful as he discusses the relationship between ethnicity, class and politics in Guyana.
12. This team also worked on the mimeographed publication *Dayclean* which was the mouthpiece of the Working People's Alliance.
13. Certificate in Pat Rodney's papers.

CHAPTER 9

Rodney's Perspectives on Caribbean and Guyanese Politics

Rodney's return to Guyana in 1974 came at a time when regional politics in the English-speaking Caribbean was moving left of centre. Ruling parties such as Michael Manley's People's National Party in Jamaica, Errol Barrow's Democratic Labour Party in Barbados, Forbes Burnham's People's National Congress in Guyana and Eric Williams' People's National Movement in Trinidad constituted a regional social-democratic axis that was nonaligned. Their social-democratic outlook had been shaped by postwar British Labour Party and left wing thinking transplanted to the Caribbean and modified according to their own native political experience and instincts which in the case of Forbes Burnham led to the breaking of the rules of social-democratic fair play as far as electoral practices were concerned. They had a strong sense of a Caribbean destiny and argued their right to shape their own foreign policy, hence their decision to establish diplomatic relations with Cuba, which displeased Washington. These political leaders were respected in the Non-Aligned Movement. However, their domestic agendas were being criticised from both the right and the left. Eric Williams had come under the sharpest attacks, in what became known as the 1970 February Revolution when mass protests and near mutiny in the military nearly overthrew his regime.[1] The political right, that was strongest in Jamaica, looked to Washington, and in the case of Edward Seaga, exploited Cold War anticommunism to his party's benefit in the late 1970s while in opposition and in the 1980s in government. Guyana's People's Progressive Party and the People's National Congress, the People's National Party and Workers'

Party of Jamaica and the New Jewel Movement of Grenada all developed party-to-party relations with the Communist Party of Cuba and the Communist Party of the Soviet Union thereby creating a political and ideological network with Havana and Moscow.

Regional politics, to some extent, mirrored the Cold War alignments of the 1970s. But it was much more than this. A generation of young people drawn from the middle classes, working class, rural and urban poor felt that through political intervention changes could be effected that could radically alter the conditions of the mass of the population for the better. Moreover, they were positioned not only in small left wing parties but in mainstream electoral parties and thus able to influence the outcome of national electoral competition or, as in Grenada, in 1979, to take power from a discredited leader. There was undoubtedly a strong idealism that motivated the postindependence radicals just as was the case with the pre-independence radicalism of the 1930s to 1950s. However, it was the political generation that had been shaped in the latter period who were to be dominant in the period after independence. The postindependence radicals were destined to function within the political framework that their parents had established.

However, although Guyanese politics has much in common with politics in the English-speaking Caribbean it has been distinctive in the region in that it has been dominated by two left of centre parties with two racial constituencies. Cheddi Jagan in his book *The West on Trial* has gone into great detail on the political machinations of the British and American governments in the 1950s and 1960s in collaboration with his political opponents to use race to divide the country along racial lines. The outcome of the political machinations against Jagan was that he was kept in political opposition for nearly 30 years.[2] Unlike Jamaica's political parties which in the 1970s were sharply divided on ideological lines with the People's National Party espousing democratic socialism and a strong role for the state in the economy and the Jamaica Labour Party defending capitalism and the market, the main Guyanese parties were not very different ideologically.[3] Divided along racial lines Guyana's two principal parties – Jagan's People's Progressive Party and Burnham's People's National Congress – were left wing and were in the 1970s respectively anchored in the Indian and African sectors of the population. This anchorage has shaped the practice of these parties. Although the rhetoric of their leaders was multiracial, the political conversations of many of their supporters and electoral mobilisation were distinctly racial.

The Working People's Alliance drew its members from families who were activists supporting either Cheddi Jagan or Forbes Burnham. The fathers of Walter Rodney and Rupert Roopnarine[4] were politically active in the early

PPP and Eusi Kwayana himself had participated in the pre-PPP, PPP and PNC politics. They all recoiled from racialist politics, had lost respect for Burnham, and maintained respect for Jagan, recognising his pioneering role in Guyana's political awakening, but they felt that his working class rhetoric was in conflict with the racial support of the PPP. According to Rupert Roopnarine, leader of the WPA, "they also felt that while PPP leadership proclaimed Marxism-Leninism and racial unity publicly, they continued to mobilise racially in the bottom-houses",[5] hence their canvassing for elections was racial.

The evolution of Guyana's socialist politics depended in part on two dominant politicians – Forbes Burnham and Cheddi Jagan. At the start of the decade of the 1970s Forbes Burnham had a strong national and regional standing especially among Afro-Guyanese and sectors of the Afro-Caribbean population, as is portrayed in Salkey's *Georgetown Journal*. Salkey's book recorded his journey to Guyana where he participated in the February 1970 Caribbean Writers and Artists Conference which coincided with the founding of the Republic of Guyana on 23 February 1970. This was the first Caribbean Festival of the Arts known as CARIFESTA. Burnham was then at the height of his political career. In 1970 a collection of his speeches was published. It was entitled *A Destiny to Mould* and included a foreword by Martin Carter, a distinguished Caribbean poet, who was then at Guyana's Ministry of Information and Culture. Carter, who later became a critic of Burnham, worked with both Cheddi Jagan and Forbes Burnham, and in 1980 wrote a very fine poem to Rodney's memory.[6] In his foreword to Burnham's speeches Carter wrote:

> I have known Forbes Burnham as a person for over twenty-five years – first when I was a rather hopeless student and he was acceptedly the most intellectually gifted of the masters at Queen's College, Guyana; later when I was a so-called 'extremist-leftist-political-activist' and he a leader in our time of standing up. In those days the period between 1949 and 1954 – we, and I include names known and unknown, all tried together to 'storm heaven' in the face of gloomy admonitions to the effect that heaven was not in fact stormable. And even now, with him Prime Minister and me a member of the government, we will continue to have very spirited discussions as to the stormability of heaven.[7]

Carter established Burnham's position in the left wing of the anticolonial movement and went on to say that "Burnham is, I feel, by nature and temperament an intellectual ... But the economic, social and psychological pressures of a country harassed by history have made him transform himself."[8] Burnham had become a political leader and a pragmatist but "his pragmatism is political and not philosophical".[9] These fine distinctions being made by Carter reflect his own involvement in the discussion of the 1950s and 1960s about Marxism and anticolonial politics and the role of political leadership in postcolonial development in the context of a racially divided society. Carter's brief foreword talks more about Burnham's past and his work habits and not very much about what Burnham had become. Burnham had changed "from the gay, witty and brilliant companion of years ago" and had become "the work-horse of the nation demanding from his colleagues and himself prodigies of effort".[10]

Salkey noted in his diary the comments of an observer who claimed:

Everybody knows Cheddi. He's been going a long time. People say he too far behind to catch up with Burnham . . . Burnham is a better politician. He's got everything, now. All the problems, too, for that matter. He's a man that most people will tell you that is tougher than Cheddi. Burnham's the sort of politician that leaves you guessing. Just not some people in Guyana, only, I mean. America doesn't really understand him the way they think they understand Cheddi . . . For instance, do you know that Burnham is the sort of man who sells the Party paper in Bourda Market on Sunday mornings? He's the Prime Minister, you know! He goes out to the market, and maybe with one or two other people, a Minister, or a Party worker, and he sells the Party newspaper, right there, and that's what I mean, when I say that Burnham is Burnham. He can do as he likes, you see. He surprises even Guyanese people. The Americans must be guessing, too. I would say that he knows what he is doing right now. He's a man who knows his politics, and he knows Guyana, as it is . . . He understands power, in the way that, maybe, Cheddi doesn't understand it. You see, I think that Burnham understands the Indian majority, Black minority thing better than most people believe . . . (Salkey 1972: 125).

This 'understanding' served Burnham well as he manipulated racial fears in Guyanese society using his intellectual and oratorical skills to effect a Machiavellian control of Guyanese society, with its small population of about 800,000.[11] No other politician in the English-speaking Caribbean of his time exerted such a powerful control over his society. Forbes Burnham was intellectually gifted but he had also developed a reputation, in some circles, as being devious and ruthless. Jagan, on the other hand, seemed a benign socialist, but was no political match for Burnham. Dr Harry Drayton, who knew both Jagan and Burnham, offered the view that "Cheddi does not have the nimbleness of wit and quality of intellect. Cheddi learnt his Marxism in Chicago in the 1930s. He couldn't decide whether he wanted to be the M.N. Roy or the J. Nehru of Guyana" (Drayton 1989).[12]

Colin Cholmondeley, whose family was close to Burnham and whose father worked in the PNC office, recalled Burnham

> as an extremely bright man, an astute individual, with a massive intellect and energy but unfortunately for Guyana this massive intellect was directed primarily at achieving overweening control over individuals, to control people for his own ends. He derived a kind of sadistic pleasure in making people be at his beck and call. He would call Ministers, bureaucrats and treat them with such abandon. I was in his office and I remember him calling a Minister who happened to be travelling the next day late at night at about 11 p.m. and then let him wait on him. He continued the conversation with me for at least 15 minutes. He then admitted the Minister to his office and made him stand for another ten minutes without ackowledging him. This was a display of such power and abject submission. He dedicated himself to suborning (Cholmondeley 1989).[13]

According to Cholmondeley, who had lectured at the University of Guyana in the 1970s, "every lecturer at the University of Guyana who was eligible for sabbatical or academic leave had to get approval from the Central Bank for foreign exchange allocations to be made and that list first went to Burnham" (Cholmondeley 1989).

Percy Hintzen[14] best explained the imperatives of Guyanese politics in the 1970s in terms of the role that coercion played in the survival of the Burnham regime. Three factors were important in determining Burnham's approach to political power. First, the Indian population was larger than the African and race was the "dominant factor in the formation and manifestation of political attitudes of the Guyanese electorate".[15] Secondly, the change in the electoral system from first-past-the-post to proportional representation in 1964 enabled Burnham to accede to power. Jagan's People's Progressive Party gained 24 seats and Burnham's People's National Congress gained 22, with the United Force (UF) gaining seven. The PNC and the UF formed a coalition government. Thirdly, anticommunism in the Cold War era worked to Burnham's benefit in that he was seen as being preferable to Jagan. Arthur Schlesinger, advisor to the Kennedy administration, explained:

> An independent British Guiana under Burnham (if Burnham can commit himself to a multiracial policy) would cause us many fewer problems than an independent British Guiana under Jagan. And the way was open to bring it about because Jagan's parliamentary strength was larger than his popular strength. He had won 57% of the seats on the basis of 42.3% of the vote. An obvious solution was to establish a system of proportional representation. This,

after prolonged discussion, the British finally did in October 1963 (Hintzen 1989: 53).

Hintzen analysed:

The use of coercion can buy a political elite enough time to develop and implement an effective long-term response to challenges to its power. In light of this, the PNC regime began to intensify its use of violent and non-violent coercion to buy time while restructuring the state machinery to control. Initially, regime survival had depended upon coercive deployment against the country's East Indian population, particularly during electoral campaigns. In 1971 this deployment was extended to ASCRIA (African Society for Cultural Relations with Independent Africa), and in 1973, to dissident formerly pro-regime unions. By 1978, the use of the regime's coercive resources came to be directed at securing the generalized political demobilization of the entire population. Singled out for particular attention were members of the WPA and all activists engaged in any overt form of political dissent. Leaders of the anti-regime movement were arrested on trumped-charges, while known political dissidents were placed under constant surveillance. The houses of anti-regime activists, and those associating with them, were constantly searched under the powers of a National Security Act which gave the police sweeping powers. Leading members of the opposition were constantly intimidated with a campaign of state-directed violence. Some including the most important and dynamic of the WPA activists, Walter Rodney, were killed. Many more were arrested, some on charges of treason (Hintzen 1989: 172).

This explanation offers a contextual basis to evaluate Rodney's involvement in Guyanese politics. In the early 1970s the authoritarian and corrupt practices leading to PNC paramountcy were already underway. Among the early targets were Clive Thomas, a University of Guyana economics professor and member of the group Movement Against Oppression (MAO), who survived an attempt to kidnap him. Thomas' colleague, Josh Ramsammy, senior lecturer in biology and active member in MAO, was shot and seriously wounded in Georgetown. In addition, a number of PPP activists were victimised. In 1973 the PNC gained 37 seats in the 53-seat Parliament, and the opposition parties – the PPP and the UF – got 14 and 2 seats respectively. This enabled Burnham to secure the two-thirds majority in the Parliament which later enabled him to impose the 1980 Constitution after eliminating the right to referendum to change certain entrenched clauses. The opposition claimed that many different techniques were used to hinder the electoral campaign of opposition parties, these included restrictions on the importation of newsprint for opposition newspapers (especially the *Mirror*, the PPP newspaper); beatings and breaking up of political meetings; refusal of permits requested by opposition politicians who wished to visit Amerindian areas; and arrests of opposition party activists . . . It was reported that the army intervened openly in the collection and transportation of ballots . . . opposition party agents were not allowed to accompany ballot boxes in transit to electoral offices (Guyana Nationals and Friends Alliance [GNFA] 1979: 6).

Burnham continued to use these tactics throughout the 1970s against the opposition. Jagan's People's Progressive Party declared a campaign of civil resistance as their line of protest against the elections.[16] The PPP conducted its campaign against Burnham's illegal actions not only in Guyana and the region but also internationally where he exposed Burnham. But Burnham refuted the charges in Moscow and Havana by affirming his anti-imperialism and his socialist convictions, and in Washington and London he played the anticommunist card against Jagan whose PPP was part of the international communist movement. In Guyana he held to the view that if Guyanese Indians gained power Guyanese of African descent would be marginalised. Burnham therefore maintained power by applying Malcolm X's maxim "by any means necessary".

In this racial and political climate the Burnham regime saw Walter Rodney as a potentially important opponent and critic. The fact that he was Afro-Guyanese and not Indian made his opposition to Burnham's regime of special significance. To the pro-Burnham Afro-Guyanese middle class, Rodney had broken ranks with his ethnic group, and to sections of the Indian community this gave his thrust towards a nonracist politics a greater degree of integrity and intellectual honesty. Rodney had close personal and political ties with Eusi Kwayana, who was a leading figure in ASCRIA. Whenever he visited Guyana he had discussions with Eusi Kwayana and it was ASCRIA which organised public meetings in his support in 1974 when the Burnham regime blocked his appointment at the University of Guyana. These meetings were also addressed by Cheddi Jagan, and Roopnarine (1996) suggests that Kwayana and Jagan were appearing on the platform for the first time since the political split of the 1950s. Rodney visited Cheddi Jagan, leader of the People's Progressive Party, at Freedom House, the party headquarters. Rodney was also close friends with C.Y. Thomas who was in the *Ratoon* group. *Ratoon* was similar to the *Abeng*[17] newspaper group of radical intellectuals in Jamaica.

The government of Forbes Burnham had a progressive image because of his cooperative socialism. Meanwhile the Manley government in Jamaica was reviving democratic socialism and had co-opted D.K. Duncan and Arnold Bertram among other young left wing persons to assist with this project. Cuba was developing diplomatic and political relations with several English-speaking countries, thus ending a long period of diplomatic isolation. Outside of the established political parties there were a number of left wing organisations that had been formed by the radical intelligentsia. Among these were the New Jewel Movement in Grenada, the Working People's Alliance in Guyana, the Workers' Liberation League which became the Workers' Party of Jamaica in 1978 declaring itself Marxist-Leninist, and intending to develop links with the international communist movement. Rodney knew many of the leaders of these organisations and had close ties with radical staff and students on the three campuses of the University of the West Indies in Trinidad, Jamaica and Barbados, and with the trade union movement, particularly the Oilfield Workers Trade Union of Trinidad and the Barbados Workers Union. He also had ties with the Caribbean Council of Churches which shared some of Rodney's ideas on issues of regional development and sovereignty. Rodney's experience in Africa and the Caribbean had made him sharply critical of the middle classes or the petty bourgeoisie and thus he did not take the Manley-Burnham rhetoric at face value. Instead he looked squarely at its social and ethnic content as well as its political limitations. His essay "Contemporary Political Trends in the English-speaking Caribbean", which was published in the *Black Scholar* of September 1975, sets out very clearly the theoretical framework within which he analysed the region. First, he saw that "constitutional decolonization almost invariably concluded with a political arrangement from which the masses are excluded and one which provides the political basis for neo-colonialism. British West Indian territories have been typical in these respects" (Rodney 1975d: 15).

This thesis which had its roots in Fanon's book, *The Wretched of the Earth*, had been extensively discussed for Jamaica by Trevor Munroe in his doctoral dissertation which was subsequently published as a book.[18] Secondly, Rodney argued that

> a deep understanding of West Indian society cannot be reached without recognising changes in the form and direction of imperialism both in the centres as well as in the peripheries. Monopoly capital has assumed new aggregations and new strategies over the last two decades. Scientific and technological advances in the metropoles have expanded the capacity of the multinational corporations so that they continue to extract surplus while adjusting to new juridical patterns of ownership of the means of production in

the Third World and while modifying the classic international division of labour which had restricted colonial areas to primary production (Rodney 1975d: 15).

This was no simple statement of dependency theory but was an attempt to locate the region within the context and changing character of global capital. Central to Rodney's analysis of Caribbean politics was his thesis that "the most significant of the set of internal and external socioeconomic contradictions which shape neocolonial politics are those that derive from the consolidation of the petty bourgeoisie as a class around the state" (Rodney 1975d: 15).

His observations on the petty bourgeoisie represent a development of Fanon's assessment in the *Wretched of the Earth*. The socialist rhetoric of many Caribbean and African leaders in the 1970s was therefore seen by Rodney as pseudosocialism. Neocolonial politics under the leadership of the petty bourgeoisie had several features which Rodney outlined. These were 1) the concentration of power in the hands of a petty bourgeoisie; 2) the destruction of popular political expression and participation; 3) the manipulation of race and other divisions amongst the people; 4) the institutionalisation of corruption; 5) the extension of political repression and victimisation; 6) the vulgarisation of "national culture" as a tool for class rule; 7) the deliberate distortion of revolutionary concepts. These points summarised his view of the political trends in the West Indies in the 1970s with an emphasis on Guyanese politics. He went on:

> various combinations of the above elements aid the implementation of policies which allow the reproduction of the petty bourgeoisie as a class in the midst of declining material standards for the vast majority and simultaneous with the accelerated expatriation of surplus by the multinational corporations (Rodney 1975d: 16).

This analysis captured the essence of the postcolonial situation and he was able to show how these characteristics cut across ethnic lines. With the Trinidadian and Guyanese experience in mind, Rodney asserted that the African petty bourgeoisie in Trinidad

> maintained a firm hold of the PNM (People's National Movement) on the unwritten but widely understood premise that they were supposedly operating in the interests of the African majority. The Indian petty bourgeoisie was dissimilar only to the extent that it had a strong commercial capitalist orientation. Both sectors of the petty bourgeoisie treated the workers and

peasants in an arrogant, bullying, contemptuous way – resorting to outright gangsterism on many occasions (Rodney 1975d: 16).

Rodney distinguished between the older and newer sections of the petty bourgeoisie. The older were the

> better established sectors of the West Indian petty bourgeoisie, such as the Syrian, Jewish, Chinese or Indian merchants and the French Creole or Indian landed proprietors. These latter are engaged in production or distribution, and they realise value through rent, the direct exploitation of labour and the exploitation of the market. On the other hand, the new petty bourgeoisie have no immediate base in production and hence their need to maintain political hegemony (Rodney 1975d: 17).

Politics was, for Rodney, rooted in the material sphere of economic interests and the evolution of corresponding social and racial hierarchies.

Rodney continued his critique by exposing the corruption that had become endemic to the political system and by condemning the growing levels of repression and electoral fraud that were being used to maintain power. He stated that "social and political repression in the English-speaking Caribbean arises directly out of the material conditions of the neo-colonial underdevelopment and the lop-sided division of the social product – as is the case everywhere else in the neo-colonial Third World" (Rodney 1975d: 9).

Rodney's alternative to the Caribbean's dependent capitalist order was socialist transformation similar to that taken by the Cuban Revolution, not the pseudosocialism of the West Indian petty bourgeois regimes. It was not a question, however, of blind imitation of the Cuban Revolution as so many Cuban officials had warned against, pointing to the high price they had had to pay,[19] but a process that was akin to the Grenadian Revolution, but with a more clear cut perspective on issues of democracy and elections. In the mid 1970s Rodney noted that

> neo-colonial politics have entered a new operational phase in which pseudo-socialism is adjudged to be more effective than anti-socialism as a means of maintaining control over the working people ... Pseudosocialism is especially concerned with its image at home and abroad and seeks support from the socialist camp and from revolutionary sectors of the imperialist world (Rodney 1975d: 20).

Similar views were expressed by veteran politician and writer Eusi Kwayana in his paper on Guyana's pseudosocialism (Kwayana 1976). Rodney was in many respects responding to the Guyanese situation and Burnham's manipulative political skills. Burnham had been succeeding in gaining support from Cuba and the Soviet Union and had developed ties with radical regimes and liberation movements in Africa. But Rodney's argument was more generalised and applied to the English-speaking region which was then experiencing a radical turn. The decade had started with the Black Power revolt of February 1970 in Trinidad and Tobago, by March 1979 Maurice Bishop was in power in Grenada, and Michael Manley dominated Jamaica's politics from 1972 to 1980.[20] It is out of this context of the promise of popular political mobilisation, especially among young people in the Caribbean, that Rodney's critique arose.

With the abortion of radicalism in the 1980s antisocialism became the prevailing rallying cry and this was speeded up with the collapse of communist states in Eastern Europe in the late 1980s and early 1990s. The petty bourgeoisie has proved itself just as capable in adopting antisocialism as it did socialist rhetoric in the 1970s. Moreover, the Cuban model, dependent as it was on the Soviet Union and the former socialist bloc, has had waning appeal because of its economic crisis and the monopoly of power by Fidel Castro and the ruling Communist Party.[21] The disintegration of socialist states in Europe, the dissolution of the Soviet Union and the capitalist policies of the Chinese communists have made implausible the socialist option in the Caribbean. However, these developments do not take away from Rodney's analysis of the class character of the petty bourgeoisie. Rather they underscore his argument that this class has had a poor record in the battle for decolonisation, albeit in circumstances that have worsened in the Caribbean and Africa since Rodney's murder in 1980. It was on the basis of the analysis discussed above that Rodney and the Working People's Alliance emerged as the junior opposition to the Burnham regime. It was Cheddi Jagan who was the main opposition figure in Guyana.

Jagan's critical support and Rodney's critical exposure

Through its extensive state sector in bauxite mining and sugar that had been nationalised in 1975–76, the creation of party paramountcy and linkages with socialist and communist parties, Burnham's party and government by the 1970s had all the trappings of a socialist state. Jagan's PPP shifted to critical support in a fashion similar to the Workers' Liberation League's (WLL) and later WPJ's support for the Manley regime in the 1970s. Cheddi Jagan stated in 1975 at the twenty-fifth anniversary conference of the PPP, that "our political line should be changed from non-cooperation and civil resistance to critical support. This can lay the basis for a political solution in our country. It will also help to frustrate the PNC's attempts to isolate the Party."[22] Jagan's policy of critical support reflected responses both to internal and international changes. On the internal side, Jagan obviously felt he was being isolated as Burnham was implementing many of the economic and foreign policy positions that Jagan had been advocating. On the international side the situation seemed more favourable to anti-imperialist radicalism. The 1975 meeting of Latin American and Caribbean communist parties held in Havana issued a declaration which was signed by the PPP and which called on communists to support national bourgeois regimes that promoted anti-imperialism and nationalist reforms. The declaration stated: "there are sectors of the Latin American bourgeoisie that can adopt positions converging with the anti-imperialist struggle."[23]

The Burnham regime represented the Afro-Caribbean middle class and had all the elements of Third World radical nationalism with a programme of nationalisation with disastrous economic consequences, anti-imperialist and socialist rhetoric combined with authoritarian political control. By the mid 1970s Guyanese politics would be assessed in Havana and Moscow as having two left wing parties with the PNC under Burnham gaining recognition as a ruling party seriously committed to transformation and internationalist solidarity.

Rodney was opposed to the PPP's policy of critical support for the PNC and argued instead for critical exposure. The line of thinking which led Rodney and the WPA to this position arose from their understanding of what Burnham and the PNC represented in Caribbean and Guyanese politics from both a class and racial standpoint.

In 1976 Rodney was of the view that "throughout the Caribbean the consciousness of the masses is at quite a high level" (Rodney 1976c: 112) and he elaborated:

> The recent history of the Caribbean has been characterised by the intervention of Caribbean Marxism on the political scene. Often this intervention has been undisciplined, sporadic, but nonetheless of historical importance. All political forms, rhetoric, institutions have had to adapt themselves to the eruption of Marxism on the scene since 1938 in one form or another. The discussion of socialism is part of a response to a popular outbreak, a demand for change (Rodney 1976c: 111).

The 'socialisms' of the ruling parties, whether it was 'cooperative socialism' in Guyana or 'democratic socialism' in Jamaica, were seen by Rodney as the response of the ruling political elite to pressures from below. C.L.R. James' very strong support of Julius Nyerere and Michael Manley was, however, never Rodney's position.[24] Rodney was more critical, looking less at personalities and more at the social bases of regimes as well as the context of international economic and political systems in which postcolonial states functioned. Comparing the petty bourgeoisie in Jamaica and Guyana, Rodney indicated.

> For example, the ties between the indigenous petit bourgeoisie and international capital have always been closer, firmer and more developed than in Guyana. More subsidiaries of multinational corporations operate in Jamaica. The involvement of the petit bourgeoisie in insurance companies, mortgage finance, etc., has been much wider. One could almost say that in Jamaica there are one or two examples of a national bourgeoisie – not a national bourgeois class – but single individuals who definitely command (from a subordinate position to international capital) certain resources which can be utilised locally. Most of Jamaica's housing development in the postwar period has been privately financed.
>
> But in Guyana we did not have a lot of multinational development. Bookers controlled many sectors of the economy. We did not have such a burgeoning period of industrialisation-by-invitation as they attempted in Jamaica. We do not have as powerful a private capitalist sector either in commerce or in industry (Rodney 1976c: 112–13).

It was therefore a weaker petit bourgeoisie that was more easily cajoled than in Jamaica. In this light Rodney saw Burnham's nationalisation in bauxite and sugar not only as an attempt to

> redistribute wealth in purely national terms as between the given dependency and the epicentres of international capitalism . . . but more than this it is a political question. Certain classes have to consolidate their social and political power and nationalisation is necessary not merely, let us say, for Guyana to get more for its sugar and bauxite, but also for the Guyanese petit bourgeoisie to reproduce itself as a class and to control the state machinery and society in its own class interest. Fundamentally it remains a political question (Rodney 1976c: 112).

Sticking to the class basis of the regime and understanding its economic weaknesses, Rodney did not make the mistake of paying undue attention to the personality of the political leader as the left in Jamaica tended to do with Manley. A sense of the relationship of social forces and the position of the

Caribbean in Washington's foreign policy making were important but this did not mean that a leader was a prisoner of his class background or the social forces he had come to represent. Instead, Rodney's position recognised socially determined and historical possibilities and ruled out miracles associated with popular belief in charismatic politicians or transitions to different socioeconomic systems based on the decisions of a single personality or a group of men and women organised in a political party.

In a letter written on 23 September 1975 to Harry and Kathleen Drayton, Walter summarised his experience after being in Guyana for over one year:

> Changes taking place over here have been incremental rather than dramatic, so that there is nothing new with which you would be unfamiliar. Even the apparent turnabout on the part of the PPP may prove to be nothing significant. So far the government has done much to indicate that they would dialogue with the PPP Jagan's critical support speech met with some rather insulting responses that he should prove himself to be genuine, and the only measurable result so far has been a tendency to allow the PPP to feature occasionally in the news.
>
> The WPA found it impossible to come to a unanimous conclusion on the implications of the actions of the PPP. One of our constituent groups took a hard line that the PPP was responding to foreign dictates and were selling out the working class. Another was more hopeful that the new policy might arrest certain neo-fascist trends and perhaps force changes within the PNC and PPP. Of course, our own work continues as before, although there is the possibility that we might be isolated as ultra-leftists (Rodney 1975e).[25]

Rodney's position was that of critical exposure not critical support. This position was one of the reasons why within sections of the regional left he was indeed regarded as an 'ultra-leftist'. In the final paragraph of his letter he said:

> As one would expect, pseudo-socialism draws fire from socialists who attack its spuriousness and it also arouses the ire of those who are ideologically opposed to socialism and are antagonised by the government's seeming efforts in that direction. The situation calls out for some serious and original theoretical analysis. We in the WPA have recognised this fact, but our manpower resources are limited and we are caught up in the immediacy of agitation. The *Ratoon* group is planning to reactivate itself this coming academic year by undertaking formal Marxist classes and possibly publishing a theoretical journal. If so, then a gap would be plugged (Rodney 1975e).

This gap arose because of the conflict that political activists face between the pull of day-to-day agitation and the need to reflect theoretically on the broader picture and identify the strategic issues. Given his work as activist, theoretician and historian, Rodney was caught up in the struggle to make time for these interconnected and time consuming undertakings. His political line of critical exposure was not given further theoretical underpinning other than what existed in the *Black Scholar* interview and in many public statements. His time was divided between political work, studying the historical development of the working class, as well as in direct political and educational work with Guyanese workers.

Study group and theoretical work

The two journals appearing in Guyana in 1978 with which Rodney was associated were *Transition* which was a radical social science publication of the Faculty of Social Sciences and Institute of Development Studies of the University of Guyana, and the independent *Georgetown Review* edited by Andaiye, Brian Rodway and Rupert Roopnarine. In *Georgetown Review* he published an essay on the "Internal and External Constraints on the Development of the Guyanese Working Class" which formed part of his *History of the Guyanese Working People*. Among the other contributors were C.Y. Thomas who also published a chapter from his book *Plantations, Peasants and State* and Rupert Roopnarine who was interviewed on his film *The Terror and the Time* (*Notes on Repressive Violence in Guyana*). There were also several new poems by Martin Carter. *Georgetown Review* had the potential of becoming a 1970s version of the *New World* journal of the late 1960s but it did not survive.

Rodney's essay entitled "Transition" was a lengthy editorial which explained the objectives of the journal, *Transition*.[26] Rodney's editorial discussed the theoretical significance of the term 'transition' from a Marxist point of view. It is, quite definitely, not one of his best essays as it lacks focus, jumps from region to region in the Third World and from one theoretical issue to another. It nevertheless provides insights into his thinking about the transition to socialism in the Third World. The main feature of Rodney's editorial was its intellectual independence in a period when many Caribbean Marxists were tied to either Moscow or Peking. But this does not save Rodney from utopian conceptions of socialism that grew out of notions of disengagement from imperialism. Nor does it save him from a conception of socialism that rests heavily on the political alignments of global power in the 1970s, hence his view that

The contradictions within the imperialist system and between imperialism and socialism provide the objective basis for the passage to socialism in dependent capitalist countries. This has to be reiterated and then qualified by the equally important variable of action by class conscious elements. Transition therefore equates with guided transformation; it means social policy directed by the working class in its own interest. Broad and challenging possibilities are opened up by the notion of workers' democracy, which has relevance both at the point of production and within the several levels and branches of the state (Rodney 1978: 8).

These views were compatible with Jagan's ideas on socialism, and went well with C.L.R. James' workerist theorising in the Facing Reality[27] group he had had in the United States in the 1950s and 1960s. Moreover, the essay was unrealistic in its approach to economic development. In the area of the relations between economics and politics the thinking was at its woolliest. It was on the issue of democracy that he was clearer, with his critique of the undemocratic practices of Marxist regimes in Congo Brazzaville, Guinea, Somalia and Ethiopia. He wrote:

Verbal adherence to Marxism in Congo Brazzaville, Guinea, Somalia and Ethiopia has accompanied social developments indistinguishable from those in states where there has been an explicit rejection of the theory of class contradictions: that is to say, Marxist intellectuals have been silenced, workers' representatives have been eliminated and the working class as a whole excluded from democratic participation in social reconstruction. For transition to have validity, it must include the widespread promotion of socialist education without caricature and it must rely firmly on workers' democracy (Rodney 1978: 8).

He went on:

Broad and challenging possibilities are opened up by the notion of workers' democracy, which has relevance both at the point of production and within the several levels and branches of the state. It should also be clear that such transition would allocate meaningful roles to strata which are closely or potentially allied to the working class: above all, the peasantry as well as independent craftsmen, shopkeepers, the lower salariat, students, technocrats and other intellectuals (Rodney 1978: 8).

The Working People's Alliance and race

From 1961 to 1964 Guyana was torn by racial and labour conflict which contributed to the removal of the Jagan government. Burnham gained power in 1964 when in alliance with the smaller United Force he defeated the PPP which had been in office from 1957 to 1964. Guyana became independent in 1966 with Burnham as Prime Minister. In the 1968 elections the PNC won 30 seats, the PPP 21 seats and the United Force 2 seats.[28] By 1970 Burnham declared Guyana a Republic.

There was in the 1970s a more favourable climate towards multiracial politics than in the 1960s and some hoped that this would help heal the wounds of racial conflict stemming from confrontations of the 1960s. This rapprochement was advocated by younger people who had grown up with attachments either to the PPP or the PNC and who saw the possibilities of creating a political force that would not promote racial politics. For example, Kwayana noted that

> one thing which kept Rodney out of Guyana for a few extra years was the racial cleavage which had taken place among the working people. A political scene which had as a main tendency political-racial polarisation would have been a very inhospitable one for him to return to (Kwayana 1988: 1).

By 1970, as elsewhere in the Caribbean, there was the formation of groups like the Working People's Vanguard Party and Movement Against Oppression which were critical of Burnham's electoral practices and spoke out against the racial polarisation of Guyanese politics and party control of the judiciary and the security forces. The PNC under Burnham with its doctrine of party paramountcy was becoming more authoritarian by the mid 1970s. In an interview with the Jamaican writer, Andrew Salkey, Walter Rodney offered his interpretation of the racial situation and the struggle for socialism.

> I think that within our community of Guyana, different ethnic groups need to assert their identity, need to put themselves together, to pull themselves together, and when they have and when they can operate on the basis of mutual respect, which they are not doing now, then I think that the way will be clear for building a new society, a society of a mixed unit, through socialism. But, the various groups must be built up, made conscious of their own potential, their own dignity, their own power, as people, as Guyanese (Salkey 1972: 387).

The relationship between ethnic identity and the struggle for socialism had posed knotty problems for twentieth century Marxism, in the Soviet Union as well as China. Many Caribbean Marxists assumed a kind of reductionist interpretation of ethnicity which saw the struggle for socialism and class solidarity across racial lines solving the problem of ethnicity. Rodney was criticised as being a 'nationalist' (a bad word in the Marxist lexicon) when he focused on the relative autonomy of ethnicity and race from class.[29] Rodney's observations, however, did have a kind of stages approach to history which could be parodied in the following manner: First, solve the racial question by purging yourself of racial antagonisms, then you'll be ready as a nation to take on the main enemy which is the international capitalist system. Rodney's political criticism of Guyanese politics was that neither leader should be content with the existing division of the country and that race should not be exploited for political office.

The Working People's Alliance was the organisational collective within which Rodney functioned and he was able to draw on the experience of middle class intellectuals and grass roots activists of African and Indian extraction. Rodney had a deep respect for Kwayana, one of his colleagues in the WPA leadership, and looked to him for personal and political guidance. Not long before he was killed, Rodney was to describe Kwayana as an outstanding intellectual and political figure, emphasising that he was "a person of tremendous quality, an individual who has remained uncorrupted, in a context of corruption and squalor" (Rodney 1980d: 3). The generation of the 1960s had become disillusioned with Jagan's PPP and more so with Burnham's PNC. The WPA brought together the African Society for Cultural Relations with Independent Africa founded by Eusi Kwayana who had been involved in anticolonial mobilisation since the 1940s, and had been a leading figure of both the PPP and the PNC. The other organisations from which the WPA drew its support were the Indian Political Revolutionary Association, the Working People's Vanguard Party (Marxist-Leninist), and then there was a university based Marxist group that had gathered around the newspaper *Ratoon*. Rodney pointed out that

> these groups came together in response to at least two important pressures. One was a new demand to overcome a racist-oriented organization, so that both ASCRIA and IPRA collaborated on issues such as the landless squatters, of both Indian and African descent. The question was dealt with in class terms rather than racial terms. Second, as questions of socialism and ideology were being raised, the aim was to provide an organization which would take the task of political and ideological education more seriously than any other existing political group (Rodney 1976c: 120).

Kwayana summed up the aims of the organisation very well when he wrote that the WPA saw itself "purely as an agency for the revolutionising of the political culture and for the reversal of political polarisation" (Kwayana 1988: 9). Rodney's political and academic writings, his intellectual contribution to the race/class dialectic, and his critique of the middle class need to be seen in the light of this statement of revolutionary idealism. It is completely 'un-Leninist' in its failure to focus on taking power and cannot be easily shoved into a capitalist or socialist pigeonhole. The concern with transforming political culture and the reversal of political polarisation speaks to the task of reconstructing the basic political values of modern Guyanese society and not to the pragmatic task of taking power. Although in 1979 the latter issue came to the fore, there was a tension between the vaguer, long-term objective of changing the political culture, empowering the working people and setting up the necessary alliances to take power from Burnham.

Rodney's work in Guyana can best be understood in terms of this tension between revolutionary idealism and the pragmatism of daily political life where idealism and abstractions are always found wanting, especially in a society prone to racial cleavage. It was the long-term issues, however, which lay behind his political educational work in bottom-house meetings, public meetings, lectures, his research and writing of Guyanese history as well as the books for children. Rodney's appeal to the working people cut across race to establish connections that had existed in the 1940s and early 1950s but had been destroyed by divisions within the nationalist movement. In Jagan, the Marxist-Leninist, his party supporters saw an Indian leader and in Burnham, the cooperative socialist, his supporters saw the Afro-Guyanese answer to Jagan. There were some Africans in the PPP leadership and some Indians in Burnham's leadership to maintain the fiction that both had tried to integrate their party machines but no one really believed that and the political culture accepted the racial polarisation as a fait accompli. Both politicians spoke in terms of Guyanese unity but racial politics to one degree or the other had become the order of the day. Under Burnham a few Indians were co-opted but the state sector became predominantly African while rural sugar labour and private economic spheres were Indian. From the point of view of both Burnham and sections of the Afro-Guyanese middle class Rodney was being disloyal to the group. It was against this racial mentality and acquiescence to racial polarisation that Rodney campaigned vigorously in the 1970s.

It was entirely consistent with Rodney's orientation that when ASCRIA organised a public meeting in Georgetown to mobilise support against the decision of the University of Guyana Board of Governors not to appoint Rodney to the post of Professor of History it had multiracial support: Cheddi Jagan of the PPP and other leaders of Indian origin were also involved.

Rodney's involvement in the Arnold Rampersaud case in 1974 indicated that his ideological commitment to multiracialism was backed up by practical involvement in defense of Indian political activists who were victims of

Afro-Guyanese victimisation.[30] Rampersaud was an activist of the PPP who had been charged with the murder of a police constable, James Henry, who "was murdered while guarding the toll station at #63 Village on the Corentyne". Rampersaud was "arrested while going to take food for his brother who had been held on the previous day in connection with the toll gate shooting" (Rodney 1982: i). Arnold Rampersaud was a well-known PPP activist in the Courentyne and his supporters contended that he was being framed by the government. In one of his speeches on behalf of Rampersaud, Rodney dealt with the issue of race and politics in Guyana. He felt that

> more than one political party has been responsible for the crisis of race relations in this country. I think our leadership has failed us on that score. I think external intervention[31] was important in bringing the races against each other from the fifties and particularly in the early 1960s. But I am concerned with the present. If we made that mistake once, we cannot afford to be misled on that score today. No ordinary Afro-Guyanese, no ordinary Indo-Guyanese can today afford to be misled by the myth of race. Time and time again it has been our undoing (Rodney 1982: 8).

Rodney opposed racial politics from the standpoint of the need to reduce the divisions among the Guyanese working people and the target of his attack was the Afro-Guyanese middle class and the leadership of the ruling party. In the struggle for justice for Rampersaud, Rodney came out against the transfer of the case from the predominantly Indian area of the Courentyne to the predominantly Afro-Guyanese area of the capital, Georgetown, where the jury was made up mainly of Afro-Guyanese men.

In a 1976 interview with the African-American scholar William Strickland, Rodney recalled that

> in the 1960s we had seen the phase of electoral politics, where people were lining up on one side or the other – the PPP if one was Indian and PNC if one was African. That was very clear. I recall very well, as late as 1961, being very confused on the question of whether one went for the PPP or the PNC. As I listed the pros and cons, I said, well the PPP says it's a Marxist party but it's not operating that way and it had Indians. On the other side, the PNC didn't even claim to be Marxist or even a serious socialist party. Yet it had the Africans. And for those of us Africans who were struggling for some clarity, struggling to take a progressive position, it was extremely difficult. Many who had joined the PPP as the better of a bad choice actually had to leave the party. And ultimately, because of those racial questions, a generation of us have actually stayed clear of the two dominant political parties. The whole history

of the 1960s was a history in which our political choices were fundamentally dictated, not by any class position but by the on-going race conflict. And it made it extremely difficult for any progressive, African or Indian, to intervene in the Guyanese situation, because it was already so formed that the moment one intervened, one was doing so in a ready-made context of Indian versus African. In this respect I was actually more comfortable in Jamaica because there the confrontations were clear. Class and ethnicity ran along the same lines. When I wrote *Groundings with my Brothers*, I referred back to the Guyanese African and Indian situation, trying to make it clear that the way in which one was using the word 'black' in (a) West Indian context must of necessity embrace the majority of African and Indian population because I knew that the word 'black' could well be interpreted in a narrow sense to mean only African, and hence anti-Indian . . . (Rodney 1976d: 8–9).

The distinction between race and class was central to Rodney's thinking. In this respect his 'black nationalism' or Black Power was quite definitely different from the meaning given to it in the United States by Stokeley Carmichael, who, when he came to Guyana used Black in the narrow racial sense. Rodney, in striving towards developing class politics in Guyana, paid attention to social differentiation within the main ethnic groups and did not treat ethnic groups as a homogenous category. He put some store by the fact that

among the Indian working people, and some of the intelligentsia, there is a growing awareness that while the petit bourgeoisie that dominates Guyana is largely African, it is not exclusively African. It is engaged in alliances with certain kinds of Indians – with the Indian businessman and other Indian petit bourgeoisie (Rodney 1976d: 9).

He could only hope that ultimately the Indian working people would see that the Burnham regime was not really benefiting the African masses either.

Left wing ideology

The other sphere of Guyanese political culture was its left wing ideological character. The nationalist movement of the 1940s and 1950s had adopted socialist anticolonial rhetoric. It was not surprising that by the end of the 1960s the PPP was Marxist-Leninist and by the mid 1970s the PNC also spoke in Marxist-Leninist terms. At the twenty-fifth anniversary conference of the People's Progressive Party in 1975 Jagan said, "We are glad that the

PNC has been forced to swallow its anticommunist and anti-Cuban sentiments and to advocate Marxism-Leninism..." and he went on to warn that socialist states

> also have a responsibility to make sure that petty-bourgeois nationalist governments like the PNC do not exploit the relations between them and make it appear that their parties are the vanguard parties to the detriment of the revolutionary process (Jagan 1975: 13).

So that both the PPP and the PNC had Marxist-Leninist profiles and the PNC, whilst seeking to maintain good relations with Washington, set about undercutting the PPP within the socialist community. Closer ties and cooperation were developed at the state and party levels between the PNC and the Communist Party of the Soviet Union and the Communist Party of Cuba. PNC cadres were sent to Communist Party schools in Moscow and Havana. Meanwhile, much of the international work of the PPP focused on trying to prove that Burnham was not really committed to socialism and warning against premature recognition of the PNC. The international communist movement on the other hand sought to promote greater cooperation between the two parties since their ideological positions were so close. Havana was more enthusiastic about the prospects for the PNC than was Moscow but the latter also saw Burnham's Guyana as one of the socialist oriented states in the Third World.[32]

Eusi Kwayana had characterised Burnham's socialism as pseudosocialism (Kwayana 1976). Rodney went further to say that the PNC

> really does incorporate . . . a large proportion of the most reactionary and right-wing elements in the country – groups that used to be in the United Force, groups that used to oppose even the nationalist struggle back in the 1950's. That is not to say that any given individual is incapable of transformation. But we are talking not just of one individual, but of a large number who are clearly representatives of a class which has given no indication, public or private, of any transformation in their world view, their life style or their social objectives. They are encrusted within the party and the government, they represent the party at the highest level inside and outside the country. Overnight they have been given new slogans to shout and it does amaze me how these slogans don't stick in their throats. It is not a matter of a small deflection here and there, the fellows actually have to turn their sentences around in exactly the opposite direction (Rodney 1976c: 117).

Thus Rodney was clearly able to see behind the smokescreen of socialist rhetoric by identifying the social substance of Burnham's regime and he dedicated himself to its exposure. This was a key element in his political education of the Guyanese working people and by the end of the 1970s many came to see in him the embodiment of part of their hope for political and socioeconomic change. Rodney was working his way through his intellectual and political struggles to make real the somewhat elusive concept of the emancipation of the working people which owed something to C.L.R. James' political writings. The idea is not really defined or developed theoretically in Rodney's writings or in WPA publications. Rodney was more inclined towards looser forms of organisation based on the self-activity of the working people and notions of spontaneity. He was therefore critical of the Leninist formations that had developed within the regional left in Jamaica and in the New Jewel Movement. His own sense of Marxism developed against this backdrop.

Rodney's Marxism was influenced by the radical politicisation of the PPP in the 1950s and the subsequent negative racialisation of Guyanese politics, by the Cuban Revolution, the decolonisation movements in Africa and its theoreticians such as Frantz Fanon and Amilcar Cabral and, of course, C.L.R. James' approach to the Marxist legacy as historian and political activist. To this must be added Rodney's own independent reading, research and political experience.

Rodney was not a Marxist-Leninist in the sense of Communist Party orthodoxy as was characteristic of the Marxist-Leninist left in Jamaica, Guyana and Grenada in the late 1970s. In political views and connections he was independent of Moscow and the thinking of the 1970s that was developed by Soviet Third World specialists such as Karen Brutents and Rostislav Ulyanovsky about the prospects of transition to socialism in newly independent countries. Nor was he keen on the Leninist doctrines of vanguard party that had been the focus and practice of much of the WPJ's theorising and which had brought political dividends by 1978 with the attendance of a CPSU delegate at the founding Congress of the WPJ. Further material and political dividends were to follow for the WPJ with financial and educational assistance both at the level of tertiary university education and party ideological schools and the gaining of a seat at the *World Marxist Review* in Prague, Czechoslovakia, in 1980 which made the WPJ and the PPP the two English-speaking Caribbean parties with formal recognition in the international communist movement.

On the other hand, in the 1970s Rodney spoke in terms of Caribbean Marxism and in a 1980 interview he critiqued the Caribbean communists.

> There is still a preference among many of the Third World Marxists and/or radicals for orienting themselves towards a very specific body of theory and

analysis at an international level to the point where it becomes an identification with a particular nation-state. We have attempted very rigorously to avoid that. We believe it is the correct position, but perhaps the correctness of the positions will only show itself in a period of time. We believe that it will be an important lesson for the Caribbean as a whole (Rodney 1980d: 2).

Rodney's insistence on an independent approach to Marxism enabled him to avoid political dogmatism arising from allegiances to either Russian or Chinese Marxism.

Political crisis, 1978–1980

The political crisis which took place in Guyana at the end of the 1970s appeared from the outside as a struggle among socialist parties using the same rhetoric. There were no conservative opposition parties to which Washington could give support and for Cuba, Burnham seemed acceptable, and even in the case of revolutionary Grenada in 1980 it was Burnham who gave the Bishop regime its initial military training, and military cooperation continued throughout the years of the People's Revolutionary Government of Grenada from 1979 to 1983.[33] Rodney appeared to be in an absurdly left position. Jagan's situation one could understand as the father of modern Guyanese nationalism from whom power had been taken through a number of rigged elections and the individual in whom the Indian majority had invested its political aspirations.

The political deterioration of the Burnham regime developed in the mid 1970s and reached crisis proportions by the end of the decade. A major issue arose in 1978 over the Constitution (Amendment) Bill which allowed the government with its two-thirds majority in the National Assembly to change important provisions in the Constitution such as those dealing with parliament and the electoral system without holding a referendum. The opposition forces formed the Committee in Defence of Democracy which included the PPP, WPA, the People's Democratic Movement and the Liberator Party. A number of the trade unions, professional and religious bodies and civic organisations made up the Citizens Committee. The two bodies worked together to oppose the referendum. Much of their attention was focused on exposing the subordination of the electoral machinery to the PNC. Among the issues were the conduct of overseas registration and voting; the organisation of registration at home; the conduct of the poll at home; the custody of the ballot boxes after a poll; the subordination of the nominally independent Elections Commission; freedom of speech; freedom of assembly; and the aggravation of ethnic tensions. In its statement on the 10 July 1978 referendum the WPA noted:

> It has been alleged that there was malpractice in every facet of the referendum procedure, and that there were incidents of violence and intimidation engineered by the regime against the opponents of the constitutional amendment. BUT THE SINGLE MOST IMPORTANT FACT ABOUT THE REFERENDUM OF JULY 10 WAS THE SILENCE OF THE STREETS AS THE PEOPLE OF GUYANA BOYCOTTED THE REFERENDUM AND STAYED HOME (WPA 1978).

The regime, of course, claimed 71.4 percent of the electorate turned out to vote and a 97.4 percent support for the bill that would give Burnham the right to change the constitution as he saw fit since they already had a two-thirds majority in Parliament. In its July 1978 issue, *Dayclean*, the much harassed two-page mimeographed organ of the WPA, presented its own evidence to prove there had been a boycott and estimated the turnout for the country at being no more than 10–15 percent. Independent sources confirmed the low turnout and there was evidence of considerable electoral malpractice (Kempe Hope 1985: 60–61). *Dayclean* July 1978 editorialised:

> Because the 1973 General Election was rigged, the 2/3 majority claimed by the PNC in the House has always been an illegal one. The referendum fraud now opens the way to complete illegality. The regime has extended the life of parliament to act as legislative and constituent assemblies, but that parliament loses all legal right to act in either of those functions at midnight on July 25. From July 26, then, Guyana will be ruled by a legislative body that will be entirely nominated, entirely unconstitutional and entirely illegal, and the so-called Constituent Assembly will itself be no more than an exercise in total illegality.

The WPA also noted the growing use of the military which had been deployed on election day in Georgetown, Linden, and villages that were populated by Afro-Guyanese, indicating that the predominantly Afro-Guyanese military was being used against all sections of the working people irrespective of race. Sharp conflicts continued between the opposition and the government but these did not weaken the political position of the Burham regime which seemed to be committed to the policy that power should be maintained, in the words of Malcolm X, "by any means necessary".

The November 1978 Jonestown tragedy involving the collective suicide-murder ritual of over 900 Americans was further evidence of the extent to which the Burnham regime was linked to unsavoury characters. Gordon Lewis, the distinguished Caribbeanist, noted that "the Guyanese high officialdom, men like Ptolemy Reid and Kit Nascimento, were impressed by Jones; he was a charmer, he knew how to speak the socialist vocabulary" (Lewis 1979: 23). Rodney took the analysis further when he contended:

> If we were to draw attention to the horrendous events of Jonestown, we would see that what occurred there was precisely an act of complicity through neglect on the part of both the US and the Guyanese Governments. The US Government had admitted in its reports that it had done far less than it should have done for US citizens who were at Jonestown and some type of intervention on behalf of those citizens might well have avoided the holocaust. The US Government had admitted this. The Guyanese Government had admitted nothing of the kind. The Guyanese government has treated the whole situation as if it were an everyday affair, as though 914 people die in the bush in Guyana every day. But the people were citizens of the US and were entitled to protection like any citizen abroad, were entitled to protection from their own country as well as from the host country. The Government of Guyana offered them absolutely no protection because it was engaged in its own opportunist links with the leadership of the People's Temple. So what I'm driving at, by drawing attention to that incident, is that the role of the US Government is not one to be taken lightly, not in our hemisphere, not in our country. It's going to continue to have a role, whether we like it or not. The point is if the US Government is going to be allowed to get away with making a lot of pious statements about human rights when, in fact, in this region, it proceeds indirectly to bolster a tyrant whose quality is no different than any dictator who arose in any other part of the world (Rodney 1980d: 3).

US foreign policy had been found wanting in the Jonestown tragedy and so had the Burnham regime. But the US government was prepared to support Burnham because the opposition party was led by Cheddi Jagan and he was a pro-Soviet Marxist-Leninist. After Jonestown the US option in Guyana remained Forbes Burnham; moreover, Burnham and the PNC had the support of the rest of the predominantly Afro-Caribbean political leadership in the region. Whether it was the Americans who committed suicide or the Guyanese people faced with the dictatorial policies of the Burnham regime, the fundamental question posed by Rodney was the issue of democracy and human rights.

Nineteen seventy-eight saw strike actions by bauxite workers, employees of the University of Guyana and the Clerical and Commercial Workers Union which helped to shape the politics of 1979, the year of resistance which culminated in the electoral boycott. No doubt encouraged by the fall of Gairy in Grenada and Somoza in Nicaragua, Guyanese opposition forces were hopeful that Burnham would be next. But Burnham, though having consolidated personal power, could not be politically located either in the Gairy or Somoza camps. Gairy's authoritarianism in Grenada in the 1970s was emerging as a caricature of Haiti's Papa Doc, while Somoza had an anticommunist campaign justifying his terror and murder of the opposition. Burnham was not that type of a leader. His political authoritarianism was similar to other left wing Third World regimes where socialist rhetoric was deployed to disguise the concentration of power in the hands of the political leader and the group around him. Simultaneously, the opposition was repressed and coerced and the weakest co-opted. In the region and in the Third World Burnham had legitimacy and his anti-imperialist sympathies were in many respects no different from those Jagan or Rodney espoused. Moreover, internally he remained in control but was experiencing his most serious political challenge from the WPA and in particular the organising and political work of Rodney among bauxite workers had extended the WPA's base outside of the confines of Georgetown. Rodney's role as a fearless and popular tribune certainly helped to stimulate sectors in the middle class who had been emboldened and were prepared to follow the example of unionised labour in making their opposition to the regime more open. Meanwhile, the PPP stepped up its activity as an opposition party and was active on the labour front.

The assessment made by both Jagan's PPP and the WPA was that Guyana too was on the edge of a revolutionary situation. Jagan published a statement following the Grenadian and Nicaraguan Revolutions in 1979 entitled "Guyana Fast Approaching Revolutionary Situation" (Jagan 1979a).[34] According to Rupert Roopnarine (1996):

> Whatever conclusions Jagan drew from the Nicaraguan and Grenadian revolutions, the PPP argued strenuously in 1979 that a revolutionary situation did not exist in Guyana. The Leninist recipe was frequently invoked to point to the missing ingredients. Jagan's speech at a village on the West Coast of Demarara (Grove) in December during the election campaign went to great lengths to establish the difference in assessment between the PPP and WPA According to Jagan's thesis, WPA and Rodney were being adventurist since the rebellion was premature. In the end, the ideal revolutionary situation was never to arrive but was to remain perpetually imminent.

Caribbean left wing groups had scrupulously studied Lenin's criteria for a revolutionary situation and tried to apply them to their local circumstances, and they were aware of the debates on these matters in the Latin American and African revolutionary movements. They very often overestimated their own political strengths and the consequences of their actions, and had a tendency to underestimate the rootedness of the parties that had been formed a generation before. Moreover, they overestimated their significance as small groups in small states caught up in the Cold War struggle between Washington and Moscow. Adventuristic tendencies were therefore a feature of left wing groups and personalities, including Walter Rodney.

Dayclean, the WPA newssheet of 20 March 1979, had a lead story entitled "De Shah Gone! Gairy Gone! Who Next?"[35] and it ended with the slogan "De Shah Gone! Gairy Gone! Dese Next!" Guyana experienced heightened political activity from the opposition but the strikes, public meetings, arrests and political murders could not be described as constituting a revolutionary situation. Burnham's control of the armed forces was intact and there was little possibility of a breakaway faction joining with the WPA in any insurrection. Moreover, the PPP would not enter into political adventures given the fact that their focus was really on securing a system of free and fair elections which would legitimately put them in office. The period certainly brought Rodney and the WPA and to a lesser extent the PPP to the forefront and was a bold challenge to Burnham's rule.

The turning point in the relations between the WPA and the Burnham regime came on 11 July 1979 when the building housing the office of the General Secretary of the PNC and the Ministry of National Development was set afire. The WPA leaders were the chief suspects, and among those arrested and charged with arson were Walter Rodney; Rupert Roopnarine – filmmaker, poet and literary critic; Omawale – consultant at the UN's Food and Agricultural Organisation; Karen De Souza – young civil servant in the Office of the Prime Minister; Bonita Bone Harris – teacher and WPA activist.

The burning down of the PNC headquarters also marked a change in the relationship between the WPA and the population as it was seen as an act of open defiance. As such, the arrest of the WPA leadership and their trial attracted considerable public attention. While on bail the WPA leaders held many public meetings which attracted several thousand people. On 20 July over 8,000 people attended a WPA rally at Bourda Mall. A week later, on 27 July at a meeting at Louisa Row in South Georgetown, the WPA declared itself a political party and announced a provisional executive with a rotating chairmanship.[36] Among the executive members were Andaiye, Moses Bhagwan, Bonita Harris, Eusi Kwayana, Diana Matthews, Maurice Odle, Wendall Persaud, Bisson Rajkumar, Josh Ramsammy, Walter Rodney, Rupert Roopnarine, Sase Omo, Tacuma Ogunseye and Clive Thomas. This executive was made up predominantly of Afro-Guyanese and Indo-Guyanese middle class intellectuals.

The idea of a rotating chairmanship meant that there was no single leader and moreover, the biracial character of the WPA could better be expressed. This was also part of the efforts of the WPA to develop collective leadership and to distinguish itself from the other two socialist parties whose leaders dominated their parties. But in the post-1979 period Walter Rodney was the personality recognised by the Guyanese people and abroad as the WPA leader.

This was never a perception shared by Rodney or encouraged by him neither did it reflect the internal mechanisms of the leadership. He certainly saw himself as a historian of Africa and the Caribbean, a theoretician of decolonisation and a political activist. Walter Rodney said in 1980 that he never conceptualised himself as a politician in terms of the struggle for power (Rodney 1980d: 2). This applied to other leaders of the WPA. Roopnarine did not conceive of himself abandoning the making of films and the writing of poetry and literary criticism for politics in the professional way that Burnham and Jagan were politicians. In his last speech Rodney compared himself to the nineteenth century Afro-Guyanese medical practitioner, Dr John Rohlehr, and the barrister Louis De Souza who at the end of the nineteenth century fought colonial discrimination and led a reform movement (Rodney 1981b: 149).[37]

Rodney and WPA cadres were more attuned to the politics of a social movement than to party politics and the institutionalisation of politics that had taken place in West Indian politics since political independence. That institutionalisation had been one of the gains of the social movement of the 1930s and 1940s. But no sooner had independence been achieved than another social movement of a somewhat lesser order of the 1960s and 1970s rose to challenge the political order. A social movement has its ups and downs and one type of social movement is replaced by others as people respond to new challenges and issues. Opposition political parties may take up some of the key issues in their programme and parties in power may try to address them. Political parties are equipped to deal with the transition to power through electoral means and in Guyana that role was being played by the PPP and the PNC. In 1979 the WPA was at the stage that the Political Affairs Committee founded by Jagan was at in the late 1940s (Jagan 1972: 64). It was an important agitational group but it would take some time before it could become a political party of consequence and in moments of upsurge such as took place in 1979 the people looked to the WPA and its leadership, not necessarily to replace the dominant parties, but to speak out for them on critical issues and put those issues on the political agenda.

Personalities like Andaiye, Rodney and C.Y. Thomas were well educated and poised if they so desired to benefit from good positions in the PNC regime but they had made certain moral and political choices which were not typical of the mainstream Guyanese middle class. In this regard the moral example of Eusi Kwayana who had served both the PPP and the PNC yet refused to become a typical West Indian middle class politician was very important. The WPA was trying to change the political culture but in terms of the realities of Caribbean and Guyanese politics once one stepped into the arena of the struggle for power it made its own demands.

Andaiye (1989), who functioned in a variety of capacities as party coordinator, editor of *Dayclean*, International Secretary and Women's Secretary of the WPA, worked closely with Rodney in the last two and a half years of his life on political matters as well as assisting him with editing his book, *A History of the Guyanese Working People, 1881–1905*. In 1978 the WPA had been a looser, informal type of structure with relaxed political discussions. There had been some mobilisation around the 1978 referendum but the organisation had no money and no vehicle and had to rely on those who were employed for funds. Andaiye described 1979 as being utterly different from the time of the burning down of the PNC building in July 1979. It was this crisis which had precipitated the launching of the fledgling party. Most of her contact with Rodney had to do with the book he was writing and he was very anxious to get it finished. He worked on it almost every day in the context of public political work and threats to his life. At each public meeting he ran the risk of being beaten, tear-gassed or arrested and after July 1979 he lived in a number of safe houses.

Andaiye pointed out that he was fully involved in the discussion and writing of the 1979 party programme but he was not as fully involved in the debate on the party's constitution. It was not a matter that organisational issues, per se, did not stimulate him, although that may have been a part of it, but he shared with C.L.R. James a hostility to Leninist notions of vanguardism which were popular in left wing circles, especially in the English-speaking Caribbean, in the late 1970s.[38] Rodney's preference was for mass agitation and Rupert Roopnarine spearheaded the work on the constitution and party building efforts. However, Roopnarine (1996) points out that Rodney was "fully in support of the cadre formation: highly motivated cadres, disciplined, with a rigorous division of labour, need to know principles of revolutionary work, round the clock availability and other forms of sacrifice unavailable in less centralist organisations. This was of course a prerequisite in the self-defence security units."

Rodney's democratism is what stood out. For instance, Rodney, as was the case with other WPA leaders, was supportive of the Grenadian Revolution but thought the New Jewel Movement should hold elections. Rodney was opposed to the banning of *Torchlight*, a privately owned newspaper that was critical of Bishop's government. Andaiye said that Walter and Maurice Bishop had meetings in 1979 and Maurice told her that Walter "was a pain in the ass". She continued, "Walter had a strong theoretical position that was totally opposed to notions of parliament and freedom of the press being bourgeois rights" (Andaiye 1989).[39] In explaining Rodney's objection, Andaiye said:

> It was a deeply felt objection to the use of other people's conclusions about their reality as a substitute for thinking about one's own reality. His point was that the rights that left-wing Caribbean people referred to, dismissively, as 'bourgeois-democratic rights' were rights which, in the Caribbean at least, had been fought for and won by working people (Andaiye 1990: 12).

The Grenadian left, as was the case with the Marxist-Leninist left in the Caribbean, used the concept of 'bourgeois democratic' as a tool of analysis. As such while there was enthusiasm in the WPA for the Grenada Revolution, given Burnham's involvement with the New Jewel Movement there were concerns in both the PPP and WPA about how this would benefit Burnham politically within Guyana. In 1979 and 1980, the WPA had no party to party relations with the NJM, although Eusi Kwayana, Rodney and Clive Thomas were highly regarded by the New Jewel Movement. One of the main political conclusions drawn by C.Y. Thomas from the defeat of the Grenadian Revolution had to do with the issue of upholding democratic norms.

> The events surrounding the self-destruction of the revolutionary process in Grenada bear directly on the organisation and future development of political formations among the popular forces of the Caribbean. The first of these is that events which led up to the execution of Maurice Bishop and others clearly indicate the importance which must be attached to the constitutionality, legality and due process, in the legitimisation of political action within the region. The success of the New Jewel Movement and Maurice Bishop Government in gathering support to overthrow the Gairy regime and subsequently capturing the imagination and minds of the West Indian peoples most in favour of the revolutionary process rested largely on their systematic exposure, when in opposition, of Gairy's methods of dictatorial rule and his gross violations of regionally accepted norms of constitutionality, legality and due process. Their subsequent failure to hold 'free and fair elections, and elections free from fear' had always, therefore, tarnished their reputation in the eyes of large sections of the popular forces. This was particularly so because immediately after the successful overthrow of Gairy a pledge was made to hold free and fair elections, to uphold the due process and to protect the human

rights of citizens which Gairy had so grossly and savagely violated (Thomas 1984: 7).

The insistence on this point was not merely a matter of political expediency but one of principle and it is one of the main contributions of the Guyanese left to the reflection on regional politics in the 1970s. The pity is that the critique of the Grenadian process was not made public during the course of Maurice Bishop's government due to self-censorship. As C.Y. Thomas admitted:

It was only fear of splitting ranks in the face of threats of imminent invasion by the USA, as well as what appeared to sympathetic outsiders to be serious efforts to develop alternative forms of so-called direct democracy which had stayed the hands of critics (Thomas 1984: 7).

A peculiarity of the Guyanese political situation, as we have pointed out, was that the three main parties were socialist. In the eyes of the WPA the PNC's socialism was pseudosocialism and the PPP's was bound up too much with the Brezhnevite model of socialism. The PPP had not done sufficient creative thinking on the specifics of the Guyanese situation as the writings of Jagan[40] and the pages of *Thunder*, the party's theoretical journal, and *Mirror*, the party newspaper, show. Jagan's published work shows a strong preference for analysis of the international situation but analysis of the national scene and alternatives do not go beyond anti-Burnhamism and the 'true' socialism of the PPP. The situation certainly created problems for all three parties as far as their relationship with the radical bloc of countries were concerned. The PPP and the PNC had good connections with the then socialist countries as well as the Non-Aligned Movement. These countries tended to ignore the repressive domestic policies being pursued by the Burnham regime. Burnham was thus in a strong position to respond to the challenges posed by the opposition. His sense was that the WPA and Rodney would be prepared to take steps outside the constitutional framework to undermine and even remove him from power while the PPP and Jagan would not take that course. For his part, Rodney had maintained the position that "if a situation has become intolerable and if all avenues for peaceful change have become exhausted, then violence would be the logical result" (Rodney 1980e: 12).[41] On the other hand, the main issue for Jagan was how to get free and fair elections, while the main issue for Burnham was how to perfect the system which kept Jagan in opposition. Thus Rodney appeared to Burnham as the fly in the ointment of a carefully worked out arrangement for maintaining power.

Burnham was therefore on the warpath in 1979 and at his Party Congress he had reportedly said "we shall match steel with more highly tempered steel" (Andaiye 1989). The opposition, particularly the WPA, was taking the fight to him. During the arson trial the WPA leadership was on centre stage and the repression continued. Some 500 persons gathered outside the court on 14 July when Rodney, Roopnarine and Omawale appeared in court and were charged with arson. WPA supporters were attacked by thugs of the infamous House of Israel. Father Bernard Darke, Jesuit priest and photographer for the *Catholic Standard*, was fatally stabbed in the back. Michael James, editor of the *Catholic Standard*, and his wife along with others were beaten. Two WPA activists, Ohene Koama and Edward Dublin, were also killed in the months before Rodney's murder. Ohene Koama was killed on 18 November 1979 and the official story was that he had "attempted to shoot at a police party which had supposedly discovered two missing army rifles in the trunk of his car". The WPA claimed that Koama was unarmed and that he was killed in cold blood (GNFA and LACAP 1980: 7). On 25 February 1980 Edward Dublin who had been Rodney's bodyguard was shot by the police outside "the Bird Palace nightclub in Linden" (GNFA and LACAP 1980: 10). The police stories on Dublin's killing varied from allegations that Dublin had been caught housebreaking to the charge that he had been stealing cement from a cinema construction site and was shot while resisting arrest.

As in his analysis of George Jackson's legacy and the political transformation of criminals into politically aware activists, Rodney used Dublin's life to exemplify this process in Guyana. Rodney referred to Dublin who came from the bauxite area of Linden when he said:

Many of you in Georgetown would not know that brother who was executed by a section of the police carrying out the orders of this regime, for political reasons. Now normally when a brother falls in the struggle, there are some political movements which try to suggest that he was a saint, that he was a perfect human being, that he was always an angel from the time of his birth. We . . . suggest nothing of the kind. What we do know is that Brother Edward Dublin was what you would call a 'street force', a brother who had been kicked out of the work force at Linden and when you get kicked out of the work force the only force you can join is the street force. So the brother was on the street force, and what was important while he was hustling a living was that he managed to acquire a certain political awareness, decided that it wasn't worth the while getting into petty crime and getting into conflict with the police. He decided that he would never again lend his services to be bought off as a mercenary and a thug by the regime. And because this brother took that stand, he became a threat to the PNC and the ruling class and their representatives in the Wismar/McKenzie area, and he was executed. What I am trying to say is simply this: The revolution is made by ordinary people, not by angels, made by people from all walks of life, and more particularly by the working class who are in the majority. And it is a sign of the times, a sign of the power of revolutionary transformation, when a street force member is developed into a fighting cadre in a political movement (Rodney 1981b: 5–6).

The murders of Dublin, Darke and Koama were symptomatic of the dangers facing politically active opponents of the Burnham regime. The Guyanese poet, Martin Carter, former political colleague of Forbes Burnham, in his open letter published in *Dayclean*, summed up the moral and ethical issues in the political situation.

> The PNC's method of ensuring self-perpetuation consists of indulging in a deliberate policy of degrading people. And the reasoning behind this is that degraded people are incapable of effective resistance.
> Of this policy, the following examples should be kept in mind. Item: In the rigging of elections in which many ordinary and by no means vicious people were cajoled into doing indecent things, and were thereby compromised. Item:
> In corruption as a way of life, in which people were made to accept that stealing, cheating, lying, bearing false witness, informing on each other was a positive sign of loyalty to the regime; ... And the greatest damage done ... is to young people who are led to believe that they can do anything, no matter how selfish, how intolerant, how mindless, how coarse, since they identify this attitude with the attitude the regime underwrites (Carter 1979: 2).

This was Martin Carter's indictment of the Burnham regime which he had served. Carter himself was beaten up by thugs loyal to the regime. It is against the background of Carter's depiction of Burnham's regime that Rodney's political speeches and the wit deployed in them can be better understood.

A feature of Rodney's speeches was that they attacked the degradation of life in Guyana and the bullying of Burnham. For fear of political victimisation many voiced their criticism in private but were afraid to air their views in public. But Rodney and the WPA led the way in this public criticism of Burnham and ridiculed him. In the pamphlet *People's Power, No Dictator* Rodney had exasperatedly propounded that the language of political opposition

> must express not only ridicule but anger and disgust. The dictatorship has reduced us all to such a level that the situation can be described only in terms befitting filth, pollution and excrement. Even our deep-rooted sense of modesty in Guyana cannot stand in the way of rough words to describe the

nation's shame. That is why the WPA repeats the legend of King Midas who was said to have been able to touch anything and turn it into gold. That was called the 'Midas touch'. Now Guyana has seen the 'Burnham Touch' – anything he touches turns to shit (Rodney 1979a: 14).

In a 1979 speech Rodney recalled that at a political meeting at Bourda an old woman had said "Burnham mek Satan cry" (Rodney 1979a: 6). These jokes always evoked laughter from the crowd especially when he spoke about Burnham's version of the Midas touch. This was vintage West Indian political campaigning. But the jokes were also on Rodney in that once during this period he had to run from a public meeting and Burnham referred to his athletic prowess.

As regards that incident on 22 August when Rodney was addressing a meeting, Eusi Kwayana had this to say.[42]

> A squad of uniformed policemen, including Rabbi Washington's men dressed in police uniform and carrying no regulation numbers, attacked the meeting which they claimed was illegal. It was a total assault with batons on the crowd of peaceful citizens by a crowd of well armed policemen of the Tactical Service Unit (Riot Squad). Soon the crowd burst and scattered from the meeting point at Delph Street and Campbell Ave and dashed for Middleton Street and then across it to Kitty. Scores of people were beaten by the police. They were on fire with a venom not noticed before. This was due to the House of Israel. Brother Moses Bhagwan who took refuge with some livestock in a nearby yard was dragged out and beaten, ending with a broken arm. After that he was arrested and charged. This led to a lawyers' strike the next day. Mr Burnham commented on the incident the following Sunday as he spoke to a rally closing the Third Biennial Congress of the ruling party. He identified himself clearly with the police action by saying it was rude of the Worst Possible Alternative (WPA) to hold a meeting just two corners off from Sophia where the opening session of his Congress was being held. He also commented on Rodney's prowess as an athlete and promised to send him to the Olympics (Kwayana 1988: 15).

When a reporter asked Rodney about the incident he pointed to the fact that he had almost been set upon by thugs disguised as policemen and jokingly said, "Fortunately, some of the skills I had as a youth had not entirely disappeared and I was able to use them" (Rodney 1980e: 12). In fact, at a certain level there was a personal rivalry going on between Burnham and Rodney which ended in the latter's death.

Political rhetoric was a means towards action. Rodney never doubted the capacity of the Guyanese people for mass action and he felt strongly that what the regime was doing was demoralising to the population. Many Guyanese activists, ranging from middle class professionals to bauxite workers as well as activists of Indo-Guyanese and Afro-Guyanese extraction I interviewed, spoke highly of the political-educational work Walter conducted in the bottom-houses. Eusi Kwayana summed it up when he wrote:

> his political students, including my wife, did not leave his courses spouting slogans and quotations from the great masters, but with some competence in the art of examining the social relations and trying to discover the social motion, or at least with a sense of the need to do this as an important political task. His students left his courses interested in discovering the story of the oppressed classes . . . and learning of their efforts and limited successes in the destiny of self-emancipation for which, Rodney taught, there was no substitute (Kwayana 1988: 4).

Rodney himself commented on his educational work in a letter to friends:

> One of the more rewarding achievements of recent weeks is that I have been able to start two Marxist study groups: one at my home and another at Linden. The latter is purely working class and was at the request of some very advanced workers who have already done a great deal of reading. The one at my home is more diluted with respect to class elements, but the whole society can and will benefit from more scientific insights. Besides, as the consequence of deliberate efforts in that direction, the group includes four sisters – their absence having been noteworthy in previous efforts (Rodney 1975e).

Rodney's work among bauxite workers, who had already started their own Organisation of Working People, was his most important practical contribution to the building of the WPA. Kwayana assessed Rodney's contribution in this area thus:

> His work among the bauxite workers was more concentrated and more intensive. Two things made it so. They had only three main locations or communities – Mackenzie, Kwakwani, Everton with Ituni as a very small township. Secondly their best elements had organised themselves into the Organisation of the Working People (OWP) sometime before. This organisation was able to organise classes running many weeks with both C.Y. Thomas for labour economics and Walter Rodney for classes in political economy and revolution, with others of us holding a class or two as reliefs or on special themes. His work among the sugar workers was less intensive and less thorough. The WPA went to the sugar estates in those days mainly by

invitation. For the sake of good understanding and mutual trust between us and the PPP we avoided establishing bases in the sugar estates. Not only the PNC, but the PPP also had fears of, and misgivings about, the long-term effect of WPA agitation and organisation in the sugar belt – and in the case of the PNC, the bauxite belt (Kwayana 1988: 8–9).

Eusi Kwayana described the educational work conducted by Rodney and C.Y. Thomas among bauxite workers as being very intensive (Kwayana 1988: 8). Thomas lectured in labour economics and Rodney taught political economy and the history of revolutions. Braving political victimisation, workers recalled the bottom-house study groups that were held on Sunday mornings for periods lasting several weeks (Afrani 1989). They recall Rodney travelling in his red Mini-Minor, not only giving classes in the homes of workers but overnighting with their families.[43] Ninteen seventy-nine was a rough period for these workers as the WPA-oriented workers were retrenched and in December, 42 of them were imprisoned for their involvement in strike and protest activities during August.

The story behind this was that bauxite workers had gone on strike in mid July to end the wage freeze on the public sector and 20,000 sugar workers had gone on a solidarity strike in August (GNFA 1980: 2–3). In this period of heightened political activity Rodney threw himself fully into the political struggles, risking his life in the same way that was being done by many of his comrades and many working people. On 13 September Rodney and four other persons were arrested in Leonara, West Demerara, "during a roadblock search for arms and ammunition" (GNFA 1980: 5). They spent twenty hours in detention "during which time Rodney's home was ransacked and political literature seized. Eventually all were released without charge" (GNFA 1980: 5). On 3 October Rodney was arrested once more in Linden "supposedly for the distribution of 'subversive literature'; however, after being held in custody for several hours he was released without charge" (GNFA 1980: 6). From 24 to 26 October, court hearings took place and Magistrate Fung Kee Fung granted the prosecution's application for a summary trial in which Walter Rodney, Rupert Roopnarine and Omawale were charged with arson. The Magistrate employed the Administration of Justice Act of 1978 under which the three men were denied the right to trial by jury. Travel restrictions were also imposed on most of the WPA leaders.

By November 1979 Rodney wrote that there was a lull in public, street activity and he attributed this to three factors:

the seizure of some of our cars and public address equipment by the police . . . the burning of one of our vehicles by the police. [Secondly, the WPA had decided to] put more of our energies into the work of party-building, and into bilateral negotiations with party and non-party groups on the question of a Government of National Unity. And thirdly, from our unwillingness to allow the state to consume our time and energy in this period in the endless round of court appearances that were resulting, and would continue to result from our confrontations with the police at every picket, demonstration or 'illegal' public meeting (Rodney, 1984: 133).

The politics of national unity promoted by the WPA assumed an alliance with the PPP.

In his letter of 2 May 1980 to friends in Hamburg he had written:

The lull in street activity has led to some sense of frustration and to loss of momentum in the mass movement. There is a feeling of the moment not being seized. While this view overestimates the possibilities of that period, it is true that the leadership – whether of the other left political party, the progressive trade unions or of the other anti-dictatorial parties and groups – did not see the possibilities that were present in the simultaneous explosion of mass militancy and worker action; they were in fact, overwhelmed by their sense that in the face of all this, the power of the state nevertheless remained intact (Rodney 1984: 134).

What these possibilities were, are not set out in the letter. Rodney was concerned with the ability of the WPA to gain strength politically and to prevent the movement from going into a trough of despair and his comments on the weakening of the state are important in that the Afro-Guyanese middle strata were expressing their criticism of the regime more openly, and to the extent that Rodney was a symbol of this disaffection among Afro-Guyanese, he was attacking the core of racial loyalty to the Burnham regime. It was Rodney's attack on black political opportunism that made him feared and hated. He himself commented on this Achilles heel of the governing party.

The real weakening of the state is, however, becoming clearer now. As it struggles to maintain itself in power without popular support, it is forced to resort to a strategy that alienates the very groups on which it must rely. Managers, corporation heads and civil servants are protesting, resigning or being fired in a developing conflict between their own sense of 'professionalism' and the regime's insistence on their toeing the party line. The regime has reorganised the police force and the army under loyal leadership; but its inability to trust the official armed services is leading to a growth in the number and size of its private armies; and this is itself a further impetus to the alienation of elements in the official forces. There is dissension in the ranks of the ruling party's leadership over how best to 'manage' the growing crisis (Rodney 1984: 134–35).

Rodney therefore pleaded with his friends in Hamburg "not to put the struggle in Guyana on the back burner in favour of those countries in which the progress of struggle was more obvious, and therefore more newsworthy" (Rodney 1984: 135).

Rodney was arrested on several other occasions in the period 1979–1980, and in the last several months of his life had virtually moved from house to house to escape harassment as he continued to travel throughout the country doing political work. Rodney even left Guyana illegally in February 1980 for Europe and Africa and returned sometime in May. His departure through Suriname to Europe and then to Tanzania and his turning up at Zimbabwe's independence celebrations[44] as an honoured guest was a shock to Burnham who himself was in attendance for the occasion. Much to Burnham's surprise Rodney not only turned up in Harare, but was given VIP treatment, when he should have been marooned in Guyana! In fact, during Rodney's visit to Zimbabwe he received an invitation to head the Institute of Development Studies at the University in Zimbabwe. Later, in his statement condemning Rodney's murder, Prime Minister Robert Mugabe of Zimbabwe disclosed that he had met with Rodney on 16 May and discussed plans for him to write a history of Zimbabwe.[45] Rodney's visit to Zimbabwe also had the political objective of gaining political support, and according to some sources,[46] he also sought weapons for the growing struggle in Guyana against the authoritarian regime but he was not successful in this mission.

Rodney was struck down when there was a lull in public activity and when the regime's popular base had been undermined, but it had sufficient strength to govern and sufficient regional and international recognition to be accepted as a legitimate regime. This lull in public activity enabled the regime to intensify its repression against the opposition, using both legal and extra-legal mechanisms. The issue of *Dayclean* which was published on 13 June 1980 had detailed the harassment of the period from 31 May to 12 June, especially of individuals in the leadership and supporters of the WPA. The newssheet reported that 39 persons had been arrested on "suspicion of political action" in support of the opposition. Thirty homes were searched for arms and ammunition and political literature put out by the opposition and one person was threatened because he had a book written by Walter Rodney. Rodney's assassination was the centrepiece of an intensive period of beatings, imprisonment and general harassment of WPA leaders and supporters by the Forbes Burnham regime.[47] His assassination on 13 June

1980 by an ex-officer of the Guyana Defense Force put an end to the life of one of the most creative Caribbean scholar-activists of the 1960s and 1970s and enabled the PNC regime to continue in power for over a decade with negative social, economic, political and moral consequences for the Guyanese people. It would not be until 1992 that a fair election was held in Guyana and the People's National Congress would be defeated and replaced by Cheddi Jagan's People's Progressive Party.

The political-moral imperatives of the Guyanese situation drew Rodney and others into combat with Burnham. To the Caribbean left, inclusive of the social democratic People's National Party of Jamaica and the Communist Party of Cuba, Burnham was an ally, a fact which isolated Rodney and the WPA in the region. Burnham also had the strong support of the United States.[48]

On the other hand, Rodney in the 1979–80 period became a symbol of resistance to an authoritarian and corrupt regime. At Rodney's funeral, George Lamming, the Barbadian novelist, was to voice this moral imperative when he said in the church:

> Today, we meet in a dangerous land, and at the most dangerous of times. The danger may be that supreme authority, the supervising conscience of the nation, has ceased to be answerable to any moral law, has ceased to recognise or respect any moral law, has ceased to recognise or respect any minimum requirement of ordinary human decency (Lamming 1992: 184).

In a memorial speech in London C.L.R. James declared that

> Rodney was absolutely made to get rid of Burnham and take his position. He was a great scholar, he was an international scholar, and he hadn't been mixed up in Guyanese politics before. He wasn't mixed up at all. He was absolutely new and Burnham would know that, and therefore, I warned them to be careful, 'be sure that you guard Rodney from assassination'. I thought that might have helped; it didn't help (James 1980: 30).

C.L.R. James was not only Rodney's mentor; he was his sharpest critic. He was of the opinion that

> Walter had not studied the taking of power. I am going to emphasize that, because you *have* to do that. The taking of power has to become the common discussion among the Caribbean people and intellectuals so that all will know it; so that, as young people grow up and develop and begin to look at history, they begin to see not only what has been done to us, but what we have done, what we have achieved, and what we have to do (James 1982: 135).

Given C.L.R. James' line of reasoning, was he inclined to the view that Rodney was a political adventurist? This was certainly the dominant critique of sections of the regional left of the 1970s, as I have pointed out. James continued:

> He recognised that Burnham meant mischief and that he was prepared to use all power, the armed power of the state, to destroy the opposition. Rodney knew that and he tried to organise against it. And he organised wrong. A key problem in the face of overwhelming state power is how to arm oneself against it. In fact, the arms for a revolution are there: the police and the army have them. What you have to do is to win over a section of the army, and you have arms. And you also take away arms from the government.
>
> A revolution is made with arms, but a revolution is made by the revolutionary spirit of the great mass of the population. And you have to wait for that (James 1982: 138).

This last sentence about waiting is the key to understanding James' critique. And it is, of course, connected to his view that the situation in Guyana was not ripe for a revolutionary overthrow of the Burnham regime.

> But they were not really ready in Guyana when Walter was there to lead them. It can come with sudden speed, but you must wait for it . . . he took on all sorts of activities, on the conception that he had to show them that he was not asking anybody to do anything that he would not do himself.
>
> That is why Walter found himself in a car with a member of Burnham's army making some arrangements about some gadget that turned out to be an explosive. *He never should have been there.* No political leader had any right to be there. Not only should he never have been there, the people around him should have seen to it that he was not in any such position. That was a fundamental mistake, and it was a political mistake. It was not a mistake in personal judgement. It was because he was doing all sorts of things to show them that a revolutionary is prepared to do anything. And that was not the way (James 1982: 139).

James and Rodney differed in their assessment of the significance of the 1979–80 period. James looked at the Guyanese political situation in 1979–80 through a Leninist interpretation of mass insurrection and his own vast political experience. But James' invocation of Leninist insurrectionary wisdom is persuasive. If Rodney had followed James' advice he would probably have saved his life but that advice failed to account for the specifics of the Burnham dictatorship and why Rodney felt compelled to confront it the way he did. Rodney felt compelled to confront the Burnham regime in the same way that he was calling on the working people to do. He did not feel that he could call on them to go on the front lines while he put out position statements from afar in the United States or Europe or elsewhere in the Caribbean. It was a moral position not a Leninist one. Political opposition involved risks and he undertook the simple task of securing a 'walkie-talkie' but the device handed to him exploded as he tried to test it, killing him instantly. Andaiye, who was one of his closest political colleagues and personal friends, had a different concern from James.

> For me what Walter misread wasn't Burnham. What worried me was his misreading of that category of person called lumpen. Always open. He was very excited by people who had come to see that Guyana was dread.[49] A category who would get to speak to him quite easily was the ex-soldier which is what this boy claimed to be and from a relatively poor background and so on. He had all the things to attract. Rodney misread him. He had mentioned him to me, a few weeks before, as an ex-soldier who had electronic skills. He knew that he was walking a thin line but he felt so strongly that the awe and fear of Burnham had to be combatted (Andaiye 1989).

Andaiye's testimony comes closest to an appreciation of why Rodney felt he had to take the risks that eventually led to him becoming a victim of the regime. It is on the level of the mundane activity of conducting opposition politics in Guyana, in the act of securing a walkie-talkie and in the decision of the regime to eliminate, not only small political fish but a big one, that the reasons for Rodney's tragic end may lie.

Death

At 5 p.m. on Friday, 13 June 1980 Pat "dropped off Walter at an executive meeting of the WPA and went on to a fund-raising film show". He told her not to bother to pick him up as he would most likely get home before her.[50] At 7.30 p.m. his younger brother Donald picked him up and in five to ten minutes drove him near the home of Gregory Smith, a former member of the Guyana Defence Force, where Walter was to receive a walkie-talkie. Donald Rodney had kept in touch with Gregory Smith on behalf of his brother and had reported on his progress with the walkie-talkie sets.[51] Smith had made several promises to deliver the sets but had proven unreliable. Friday, 13 June was the date that had been set to test finally whether Smith could deliver since he had claimed to be a radar and electronics technician. Some of Walter's closest colleagues have said he was too trusting of people and that there were other people who could have been asked to undertake the task of checking on the walkie-talkies. He had made a bad political judgement on Smith, taking him for someone who was prepared to assist his political efforts. Moreover, not being a superstitious person, Friday, 13 June had no significance. Donald's testimony went as follows:

> The purpose of my visit to Smith on the night of June 13, 1980 was to collect one walkie-talkie set for testing. When I went to his home, Smith came to the door and appeared surprised at seeing me. He asked me where Walter was, I told him that Walter was around the corner. He asked me if we were walking or driving and whether we would test the set in the car or on foot. I replied that Walter would decide that. He told me the set was ready. He then went inside. I remained at the door. Smith returned with an object in his hand. The object was in a brown paper bag. He pointed to a knob on one side of the object; by pressing the paper bag against it, the knob protruded. He explained that the set would be tested at two positions. After the first test, the knob was to be turned. He demonstrated by turning the knob clockwise. He made me repeat the action (Donald Rodney 1980).

Donald had no reason to suspect that Smith was handing him a time bomb and not a walkie-talkie set.

Smith gave Donald directions where he should go to carry out the first test, and the second test was to take place outside the Georgetown prison which was nearby. Smith said that he "wanted to observe whether the transmission would be interfered with by the extensive metal wall". Smith and Rodney stepped out of the house and into the street light where they synchronised their watches at 7.50 p.m. The first test was to take place at 8 p.m. Smith handed Donald the set.

> I left the yard with the package in my hand and returned to my motor car. I went into the driver's seat and told Walter, who was still sitting on the left side front seat that we should start walking immediately and I would relay Smith's instructions as we walked. He said that we should drive. I replied that the instructions included walking along Camp St. He said that we would drive along Adelaide Street as he didn't think the difference mattered. I agreed and handed over the package to him and then started the car.
>
> As I drove on to Broad St. I explained that we were required to make trials at two positions: the first, at Princess St. at 8 o'clock and the second some time after by the prison. We waited until 8 o'clock. At 8 o'clock by my watch Walter looked down at the package which he held in his lap. The signal light flashed. Walter remarked that was very good. I then reminded him to turn the knob

which he immediately did. I then drove off north along John Street across D'Urban St. and passed the prison. I parked the car on the western side of John St. approximately 20 yards from Hadfield St. and turned off the ignition and all the lights.

We waited for a signal from the package. There was no signal. Within a minute from the time I parked the vehicle, Walter started saying something in reference to Gregory. I turned slightly to look through the driver's window which was open. Suddenly, I heard a loud noise and at the same time I felt my body being twisted against the driver's door which flew open. I became blinded on the left side, and became aware of the dashboard lights coming on. There was no feeling in either of my hands, even though I instinctively raised both hands to secure my spectacles as I was getting out of the car.

I realised then that there had been an explosion on Walter's side of the car and that he was seriously injured. I thought immediately of getting help for him. I pushed back the driver's door with one hand and ran north along John St. to the home of Dr Omowale on Croal St. When I arrived there I shouted and the door was opened by someone whom I told that something terrible had happened in my car at John and Hadfield Sts. and that Walter was still there and needed help. I went upstairs and then realised that I was bleeding profusely. I told Andaiye and Karen (de Souza) to go to the scene . . . (Donald Rodney 1980: 1–2).

On the night of Rodney's assassination the home of his mother, Mrs Pauline Rodney, was searched for arms and ammunition and his own home was searched in the presence of his widow and children. Statements by the Burnham regime following Rodney's death claimed that he and his brother, Donald, were on their way to blow up the Georgetown jail and the device went off prematurely (Mentus 1980: 38). And pamphlets appeared in Georgetown saying: "He who lives by the bomb shall die by the bomb. Rodney blows himself up on the way to blow up prison. WPA don't look for scapegoats now" (Mentus 1980: 38). Another pamphlet was headed "To Walter" and it read:

Hickory Dickory, Doc/ Appointment at 8 o'clock/We wouldn't need no bail/ When we done with the jail/And this walkie-talkie start talk. Rockabye Rodney now lives in the past/ Dispatched to his master so quick and so fast/ Twas never the intention that his fiendish invention/Would choose his own lap for the blast (Mentus 1980: 41).

Gregory Smith was flown out of Guyana on a army helicopter on 16 June and some years later was traced by journalist Rickey Singh to French Guiana where he was working with a fishing company (Singh 1994).[52] Several days later Forbes Burnham appeared on Trinidad and Tobago television speaking on the issue with "smug complacency", underlining his message that Rodney had taken his own life.

The murder of Walter Rodney, at age 38, shocked the region and was a severe blow in personal, political and academic terms. His friend and one of the Caribbean's leading literary critics and cultural historians, Gordon Rohlehr, best summed it up as "a devastating body blow to an entire generation; the literal reduction to ashes of passion, energy, commitment, courage, laughter and intelligence" (Rohlehr 1991: 6). Comparing Rodney's 1968 expulsion from Jamaica with his murder in Guyana in 1980, Rohlehr wrote:

> Jamaica made him into an issue: not the issue that Shearer defined – that of Rodney being a security risk – but the question of how was the academic to translate analysis of society into political action, and thereby rescue intellectual activity from being a sort of privileged paralysis. Guyana, with the barbarism that has been the norm of political activity there for the last twenty years, answered the question by annihalating him (Rohlehr 1980: 1).

The Caribbean region went into mourning and over 35,000[53] people joined in the funeral procession which ended in Georgetown. The turnout to the funeral of the Guyanese people and representatives from the region's political and social organisations fully justified Kamau Brathwaite's line in his poem to Walter Rodney, "the caribbean bleeds near georgetown prison" (Brathwaite 1983: 68).[54] Rodney's body

> was taken twelve miles out of Georgetown to a village on the East Coast, Demarara, called Buxton from where it would begin its journey in procession back to the city. Why Buxton? This is a village that holds revolutionary memories for the Guyanese people. It was named for the anti-slavery campaigner Charles Buxton, and it was one of the villages that the slaves pooled their money to buy (Mentus 1980: 48).

Memorial events were held in the United States, Germany, Britain, Tanzania and Nigeria and statements were made by several Caribbean governments, among them the Jamaican government of Prime Minister Manley, the Communist Party of Cuba, the Antiguan government and the Grenadian government of Prime Minister Maurice Bishop.[55]

Rodney's murder took place during a downturn in the popular movement and notwithstanding the slogan of the WPA which went "Don't mourn, Organise" his murder had the required impact of achieving Burnham's objective of intimidating the opposition. As Ric Mentus pointed out:

Those who had expected Rodney's death and the circumstances surrounding it would have sparked a violent revolution among the people will be disappointed. It is not that the people are cowards or complacent. It is just that they know with a certainty those outside will never have, that the day they take to the streets in protest is the day their blood will wash the pavements, mowed down with the same callousness and smug complacency that those who saw the Burnham interview on TTT (Trinidad and Tobago Television) must remember[56] (Mentus 1980: 41).

While the period following the expulsion of Rodney from Jamaica in 1968 saw a regional political upsurge in radical politics, 1980 was a turning point of a different kind that was influenced by a shift to the right. There was the election of Ronald Reagan in the United States and the electoral defeat of Michael Manley in Jamaica in 1980. The Grenada Revolution lasted for a further three years before factional disputes within the leadership of the New Jewel Movement led to the murder of Maurice Bishop and provided a pretext for the American invasion which put an end to the regime. By the end of the decade not only was the regional left in disarray but Eastern European communism had crumbled and the Cuban Revolution itself began its descent into a penurious economic state and once more became dependent, as is the case with other Caribbean states, on private foreign capital. These circumstances pose new challenges to the peoples of the region and require the reconsideration of the role of its intellectuals. In making this evaluation Rodney's intellectual and political legacy has an important place. That legacy has deep roots in two important struggles. These are, first, his efforts to understand the role of Africa and African peoples in the development of the modern world over the past half a millennium and the negative impact of that role on African peoples themselves in the form of our own underdevelopment. Secondly, there are his efforts to define his role as a West Indian or Caribbean intellectual participating in the late twentieth century postcolonial struggles. With regard to this latter role he was constantly clarifying what this meant for him in his sojourns in Jamaica, Tanzania and at home in Guyana. His work constitutes an important chapter in the radical West Indian intellectual tradition that concerned itself both with regional issues as well as with freedom in Africa.

Calls for an investigation into the circumstances of his death have been made since 1980 but no action was taken until 1994.[57] The vigil of his son, Shaka Rodney, outside the Chambers of the Attorney General in January 1994, once more brought to public attention the need for the government (this time of Cheddi Jagan) to initiate an inquiry into the circumstances of Walter's death and such a commitment was made.[58] After the election of Cheddi

Jagan's PPP in 1992 Guyana belatedly gave official recognition to Rodney with the decision to establish a professorial chair to honour his memory and scholarship.[59] He has also been posthumously awarded Guyana's highest honour, the Order of Excellence.[60]

NOTES

1. See Pantin (1990), Meeks (1977), and Ryan (1989) for descriptions and analyses of the February 1970 demonstrations in Trinidad which almost led to the fall of the Eric Williams regime.
2. Jagan became President of Guyana in 1992 after the first fair election in nearly 30 years. He died on 6 March 1997 after suffering a heart attack.
3. The critiques made by Cheddi Jagan and Walter Rodney of Burnham are quite unlike the debates between Jamaican political leaders Michael Manley and Edward Seaga in the 1970s and 1980s. Jagan and Rodney spend a lot of time saying that Burnham is not a true socialist, he is an opportunist, he is debasing socialism, he is corrupt, and his rule is authoritarian etc. While Jagan was politically close to Havana and Moscow, Burnham also had exceptionally good ties there as well. His links with Washington and London were also intact as he exploited the anticommunist card used against Jagan. In London and Washington Burnham was the better of two evils. In Havana and Moscow Jagan and Burnham were accepted as socialists and as anti-imperialist politicians.
4. I am grateful to Rupert Roopnarine for this comment contained in his report on the Guyana chapter of this book.
5. See Roopnarine (1996).
6. See "For Walter Rodney" in Martin Carter (1989). Carter was a poet with a philosophical style and it is not easy to deconstruct this poem. Each reading offers a different perspective.
7. See foreword by Martin Carter to Forbes Burnham (1970). This collection represents Burnham at his best. The decade of the 1970s saw the cynical abuse of power coupled with the use of an increasingly turgid socialist rhetorical style.
8. Burnham (1970).
9. Burnham (1970).
10. Burnham (1970: xii).
11. In 1982 the population of Guyana was 803,000. East Indians made up 51 percent of the population and Africans 31 percent, Creoles 11 percent, Amerindians 5 percent, Chinese and Portuguese percent, others 1 percent. See Latin American Bureau (1984: 7).
12. M. N. Roy was an Indian Communist of the 1920s and 1930s and J. Nehru was the nationalist Anglophile politician who led India to independence in 1947.
13. Colin Cholmondeley said his father had been Burnham's close friend and advisor for many years. His father had been former President of the Teachers' Association, Headteacher, Chief Education Officer and retired early to run the PNC office and electoral campaigns. He died in 1971. At the time of the interview, Colin Cholmondeley, a former insurance executive, was a management consultant.

14. Percy Hintzen offers a good comparative discussion of ethnicity and politics in Trinidad and Guyana. He argues that political leaders in developing countries face a "conflict between the prerequisites for satisfying the collective needs of society on the one hand and the imperative of servicing the power, security, exploitative, and accumulative interests of metropolitan actors and their local allies, dependents, and clients on the other" (Hintzen 1989: 1).
15. While the PPP saw the 1968 election as a fraudulent one, UWI political scientist J.E. Greene argued that the PNC benefited from "a switch of party support across the traditional lines of race" (Greene 1974: v).
16. See Janet Jagan (1973).
17. For brief discussion on the Abeng group and its political significance see Lewis (1997).
18. See Trevor Munroe (1972).
19. Cuban officials who attended the conferences of the People's National Party and the Workers' Party of Jamaica in the 1970s always stressed the political peculiarities of their revolution and had an appreciation of the importance of the left working within the Westminster political system which the English-speaking Caribbean had inherited.
20. In a speech made at the Caribbean Unity Conference held at Howard University on 21 April 1972, Rodney said:

    Take James who is sitting beside me. He admits, as does Nkrumah, as does Nyerere, that the movement towards African independence went faster and further than they could envisage. They did not see that the masses were going that far and that fast. Just recently after I had left the Caribbean, back in Africa, I kept saying to myself – Jamaica first, the forces are ready . . . Trinidad and Guyana, we have to wait. But the people of Trinidad did not wait. They moved (Rodney 1972e: 6).

    Rodney was referring to the 1970 uprising in Trinidad.
21. Certainly the US blockade of Cuba of over three decades has contributed in large measure to the economic crisis and the stalemate in the political system.
22. See Cheddi Jagan (1975).
23. See Jorge Castaneda *Utopia Unarmed: the Latin American Left After the Cold War* (New York: Alfred A. Knopf 1993) 83, for discussion of this document and its implications for communist parties in Latin America. "The Declaration of the Meeting of Communist Parties of Latin America and the Caribbean" was published by the PPP in Guyana and in Jamaica it was serialised in *Socialism* – theoretical organ of the Workers' Liberation League – September, October and November 1975. *Socialism* had a circulation among left wing groups in the English-speaking Caribbean and this article was used in study group discussions. This document was important in helping to shape a more supportive attitude of the Marxist-Leninist left in Jamaica towards the Manley administration.
24. C.L.R. James wrote about the Arusha Declaration of Julius Nyerere in passionate terms.

    I was able to pass into Tanzania and read, hear and see for myself what was going on. I remain now, as I was then, more than ever convinced that once again something new had come out of Africa, pointing out the road not only for Africa and Africans but for all those seeking to lift ourselves from the parlous conditions of our collapsing century (James 1977: 24).

    He referred to the Arusha Declaration "as something new in the history of political thought" (James 1977: 218). James concluded:

socialist thought has seen nothing like this since the death of Lenin in 1924, and its depth, range and the repercussions which flow from it, go far beyond the Africa which gave it birth. It can fertilise and reawaken the mortuary that is socialist theory and practice in the advanced countries . . . " (James 1977: 223)

James was also very enthusiastic about Michael Manley in the 1970s. With reference to Manley's 1976 Speech to the 38th Annual Conference of the People's National Party on 19 September 1976, James said, "I would like to say that in fifty years of political activity and interest in all sorts of politics, I have never heard or read a speech more defiant of oppression and in every political way more suitable to its purpose" (James n.d.).

25. Walter Rodney was dogged by this criticism throughout his political life especially in the Caribbean. At an African Studies Association panel in 1990 Ali Mazrui implied this when he said that Rodney was to the left of Nyerere and Burnham, whose countries were to the left of their region (Mazrui 1990a). According to Andaiye, Maurice Bishop regarded Walter as a "pain in the ass" (Andaiye 1989). In discussions in the late 1970s among Caribbean groupings such as the PPP and the WPJ which shared a close link with Cheddi Jagan and the PPP it was felt that Rodney was an ultraleftist because of his position towards the PNC. The criticism is also implicit in C.L.R. James (1982). Officials of the Communist Party of Cuba also took that view but given their close ties to the Burnham regime it is not surprising. Burnham was said to have had a dossier on Rodney which he used to try and discredit him politically as an ultraleftist.

26. Chairman of *Transition's* editorial board was economist, Maurice Odle. General editor was Perry Mars and among the associate editors were Walter Rodney and University of the West Indies scholars George Beckford, Norman Girvan, and Trevor Munroe. Rodney saw the Guyana based *Transition* as a Marxist version of Rajat Neogy's Uganda based *Transition* journal that was one of Africa's principal English-language intellectual periodicals in the 1960s and 1970s. Since 1991 *Transition*, now an American cultural journal, is published by Oxford University Press in the United States and is edited by Kwame Anthony Appiah and Henry Louis Gates, Jr.

27. For comments on *Facing Reality* see Paul Buhle (1988: 121–22).

28. Massive electoral fraud characterised the Guyanese electoral process until the election of 1992 when Jagan was returned to power.

29. See Alex Dupuy (1996) for an assessment of Rodney which uses the oversimplified Marxist idea of his nationalist and Marxist phases with the latter being much richer than the former. While this distinction can be made there is a sense in which the class basis of phenomena is seen as having all the insights into the problems of race, class and ethnicity with the previous nationalist phase being narrow-minded.

30. In 1982 the Working People's Alliance published the text of a speech Rodney made some time in 1977 in defence of Arnold Rampersaud. The pamphlet was entitled "In Defence of Arnold Rampersaud". Eusi Kwayana (1988) uses long excerpts from it in the section "Rodney on Racial Justice, A Legacy For All". After spending 1,250 days in jail Rampersaud was freed on 4 December 1977.

31. Reference to the British military suppression of the 1953 Jagan government.

32. The attitudes towards the Burnham regime within the international communist movement in the early 1980s were quite positive. This became very clear to me during my tenure on the editorial board of the *World Marxist Review* from 1982 to

1984 in Prague, Czechoslovakia. The PPP through their leader, Cheddi Jagan and representative, Clement Rohee and later Donald Ramoutar on the editorial council, in their political reports tried to give more realistic assessments of the character of the PNC. But the PNC was nevertheless assessed as being ideologically close to Marxism by several international departments of Eastern European communist parties.

33. According to Roopnarine (1996) "military personnel from the Guyana Defence Force were on the ground in Grenada at the time of the assault. Burnham had a real panic in 1983 that this would become known to the USA."

34. In an unpublished article "Rodney – I'm Here to Stay" Cheddi Jagan argued that there was no revolutionary situation in Guyana in 1978–79. Jagan was kind enough to show me this article which he had written in tribute to Rodney. While the article noted differences such as the PPP's critical support of the PNC and Rodney's position of critical exposure, it stressed their similar ideological positions as Marxists. This article is interesting because it highlights different assessments of the political situation in Guyana and their consequences for political action (Jagan 1989).

35. Reference to the overthrow of the Shah of Iran.

36. According to Roopnarine (1996), "The leadership arrangements of the WPA, much criticised by the Marxist-Leninist Caribbean parties, had also to do with the rejection of the Stalinist cult of personality then in vogue among Marxist-Leninist parties as well as security considerations."

37. See Rodney (1981c: 149) for reference to the political activism of barrister De Souza and the medical practitioner, Dr Rohlehr, at the end of the nineteenth century.

38. Foremost among the advocates and practitioners of Leninism were the People's Progressive Party led by Cheddi Jagan and the Workers' Party of Jamaica led by Trevor Munroe. With the Grenadian Revolution of 1979 Leninist influence spread in the Eastern Caribbean especially with the influence of Bernard and Phyllis Coard in the New Jewel Movement. Munroe was responsible for a number of locally produced texts seeking to apply Marxist-Leninist ideas to the Caribbean. One of Munroe's texts that was used intensively was his *Organizational Principles of the Proletarian Party* (Munroe 1978). Cadres from the Caribbean were also sent to party schools in Moscow and Cuba.

39. For an important discussion of the theoretical issues underlying this debate, see Thomas (1986).

40. Cheddi Jagan *The Caribbean – Whose Backyard*? (1984) was 374 pages long and was a poor follow-up to *The West on Trial*. While the latter provided an insightful mix of biography and analysis of Guyanese politics in the early years of the Cold War, *The Caribbean – Whose Backyard*? was anti-imperialist but weak in analysis of Caribbean politics. This is also true of his collection of articles *The Caribbean Revolution* (1979b). They seemed to be written principally with the international communist left in mind.

41. My conversations with Elvin McDavid, a former political assistant to Forbes Burnham, suggests that the PNC suspected that the WPA and Rodney in particular were in 1979 pursuing a course of action that would lead to the overthrow of the regime. Rodney and others were blamed for burning down the PNC headquarters and preparing for the violent overthrow of Burnham's government (McDavid 1988). Security files on Rodney and the WPA are not available to researchers so it is not possible to assess the

PNC's charges against Rodney.

42. See Shiva Naipaul's *Journey to Nowhere – A New World Tragedy* where he writes: the most notorious of Burnham's criminal courtiers is a black preacher from Tennessee calling himself Rabbi Washington. Back home, where he is known as David Hill, he is wanted by the police on charges of blackmail and violence. But in Guyana, where he surfaced in 1972, he is a figure of consequence. He has created around himself a religious sect – the House of Israel – which espouses a messianic doctrine of black redemption. His Guyanese followers adorn themselves in the colours of the ruling party, which also happen to be the national colors. They arrive by the busload to take part in Government-sponsored rallies and parades; they help to break up Opposition meetings. In a sugar strike called by a union unfriendly to the Government, they played the part of scab labor. The Rabbi lives in considerable style. His benefactors have, in addition, provided his organization with two farms. The House of Israel calls itself "Burnham's Church", It has even included him in its theology: the Comrade Leader is Moses; the Rabbi is Aaron (Naipaul 1981: 63–64).

43. In conducting my interviews with workers some were very enthusiastic about my efforts and cooperated. Others were bitter and felt that the middle class in the WPA leadership hadn't done sufficient to preserve Walter Rodney. Some noted that on his trips abroad he always brought gifts for them (K. Afrani and Frank Fyffe 1989).

44. It is significant that both Walter Rodney and Bob Marley were in Zimbabwe at the same time. Marley's music was in a sense the counterpart to what Rodney had done in his historical writings and teaching (Campbell 1986: 146).

45. See *Sunday Sun* (Barbados), 22 June 1980: 25.

46. Some informants in Guyana and in Tanzania suggest that this was the case. This remains a matter of national security in Guyana and researchers will have to wait until security files become available or people in the know think it judicious to speak about these matters.

47. For a detailed statement on the police and military harassment of the WPA see Roopnarine (1995).

48. See *Dayclean*, 9 May 1980 for WPA's criticism of the US ambassador to Guyana who was accused of turning a blind eye on human rights violations in Guyana.

49. Gordon Rohlehr captures the essence of dread when he wrote:
    Dread is that quality which defines the static fear-bound relationship between the 'have-gots' and the 'have-nots'. It is the historic tension between slaver and slave, between the cruel ineptitude of power on the part of the rulers, and the introspective menace and dream of Apocalypse on the part of the down-trodden. This is why Dread remains a constant quality in Jamaica's creative life (Rohlehr 1992a: 125–26).

50. See the Barbadian newspaper *Sunday Sun*, 22 June 1980: 25, for interview with Pat Rodney.

51. The WPA needed some means of communication because they were denied access to the state-owned radio and newspapers, and telephones were not easily accessible and when accessed were bugged (Mentus 1980: 41).

52. See report in *Sunday Chronicle*, 9 January 1994.

53. In a statement issued on 13 September 1980 the WPA claimed that the crowds reached between 35 and 40 thousand persons. I attended the funeral as a representative of the Workers' Party of Jamaica and can confirm the estimate of over 35,000 people. Journalist Ric Mentus put the turnout "at a low of 30,000 and a high of 50,000" (Mentus 1980: 48).

54. Rodney's tragic death stimulated the muse in a number of poets. See the 1985 collection *Walter Rodney, Poetic Tributes* with an introduction by Andrew Salkey and a foreword by David Dabydeen (Bogle L'Ouverture 1985). Martin Carter's (1989) poem to Walter Rodney and Braithwaite's (1983) are among the most powerful evocations of what Rodney represented to the Caribbean region. Rodney's activism was also used for fictional purposes by Andrew Salkey. Andrew Salkey's 1974 novel *Joey Tyson* is a fictional reconstruction of what happened in Jamaica in October 1968 when Rodney was declared persona non grata. Salkey's 1984 story "*The One – the story of how the people of Guyana avenge the murder of their Pasero with help from Brother Anancy and Sister Buxton*" depicts Anancy as a freedom fighter against Burnham's One-manism following the death of Rodney.
55. The Jamaica Labour Party whose government had banned Rodney in 1968 issued a statement above the signature of its Deputy Leader, Pearnel Charles. The People's Progressive Party of Guyana issued a statement and gave coverage of the events in its newspaper, the *Mirror*. Statements were made by the Oilfield Workers Trade Union of Trinidad and Tobago, the Council of Progressive Trade Unions of Trinidad and Tobago, the United Labour Front of Trinidad and Tobago, the Jamaica Council for Human Rights; the Jamaica Committee for Human Rights and Democracy in Guyana; the National Workers Union, Dominica; University of the West Indies, St Augustine, Students and Guild Council in Trinidad and Tobago; concerned members of staff and former colleagues of Walter Rodney at the University of the West Indies in Barbados; the Caribbean Council of Churches; Movement for National Liberation in Barbados; Workers' Party of Jamaica; Guyana Solidarity Committee of the Federal of Germany; Kwame Ture (formerly Stokely Carmichael) on behalf of the All African People's Revolutionary Party, Washington DC (Mentus 1980: 50–52). The Antigua-Caribbean Liberation Movement led by Tim Hector dedicated the 30 June issue of the newspaper *Outlet* to Rodney's memory.
56. Reference to an interview with President Forbes Burnham conducted by Trinidad and Tobago Television. Burnham came across as not only smug but arrogant. There was no regret that Rodney had died and this shocked many people.
57. On the thirteenth anniversary of his assassination calls were made for a public investigation into the circumstances of his death. See Eddi Rodney (1994).
58. See *Guyana Chronicle*, 1 January 1994.
59. See *Sunday Gleaner*, 31 January 1994.
60. See *Sunday Gleaner*, 31 January 1994.

Conclusion

I have tried to trace the evolution of Walter Rodney's intellectual and political thought in the context of the period immediately following political independence in the Caribbean and Africa. He functioned in an intellectual context that had been shaped by C.L.R. James to whom Rodney and many of his generation owed a major intellectual debt. There was a remarkable congruence between Rodney's academic and intellectual endeavours, on the one hand, and his political concerns, on the other. He extended James' work in the area of African history and in activism in Tanzania, Jamaica, as well as in Guyana. Rodney's studies of African and Caribbean history were integrally related to his activism as they contextualised the passage of Africans and peoples of African descent through the slave trade and plantation slavery to the late twentieth century. Rodney, thereby, enriched the Jamesian Marxist and Pan-Africanist legacy by his involvement at an academic and political level in Tanzania and the Caribbean. However, Rodney often spoke of the inadequacy and paucity of Marxist enquiry and analyses of the Third World and as a scholar saw himself as contributing to the creation of that body of work. He emerged in the 1970s as one of the best-known postcolonial thinkers and activists in Africa and the Caribbean due to the reputation established by his book *How Europe Underdeveloped Africa*. While *How Europe Underdeveloped Africa* explained the significance of Africa in Western political economy in the last 500 years from the slave trade through to colonialism his activism was geared towards realising the empowerment of working people in the Caribbean and Africa.

In Jamaica, in 1968, Rodney was caught up in grass roots cultural politics which fought entrenched racism in Jamaican society. The social movement of the 1960s, that had been influenced by Rastafarianism, had engaged the Jamaican oligarchy and the brown and black middle class in sharp ideological and cultural confrontation about race, colour, and power in Jamaican society. Rodney's links with radicalised youth and Rastafarians caused the political elite to panic. His knowledge of African history and his willingness to share this with the grass roots young people contributed to the growth of self-respect and dignity among young people that had been preached by the Garvey movement in the 1920s and continued by the Rastafarian movement in the 1950s and 1960s. This had been done in opposition to some in the nationalist movement in Jamaica and elsewhere in the Caribbean who wanted to sweep issues of race and colour under the carpet or to treat them at a superficial level.

Connected to this was the struggle Rodney waged in Guyana in the 1970s against the politics of Forbes Burnham, who maintained power through a system of unfair elections, political intimidation of the opposition and the manipulation of racial insecurities.

Rodney's brief life coincided with the early years of decolonisation in Africa and the Caribbean, the Cuban Revolution, the gains of the Civil Rights movement in the United States and America's defeat in Vietnam. He had direct contact with the participants in the struggles in Southern Africa against Portuguese rule and in South Africa against apartheid. He was in Tanzania for its attempts at radical reforms under Julius Nyerere and in the Caribbean during the 1970s. He was living in Guyana when the revolutions in Nicaragua and Grenada took place in 1979, the year of his most active opposition to Burnham's regime. He is often described as being to the left of Caribbean politics in the 1970s while in Tanzania he was criticised for being too supportive of Nyerere's efforts at radical reforms. His activism speaks to the political promise of those years insofar as they reflected a heightened level of mass political activity geared towards the achievement of particular economic, social and political goals.

I have examined the content of his political positions and looked at the merits and weaknesses of his theoretical points of view and political practice. His critical focus on the role of the African and Caribbean middle classes as the social group which inherited power from the colonial powers and their relationship with the working people was very Jamesian. How this relationship was developed provided a litmus test of the extent to which substantial changes were being made in the heritage of colonial authoritarian politics in both the Caribbean and Africa. His focus on the role of the middle class, its control and use of the state, and its general evolution, remains a very important issue in contemporary politics.

His interpretations of African and Caribbean history, his analyses of the relationship between social class and race, the role of working people and his insistence on understanding the global context shaping the evolution of the postcolonial world, continue to provide points of departure for academic research and political analyses and action. The changes that have taken place in the world, since his death, have in a sense realised Rodney's worst fears about the prospects facing the postcolonial world of Africa and the Caribbean and would have probably led him to speak more emphatically about recolonisation. But he would have been forced to look more pragmatically at these conditions, at issues of economic development and politics in Africa and the Caribbean. The content of this pragmatism would be guided by the experience of the working people and their efforts to find solutions to new structures and circumstances of subordination.

Rodney's intellectual legacy, as a historian and as an activist, forms an important part of the unfolding Caribbean intellectual tradition, a tradition that requires far more scholarly attention than it has so far received. The central feature underlying Rodney's contribution to this tradition was his positive awareness of himself as a person of African descent in the Caribbean, the link he forged with Africa and the intellectual agenda that emerged in relation to the major challenges of decolonisation.

Bibliography

Afrani, K. 1989. Interview by author. Linden, Guyana. (26 July).

Africa Books. 1991. *Africa Today*. London: Africa Books.

Alpers, Edward A. 1973. Rethinking African economic history: a contribution to the discussion of the roots of under-development. *Kenya Historical Review* 1 (2): 163-88.

——. 1982. The weapon of history in the struggle for African liberation: the work of Walter Rodney. In *Walter Rodney – Revolutionary and Scholar: a Tribute*, edited by Edward Alpers and Pierre-Michel Fontaine. Los Angeles: Center for Afro-American Studies and African Studies Center, University of California.

Amin, Samir. 1990. *Delinking – Towards a Polycentric World*. Translated by Michael Wolfers. London: Zed Books.

——. 1992. *Empire of Chaos*. Translated by W.H. Locke Anderson. New York: Monthly Review Press.

Andaiye. 1989. Interview by author. Bridgetown, Barbados (12 July).

——. 1990. Rodney not tied to dogma. *Caribbean Contact* (May-June): 10, 12.

Augustus, E., and Walter Rodney. 1961–1962. Some political aspects of independence. *Pelican Annual – University of the West Indies*: 90-95.

Babu, Abdul. 1981. *African Socialism or Socialist Africa*. Dar es Salaam: Tanzania Publishing House.

Bagoya, Walter. 1990. Interview by author. Dar es Salaam (28 July).

Bascom, William. 1972. *Shango in the New World*. Austin: University of Texas Press.

——.1983. Caribbean man: the life and times of Philip Sherlock. *Jamaica Journal* 16 (3): 22-30.

Baugh, Edward. 1993. Walcott's Jamaica. *Jamaica Observer* (11 April): 50-51.

Beauvoir, Simone de. 1968. *Force of Circumstances*. Harmondsworth, Middlesex: Penguin Books.

Benn, Denis. 1987. *The Growth and Development of Political Ideas in the Caribbean 1774–1983*. Kingston: Institute of Social and Economic Research, University of the West Indies.

Bernal, Martin. 1987. *Black Athena – the Afroasiatic Roots of Classical Civilisation.* Vol. 1: *The Fabrication of Ancient Greece 1785–1985.* New Brunswick, New Jersey: Rutgers University Press.

———. 1991. *Black Athena – the Afroasiatic Roots of Classical Civilisation.* Vol. 2: *The Archaeological and Documentary Evidence.* New Brunswick, New Jersey: Rutgers University Press.

Bess, Michael. 1993. E.P. Thompson – the historian as activist. *American Historical Review* 98 (1): 19-38.

Best, Lloyd. 1990. Placing ourselves in history – a tribute to C.L.R. James. *Trinidad and Tobago Review* 12 (9): 17-20.

———. 1993. Our intellectual father (Sir Arthur Lewis) – an appreciation. *Trinidad and Tobago Review* 15 (7): 16-17.

Bishop, Maurice. 1984. Maurice Bishop, Grenada is building a new life. Interview by Rupert Lewis. In *Grenada: History, Revolution, US Intervention*. Latin America – Studies by Soviet Scholars. Moscow: *Social Sciences Today* Editorial Board and USSR Academy of Sciences.

Boahen, Albert, ed. 1990. *General History of Africa,* Vol. 7 – *Africa Under Colonial Domination.* London and Paris: James Currey Publishers and UNESCO.

Bogle L'Ouverture Publications. 1985. *Walter Rodney – Poetic Tributes* (with an introduction by Andrew Salkey and a foreword by David Dabydeen). London: Bogle L'Ouverture Publications.

Bogues, Barrymore Anthony. 1993. Political Thought of C.L.R. James (1934–1950). Ph.D. thesis, University of the West Indies.

———. 1997. *Caliban's Freedom – the Early Political Thought of C.L.R. James.* London and Chicago: Pluto Press.

Bonnett, Aubrey W., and G. Llewellyn Watson, eds. 1990. *Emerging Perspectives on the Black Diaspora.* Maryland: University Press of America.

Brathwaite, Edward. 1971. *Development of Creole Society in Jamaica, 1770–1820.* Oxford: Clarendon Press.

———. 1973. Dialect and dialectic. Review of *How Europe Underdeveloped Africa. Bulletin of the African Studies Association of the West Indies* 6 (December): 89-99.

———. 1976. The love axe/1: developing a Caribbean aesthetic 1962–1974. In *Reading Black: Essays in the Criticism of African, Caribbean & Black American Literature*, edited by Houston Baker. Cornell: Cornell University, Africana Studies and Research Center.

———. 1983. *Third World Poems.* London: Longman Group.

———. 1985. *Contradictory Omens – Cultural Diversity and Integration in the Caribbean.* 2nd reprint. Kingston: Savacou Publications.

Buhle, Paul. 1988. *C.L.R. James – the Artist as Revolutionary.* London and New York: Verso.

Burnham, Forbes. 1970. *A Destiny to Mould: Selected Discourses by the Prime Minister of Guyana.* Compiled by C.A. Nascimento and R.A. Burrowes. London: Longman Caribbean.

Bryan, Patrick. 1991a. Black perspectives in late nineteenth-century Jamaica: the case of Dr Theophilus E.S. Scholes. In *Garvey – his Work and Impact*, edited by Rupert Lewis and Patrick Bryan. New Jersey: Africa World Press.

———. 1991b. *The Jamaican People 1880–1902. Race, Class and Social Control*. London: Macmillan Caribbean.

Cabral, Amilcar. 1980. *Unity and Struggle. Speeches and Writings*. Texts selected by the PAIGC. Translated by Michael Wolfers. London: Heinemann.

Cabrera, Lydia. 1986. *El Monte, igbo-finda, ewe orisha, vititi nfinda*. Miami: Colección del Chichurekú.

Campbell, Horace. 1973. Review of *How Europe Underdeveloped Africa* by Walter Rodney. *Mawazo* 4 (1): 62-68.

———. 1986. The impact of Walter Rodney and progressive scholars on the Dar es Salaam school. *African Association of Political Science Newsletter* (July-September): 14-30.

———. 1988. The teaching and research of political economy in Africa with specific reference to East Africa. *African Review* 15 (1).

———. 1990. Interview by author. African Studies Association meeting. Baltimore (4 November).

Campbell, Trevor. 1981. The making of an organic intellectual – Walter Rodney 1942–1980. *Latin American Perspectives* 8 (1): 49-63.

Carter, Martin. 1979. Open letter to the people of Guyana. *Dayclean Special*; also published in *Kyk-Over-Al* – (A Martin Carter Prose Sampler), Special Issue 44, (May 1993): 88-89.

———. 1989. *Selected Poems*. Guyana: Demarara Publishers.

Castañeda, Jorge. 1993. *Utopia Unarmed: the Latin American Left After the Cold War*. New York: Alfred A. Knopf.

Chevannes, Alston Barrington. 1976. The repairer of the breach: Reverend Claudius Henry and Jamaican society. In *Ethnicity in the Americas*, edited by Frances Henry. The Hague: Mouton.

———. 1989. Social and Ideological Origins of the Rastafari Movement in Jamaica. Ph.D. diss., Columbia University.

———. 1994. *Rastafari – Roots and Ideology*. Syracuse: Syracuse University Press.

Chevannes, Alston Barrington, ed. 1995. *Rastafari and Other African-Caribbean Worldviews*. The Hague: Macmillan in association with the Institute of Social Studies.

Cholmondeley, Colin. 1989. Interview by author (6 August). Port of Spain, Trinidad.

Cliffe, Lionel, and John Saul, eds. 1972. *Socialism in Tanzania – an Interdisciplinary Reader*. Vol. 1. Nairobi: East African Publishing House.

———. 1973. *Socialism in Tanzania – an Interdisciplinary Reader*. Vol. 2. Nairobi: East African Publishing House.

Coulson, Andrew. 1978. *African Socialism in Practice – the Tanzanian Experience*. Nottingham: Spokesman Books.

———. 1982. *Tanzania – a Political Economy*. Oxford: Clarendon Press.

Crahan, Margaret E., and Franklin Knight. 1979. *Africa and the Caribbean – the Legacies of a Link*. Baltimore: Johns Hopkins University Press.

Cudjoe, Selwyn, ed. 1993. *Eric E. Williams Speaks – Essays on Colonialism*. Wellesley: Calaloux Publications.

Cudjoe, Selwyn and William Cain. 1995. *C.L.R. James: His Intellectual Legacies*. Boston: University of Massachusetts.

Curtin, Philip. 1969. *The Atlantic Slave Trade: a Census*. Madison: University of Winsconsin Press.

———. 1970. Review of *A History of the Upper Guinea Coast 1545–1800*, by Walter Rodney. *Journal of African History* 11, (3): 453-55.

Davidson, Basil. 1994. *The Search for Africa: History, Culture, Politics*. New York: Random House.

Davis, Frank. 1991. Interview by author. Kingston (3 June).

Devonish, Hubert. 1991. Nature of African-East Indian contact in 19th century Guyana – the linguistics evidence. Paper presented to Seminar, Department of History, University of the West Indies, June.

Diop, Cheikh Anta. 1991. *Civilization or Barbarism: an Authentic Anthropology*. Translated by Yaa-Lengi Meema Ngemi. Edited by Harold J. Salemson and Marjolijn de Jager. Brooklyn, New York: Lawrence Hill Books.

Dizzy, Ras. 1969. *The Human Guide Line – Poems and Inspirations*. Kingston: no publisher.

Drayton, Harold. 1989. Interview by author (18 August). Bridgetown, Barbados.

Du Bois, W.E. Burghardt. 1986. *W.E.B. Du Bois Writings – The Suppression of the African Slave-trade; The Souls of Black Folk; Dusk of Dawn; Essays and Articles*. Cambridge: Library of America.

Duggan, William, and John R. Civille. 1976. *Tanzania and Nyerere*. New York: Orbis Books.

Dupuy, Alex. 1996. Race and class in the postcolonial Caribbean: the views of Walter Rodney. *Latin American Perspectives* 89, 23 (2):107-29.

Edmondson, Locksley. 1985. African history and African studies in the black diaspora. In *The Educational Process and Historiography in Africa*. Paris: UNESCO.

Eltis, David, and David Richardson. 1997. Patterns of slave shipments from West Africa: Comparing the Gold Coast, Bight of Benin and Bight of Biafra, 1660–1867. Paper presented to conference *West Africa and the Americas: Repercussions of the Slave Trade*. University of the West Indies, 20-22 February.

Emeagwali, Gloria Thomas. 1981. Alternative perspectives on the reconstruction of the African past – the case of Walter Rodney. *Kiabàrà* 4 (2): 127-38.

Ewald, Janet J. 1992. Slavery in Africa and the slave trades from Africa. *The American Historical Review* 97 (2): 465-85.

Fage, J. D. 1989. African societies and the Atlantic slave trade. *Past and Present* 125 (November): 97-115.

Fanon, Frantz. 1966. *The Wretched of the Earth*. New York: Grove Press.

———. 1970. *Towards the African Revolution*. London: Penguin.

Fatton, Robert. 1992. *Predatory Rule State and Civil Society in Africa*. Boulder and London: Lynne Rienner Pubs.

Ferguson, Douglas. 1982. Walter Rodney's application of Marxist theory to the African past and present. In *Walter Rodney – Revolutionary and Scholar: a Tribute*. Los Angeles: Center for Afro-American Studies and African Studies Center, University of California.

Figueroa, Mark. 1993. W. Arthur Lewis's legacy – industrialization or agricultural development? Paper presented to seminar series, Department of Economics, University of the West Indies, Jamaica.

Fyffe, Frank. 1989. Interview by author, Georgetown, Guyana (26 July).

Freund, Bill. 1984. *The Making of Contemporary Africa – the Development of African Society since 1800*. Bloomington: Indiana University Press.

Gibbs, Roxanne. 1980. Last Friday with the Rodneys. *Sunday Sun* (22 June).

Gibbons, Arnold. 1994. *Walter Rodney and his Times*. Vol. 1. *Identity and Ideology*. Georgetown: Guyana National Printers.

Girvan, Norman. 1961–1962. Walter Rodney. *Pelican Annual*: 110–111.

———. 1968. After Rodney – the politics of student protest in Jamaica. *New World Quarterly* (4) 3: 59-68.

———. 1973. An economic assessment. Review of *How Europe Underdeveloped Africa*. *Bulletin of the African Studies Association of the West Indies* 6 (December): 83-87.

———. 1990. Foreword to Tribute to a Scholar: Appreciating C.L.R. James, edited by Bishnu Ragoonath. Kingston: Consortium Graduate School of Social Sciences, University of the West Indies.

———. 1995. Letter to Brian Meeks (18 July).

Gonsalves, Ralph. 1979. The Rodney affair. *Caribbean Quarterly* (25) 3: 1-24.

Gray, Obika. 1991. *Radicalism and Social Change in Jamaica, 1960–1972*. Knoxville: University of Tennessee Press.

Gray, Richard. 1975. Introduction to *The Cambridge History of Africa*. Vol. 4. *c.1600–c.1790*. Cambridge: Cambridge University Press.

Greene, J.E. 1974. *Race vs Politics in Guyana*. Kingston: Institute of Social and Economic Research, University of the West Indies.

Grimshaw, Anna, ed. 1992. *The C.L.R. James Reader*. Oxford: Blackwell Publishers.

Guyana Nationals and Friends Alliance (GNFA), and Los Angeles Committee for Academics in Peril (LACAP). 1980. *Chronology of Political Oppression and Official Murder in Guyana*. Los Angeles: Guyana Nationals and Friends Alliance and Los Angeles Committee for Academics in Peril.

Hair, P.E.H. 1978. *The Atlantic Slave Trade and Black Africa*. London: The Historical Association.

Hall, Kenneth. 1973. Europe in Africa. Review of *How Europe Underdeveloped Africa*. *Bulletin of the African Studies Association of the West Indies* 6 (December): 87-89.

Hamilton, Ruth Simms, ed. 1990. *Creating a Paradigm and Research Agenda for Comparative Studies of the Worldwide Dispersion of African Peoples*. Monograph No. 1. Michigan: African Diaspora Research Project, Michigan State University. East Lansing.

Harris, Joseph. 1992. *Global Dimensions of the African Diaspora*. Washington, D.C.: Howard University Press.

Hauner, Magdalena. 1981. Kiujamaa – Notes on political language. *Studies in African Linguistics – Precis of the 12th Conference on African Linguistics* (April): 46-50.

Henry, Paget, and Paul Buhle, eds. 1992. *C.L.R. James's Caribbean*. Durham and London: Duke University Press and Macmillan Caribbean.

Hill, Robert. 1982. Walter Rodney and the restatement of Pan-Africanism in theory and practice. In *Walter Rodney – Revolutionary and Scholar: a Tribute*, edited by Edward Alpers and Pierre-Michel Fontaine. Los Angeles: Center for Afro-American Studies and African Studies Center, University of California.

Hilton, Anne. 1985. *The Kingdom of Kongo*. Oxford: Clarendon Press.

Hintzen, Percy. 1989. *The Costs of Regime Survival: Racial Mobilization, Elite Domination and Control of the State in Guyana and Trinidad*. Cambridge: Cambridge University Press.

Hoare, Quintin, and Geoffrey Nowell Smith, eds. 1978. *Antonio Gramsci – Selections from Prison Notebooks*. London: Lawrence and Wishart.

Hope, Kempe Ronald. 1985. *Guyana – Politics and Development in an Emergent Socialist State*. Oakville: Mosaic Press.

Hooker, James. 1967. *Black Revolutionary – George Padmore's Path from Communism to Pan-Africanism*. London: Pall Mall Press.

———. 1975. *Henry Sylvester Williams: Imperial Pan-Africanist*. London: Rex Collings.

Huntley, Jessica. 1973. Letter to Walter Rodney. London (30 July).

Hutton, Clinton. 1992. 'Colour for colour, skin for skin': The ideological foundation of some of the ideas justifying the Morant Bay rebelsion and its suppression. Ph.D. thesis, University of the West Indies.

Inikori, Joseph. 1992a. *The Chaining of a Continent: Export Demand for Captives and the History of Africa South of the Sahara*. Kingston: Institute of Social and Economic Research, University of the West Indies.

———. 1992b. Ideology versus the tyranny of paradigm: Historians and the impact of the Atlantic slave trade on African societies. Paper presented to the meeting of the African Studies Association, Seattle, 20-23 November.

———. 1993a. *Slavery and the Rise of Capitalism*. (The 1993 Elsa Goveia memorial lecture, presented at the University of the West Indies, Jamaica, 29 March 1993.) Kingston: Department of History, University of the West Indies.

———. 1993b. Ideology versus the tyranny of paradigm: Walter Rodney and the debate on African development and underdevelopment. Paper sent to author.

———. 1994. History in breadth and history in depth – grand theories and empirical evidence in the expanding historiography of the Atlantic slave trade. Paper presented at conference on *The State of African Diaspora Studies – Present Realities and Future Prospects*, 18-19 February, University of North Carolina, Chapel Hill.

Inikori, Joseph, and Stanley L. Engerman, eds. 1994. *The Atlantic Slave Trade – Effects on Economies, Societies, and Peoples in Africa, the Americas, and Europe*. Durham and London: Duke University Press.

Jagan, Cheddi. 1972. *The West on Trial: the Fight for Guyana's Freedom*. New York: International Publishers.

———. 1975. Cheddi Jagan on critical support. Toronto: Association of Concerned Guyanese.

———. 1979a. Guyana fast approaching revolutionary situation. Georgetown. Mimeographed.

———. 1979b. *The Caribbean Revolution*. Prague: Orbis Press Agency.
———. 1984. *The Caribbean – Whose Backyard?* Prague: Orbis Press Agency.
———. 1989. Rodney – I'm here to stay. 18-page manuscript in Jagan's papers, Freedom House, Georgetown, Guyana.
Jagan, Janet. 1973. Army intervention in the 1973 elections in Guyana. Georgetown: PPP Education Committee.
Jamaica Hansard. 1968-1969. Proceedings of the House of Representatives of Jamaica. 28 March–22 October.
James, Adeola. 1989. Interview by author. Georgetown, Guyana (23 July).
James, C.L.R. 1960. "Modern politics". A series of lectures on the subject given at the Trinidad Public Library in its adult education programme. Port of Spain: PNM Publishing.
———. 1962. *Party Politics in the West Indies*. San Juan, Trinidad: Vedic Enterprises.
———. 1963. *Black Jacobins – Toussaint L'Ouverture and the San Domingo Revolution*. New York: Random House.
———. 1968. Walter Rodney and Caribbean misrule. *Bongo-man* (December): 16-19.
———. 1974. Letter to Walter Rodney. 18 May. In Walter Rodney Papers a.
———. 1977. *Nkrumah and the Ghana Revolution*. London: Allison and Busby.
——— 1980. C.L.R. James on Walter Rodney. *Race Today* (November): 28-30.
———. 1982. Walter Rodney and the question of power. In *Walter Rodney – Revolutionary and Scholar: a Tribute*, edited by Edward Alpers and Pierre-Michel Fontaine. Los Angeles: Center for Afro-American Studies and African Studies Center, University of California.
———. 1986. *Beyond a Boundary*. London: Stanley Paul.
———. 1992. Notes on the life of George Padmore. In *The C.L.R. James Reader*, edited by Anna Grimshaw. Oxford: Blackwell Publishers.
———. 1993. *World Revolution 1917–1936: The Rise and Fall of the Communist International*. New Jersey: Humanities Press International.
———. n.d. An analysis of the political situation in Barbados. Photocopy in author's possession.
———. n.d. A relevant supplement to Michael Manley: "*Not for Sale*". San Francisco: Editorial Consultants.
James, George G.M. 1985. *Stolen Legacy. The Greeks Were not the Authors of Greek Philosophy, but the People of North Africa, Commonly Called the Egyptians*. San Francisco: Julian Richardson Associates.
Jeyifo, Biodun. 1980. Salute to a fallen revolutionary intellectual. In *And Finally They Killed Him. Speeches and Poems at a Memorial Rally for Walter Rodney (1942–1980)*. Oduduwa Hall, University of Ife, Nigeria, Friday, 27 June 1980. Ife: Editorial Collectives of *Socialist Forum* and *Positive Review*.
Jewsiewicki, Bogumil. 1989. African historical studies – academic knowledge as 'usable past' and radical scholarship. *African Studies Review* 32 (3): 1-76.
Kaba, Lasiné. 1982. Walter Rodney – a Pan-Africanist historian. In *Walter Rodney – Revolutionary and Scholar: a Tribute*, edited by Edward A. Alpers and Pierre-Michel Fontaine. Los Angeles: Center for Afro-American Studies Center, UCLA.

Kaijage, Fred. 1991. Interview by author. Univerity of Florida, Gainesville (9 January).

Kanywanyi, Joe. 1990. Letter to author. Dar es Salaam (10 December).

Karioki, James. 1974. African scholars versus Ali Mazrui. *Transition* 45 (9): 55-63.

Kissinger, Henry. 1994. *Diplomacy*. New York: Simon and Schuster.

Knight, Franklin. 1988. Interview by author. Kingston (25 March).

Knight, Franklin, and Richard Price. 1981. Editors' note to *A History of the Guyanese Working People, 1881–1905*, by Walter Rodney. Kingston and London: Heinemann Educational Books.

Kwayana, Eusi. 1976. Some aspects of pseudo-socialism in Guyana. Paper presented at a seminar on the Caribbean, University of the West Indies, St Augustine campus, 22 June.

———. 1988. Walter Rodney. Georgetown: Working People's Alliance.

Lacey, Terry. 1977. *Violence and Politics in Jamaica, 1960–1970*. Manchester: Manchester University Press.

La Guerre, John Gaffar. 1982. *The Social and Political Thought of the Colonial Intelligentsia*. Mona: Institute of Social and Economic Research, University of the West Indies.

———. 1987. Pluralism and the Guyanese intelligentsia. *Caribbean Quarterly* 33 (1 & 2): 44-60.

Lamming, George. 1981. Foreword to *A History of the Guyanese Working People, 1881–1905*, by Walter Rodney. London, Kingston, Port of Spain: Heinemann Educational Books.

———. 1992. *Conversations, George Lamming – Essays, Addresses and Interviews 1953–1990*. Edited by Richard Drayton and Andaiye. London: Karia Press.

Latin American Bureau. 1984. *Guyana – Fraudulent Revolution*. London: Latin American Bureau with the assistance of the World Council of Churches.

Lawi, Y. 1986. A biographical-historiographical sketch of Walter Rodney. M.A. paper, Department of History, University of Dar es Salaam.

Legum, Colin. 1972. *Africa – The Year of the Students. A Survey of Student Politics in Universities and Schools*. London: Rex Collings.

Legum, Colin, and Geoffrey Mmari, eds. 1995. *Mwalimu – The Influence of Nyerere*. London, Dar es Salaam, Trenton: British – Tanzania Society in association with James Currey, Mkuki Na Nyota, Africa World Press.

Lewis, Arthur. 1961–1962. The University – statement by Dr Arthur Lewis, Vice Chancellor, at press conference, 25 April. *Pelican Annual*.

———. 1965. *Politics in West Africa*. London: George Allen and Unwin.

———. 1983. *Selected Economic Writings of W. Arthur Lewis*. Edited by Mark Gersovitz. New York: New York University Press.

Lewis, David Levering. 1993. *W.E.B. Du Bois, 1869–1919. Biography of a Race*. New York: Henry Holt and Company.

Lewis, Gordon. 1979. "Gather with the Saints at the River": the Jonestown Guyana holocaust of 1978. A descriptive and interpretative essay on its ultimate meaning from a Caribbean viewpoint. Rio Piedras: Institute of Caribbean Studies, University of Puerto Rico.

———. 1983. *Main Currents in Caribbean thought: the Historical Evolution of Caribbean Society in its Ideological Aspects, 1492–1900*. Kingston and Port of Spain: Heinemann Educational Books (Caribbean).

———. 1987. *Grenada – the Jewel Despoiled*. Baltimore and London: Johns Hopkins University Press.

Lewis, Rupert. 1968. Personal journal.

———. 1973. A Marxist approach. Review of *How Europe Underdeveloped Africa*. *Bulletin of the African Studies Association of the West Indies* 6 (December): 77-82.

———. 1988. *Marcus Garvey: Anti-Colonial Champion*. New Jersey: Africa World Press.

———. 1994. Walter Rodney: 1968 revisited. *Social and Economic Studies* 43 (3) : 7-56.

———. 1997. Learning to blow the Abeng: a critical look at anti-establishment movements of the 1960s and 1970s. *Small Axe* 1 (March): 5-17.

———. *The Lictor, – The Queen's College Magazine*. 1958/59.

Lovejoy, Paul. 1997. Electronic mail (hard copy): Late 90s historians and transatlantic figures. 29 April.

McDavid, Elvin. 1988. Conversation with author. Kingston (5 July).

McGowan, Winston. 1993. The life and work of Walter Rodney. *Stabroek News* November 16–December 6.

Manley, Michael. 1975. *A Voice at the Workplace – Reflections on Colonialism and the Jamaican Worker*. London: André Deutsch.

Manley, Rachel, ed. 1989. *Edna Manley: the Diaries*. London: André Deutsch.

Marable, Manning. 1986. Black studies – Marxism and the Black intellectual tradition. In *The Left Academy – Marxist Scholarship on American Campuses*, edited by Bertell Ollman and Edward Vernoff. New York: Praeger.

———. 1987. Race, class and democracy. Walter Rodney's thought on the Black American struggle. The third Walter Rodney Memorial Lecture. Delivered at Ealing Town Hall, Ealing, London, on 13 June 1987. London: Friends of Bogle.

Mars, Perry. 1990. Ethnic conflict and political control – the Guyana case. *Social and Economic Studies* 39 (3): 65-94.

Mathurin, Owen. 1976. *Henry Sylvester Williams and the Origins of the Pan-African Movement 1869–1911*. Westport, Connecticut: Greenwood Press.

Maynier-Burke, Shirley. 1988. Strength and subtle shades – Albert Huie interviewed. *Jamaica Journal* 21 (3): 30-38.

Mazrui, Ali. 1978. *Political Values and the Educated Class in Africa*. Berkeley and Los Angeles: University of California.

———. 1990a. Presentation on Walter Rodney, at African Studies Association meeting. Baltimore (1 November). Audiotape.

———. 1990b. Interview by author. African Studies Association meeting. Baltimore (2 November).

Meeks, B. 1977. The development of the 1970 revolution in Trinidad and Tobago. Master's thesis. University of the West Indies.

———. 1993. *Caribbean Revolutions and Revolutionary Theory – an Assessment of Cuba, Nicaragua and Grenada*. Warwick: Warwick University Caribbean Studies, Macmillan Caribbean.

———. 1996. Obscure revolts, profound effects: the Henry rebellion, counter hegemony and Jamaican society. Paper presented to the panel "History, hegemony and political identity: contesting he canon", 21st Annual Caribbean Studies Association conference, Puerto Rico, 27-31 May.

Mentus, Ulric. 1980. The Walter Rodney killing. Was the Burnham government in any way responsible? *People – Caribbean Magazine* (July): 37-52.

Mills, Charles. 1990. Getting out of the cave: tension between democracy and elitism in Marx's theory of cognitive liberation. *Social and Economic Studies* 39 (1): 1-50.

Moore, Brian. 1982. Walter Rodney, his contribution to Guyanese historiography. *Bulletin of Eastern Caribbean Affairs* 8 (2): 23-29.

———. 1987. *Race, Power and Social Segmentation in Colonial Society. Guyana after Slavery 1838–1891*. New York, London: Gordon and Breach Science Publishers.

———. 1995. *Cultural Power, Resistance and Pluralism: Colonial Guyana 1838–1900*. Kingston and Montreal: The Press UWI and McGill-Queen's University Press.

Morris, Mervyn. 1992. Dennis Scott, a remembrance. *Jamaica Journal* 24 (2): 53-54.

Mulei, Christopher. 1972. The predicament of the left in Tanzania. *East Africa Journal* 9 (8): 29-34.

Mulvaney, Rebekah. 1990. *Rastafari and Reggae: a Dictionary and Sourcebook*. (Bibliography by Carlos I.H. Nelson. Illustrations by Barbara Boyle). Westport, Connecticut: Greenwood Press.

Munroe, Derwin. 1989. Riots in post colonial Jamaica. Master's thesis, University of the West Indies.

Munroe, Trevor. 1969. Black power as a political strategy in Jamaica. *Bongo-Man* (June): 1-14.

———. 1972. *The Politics of Constitutional Decolonization: Jamaica 1944–1962*. Kingston: Institute of Social and Economic Research, University of the West Indies.

———. 1978. *Organisational Principles of the Proletarian Party*. Kingston: Workers' Party of Jamaica.

———. 1992. *The Cold War and the Jamaican Left, 1950–55*. Kingston: Kingston Publishers.

Museveni, Yoweri. 1970. My three years in Tanzania. *Cheche* 2 (July): 12-14.

———. 1986. *Selected Articles on the Ugandan Resistance*. Nairobi: National Resistance Movement.

Nabudere, Dan. 1981. The role of Tanzania in regional integration in East Africa – old and new patterns. In *Foreign Policy of Tanzania 1961–1981: a Reader*, edited by K. Matthews and S. Mushi. Dar es Salaam: Tanzania Publishing House.

Naipaul, Shiva. 1979. *North of South – an African Journey*. New York: Simon and Schuster.

———. 1981. *Journey to Nowhere: a New World Tragedy*. New York: Penguin Books.

Naipaul, Vidia. 1994. *A Way in the World*. New York: Alfred A. Knopf.

Negus, Ras. 1969. Interview in *Abeng* (12 April).

Nettleford, Rex. 1970. *Mirror Mirror: Identity, Race and Protest in Jamaica*. London and Kingston: William Collins and Sangster (Jamaica).

———. 1978. *Caribbean Cultural Identity: the Case of Jamaica. An Essay in Cultural Dynamics*. Kingston: Institute of Jamaica.

——. 1985. *Dance Jamaica – Cultural Definition and Artistic Discovery. The National Dance Theatre Company of Jamaica, 1962–1983*. New York: Grove Press.

Nyang'oro, Julius. 1989. *The State and Capitalist Development in Africa*. New York and London: Praeger.

Nyerere, Julius. 1967. Education for self-reliance. Dar es Salaam: Ministry of Information and Tourism.

——. 1972. Tanzania – ten years after independence. *The African Review* 2 (1): 1-54.

Oliver, Roland, and J.D. Fage. 1989. *A Short History of Africa*. New York: Facts on file.

Othman, Haroub. 1977. *The State in Tanzania*. Dar es Salaam: Institute of Development Studies.

——. 1987. A crumbling ivory tower. *Africa Events* (May): 40-42.

——. 1990. Interview by author. Dar es Salaam (29 July).

Owens, Joseph. 1976. *Dread – The Rastafarians of Jamaica*. Kingston: Sangster's Bookstores.

Padmore, George. 1956. *Pan-Africanism or Communism? The Coming Struggle for Africa*. New York: Roy Press.

Pantin, R. 1990. *Black Power Day: the 1970 February Revolution. A Reporter's Story*. Trinidad and Tobago: Hatuey Productions.

Patterson, Orlando. 1967. *The Sociology of Slavery: an Analysis of the Origins, Development and Structure of Negro Slave Society in Jamaica*. London: MacGibbon and Kee.

——. 1979. Commentary on Walter Rodney's paper "Slavery and Underdevelopment". In *Roots and Branches – Current Directions in Slave Studies*, edited by Michael Craton. London and New York: Pergamon Press.

——. 1982. *Slavery and Social Death: a Comparative Study*. Cambridge and London: Harvard University Press.

—— 1991. *Freedom: Freedom in the Making of Western Culture*. London: I.B. Tauris and Co.

Payne, Anthony J. 1988. *Politics in Jamaica*. London: C. Hurst and Company and Heinemann Educational Books (Caribbean).

——. n.d. *Government, Intellectuals and International Relations: the Politics of the University of the West Indies 1968–1984*. Occasional papers in Caribbean Studies. Warwick: University of Warwick, Centre for Caribbean Studies. .

Pike, Ruth. 1972. *Aristocrats and Traders: Sevillian Society in the Sixteenth Century*. Ithaca: Cornell University Press.

Pollard, Velma. 1980. Dread talk – the speech of Rastafarians in Jamaica. *Caribbean Quarterly* 26 (4): 32-41.

Polomé, Edgar, and C.P. Hill. 1980. *Language in Tanzania*. London: Oxford University Press.

Premdas, Ralph, and Eric St Cyr, eds. 1991. *Sir Arthur Lewis: an Economic and Political Portrait*. Kingston: Regional Programme of Monetary Studies, Institute of Social and Economic Research, University of the West Indies.

Public Relations Office. 1987. *University of the West Indies Mona*. Kingston: Public Relations Office, UWI.

Ramkissoon, Peter. 1972. Letter to Walter Rodney. Georgetown, Guyana (29 December).

Ranger, T. 1968a. *Aspects of Central African History*. Evanston: Northwestern University Press.

———. 1968b. Students and the nation. In *Tanzania – Revolution by Education*, edited by Idrian R. Resnick. Arusha: Longmans of Tanzania.

———. 1981. Towards a radical practice of academic freedom: the experience of East and Central Africa. (The twenty-second T.B. memorial lecture. Delivered in the Jameson Hall, University of Cape Town on 4 September 1981) University of Cape Town.

Reid, Victor. 1985. *The Horses of the Morning: About the Rt. Excellent N.W. Manley, Q.C., M.M. National Hero of Jamaica. An Understanding*. Kingston: Caribbean Authors Publishing Co.

Rigby, Peter. 1992. Practical ideology and ideological practice: on African episteme and Marxian problematic – Ilparakuyo Maasai transformations. In *The Surreptitious Speech – Présence Africaine and the politics of otherness 1947–1987* edited by V.Y. Mudimbe. Chicago and London: University of Chicago Press.

Rising Star. 1963. Editorial (27 October).

Robinson, Cedric J. 1983. *Black Marxism: the Making of the Black Radical Tradition*. London: Zed Press.

Robertson, Claire C., and Martin A. Klein, eds. 1983. *Women and Slavery in Africa*. Wisconsin: The University of Wisconsin Press.

Robotham, Don. 1980. Pluralism as an ideology. *Social and Economic Studies* 29 (1): 69-89.

Rodney, Donald. 1980. Statement on death of Walter Rodney. Georgetown, Guyana. Mimeographed.

Rodney, Eddie. 1989. Interview by author. Georgetown, Guyana (25 July).

———. 1994. Genuine Rodney killing inquiry needed. *Guyana Chronicle* (22 June).

Rodney, Pat. 1989. Interview by author. Bridgetown, Barbados (5-6 April).

Rodney, Walter. 1958 /1959. What price patriotism? *Lictor – Queen's College Magazine*.

———. 1963a. The role of the historian in the developing West Indies. *The Social Scientist* (18 December): 13-14, 16.

———. 1963b. B.G. – some new dimensions. *Pelican* (March): 9

———. 1965a. Letter from Walter Rodney to Professor T. O. Ranger. London (30 November).

———. 1965b. Portuguese attempts at monopoly on the Upper Guinea Coast. *Journal of African History* 6 (3): 307-22.

———. 1965c. Aspects of the inter-relationship between the Atlantic slave trade and "domestic slavery" on the Upper Guinea Coast. Paper for discussion at African History seminar, School of Oriental and African Studies and Institute of Commonwealth Studies, 17 November.

———. 1966a. A History of the Upper Guinea Coast, 1545–1800. Ph.D. diss., University of London.

———. 1966b. African slavery and other forms of social oppression on the Upper Guinea Coast, 1580–1650. *Journal of African History* 7 (3): 431-43.

———. 1966c. Masses in action. *New World*. Guyana independence issue, edited by George

Lamming and Martin Carter.

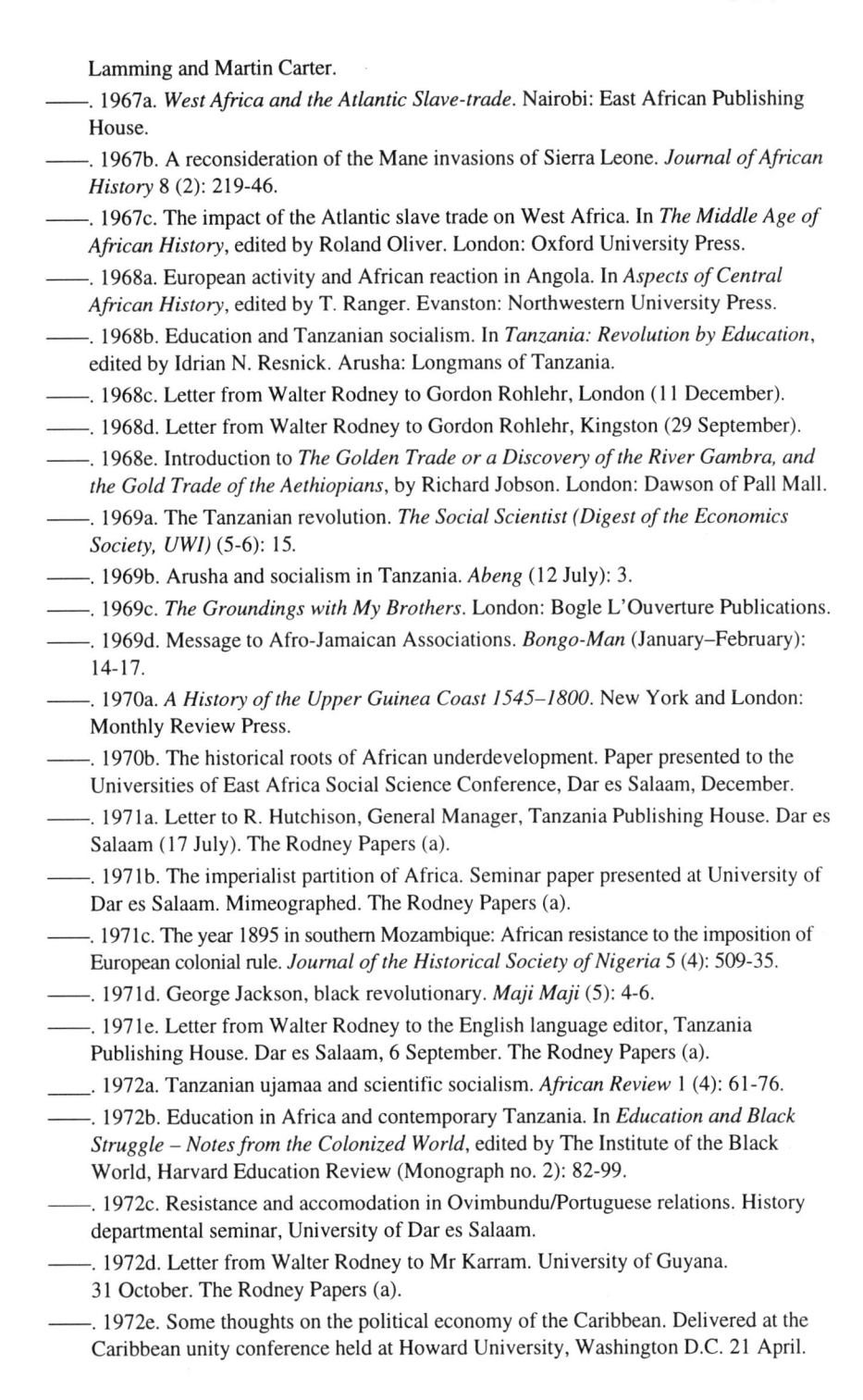

———. 1967a. *West Africa and the Atlantic Slave-trade*. Nairobi: East African Publishing House.

———. 1967b. A reconsideration of the Mane invasions of Sierra Leone. *Journal of African History* 8 (2): 219-46.

———. 1967c. The impact of the Atlantic slave trade on West Africa. In *The Middle Age of African History*, edited by Roland Oliver. London: Oxford University Press.

———. 1968a. European activity and African reaction in Angola. In *Aspects of Central African History*, edited by T. Ranger. Evanston: Northwestern University Press.

———. 1968b. Education and Tanzanian socialism. In *Tanzania: Revolution by Education*, edited by Idrian N. Resnick. Arusha: Longmans of Tanzania.

———. 1968c. Letter from Walter Rodney to Gordon Rohlehr, London (11 December).

———. 1968d. Letter from Walter Rodney to Gordon Rohlehr, Kingston (29 September).

———. 1968e. Introduction to *The Golden Trade or a Discovery of the River Gambra, and the Gold Trade of the Aethiopians*, by Richard Jobson. London: Dawson of Pall Mall.

———. 1969a. The Tanzanian revolution. *The Social Scientist (Digest of the Economics Society, UWI)* (5-6): 15.

———. 1969b. Arusha and socialism in Tanzania. *Abeng* (12 July): 3.

———. 1969c. *The Groundings with My Brothers*. London: Bogle L'Ouverture Publications.

———. 1969d. Message to Afro-Jamaican Associations. *Bongo-Man* (January–February): 14-17.

———. 1970a. *A History of the Upper Guinea Coast 1545–1800*. New York and London: Monthly Review Press.

———. 1970b. The historical roots of African underdevelopment. Paper presented to the Universities of East Africa Social Science Conference, Dar es Salaam, December.

———. 1971a. Letter to R. Hutchison, General Manager, Tanzania Publishing House. Dar es Salaam (17 July). The Rodney Papers (a).

———. 1971b. The imperialist partition of Africa. Seminar paper presented at University of Dar es Salaam. Mimeographed. The Rodney Papers (a).

———. 1971c. The year 1895 in southern Mozambique: African resistance to the imposition of European colonial rule. *Journal of the Historical Society of Nigeria* 5 (4): 509-35.

———. 1971d. George Jackson, black revolutionary. *Maji Maji* (5): 4-6.

———. 1971e. Letter from Walter Rodney to the English language editor, Tanzania Publishing House. Dar es Salaam, 6 September. The Rodney Papers (a).

———. 1972a. Tanzanian ujamaa and scientific socialism. *African Review* 1 (4): 61-76.

———. 1972b. Education in Africa and contemporary Tanzania. In *Education and Black Struggle – Notes from the Colonized World*, edited by The Institute of the Black World, Harvard Education Review (Monograph no. 2): 82-99.

———. 1972c. Resistance and accomodation in Ovimbundu/Portuguese relations. History departmental seminar, University of Dar es Salaam.

———. 1972d. Letter from Walter Rodney to Mr Karram. University of Guyana. 31 October. The Rodney Papers (a).

———. 1972e. Some thoughts on the political economy of the Caribbean. Delivered at the Caribbean unity conference held at Howard University, Washington D.C. 21 April.

———. 1972f. Letter from Walter Rodney to Ewart Thomas. The Rodney Papers (a).

———. 1973a. Recruitment of askari in colonial Tanganyika, 1920–1961. Departmental seminar paper, University of Dar es Salaam.

———. 1973b. Policing the countryside in colonial Tanganyika. Paper presented to the Council for the Social Sciences in East Africa, Annual Social Science Conference.

———. 1973c. African history and development planning. Seminar paper, University of Dar es Salaam.

———. 1974a. Some implications of the question of disengagement from imperialism. In *The Silent Class Struggle*, edited by Issa Shivji, et al. Dar es Salaam: Tanzania Publishing House.

———. 1974b. Lectures on the occasion of Southern African week in Nairobi, March, mimeographed text.

———. 1974c. The *Black Scholar* interviews – Walter Rodney. *Black Scholar* (6) 3: 38-47.

———. 1974d. Statement by Dr Walter Rodney – 18 September, Georgetown, Guyana.

———. 1975a. An interview with Rodney. *Insight* (a student publication of the St Augustine campus of the University of the West Indies).

———. 1975b. The Guinea Coast. In *The Cambridge History of Africa*. Vol. 4. *c.1600–c.1790*, edited by Richard Gray. London: Cambridge University Press.

———. 1975c. Africa in Europe and the Americas. In *The Cambridge History of Africa*. Vol. 4. *c.1600–c.1790*, edited by Richard Gray. London: Cambridge University Press.

———. 1975d. Contemporary political trends in the English-speaking Caribbean. *Black Scholar* (September): 15-21.

———. 1975e. Letter to Harry and Kathleen Drayton. Georgetown, 23 September. The Rodney Papers (b).

———. 1975f. Strategies for development. Toronto. Audiotape in The Rodney Papers. Lincoln University, Pennsylvania.

———. 1976a. *World War II and the Tanzanian Economy*. Ithaca: Africana Studies and Research Center, Cornell University.

———. 1976b. Towards the sixth Pan-African congress. Dar es Salaam: Tanzania Publishing House. In *Resolutions and Selected Speeches from the Sixth Pan-African Congress*. Dar es Salaam: Tanzania Publishing House. Also published in Horace Campbell, ed., n.d. *Pan-Africanism – the Struggle Against Imperialism and Neo-colonialism. Documents of the Sixth Pan-African Congress*. Toronto.

———. 1976c. Guyana's socialism: an interview with Walter Rodney. Interviewed by Colin Prescod. *Race and Class* 18 (2): 109-28.

———. 1976d. The politicization of race in Guyana – a conversation with Walter Rodney. *Black-World-View* 1 (4): 8-10.

———. 1976e. The colonial economy – observations on British Guiana and Tanganyika. Paper for discussion at Postgraduate seminar on "Race and Class in a Colonial Economy". Institute of Commonwealth Studies, 14 June.

———. 1976f. Immigrants and racial attitudes in Guyanese history. Paper for discussion at Postgraduate seminar on "Race and Class in a Colonial Economy". Institute of Commonwealth Studies, 17 May.

———. 1976g. Subject races and class contradictions in Guyanese history. Paper for discussion at Postgraduate seminar on "Race and Class in a Colonial Economy". Institute of Commonwealth Studies, 31 May.

———. 1977. Barbadian immigration into British Guiana 1863–1924. Paper presented at the ninth annual conference of Caribbean historians, University of the West Indies, Cave Hill, Barbados, 3-7 April.

———. 1978. Transition. *Transition* 1 (1): 1-8.

———. 1979a. People's power, no dictator. Georgetown: Working Peoples' Alliance.

———, ed. 1979b. *Guyanese Sugar Plantations in the Late Nineteenth Century: a Contemporary Description from the Argosy*. Georgetown: Release Publishers.

———. 1979c. Slavery and underdevelopment. In *Roots and Branches: Current Directions in Slave Studies,* edited by Michael Craton. London and New York: Pergamon Press.

———. 1980a. *A History of the Upper Guinea Coast 1545–1800*. New York: Monthly Review Press.

———. 1980b. The political economy of colonial Tanganyika 1890–1930. In *Tanzania Under Colonial Rule*, edited by M.H. Kaneki. London: Longman.

———. 1980c. Class contradictions in Tanzania. In *The State in Tanzania: Who Controls it and Whose Interest Does it Serve*. Dar es Salaam: Dar es Salaam University. Press.

———. 1980d. Will the world listen now? Dr Walter Rodney: recent interview by Margaret Arkhurst. *Guyana Forum* (June): 2-3. [Parts of this interview also appeared in *Caribbean Contact* (August 1980): 8.]

———. 1980e. My recipe for Guyana. (In March this year Walter Rodney gave this interview to Carl Blackman, Guyana's most senior journalist.) *The Nation* (20 June): 12-13.

———. 1980f. *Afrika – Die Geschichte einer Unterentwicklung*. Berlin: Verlag Klaus Wagenbach.

———. 1980g. *Kofi Baadu – Out of Africa*. Georgetown: Guyana National Lithographic Co.

———. 1981a. *Marx in the liberation of Africa*. Georgetown: Guyana. Also published in 1985 under the title *Yes to Marxism*. Georgetown: People's Progressive Party.

———. 1981b. *Sign of the Times – Rodney's Last Speech*. A memorial booklet to commemorate our fallen teacher on the first anniversary of his death, 13 June 1981. With tributes by Rupert Roopnarine, Eusi Kwayana and Horace Campbell. London: Walter Rodney Memorial Committee and WPA Support Group.

———. 1981c. *A History of the Guyanese Working People, 1881–1905*. Kingston and London: Heinemann Educational Books.

———. 1981d. The African Revolution. *Urgent Tasks* (Sojourner Truth Organization, Chicago) 12: 5-13. Address delivered at a symposium on C.L.R. James at the University of Michigan, Ann Arbor, 31 March 1972.

———. 1981e. Plantation society in Guyana. (Reprint from the text of a talk given by Walter Rodney at the Ferdinand Braudel Center, 11 December 1978. *Review* 4 (4): 643-66. Also published under the title, The birth of the Guyanese working class and the first sugar strikes 1840/41 and 1847. Georgetown: Working People's Alliance.

———. 1982. In defense of Arnold Rampersaud. Guyana: Working Peoples' Alliance.

———. 1983. *How Europe Underdeveloped Africa*. London: Bogle L'Ouverture Publications.

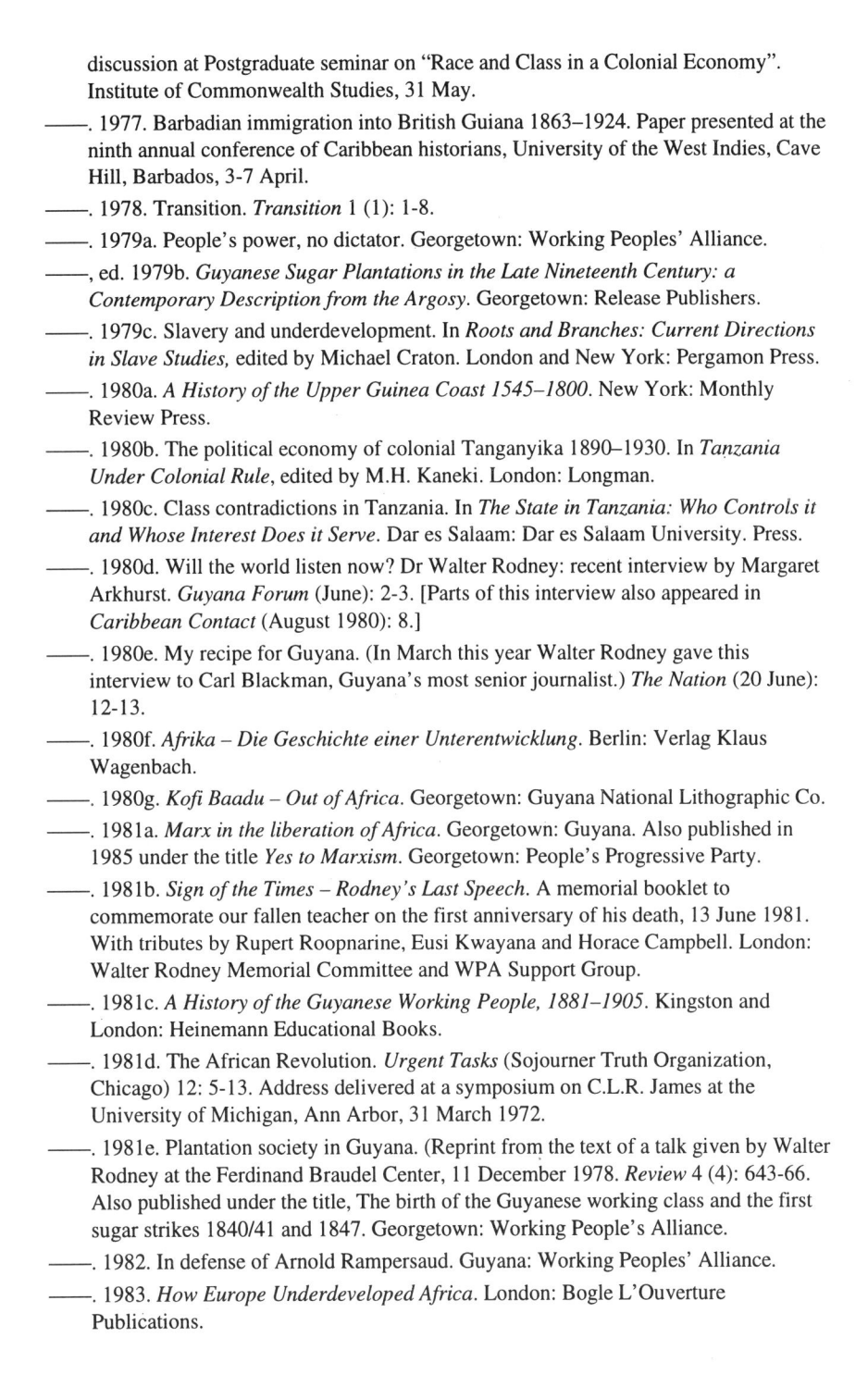

———. 1984. *A Tribute to Walter Rodney: One Hundred Years of Development in Africa*. Lectures given at the University of Hamburg in summer 1978. Hamburg: Institut fur Politische Wissenschaft der Universitat Hamburg.

———. 1985. The colonial economy. In *Africa Under Colonial Domination 1880–1935*, edited by A. Adu Boahen. California: Heinemann and UNESCO.

———. 1986. *Et L'Europe sous développa L'Afrique: Analyse historique et politique du sous-développement*. Paris: Editions Caribéennes.

———. 1987. Support for liberation struggles in Southern Africa. Address to a meeting of the Afro-Asian Cultural Society at Sussex University, United Kingston in June 1977. Georgetown: Working People's Alliance.

———. 1990. *Walter Rodney Speaks*. New Jersey: Africa World Press.

———. Up from slavery in Seychelles. Manuscript in the Rodney Papers (a).

———. Lectures on the Russian Revolution. Photocopy courtesy of Dr Robin Kelley. The Rodney Papers (b).

Rodney, Walter, Kapepwa Tambila, and Laurent Sago. 1983. *Migrant Labour in Tanzania during the Colonial Period – Case Studies of Recruitment and Conditions of Labour in the Sisal Industry*. Hamburg: Institut fur Afrika Kunde im Verbund der Stiftung Deutsches Ubersee-Institut.

Rohlehr, Gordon. 1980. Blues for brother Walter. *Trinidad and Tobago Review* 3 (10): 1, 3, 6, 16.

———. 1989. Our truest ancestor (a tribute to C.L.R. James). *Trinidad and Tobago Review* 11 (9): A and C.

———. 1991. Trophy and catastrophe – an address. *Caribbean Quarterly* 37 (4): 1-8.

———. 1992 a. *My Strangled City and Other Essays*. Port of Spain: Longman Trinidad.

———. 1992 b. *The Shape of that Hurt and Other Essays*. Port of Spain: Longman Trinidad.

Roopnarine, Rupert. 1995. Walter Rodney: murder they wrote. *Friends of Jamaica – Caribbean Newsletter* 15 (4-6): 2-4.

———. 1996. Reader's report on R. Lewis, *Walter Rodney's Intellectual and Political Thought*. The Press UWI: on file.

Rweyemamu, Justinian. 1973. Underdevelopment and Industrialization. London: Oxford University Press.

Ryan, Selwyn. 1989. *Revolution and Reaction: Parties and Politics in Trinidad and Tobago 1970–1981*. Trinidad and Tobago: Institute of Social and Economic Research, University of the West Indies.

Said, Edward. 1993. *Culture and Imperialism*. New York: Alfred A. Knopf.

Salkey, Andrew. 1972. *Georgetown Journal*. London: New Beacon.

———. 1974. *Joey Tyson*. London: Bogle L'Ouverture Publications.

———. 1985. *The One. The Story of How the People of Guyana Avenge the Murder of Their Pasero with Help from Brother Anancy and Sister Buxton*. London: Bogle L'Ouverture Publications.

Sankatsingh, Glenn. 1989. *Caribbean Social Science – an Assessment*. Caracas: URSHSLAC-UNESCO.

Saul, John. 1970. Radicalism and the Hill. *East Africa Journal* 7 (12): 27-30.

Saunders, A. C. DeC. 1982. *A Social History of Black Slaves and Freedmen in Portugal,*

1441–1555. Cambridge: Cambridge University Press.

Scott, Kathleen. 1989. Interview by author. Georgetown, Guyana (25 July).

Schuler, Monica. 1970. Akan slave rebellions in the British Caribbean. *Savacou* 1 (1): 8-31.

———. 1980. *Alas, Alas Kongo*. Baltimore: Johns Hopkins University Press.

Shamuyarira, Nathan. 1975. *Essays on the Liberation of Southern Africa*. Dar es Salaam: Tanzania Publishing House.

Shenton, Robert. 1983. Introduction. In *How Europe Underdeveloped Africa*, by Walter Rodney (sixth reprint). London: Bogle L'Ouverture Publication.

Shepperson, George. 1972. Review of *Groundings with my Brothers*, by Walter Rodney. *Journal of African History* 13 (1): 173.

Sherlock, Philip, and Rex Nettleford. 1990. *The University of the West Indies: a Caribbean Response to the Challenge of Change*. London: Macmillan.

Shivji, Issa. 1973. The silent class struggle. In *Socialism in Tanzania: an Interdisciplinary Reader*, edited by Lionel Cliffe and John Saul. Nairobi: East African Publishing House.

———. 1975. *Class Struggles in Tanzania*. London and Dar es Salaam: Heinemann Educational Books and Tanzania Publishing House.

———. 1980. Rodney and radicalism on the Hill, 1966–1974. *Maji Maji* 43 (August): 29-39.

———. 1985. *The State and the Working People in Tanzania*. Senegal: Codesria.

———. 1990. Tanzania – the debate on delinking. In *Adjustment or Delinking? The African Experience*, edited by Azzam Mahjoub. London: Zed Press.

Singh, Rickey. 1994. Probes and priorities. Political murders and 'deals' in Guyana. *Sunday Chronicle* (9 January).

Singham, A.W. 1990. James and the creation of a Caribbean intellectual tradition. *Social and Economic Studies* 39 (3): 181-89.

Slater, Henry. 1986. Dar es Salaam and the postnationalist historiography of Africa. In *African Historiographies: What History for Which Africa?* edited by Bogumil Jewsiewicki and David Newbury. London: Sage Publications.

Small, Robin. 1989. Interview by author. Kingston, Jamaica. (11 May).

Smith, M. G., Roy Augier, and Rex Nettleford. 1967. The Rastafari movement in Kingston, Jamaica, Parts 1 and 2. *Caribbean Quarterly* 13 (3): 3-20; and (4): 3-14.

Smith, M. G. 1974. *The Plural Society in the British West Indies*. Kingston and Los Angeles: Sangster's Bookstores in association with University of California Press.

———. 1984. Culture, race and class in the Commonwealth Caribbean. Kingston: Department of Extra-Mural Studies, University of the West Indies.

Sosa Rodríquez, Enrique. 1982. *Los ñañigos*. Havana: Casa de las Américas.

Soyinka, Wole. 1980. The man who was absent. In *"And Finally They Killed Him." Speeches and Poems at a Memorial Rally for Walter Rodney (1942–1980)*. Oduduwa Hall, University of Ife, Nigeria, Friday, 27 June 1980. Ife: Editorial Collectives of *Socialist Forum* and *Positive Review*.

Stone, Carl. 1973. *Class, Race and Political Behaviour in Urban Jamaica*. Kingston: Institute of Social and Economic Research, University of the West Indies.

Sutton, Paul. 1992. The historian as politician: Eric Williams and Walter Rodney. In *Intellectuals in the Twentieth Century Caribbean*, Vol. 1. *Spectre of the New Class:*

the Commonwealth Caribbean, edited by Alistair Hennessy. London: Macmillan Caribbean.

Swai, Bonaventure. 1981–1982. Rodney on scholarship and activism. Parts 1 and 2. *Journal of African Marxists* 1 (November): 31-43; 2 (August): 38-52.

Szentes, Tamas. 1985. *Theories of World Capitalist Economy: a Critical Survey of Conventional, Reformist and Radical Views*. Budapest: Akademiai Kiado.

TANU. 1967. *The Arusha Declaration and TANU'S Policy on Socialism and Self-Reliance*. Dar es Salaam: TANU.

TPH. (Tanzania Publishing House). 1976. *Resolutions and Selected Speeches from the Sixth Pan-African Congress*. Dar es Salaam: Tanzania Publishing House.

Temu, A.J. 1973. Problems of creating the African university: the case of the University of Dar es Salaam. *Social Praxis* 1 (2): 141-51.

Temu, A.J., and Bonaventure Swai. 1981. The intellectual and the state in postcolonial Africa: the Tanzanian case. *Social Praxis* 8 (3/4): 25-52.

Thomas, Ewart. 1982. Towards the continuance of Walter Rodney's work. In *Walter Rodney–Revolutionary and scholar: a Tribute*, edited by Edward A. Alpers and Pierre-Michel Fontaine. Los Angeles: Center for Afro-American Studies and African Studies Center.

——. 1989. Interview with author. Kingston, Jamaica (6 May).

Thomas, Clive. 1973. *Dependence and Transformation*. New York: Monthly Review Press.

——. 1984. Hard lessons for intellectuals. *Caribbean Contact* (September): 7, 12.

——. 1986. *The Rise of the Authoritarian State in Peripheral Societies*. New York: Monthly Review Press.

Thomas, J.J. 1969 [1889]. *Froudacity: West Indian Fables Explained*. Reprint, London: New Beacon Books.

Thornton, John K. 1983. *The Kingdom of Kongo: Civil War and Transition, 1641–1718*. Wisconsin: The University of Wisconsin Press.

——. 1992. *Africa and Africans in the Making of the Atlantic World, 1400–1680*. New York: Cambridge University Press.

Tordoff, William, and Ali Mazrui. 1972. The left and the super-left in Tanzania. *The Journal of Modern African Studies* 10 (3): 427-45.

University College of the West Indies. 1960–61. *Pelican Annual*: Annual Report of the Guild Council, 9-19.

University of the West Indies. 1963. UWI comes of age. *Pelican* (March): 2, 13.

Van Sertima, Ivan. 1976. *They Came before Columbus: the African Presence in Ancient America*. New York: Random House.

Vansina. Jan. 1986. One's own past: African perceptions of African history. In *Africa in World History: a Teaching Conference*, edited by Bryant P. Shaw. Proceedings of a conference held 25-26 April at the US Air Force Academy, sponsored by the Department of History USAF Academy and the Rocky Mountain Regional World History Organization.

Venner, Dwight. 1993. The great man (tribute to Sir Arthur Lewis). Trinidad and Tobago Review 15 (6): 16-17.

Walcott, Derek. 1993. The land of look behind. *Money Index* (27 April): 24c-24f.

Walmsley, Anne. 1992. *The Caribbean Artist Movement 1966–1972: a Literary and Cultural History*. London and Port of Spain: New Beacon Books.

Walters, Ronald. 1993. *Pan Africanism in the African Diaspora: an Analysis of Modern Afrocentric Political Movements*. Detroit: Wayne State University Press.

Ward, June. 1990. Interview by author. Dar es Salaam, Tanzania (2 August).

Warner-Lewis, Maureen. 1991. *Guinea's Other Suns: The African Dynamic in Trinidad Culture*. Dover, Massachusetts: The Majority Press.

———. 1993. African continuities in the Rastafari belief system. *Caribbean Quarterly* 39 (3 & 4): 108-23.

———. 1996a. *Trinidad Yoruba: from Mother Tongue to Memory*. Tuscaloosa: University of Alabama Press.

———. 1996b. African continuities in the linguistic heritage of Jamaica. *African-Caribbean Institute of Jamaica Research Review* (3).

White, Garth. 1967. Rudie, oh rudie! *Caribbean Quarterly* 13 (3): 30-44.

Williams, Denis. 1974. *Icon and Image: a Study of Sacred and Secular Forms of African Classical Art*. London: Allen Lane.

Williams, Eric. 1944. *Capitalism and Slavery*. Chapel Hill: University of North Carolina Press.

———. 1963. Pro-Chancellor addresses 1962 graduating class. *Pelican* (March): 4-7.

———. 1969. *Inward Hunger: the Education of a Prime Minister*. London: André Deutsch.

Working People's Alliance. 1978. Statement on the referendum. *Dayclean* (July).

PAPERS

The Rodney Papers (a) have been stored at the Langston Hughes Library, Lincoln University, Pennsylvania. There is as yet no proper collection that has been catalogued for the use of researchers.

The Rodney Papers (b) refer to copies of papers from a variety of private sources that I gathered for this project.

Index

Abeng, 100, 105, 115, 121n.32, 208
Abolition, 62
Abrahams, Anthony, 30n.13
Abrahams, Eric, 25
Afghanistan, 181n.12
Africa: British colonial rule in, 2; and Caribbean, 26, 83n.14; colonialism in, 47, 54, 63–64, 69–70, 73–74, 145; and decolonisation, xvi, 11, 54, 63; economic development in, 69, 72–74, 78–79, 81; ethnic rivalry in, 64, 141; gold mining in, 60; and Henry, 89; imperialism in, 168; Islamic versus Atlantic Africa, 83n.9; and Latin American dependency theory, 48; Lenin on, 168; Marxism in, 39, 72, 148, 177, 217; and nationalist versus materialist historical reconstructions, 55–56; neo-colonialism in, 117; political fragmentation of, 61; Portuguese in, 63–66; postcolonial historians of, 47–48; precolonial Africa, 50, 53, 82n.5; and racist constructions, 54–55; Rastafarian repatriation, 101, 106; and recolonisation by domestic political elite, xvii; revolutionary movements in, 228–229; and Rodney's ban from Jamaica, 117; Rodney's *Cambridge History of Africa* essays, 56–61; Rodney's criticism of African political leadership, 172–173; Rodney's doctorate in African history, 31, 40–45; Rodney's historical approach to, xi, 11–12, 26, 39, 47–63, 69–70, 78 107, 188, 199, 247, 254–256; and Rodney's political thought, xiv; slave trade advantages of, 51–52, 71; slave trade consequences for, xii, 52, 59–60, 61; and slave trade history, 50–51; slave trade relations and, 56; and slavery resistance, 62; social differentiation in, 50–51, 56–57, 68, 82n.5; socialism of, 140–141, 179; sovereignty in, 67; state building in, 56–61; underdevelopment of, 48, 70–72; unity of, 176–177; women's role in, 82n.6; working class in, 74–75. *See also* Slave trade; Slavery
Africa Reform Church, 89
African diaspora: as growing field, 83n.15; and heritage of social organisation, 63; and Pan-Africanism, 172; Rodney's historical research on, 61–63; and Rodney's political thought, xiv, xvii; and slave trade, 56
African National Congress (ANC), 125, 135, 180n.7
African Party for the Independence of Guinea and Cape Verde (PAIGC), 125
African ruling groups: consumption patterns of, 59–60, 67; critique of, 55; and European contact, 59; predatory characteristics of, 75, 84n.22; and slave raiding, 56, 58–60, 67; and slave trade, 50–53, 55–56, 58, 66–67; and state building, 58
African Society for Cultural Relations with Independent Africa (ASCRIA), 207, 208, 219, 220
African soldiers, as colonial collaborators, 64–65
African Studies Association, 250n.25
African Studies Association of the West Indies, 108, 122n.43
Africanus, Leo, 61
Afro-Caribbean League, 101
Afro-Guyanese: and Burnham, 204, 208, 220; education of, 11, 193–194; and free village movement, 192, 195; middle class of, 3, 11, 193–194, 208, 213, 220–222, 239; in military, 226; and People's National Congress, 221; and political parties, 203; population of, 206; and racial issues, 221–222; social formation of, 189; social stratification among, 193; victimisation of, 221; working class struggles of, 194–195, 198; and Working People's Alliance, 229
Afro-West Indian League, 101
Agaja Trudo (King of Dahomey), 58, 83n.12

Agriculture, 27, 58, 180n.3, 190–191, 198
Aja country, 57
Akan culture, 56, 60
Akivaga, Simon, 135–136
Algeria, 116, 137, 178
Alice, Princess, 120–121n.26
All African People's Revolutionary Party, 253n.55
Allied Forces, 2
Alpers, Edward A., xiv, 53–54
Alphonso, Roland, 103
Alvaranga, Filmore, 101
American Historical Association, 199
Americas: African contribution to, 62; African presence in, 69; slave trade consequences for, xiv; and slave trade relations, 56. *See also* specific countries
Amerindians, 3, 4, 62–63
Amin, Idi, 126, 175
Amin, Samir, 39, 78, 147, 148
ANC (African National Congress), 125, 135, 180n.7
Andaiye: and Bishop, 232, 250n.25; and *Georgetown Review*, 216; return to Guyana, 187; and Rodney's assassination, 243, 245; on Rodney's associations, 181n.11; and Rodney's research, 199; and Working People's Alliance, 229, 230, 231
Anglican Church, 5
Angola: Cuba in, 178–179, 181n.12; liberation movement in, 170; Portuguese rule in, 64–69, 116; and race, 139; and slave trade, 66
Annalistes, 48, 80, 82n.2
Anticolonial movement: and black nationalism, 116, 222; and Burnham, 204; and capitalism, 75; and class, 189; in English-speaking Caribbean, 2; and ethnicity, 189; and James, 176; and Kwayana, 219; and Marxism, 205; and middle class, 193; and Padmore, 40; racial solidarity of, 170; and West Indian Caribbean intellectual tradition, 69
Antigua, 115, 247
Antigua-Caribbean Liberation Movement, 253n.55
Apartheid, 116
Appiah, Kwame Anthony, 250n.26
Arusha Declaration: debates surrounding, 130–131; and James, 250n.24; and middle class, 151–153; political context of, 125–126; radical reform of, 44, 163, 165n.16; Rodney on, 137–145

Asante, 60, 82n.6
ASCRIA (African Society for Cultural Relations with Independent Africa), 207, 208, 219, 220
Asia: and African trade, 61; Asians as middlemen, 74; British colonial rule in, 2; Marxist analysis of, 72; underdevelopment in, 78
Asiatic Indians, 153, 210–211. *See also* Indo-Guyanese
Association of Caribbean Historians, 199
Augier, Roy, 8, 18, 23, 25
Augustus, Earl, 21–23, 25–26
Austen, Ralph, 83n.9

Babu, Abdulrahman Mohamed, 129, 163–164n.4
Bailundu war, 65, 84n.19
Banda, Hastings, 126
Bangalas, 67
Banks and banking: and Arusha Declaration, 126; and slavery market, 52; and University of Guyana, 206
Baraka, Imamu, 180n.7
Barbados: political parties of, 202; social differentiation in, 27; and United States, 178–179; University of the West Indies at Mona students from, 14; West Indian writers from, 17
Barbados Labour Party, 45n.4
Barbados Workers Union, 209
Barrow, Errol, 202
Basorun Gaha, 58
Bauxite industry: in Guyana, 198, 212, 214; in Jamaica, 27; Rodney's work with bauxite workers, 237–238, 252n.43; strike actions in, 227–228
Beauvoir, Simone de, 179n.2
Beckford, George, 112–113, 121n.32, 122n.50, 250n.26
Beckles, David, 25
Belize, 115
Benin, 56–57
Bennett, Vin, 121n.32
Bertram, Arnold, 114, 120n.21, 209
Bhagwan, Moses, 229, 236
Bhojpuri, 197
Bight of Biafra, 60
Bishop, Maurice: and Burnham, 225; execution of, 232, 246; and Grenada, 212; and left, 117; and New Jewel Movement, 46n.6, 117; and radical scholars, 158; on Rodney, 232, 250n.25; and Rodney's assassination, 247; Rodney's critique of left-authoritarian position of, 76
Black consciousness, 89–95, 182–183
Black Man Speaks, 98–99, 103, 105
Black nationalism: and Angola, 178–179; and

anticolonial movement, 116; and decolonisation, 145; Gray on, 109–110; and historiography, 161; in Jamaica, 85, 110; and nationalist versus materialist historical reconstructions, 55–56; and Rastafarian movement, 29; repression of, 100; Rodney as nationalistic, 80, 161, 250n.29; Rodney's criticism of, 174; and Rodney's Jamaican activism, 98; and Robin Small, 98; and socialism, 105, 110, 126; in Tanzania, 126, 161. *See also* Nationalist movements
Black Power: Caribbean impact of, 89, 94, 117; and class, 177; in Jamaica, 92–93, 95, 98; revolts in Trinidad and Tobago, 212; Rodney's Jamaican activism and, xiii, 95, 107–108; and Rodney's marriage, 32; and Scandinavian social democracy, 164n.6
Black Writers' Congress, 107, 113, 123n.56
Boer allies, 66
Bogle L–Ouverture, 81, 97, 117
Bogle, Paul, 109
Bogues, Anthony, xv
Bokassa, Emperor, 126
Bongo-Man, 105, 107, 122n.40
Bonny, 59
Bookers Sugar Estates, 184
Booth, Ken, 104
Botchwey, Kwesi, 129
Bottom-house meetings, 220, 237, 238
Bourgeoisie. *See* Middle class; Political elite
Brathwaite, Edward Kamau: career of, 12n.4; on black culturalism, 105–106; and Rodney's African history work, 35, 80; and Rodney's assassination, 246, 253n.54; as West Indian writer, 17
Braithwaite, Lloyd, 23
Braudel, Fernand, 82n.2
Brazil, 66
Brezhnev, Leonid, 20, 233
British colonial rule: and capitalism, xvii; and coercive labour regimes, 48; dissolution of, 145; and James, 36; political developments in 1940s, 2; and Caribbean intellectual thought, xv–xvi
British Guiana, 6. *See also* Guyana
British Labour Party, 2, 22, 202
British Ministry of Overseas Development, 43
Brown, Adlith, 25
Brown, Sam, 99, 121n.31
Brutents, Karen, 46n.6, 224
Brutus, Dennis, 129
Buganda, 82n.6
Buhle, Paul, 45n.4

Burke, Aggrey, 110
Burnham, Forbes: and African solidarity, 178–179; electoral practices of, 202, 206–208, 218, 225–226, 233–234, 255; and ethnic differences, 195; and Guyana's Nationalist Movement, 1; and Jonestown tragedy, 227; and Nationalist Movement, 4, 10, 25; and New Jewel Movement, 232; opposition to, 220, 228–229; and Pan-African Congress of 1974, 170; political deterioration of, 225; and Queen's College, 193; and race, 205, 220, 239–240; Rodney as left of, 250n.25; Rodney as opponent of, 10, 208, 224, 233, 235–237, 241, 243, 255; and Rodney family discussions, 5; and Rodney's assassination, 245–246, 246, 253n.56; Rodney's critiques of, 76, 208, 212, 248n.3; and Rodney's political victimisation, 11; Rodney's professorship blocked by, 44, 185, 208; Rodney's struggles against dictatorial regime of, 187; Rodney's support of, 10, 25; role of coercion, 206–207; and socialism, 195, 204, 208, 223, 228, 248n.3; and United Force, 217–218; and Working People's Alliance harassment, 241
Burnham, Jessica, 10
Burundi, 126
Bustamante, Alexander, 28
Buster, Prince, 105

Cabral, Amilcar, 12, 39, 140–150, 224
Calabar High School, 120n.16
Cambodia, 181n.12
Campbell, Clifford, 88
Campbell, Horace, xiv-xv, 79–80, 129–130, 180n.6
Campbell, Trevor, xv
Canoe Houses, 59
Capitalism: and African development, 74–75, 77–78, 81; and African resistance, 79; and African socialism, 140; and British Empire, xvii; capitalist globalisation, 148, 210; of China, 212; and class, 64; and colonialism, 66, 68, 148; of East Indians of Trinidad, 210–211; and imperialism, 168; industrial capitalism, 68, 141; and industry, 74–75; and Jamaica Labour Party, 203; and Lewis, 143, 165n.20; and lumpenisation, 177; and nationalisation, 147; and Pan-Africanism, 176, 186; and Portugal, 64–65; qualitative character of, 73; and Rodney's African history, 48; and slave trade, 51, 52, 55, 143; and Tanzania, 126, 138, 143, 144, 146–148; and underdevelopment, 200n.3; uneven development of, 66; and Western

political alignment, xvii; and world economy, 76
Caribbean: African history's relationship to, 83n.14; Africa's relevance to, 26; anticolonial movement in, 2; black consciousness in, 183; British colonial rule in, 2; British institutions' role in, 14–15, 29n.2; and Cuban diplomatic relations, 202; and decolonisation, xvi, 11, 54; decolonisation in, 116; democratic evolution of, 35; and French Revolution, 62; Great Britain's educational bias in, 8; history of, 8; Marxism of, 38, 105, 117, 216, 218, 224–225; middle class's role in, 22–23; neocolonialism in, 117; and Pan-African Congress of 1974, 171; and Pan-Africanism, 167; plantation economies in, 60; political activism in, 202–203; political leadership of, 71; radicalism in, 115, 117, 203; and recolonisation by domestic political elite, xvii; revolutions of, 186; and Rodney's assassination, 246; Rodney's historical approach to, 11–12, 39, 48, 187–200, 254–256; Rodney's political thought on, xiii, xiv, xv, 210; Rodney's public speaking on, 31; Rodney's regional influence, 115; Rodney's regional perspective of, 26–27; and slave trade, 52; social differentiation in, 27; socialism in, 213–214; Southern African solidarity of, 179
Caribbean Council of Churches, 209, 253n.55
Caribbean Unity Conference, 249n.20
Caribbean Writers and Artists Conference, 204
CARIFESTA, 204
Carmichael, Stokely: on Castro, 105; on race, 222; and Rastafarian movement, 95; restrictions on books by, 109, 112; and Rodney's assassination, 253n.55; in Tanzania, 135
Carr, E. H., 180n.3
Carter, Martin, 204–205, 216, 235, 253n.54
Carto, Colin, 199
Castro, Fidel: and *Black Man Speaks* issue, 105; Burnham as ally of, 10; and Cuban Revolution, 180n.4; and Henry, 90, 119n.10; Manley compared to, 181n.12; monopoly of power, 212; Rodney on, 105; and Rodney's ban from Jamaica, 100
Center for Afro-American and African Studies, 127
Central Bank of Guyana, 206
Central Intelligence Agency (CIA), 181n.12
Césaire, Aimé, 36, 165n.18

Charismatic leadership, 22–23
Charles, Pearnel, 114, 253n.55
Cheche, xiv, 136, 146
China: capitalist policies of, 212; communism of, 145; Communist Party of China, 140; and economic development, 75; and ethnicity, 218; and Jamaica's publications ban, 112; and Marxism, 34, 39; Rodney on, 39; socialism in, 71, 134; and Soviet Union, 142; and Tanzania, 125, 142
Chinese people: anti-Chinese riots, 89, 90; in Guyana, 3, 198; in Jamaica, 28, 89; as middle class, 211
Chinese Revolution, 147
Cholmondeley, Colin, 206, 249n.13
Chou En-lai, 125
Churchill, Winston, 2
CIA (Central Intelligence Agency), 181n.12
Citizens Committee, 225
Civil rights movement, 31, 89, 95, 116–117
Civil service, 9
Class: and African socialism, 141; and colonialism, 75–76, 150, 189; differentiation between, 196; and ethnicity, 158; and European views of Africa, 61; in Guyana, 2–3, 27, 64, 192, 198, 222; and historiography, 161; and intellectuals, xv, 9; in Jamaica, xiii, 27–28, 92, 94; and national movements, 170, 171; and organic intellectuals, xv; and Pan-Africanism, 177; and race, xvi, 4, 105, 109, 222, 256; and Rastafarian movement, 107; and revolutions, 39; Rodney on, 250n.29; role of masses in history, 21–22; and Russian Revolution, 169; and slave trade, 51, 53, 83n.11; and social differentiation, 27–28, 50–51, 56–57, 68, 82; and socialism, 105; in Southern Mozambique, 63–64; in Tanzania, 48, 146, 148–151, 163. *See also* Middle class; Working class/people
Clerical and Commercial Workers Union, 227
Cliffe, Lionel, 128, 160
Coard, Bernard, 117, 251n.38
Coard, Phyllis, 251n.38
Cold War: and anticommunism, 85, 171, 202, 206; Communist fears during, 6; and decolonisation, 145, 146; end of, 159; and Guyanese politics, 25; and Jamaican politics, 114; and nonaligned movement, 145–146; and revolutionary movements, 229; and socialism, 142
Colonialism: and Africa, 47, 54, 63–65, 69–70, 73–74, 79, 145; and African women, 82–83n.6; and capitalism, 66, 68, 148; and class, 75–76, 150, 189; and coercive labor regimes, 48; and concessions companies, 77; and economic

development, 69, 72; and education, 40–41; and ethnicity, 189; of Europe, 43, 47; and industry, 75; and James, 48; and middle class, 76; and middle class social mobility, 93; and oppression, 180n.7; and peasantry, 77; political consequences of, 75–76; and race, 71; and Rastafarian movement, 28; and recolonisation by domestic political elite, xvii; and slave trade, 48, 71–72, 79, 143; and technology, 66; and working people, xv. *See also* Decolonisation; Neocolonialism
Comintern, 167
Committee in Defence of Democracy, 225
Common Course, 159–160, 161
Communications: and colonialism, 66; and Working People's Alliance, 253n.51
Communism: and anticommunism, 85, 171, 202, 206, 208, 248n.3; and anti-imperialism, 213; and Burnham, 251n.32; and Caribbean political parties, 224; fall of, 158–159, 212; Great Britain's fear of, 6; and Jagan, 25, 208; Jamaica's anticommunist atmosphere, 19; and Marxism, 224; and Pan-Africanism, 167, 171; and working class movements, 178
Communist International movement, 40
Communist Party of China, 140
Communist Party of Cuba, 203, 212, 223, 241, 247, 250n.25
Communist Party of Great Britain, 39
Communist Party of the Soviet Union, 46n.6, 140, 168, 203, 223, 224
Concessions companies, 77
Congo, 66, 175
Congo Brazzaville, 217
Conservative Party, 2
Constantine, Learie, 36
Constitution (Amendment) Bill, 225
Convention Peoples Party, 151
Coral Gardens incident, 28, 88, 89, 90, 107
Coulson, Andrew, 128
Coulthard, Gabriel, 118n.1
Council of Progressive Trade Unions of Trinidad and Tobago, 253n.55
Creolese language, 197–198
Creolisation, 195–198
Cricket, 35–36, 123n.56
Croal, James, 8, 21
Crusader, 112
Cuba: and Angola, 178–179, 181n.12; and Burnham, 208, 212, 225, 248n.3; Caribbean diplomatic relations with, 202; communism of, 145; Communist Party of Cuba, 203, 212, 223, 241, 247, 250n.25; diplomatic relations of, 209; and Guyana, 213; and Jagan, 248n.3; and Jamaica's publications ban, 112; liberation movements of, 178; radicals visits to, 113; Rodney's visit to, 19–20, 113, 115–116; and Southern Africa, 178; United States blockade of, 249n.21
Cuban Revolution: and foreign capital dependence, 247; as model, 212, 249n.19; and radicalisation of Guyanese politics, 224; and Rodney, 20, 39, 211; and Russian Revolution, 180n.4
Cudjoe, Selwyn, 45n.3, 81n.1
Curaçao, 1
Curtin, P. D., 47, 53, 61
Czechoslovakia, 131

Daaga, Makandal, 117
Dabydeen, David, 25, 253n.54
Dahomey, 56–58
Daley, Dennis, 121n.32
Dar es Salaam University Students' Organisation (DUSO), 136
Darke, Bernard, Father, 234, 235
Davis, Frank, 113
Davis, Winston, 19, 112, 117–118n.1, 122n.48
Dayclean, 187, 201n.12, 226, 229, 231, 235, 240–241
De Souza, Karen, 229, 245
De Souza, Louis, 230
Decolonisation: and Africa, xvi, 11, 54, 63; and black nationalism, 145; and capitalism, 147; in Caribbean, 116; and independence, 23; James on, 35–36; mass party's role in, 35; and middle class, 212; and national relationships, xvi; and Nationalist Movement, 14; and neo-colonialism, 209–210; and People's Progressive Party, 2; and revolutionary pedagogy, 154–159; Rodney's historical research related to, xiv, 11, 54, 69, 81, 183, 256; and Russian Revolution, 169; and School of Oriental and African Studies' mission, 41; and socialism, 142; subjective factor in, 150–151; in Tanzania, 40, 134, 147
Delinking, 147, 166n.24
Democracy: and Arusha Declaration, 152; development problems in, 48; James on, 35; and Marxism, 38, 217; multiparty approaches to, 75; and pseudosocialism, 211; Rodney on, 21–22, 38, 227, 231–232; social democracy, 2, 126, 164n.6, 202; in Tanzania, 136, 139. *See also* Social democracy
Democratic Labour Party, 45n.4, 202
Democratic socialism, 29, 90, 94, 203, 209
Depelchin, Jacques, 161

Dependency theory: and African history, 48, 69, 78; and Tanzania, 148
Deutscher, I., 180n.3
Devonish, Hubert, 197–198
Diamond mining, 198
Dizzy, Ras, 104
Dodd, Clement, 103
Doggett, Bill, 104
Dogmatism: of left, 169; of Marxism, 38, 39, 144, 225
Dominican Republic, 1
Domino, Fats, 104
Dos Santos, Marcelino, 129, 180n.6
Drayton, Harold, 112, 122n.51, 205, 215
Drayton, Kathleen, 112, 122n.51, 215
Dread, 243, 252n.49
Dread, Judge, 105
Drummond, Don, 102
Du Bois, W.E.B., xv, 17, 36, 172
Du Bois Institute Slave Trade Data Base, 53
Dublin, Edward, 234–235
Duncan, Ann, 165n.12
Duncan, D. K., 114, 117, 120n.21, 209
Duncan, Virgil, 32, 33, 165n.12
Dungles, 87, 118n.3
DUSO (Dar es Salaam University Students' Organisation), 136
Duvalier, F. 'Papa Doc', 228

East Germany, 124–125
East Indians, 153, 210–211. *See also* Indo-Guyanese
Eastern Europe: and People's National Congress, 251n.32; political changes in, 75, 247; socialism in, 71, 176, 212
Economic development: in Africa, 69, 72–74, 78–79; and delinking, 147, 166n.24; in Europe, 71, 73; and fall of communism, 158–159; of Guyana, 25; and ideology, 145; of Jamaica, 27, 92; and Lewis, 155–156; and middle class, 153; and Pan-Africanism, 176; requirements for, 150; and revolutions, 39; and slavery, 191; in Tanzania, 70, 138, 142–143, 147, 148, 153, 163; and underdevelopment problems, 69, 78, 200n.3, 211; uneven development, 72; and West Indian Caribbean intellectual tradition, 116
Economics: in Gambia, 76–77; global economic system, 48, 74, 76–79, 143, 148; left's emphasis on, 106; of plantations, 60; and slave trade, 56, 62, 66–67; and Ujamma, 141
Education: and colonialism, 40–41, 154; competition with Native Americans, 3; expansion of opportunities in, 6–7; Great Britain's educational bias in Caribbean, 8; invisible education, 6; and Lewis, 155–158, 159, 166n.30; and middle class, 22–23, 134, 156; premium place on, 11; regional universities, 13, 17, 127, 134; and Rodney family, 5–6; and Rodney's revolutionary pedagogy, 154–159; role of, 159, 193; scholarships for, 5, 6–8, 13, 33; and social advancement, 9, 11; in Tanzania, 70, 154; and working class families, 5
Edwards, Adolph, 37, 38
Edwards, David, 23
Edwards, Lucille, 120–121n.26
Efik ekpe society, 49
Ekine, 59
Elections Commission, 225
Elizabeth II (queen of United Kingdom of Great Britain and Ireland), 7
Engels, Friedrich, 142
English Civil War, 39
Entrepreneurial class, 138, 153
Environment, impact of, in Guyanese history, 189–191
Equatorial Guinea, 126
Ethiopia, 90–91, 101, 181n.12, 217
Ethiopian World Federation (EWF), 97, 101
Ethnicity: and African ethnic rivalry, 64, 141; and Angola, 178; and black nationalism, 146, 149, 151–152, 169; and class, 158, 222; and colonialism, 189; and conflict, 195–198; ethnic diversification, 196–197; and free village movement, 195–196; in Guyana, 34; in Jamaica, xiii, 28, 114; and Marxism, 218–219, 250n.29; and neocolonialism, 210; and political activism, 112, 249n.14; and political parties, 195; and Rodney's breaking ranks with Afro-Guyanese middle class, 208; and Rodney's popularity across ethnic lines, 160; and slave trade, 51, 53; and socialism, 218–219; in Southern Mozambique, 63–64; in Soviet Union, 169; and working class divisions, 192, 194–195
Europe: African contributions to, 62; and African rulers' consumption patterns, 59–60, 67; Africa's image within, 61; Africa's subordination to, 56; colonialism of, 43, 47, 54; and decolonisation, xvi; economic development in, 71, 73; Marxist analysis of, 72; and plantation investments, 52; political developments in 1940s, 2; relevance to Caribbean, 26; and slave trade advantages, 51, 53; slave trade consequences for, xiv; and slave trade relations, 55, 56, 58, 66–67; and socialism,

xvi; uneven development in, 72
Europeans, in Jamaica, 28
Ewald, Janet, 83n.9
EWF (Ethiopian World Federation), 97, 101

Fabianism, 126
Facing Reality group, 217
Fage, John D., 41, 47
Fanon, Frantz: on Africa, 170; and Algeria, 178; and decolonisation, 224; influence on left, 106, 122n.41; influence on Rodney, 12, 94, 209–210; on lumpenproletariat, 177; and Ras Negus, 99; and Pan-Africanism, 167; Rodney compared to, 79; and Sartre, 179n.2; and socialism, 141
Fascism, 2, 42–43, 170
Febure, Lucien, 82n.2
Ferry, Jules, 75
Fifth Pan-African Congress, 170–171
First Africa Corps, 89–90, 118–119n.10
Fletcher, Richard, 19
Fontaine, Pierre-Michel, xiv
France: African presence in, 62; and Algeria, 116; French colonial rule, 145; French Communist Party, 167; French Revolution, 39, 62, 75, 82; and Second World War, 2
Frank, André Gunder, 69, 80
Franklin, Rudolph, 90
Free village movement, 192, 195–196
FRELIMO (Front for the Liberation of Mozambique), 125, 129, 135, 173
French colonial rule, 145
French Communist Party, 167
French, Joan, 37
French Revolution, 39, 62, 75, 82n.3
French, Stanley, 37
Freund, Bill, 80
Front for the Liberation of Mozambique (FRELIMO), 125, 129, 135, 173
Fulas, 52
Fung, Fung Kee, 238
Fyffe, Christopher, 51–52

Gairy, Eric, 170, 187, 227, 232–233
Gambia, 76–77
Garrison constituencies, 92, 120n.18
Garvey, Amy Jacques, 109
Garvey, Marcus: and African repatriation, 106; Edwards on, 38; intellectual tradition of, xviii; Jamaican importance of, 109; and Johnson, 89; shrine of, 95–96; Robin Small influenced by, 88, 98; and working class, 93
Garvey movement: and black consciousness, 183; and Rastafarian movement, 29, 98, 118n.8; and Rodney, 109, 255
Gates, Henry Louis, Jr., 250n.26
Gaza monarchy, 63–64
Gender: and Rastafarian movement, 106; in slave trade, 52, 53, 82–83n.6; of slaves, 83n.8
Georgetown Review, 216
German colonial rule, 48, 77, 124
German East African Company, 77
German language, 7
Germany, 48, 77, 124, 246
Ghana, 43, 101, 151, 155
Giddings, C.D., 6
Girvan, Norman: and James' study group, 37, 38; in London, 32; and New World Group, 25; on Rodney, 20–21; and Rodney's African history work, 80; and *Transition,* 250n.26
Gold Coast, 60
Gold mining, 60, 193, 198
Golding, Bruce, 114
Gonsalves, Ralph, 114
Goveia, Elsa, 8, 18, 23, 25, 189, 200n.4
Government of National Unity, 239
Gramsci, Antonio, xv, xvi
Gray, Obika, 109–110
Gray, Richard, 42, 43, 56, 83n.12
Great Britain: African presence in, 62; and bourgeois intellectual process, 41; British colonial rule, xvi, xvii, 2, 36, 48, 145; and British institutions' role in Caribbean, 14–15, 29n.2; and Burnham, 4, 208, 248n.3; Caribbean political involvement of, 5; Cold War interests of, 6; Communist Party of, 39; Communist Party of Great Britain, 39; and constitutional suspension, 6; educational bias of, 8, 134; and English Civil War, 39; and Guyana's racial issues, 203; and industrial capitalism, 68; and Nyerere, 124; racism in, 27, 31, 33, 34, 39; Rastafarian movement's rejection of, 91, 121n.26; and Rodney's ban from Jamaica, 117; Rodney's friends in, 31–32; and Rodney's memorial events, 246; and Rodney's political thought, xvii; and Second World War, 2; and Tanganyika, 124; West Indian working class in, 33–34; West Indian writers migration to, 17
Greece, 61, 83n.16
Greene, J. E., 249n.15
Grenada: and Burnham, 225; and Gairy's removal, 187, 228; and Marxism, 224; New Jewel Movement in, 115, 117; political activism in, 203; University of the West Indies at Mona students from, 14
Grenadian Revolution: defeat of, 232–233, 247;

and Guyana's revolution, 228; and Leninism, 251n.38; Rodney on, 211, 231
Groundings, 95, 97–99, 106, 110, 120n.22
Guevara, Che, 111
Guinea, 43, 49–50, 217
Guinnea-Bisseau, 49–50, 116, 150, 170
Guyana: class in, 2–3, 27, 64, 192, 198, 222; and Cold War rivalry, 25; development of, 25; educated young people spending adult lives outside of, 9–10; and electoral boycott, 228; electoral fraud in, 225–226, 250n.28; founding of, 204; independence of, 249n.20; Indian population of, 108; interethnic relations in, 34; Jonestown tragedy of 1978, 226–227; left in, 203, 213, 222–225; and Marxism, 224; middle class in, 214; nationalisation in, 214; and Pan-African Congress of 1974, 170; and political activism, 249n.14; political crisis of 1978–1980, 225–243; political parties of, 116, 202; pseudosocialism of, 211–212, 233; race in, 3, 4, 197–198, 203, 206, 218, 221–222; radical politics in 1940s and 1950s, 2–3; radical publications of, 115; revolution in, 228–229, 242, 251n.34; riots of 1905, 194; Rodney's arson trial in, 88, 229, 234, 238; and Rodney's ban from Jamaica, 117, 184; and Rodney's grassroots appeal, 86; Rodney's historical approach to, 183–184, 187–200, 200n.2, 220; Rodney's political activism in, xiv, xvi, xvii, 1, 39, 183, 185, 187–189, 200n.2, 213–216, 225–248, 254; Edward Rodney's political activism in, 1; and Rodney's political thought, xvii, 2–3; Rodney's professorship blocked in, 44, 185, 208, 220; Rodney's return to, 116, 183–184; Rodney's study groups in, 38; socialism in, 213, 225, 233; and Southern African liberation movements, 178; University of the West Indies at Mona students from, 14; West Indian writers from, 17
Guyana Solidarity Committee of the Federal of Germany, 253n.55

Haiti, 175, 228
Haitian Revolution, 36, 62, 82n.3
Hall, Douglas, 18, 25
Hall, Ken, 80
Harris, Bonita Bone, 229
Harris, Wilson, 17, 38
Hart, Richard, 122n.51
Hasfal, Frank, 97, 99, 121n.30
Hatch, John, 108, 122n.43

Hearne, John, 17
Heartman, Daniel, 99, 102
Hector, Tim, 117, 123n.23, 253n.55
Hegel, Georg, 35, 38, 168
Heidegger, Martin, 38
Henry, Claudius, 89–90, 96–97, 108, 118–119n.10
Henry, James, 221
Henry, Louisa, 10–11
Henry, Paget, 45n.3, 45n.4
Henry, Pat. *See* Rodney, Pat Henry
Henry, Reynold, 89, 118n.10
Henry, Wilfred, 10–11
Hill, David, 252n.42
Hill, Robert, 121n.32
Hintzen, Percy, 206–207, 249n.14
History Teachers Association, 159
Hobbes, Thomas, 157
Holness, John, 164n.5
Holness, Marga, 164n.5
Hope, Margaret Carter, 37
Houphet-Boigny, F., 175
House of Israel, 234, 236, 252n.42
Howell, Neville, 97
Huie, Albert, 17

Ibos, 56, 58
Ife, 57
IMF, 75, 153
Imperialism: in Africa, 168; and African socialism, 140; anti-imperialist regimes, 213; Burnham's anti-imperialism, 228; in Caribbean, 209; and industrial capitalism, 68; and production control, 73; and socialism, 216–217; and Tanzania, 144, 148
Independence: in Africa, 249n.20; of Algeria, 178; and class, 151; false multiracialism of, 108; of Jamaica, 85, 249n.20; of Kenya, 124, 137; and neocolonialism, 149; and political elite, 146; and recolonisation by domestic political elite, xvii; of Rhodesia, 125; Rodney on, 9–10, 21–23; and socialism, 75, 224; of Tanzania, 124–126, 127, 135; of Trinidad, 16, 21, 249n.20; and Williams, 16
Independence Constitution of Jamaica, 90
Independent Africa, 219
India, 2, 78
Indian Political Revolutionary Association (IPRA), 219
Indochina, 181n.12
Indo-Guyanese: and Burnham, 207, 208, 220; and education, 3; family devotion of, 3; immigration of, 192; as indentured labourers, 184, 195, 198; and Jagan, 195, 220; middle class, 222; and

People's Progressive Party, 221; and political activism, 220–221; and political parties, 203; population of, 206; and racial issues, 108, 206, 221–222; social formation of, 189; social stratification among, 193; working class of, 189, 194–195; and Working People's Alliance, 229
Industry, and capitalism, 74–75
Inheritance, 82n.6
Inikori, Joseph, xiv, 51, 53, 60–61
Institute of Commonwealth Studies, 188
Intellectuals, xv, 9. *See also* West Indies Caribbean intellectual tradition
International Development Research Centre, 187
International Union of Students, 20
International Year of Human Rights, 93, 120n.19
Invisible education, 6
IPRA (Indian Political Revolutionary Association), 219
Iran, 181n.12
Iskra, 136
Italian language, 42
Italian socialism, xv, xvi

Jackson, George, 177–178, 234
Jackson, Grace, 21
Jagan, Cheddi: Burnham critique of, 248n.3; Burnham's defeat of, 217–218; and critical support stance, 212–216; and Draytons, 122n.51; and ethnic differences, 195; and Guyana's Nationalist Movement, 1; and Guyanese nationalism, 225; on Guyanese politics, 233, 251–252n.40; and Guyanese revolution, 251n.34; and Kwayana, 208; and Leninism, 251n.38; as main opposition figure, 212; and nationalist hopes of people, 10; and People's National Congress, 251n.32; and People's Progressive Party, 4, 6, 45n.1; political expertise of, 205; as President of Guyana, 241, 248n.2, 250n.28; as pro-Moscow, 39; and race, 203; and Rodney family discussions, 5; and Rodney's assassination, 247–248; Rodney's perspective on, 25; and socialism, 217, 222–223; and United States, 206; and United States' support of Burnham, 227; and University of Dar es Salaam, 135; and working class, 204
Jagan, Janet, 1, 4
Jagas, 67
Jamaica: anticommunist atmosphere of, 19; black consciousness in, 89–95; bulldozing of low-income housing, 92, 107; and Cuba in Angola, 181n.12; distinguishing characteristics of, 26–27; education in, 70; and Henry protest, 90, 119n.10; independence of, 85; intelligentsia's relationship with, 112–116; Jamaican students in London, 32; Marxism in, 109–110, 224; middle class in, 27–28, 93, 214, 255; Moore banned from, 30n.12; national state of emergency of 1966–1967, 89, 92; neocolonialism in, 107–108; political parties of, 202; race in, xiii, 28, 88, 89–95, 114, 123n.58, 222, 254–255; and Rodney's Caribbean regional perspective, 26–27; Rodney's expulsion from, 44, 85, 100, 109, 112–115, 117, 121n.32, 128, 184, 246, 247; Rodney's political activism in, xiii, 85, 87–88, 93–97, 100, 117, 188 254–255; and Rodney's political thought, xvii, 85; social differentiation in, 27–28; socialism in, 213; and Southern African liberation movements, 178; two-party system in, 90; University of the West Indies at Mona students from, 14; West Indian writers from, 17; and West Indies Federation, 15–16, 17. *See also* Rastafarian movement
Jamaica Agricultural Society, 122n.50
Jamaica Broadcasting Corporation, 88, 109, 118n.9
Jamaica College, 89, 91, 120n.16
Jamaica Committee for Human Rights and Democracy in Guyana, 253n.55
Jamaica Council for Human Rights, 253n.55
Jamaica Labour Party (JLP): and capitalism, 203; and garrison constituencies, 120n.18; Garvey's name used by, 109; and Rodney's assassination, 253n.55; and Rodney's ban from Jamaica, 85, 112, 114; and Shearer, 119n.12; and two-party system, 90; working class and peasantry following, 28
James, C.L.R.: and African independence, 249n.20; and colonialism, 48, 176; Du Bois' influence on, 172; generational difference of, 36–37; and Hector, 123n.56; and Hegel, 168; influence on Rodney, 12, 15, 76, 81, 97, 168, 224, 254; intellectual tradition of, xvii–xviii; and Manley, 214, 250n.24; and Marxism, 15, 34–38, 224; and Nyerere's regime, 172, 214, 250n.24; and Pan-Africanism, xvi, 167, 172, 176; on racism, 62; and radical black intellectual tradition, xv; on Rodney, xiv, xv–xvi, 179, 241–243; and Rodney as ultra-leftist, 250n.25; Rodney's criticism of, 171–172; and Rodney's Marxism, 34–38; Rodney's memorial speech, 241–242; Rodney's perception of political role

of, 23; and Russian Revolution, 40, 169; and slave trade, 81n.1, 82n.3; on socialism, 35, 217; study group of, 37–38, 88; tribute to Rodney, 36–37; and Trotsky, 169; and University of Dar es Salaam, 135; on vanguardism, 231; and Caribbean intellectual tradition, xv-xvi, 15, 23, 35, 45n.3, 69, 188; and Williams, 34–35, 45n.2, 45n.4; on working class, 178, 255
James, George, 69
James, Michael, 234
James, Selma, 37–38
James, Winston, 45n.3
Jayawardena, Chandra, 23
Jews, 28, 211
Jeyifo, Biodun, xv
JLP. *See* Jamaica Labour Party (JLP)
Jobson, Richard, 84n.17
Johnson, Millard, 88, 89, 90, 118n.8
Jones, Jim, 227
Jonestown tragedy of 1978, 226–227
Jordan, Louis, 104
Journal of African History, 44, 48, 49
Jumbe, Aboud, 163n.4

Kaijage, Fred: and Common Course, 159–160; and national service, 132–133; on Ranger, 128; on Rodney, 136–137, 163; and Rodney's Russian Revolution lectures, 179–180n.3
Kalabari, 59
Kant, Immanuel, 35
KANU (Kenya African National Union), 165n.18
Kanywanyi, Joe, 139–140
Karume, Sheikh Abeid, 163n.4
Kaunda, Kenneth, 126
Kennedy, John F., 89, 206
Kenya, 124, 125, 126, 127, 137
Kenya African National Union (KANU), 165n.18
Kenyatta, Jomo, 99, 165n.19
Kgositsile, Keorapetse, 129
Khrushchev, Nikita, 20
Kimambo, I., 128, 161
King, Audvil, 97
King, Martin Luther, Jr., 89
Kingston College, 120n.16
Kissinger, Henry, 178, 181n.12
Kiswahili, 7, 127, 139, 164–165n.11, 182
Kiujamaa, 139
Knight, Franklin, 18, 19
Koama, Ohene, 234, 235

Kropatschek, 64–65
Kwayana, Eusi: and New Jewel Movement, 232; political activism of, 204, 208, 211, 231; and pseudosocialism, 223; on race, 218; on Rodney, xiv, 237–238; and Rodney on racial justice, 251n.30; and Rodney's opposition to Burnham, 236; and victimisation, 187; and Working People's Alliance, 219–220, 229

Labour: international division of, 210; migration of, 188–189, 192
Lacey, Terry, 118n.10
Lamming, George, 17, 183, 241
Land reform, 125
Lannaman, Gloria, 19, 21
Latin America, 78, 213, 228–229
Latin American dependency theory, 48, 69, 70
Layne, Aidan, 19
Left: in Caribbean, 105, 117, 247; and Cuba, 249n.19; dogmatism of, 169; economics emphasis of, 106; in Grenada, 232; in Guyana, 203, 213, 222–225; in Jamaica, 209, 224; marginalisation of, in Tanzania, 163n.4; New Left, 39; political activism in, 203; and Rodney as ultra-leftist, 215, 225, 250n.25; and Rodney's adventuristic tendencies, 228–229, 242; of Third World, 168
Lenin, Vladimir Ilyich: and Arusha Declaration, 250n.24; influence on Tanzanian politics, 134, 136; and James' Marxist study group, 37; on revolutionary situation, 228–229; Rodney on, 168; theories applied to Africa, 141; and vanguardism, 231; and working people's emancipation, 224
Leningrad, 20
Leninism, 224, 243, 251n.38. *See also* Marxism-Leninism
Leonardo da Vinci, 111
Lewis, Arthur: and capitalism, 143, 165n.20; on class, 149; and education, 155–158, 159, 166n.30; generational difference of, 17; and James, 30n.15; and Rodney, 15–16, 20; and West Indies educational orientation, 14–15, 29n.2
Lewis, Gordon, 227
Lewis, Rupert, 80, 121n.32, 122n.40
Liberation movements: in Angola, 170; and Burnham, 212; defence of, 176; information from, 175; and Pan-African Congress of 1974, 180n.7; and Portuguese colonial rule, 43; and radicals, 172; and Tanzania, 125, 129, 163; United States' contacts of, 178. *See also* names of specific groups

Liberator Party, 225
Liberia, 101
Lictor, 7, 9
Literary Society, 17
Little, Malcolm. *See* Malcolm X
London School of Economics, 39, 42
Look-Lai, Wally, 37
Lovejoy, Paul, 83n.8, 83n.9
Lumpenisation, 177–178
Lumpenproletariat, 94, 177–178, 194, 243
Lumumba, Patrice, 175
Luthuli, Albert, 135

Mack, Douglas, 101
Mais, Roger, 17
Maji Maji, 136, 147, 177
Maji Maji wars, 77
Malcolm X: ban on books of, 95, 109, 112; and Burnham, 208, 226; Caribbean impact of, 89; Jackson compared to, 177; Planno compared to, 101
Mali, 82n.6
Mande, 52, 56, 60
Manderson-Jones, Ronny, 19
Mandle, Jay, 112
Manley, Edna, 17
Manley, Michael: as charismatic politician, 214; defeat of, 247; and democratic socialism, 90, 94, 209; domination of Jamaican politics, 212; and Henry, 90; and Jamaica Broadcasting Corporation strike, 118n.9; James' endorsement of, 172, 214, 250n.24; and People's National Party, 94, 114, 119n.12, 120n.21, 202; as prime minister, 119n.12; and Rastafarian movement, 29; and Rodney's assassination, 246–247; and Seaga, 248n.3; and Selassie, 120n.16, 122n.42; and United States, 178–179, 181n.12; and University of the West Indies, 158; and Workers' Party of Jamaica, 212
Manley, Norman: and Henry, 90; and Mission to Africa, 101; and People's National Party, 15, 22, 28; and West Indies Federation, 119n.11
MAO (Movement Against Oppression), 207, 218
Mao Tse-tung, 126
Marable, Manning, xv
Marakwene, 64
Marginalisation, 89
Marketing boards, 73
Marley, Bob: creativity of, 102; and Planno, 101, 120n.15; and Rastafarian movement, 118n.7; and ska music, 121n.37; and Tosh, 122n.38; in Zimbabwe, 252n.44
Marley, Rita, 101
Mars, Perry, 250n.26
Marx, Karl, 35, 38, 134, 142
Marxism: in Africa, 39, 72, 148, 177, 217; and anticolonial movement, 205; and Burnham, 195; of Caribbean, 38, 105, 117, 216, 218, 224–225; and China, 34, 39; and decolonisation, 145; and democracy, 38, 217; dogmatism of, 38, 39, 144, 225; and ethnicity, 218–219, 250n.29; and historical modes of production, 72; and Jagan, 195; in Jamaica, 109–110, 224; and James, 15, 34–38, 224; and Pan-Africanism, 167, 171; and People's National Party, 28, 251n.32; and People's Progressive Party, 2; and race, 105, 221; and radical black intellectual tradition, xv; and Rastafarian movement, 28–29; and *Ratoon,* 215; and Rodney's historical approach, 12, 20, 26, 39, 48–50, 54, 70, 81, 137, 168; Rodney's nondogmatic approach to, xvi–xvii, 39, 112, 140, 144, 225; and Rodney's political thought, xv–xvii, 15, 33–40, 70, 137, 224, 250n.29, 254; and School of Oriental and African Studies, 42; study groups on, 37–38, 39, 131, 237; and Tanzania, 126, 146; and Third World, 39, 168, 177, 181n.10, 224; and working class, 196, 237
Marxism-Leninism: dogmatic approach to, 140; in Guyana, 222–223; in Jamaica, 209, 224; and middle class, 22; of Soviet Union, 126
Masked dancing societies, 59
Matamba, 68
Matthews, Diana, 229
Mau Mau, 137
Maxwell, John, 37
Mazrui, Ali, 129, 157–158, 179, 250n.25
Mboya, Tom, 140, 165n.19
Mbundu, 67, 68
McDavid, Elvin, 252n.41
McIntosh, Winston Herbert. *See* Tosh, Peter
McNeil, Roy, 112, 113
Mentus, Ric, 247, 253n.53
Mercantile sector, 153
Middle class: in Africa, 75–76; Afro-Guyanese middle class, 3, 11, 193–194, 208, 213, 220–222, 239; and anticolonial movement, 193; and colonialism, 76; and differentiation of class, 196; and education, 22–23, 134, 156; false multiracialism of, 108; in Ghana, 151; in Guyana, 214; hegemony of, 117; and historiography, 161; on history, xiv, 179–180n.3; and Indo-Guyanese, 222; in

Jamaica, 27–28, 93, 214, 255; and Marxism, 105; and nationalist movement's political advances, 11; and Négritude, 175; and neocolonialism, 210–211; political activism of, 203, 231; and race, 210; radicals in, 94; and Rastafarian movement, 88, 94, 102–103, 107, 110; Rodney's critique of, 32, 134, 159, 174–175, 209–211, 220, 221; Rodney's rejection of lifestyle of, 86, 111; role of, in Caribbean politics, 22–23, 35, 114, 255; role of, in Guyana, 194; role of petty bourgeoisie, xvi, 138, 150–153, 157, 172, 174; and rudie culture, 104; and School of Oriental and African Studies, 41; and Selassie's visit, 91, 120n.16; in Tanzania, 133, 138, 149–152. *See also* Political elite
Middle East, 61
Military campaigns, 65–66
Millette, James, 115
Mirror, 208, 233
Mission to Africa, 101
Mittelholzer, Edgar, 17
Mkapa, Ben, 129
Mobutu Sese Seko, 126, 175
Mondlane, Eduardo, 129, 135
Moore, Brian, 196–197
Moore, Colin, 19, 30n.12
Moore, Robert, 8
Mordecai, John, 16
Morgan, Michael, 87, 118n.5
Mother-right, 82n.6
Movement Against Oppression (MAO), 207, 218
Movement for National Liberation in Barbados, 253n.55
Mozambique: balance of power in, 66; China's influence in, 142; ethnicity in Southern Mozambique, 63–64; liberation movements in, 125, 129, 135, 170, 173; Portuguese colonial rule in, 116; race in, 139
MPLA (Popular Movement for the Liberation of Angola), 125, 129, 164n.5, 173
Mr Bailey's church, 5
Msekwa, Pius, 136
Mugabe, Robert, 240
Muhammad, Elijah, 95, 112
Muhammad Speaks, 98
Mulattoes, 52, 62, 68
Multinational corporations, 209–210, 214
Munroe, Trevor: and *Abeng,* 121n.32; on black culturalism, 105–106; and Caribbean left, 117; and debating team, 30n.13; on decolonisation, 209; and Leninism, 251n.38;

and *Transition,* 250n.26
Museveni, Yoweri, 129, 134–135
Muslim leaders, 52
Mwogozo declaration, 136

Nabudere, Dan, 129, 165n.21
Naipaul, Shiva, 126, 164n.8, 252n.42
Naipaul, Vidia, 17, 35
Nascimento, Abdias do, 180n.7
Nascimento, Kit, 227
Nation, 23, 34–35, 45n.2
National Dance Theatre Company (NDTC), 18
National Joint Action Committee, 115
National Union of Kenyan Students, 173
National Union of the Students of Uganda, 173
National Workers Union, 253n.55
Nationalisation: in Guyana, 214; in Tanzania, 126, 139, 147
Nationalism. *See* Black nationalism; Nationalist movements
Nationalist, 129, 173
Nationalist movements: and British educational bias, 8; and Burnham, 4, 10, 25; and class, 170, 171; and decolonisation, 14; in Guyana, 1, 6, 222; ideological independence of, 171; in Jamaica, 255; and race, 4, 220; Rodney's participation in, 25; and social advancement, 11; in Tanzania, 150. *See also* Black nationalism
Native Americans, 3, 4, 62–63
NATO (North Atlantic Treaty Organization) weapons, 66
Ndongo, 67
NDTC (National Dance Theatre Company), 18
Négritude, 165n.18, 174–175
Negus, Ras, 99–101
Nehru, J., 205, 249n.12
Neocolonialism: in Caribbean, 117; and decolonisation process, 209–210; in Jamaica, 107–108; and middle class, 210; and Négritude, 175; Nkrumah on, 149; and political corruption, 210, 211; in Tanzania, 70, 138–140, 147
Neogy, Rajat, 250n.26
Neto, Agostinho, 129, 164n.5
Nettleford, Rex, 16, 17, 18, 28, 106
New Creation Peacemakers' Association, 90
New Jewel Movement: and Bishop, 117; and Burnham, 232; and Caribbean radicalism, 115; communist links of, 203; factional disputes within, 247; and Gairy's removal, 187, 232; ideological deterioration of, 38–39, 46n.6; and left, 224; and Leninism, 251n.38; and Pan-African Congress of 1974, 170; and radicals, 209; Rodney on, 231; and Working

People's Alliance, 232
New Left, 39
New Left Review, 39
New World, 188, 216
New World Group, 24–25, 113, 115, 122n.50, 143
Nicaragua, 187, 228
Niger-Delta, 58
Nigeria, 43, 58, 101, 126, 246
Nkrumah, Kwame: and African independence, 249n.20; and Lewis, 155; and Negus, 99; and neocolonialism, 149; Padmore as influence on, 40; party of, 166n.27; Rodney on, 175; and Rodney's choice of teaching position, 43
Nonaligned movement, 145–146, 202, 233
North Africa, 61
North Atlantic Treaty Organization (NATO) weapons, 66
Nyerere, Julius: and African independence, 249n.20; and Arusha Declaration, 44, 125–126, 138–139; on colonialism, 180n.7; and education, 154; and James, 172, 214, 250n.24; and national unity, 151–152; radical reforms of, 110, 141–143; reputation of, 126, 164n.7; Rodney as left of, 250n.25; Rodney's criticism of, 165–166n.22, 175; and student protests, 132–133; and Tanzania's independence, 124–126; and Ujamaa, 139–140; and University of Dar es Salaam faculty, 128, 129
Nzinga Nbandi (queen of Mbundu), 68

OAU. *See* Organisation of African Unity (OAU)
Oba, 57
Obote, Milton, 157–158
Odle, Maurice, 229, 250n.26
Ogunseye, Tacuma, 229
Oilfield Workers Trade Union of Trinidad and Tobago, 209, 253n.55
Oliver, Roland, 41, 43, 47, 83n.11
Ollman, Bertell, 112
Omawale, 229, 234, 238
Omo, Sase, 229
Omowale, Dr, 245
Oranmiyan, 56
Organic intellectuals, xv
Organisation of African Unity (OAU): information from, 175; liberation committee of, 125; and Rodney, 87, 174; and Robin Small, 88
Organisation of Working People (OWP), 237
Ossie, Count, 102

Othman, Haroub, 129, 164n.6
Our Own, 97, 99, 103, 107
Ovimbundu, 67
OWP (Organisation of Working People), 237
Oxford University Delegacy for Extra-Mural Studies, 44
Oyo, 56–58
Oyo Mesi, 58

PAC (Pan-African Congress), 125, 180n.7
Padmore, George: and Marxism, 36; and Pan-Africanism, 167; Rodney's criticism of, 171; and Russian Revolution, 40; and Caribbean intellectual tradition, xviii; on working class, 178
PAIGC (African Party for the Independence of Guinea and Cape Verde), 125
Palestine Liberation Organisation (PLO), 180n.7
Pan-African Congress of 1945, 170–171
Pan-African Congress of 1974, 170–171, 180–181n.7
Pan-African Congress (PAC), 125, 180n.7
Pan-African Youth Movement, 173
Pan-Africanism: and capitalism, 176, 186; and communism, 171; as international revolution, 186; and James' political thought, xvi, 167, 172, 176; and Lewis, 155; and Marxism, 167, 171; and Padmore, 40, 171; and Rodney's African history, 48; and Rodney's political thought, xv, xvi, 167–179, 254; Rodney's Tanzania activism concerning, xiii
Parkes, Al, 31, 32–33
Partido Socialista Popular (PSP), 180n.4
Patterson, Orlando: and dungles, 87, 118n.3; and James' influence, 45n.3; and James' study group, 37; in London, 32; and Rastafarian movement, 28; on underdevelopment, 200n.3; and University of West Indies at Mona, 17; and West Indian Society for the Study of Social Issues, 25
Patterson, P.J., 118n.4
Payne, Anthony, 92
Peasantry: and capitalism, 177; and class formation, 192–193, 196; and colonialism, 77; and Jamaica Labour Party, 28; of Trinidad, 211; and working class, 192–193, 198–199. *See also* Working class/people
People's Defence Force, 125
People's Democratic Movement, 225
People's National Congress (PNC): and bauxite industry, 238; and Burnham, 202–208; Caribbean support of, 227; communist links of, 202–203, 213, 223; and Dublin, 235; electoral

practices of, 225; and Marxism, 28, 251n.32; orientation of, 25; party paramountcy of, 207, 218; and People's Progressive Party, 223; pseudosocialism of, 233; and race, 95, 203, 249n.15; and Rodney as ultra-leftist, 250n.25; and Rodney's arrest for arson, 200n.5, 229, 252n.41; and Rodney's assassination, 241; and Rodney's critical exposure stance, 213–216, 251n.34; and United States, 223

People's National Movement (PNM), 23, 34–35, 45n.2, 45n.4, 202, 210

People's National Party (PNP): and Burnham, 241; communist links of, 202–203; and democratic socialism, 29, 203; and Drayton, 122n.51; garrison constituencies of, 92, 120n.18; Garvey's name used by, 109; and Norman Manley, 22, 28; and Michael Manley, 94, 119n.12, 120n.21, 202; and race, 94–95, 220–221; and Rodney's ban from Jamaica, 85–86; and Selassie, 120n.16; and two-party system, 90; and West Indies Federation, 15; and Young Socialist League, 88, 118n.1, 122n.48; youth drawn to, 114

People's Political Party, 89, 90, 118n.8

People's Progressive Party (PPP): and British colonial rule, 2; in British Guiana, 6; Burnham's defeat of, 217–218; civil resistance campaign of, 208; and class, 2–3; and Committee in Defence of Democracy, 225; communist links of, 202–203, 208; critical support stance of, 212–216, 251n.34; defeat of People's National Congress, 241; and election of 1968, 249n.15; and Leninism, 251n.38; opposition to Burnham, 228, 232; and race, 203, 204, 220–221; and racial riots of 1963–64, 4; and Rampersaud, 221; and Rodney as ultra-leftist, 250n.25; Eddie Rodney in, 45n.1; and Rodney's assassination, 253n.55; and Rodney's Marxism, 34; and scholarship availability, 6; and socialism, 223, 233; and sugar industry, 238; supporters of, 203–204; victimisation of, 207; and Working People's Alliance, 239; and *World Marxist Review,* 224

People's Temple, 227

Perkins, Wilmot, 121n.32

Persaud, Wendall, 229

Personal cultism, 22–23, 214–215

Petty bourgeoisie. *See* Middle class; Political elite

Phillips, Peter, 87–88, 118n.4

Pittsburgh University, 18

Planno, Mortimo: and Rastafarian movement, 29, 99, 101–102; and Rodney's groundings, 97; and Selassie's visit, 91, 119–120n.15

Plantations: and agricultural exports, 192; business cycles of, 191; economies of, 60; and environment, 190–191; and estate labor, 192; and ethnic conflict, 195–196, 198; and racism, 62; and slavery market, 52, 56; and working class resistance, 194

PLO (Palestine Liberation Organisation), 180n.7

PNC. *See* People's National Congress (PNC)

PNM (People's National Movement), 23, 34–35, 45n.2, 45n.4, 202, 210

PNP. *See* People's National Party (PNP)

Political activism: and black nationalism, 116; and Burnham's opposition, 237; in Caribbean, 202–203; and ethnicity, 112, 249n.14; in Guyana, xiv, xvi-xvii, 1; of Indo-Guyanese, 220–221; of Kwayana, 204, 208, 211, 231; legitimisation of, 232; of middle class, 203, 231; of Edward Percival Rodney, 1, 2–3, 5; Rodney's historical approach to, 11, 54, 69–70, 76, 81, 150–151, 163, 168, 199, 254; and Rodney's political role, xvi-xvii; of Roopnarine's father, 203–204; and scholarly work, 69; and strikes, 229; in Tanzania, 134–136; in Trinidad, 34, 35, 249n.14. *See also* Rodney, Walter, political activism; and specific political parties and leaders

Political Affairs Committee, 230

Political corruption, 126, 138, 210, 211

Political economy: of Guyana, 188, 189, 191; of slave trade, xiv; of Tanzania, 48, 141, 161

Political elite: and black consciousness, 89; and black nationalism, 85; and Burnham's coercive practices, 207; and education, 7, 13; ideology of, 145; and independence, 146; middle class's role and, 22–23; and Pan-Africanism, 177; and recolonisation, xvii; and Rodney as subversive, 115; Rodney's criticism of, 174, 214; satire of, 166n.26; and socialism, 214; in Tanzania, 130, 138, 147

Political parties: of Caribbean, 202–203; of Guyana, 116, 195, 202, 203, 225; of Jamaica, 28, 202–203; Jamaica's youth disillusioned with, 92; and Marxist study groups, 38; of radicals, 209; and revolutionary movements, 229; role of, 230; and working class, 117. *See also* specific parties

Politricks, 92, 106

Popular Movement for the Liberation of Angola (MPLA), 125, 129, 164n.5, 173

Portugal: and African colonisation, 63–68, 145,

150; and Africa's European presence, 61–62; Afro-Portuguese traders, 52; colonial rule of, 63–68, 116, 145, 150; fascism's fall in, 170; liberation movements in African territories of, 43; Rodney's historical research in, 50; Rodney's residence in, 43; and slave trade, 66–69; and Southern Africa, 40
Portuguese colonial rule, 63–68, 116, 145, 150
Portuguese language, 42
Portuguese people, in Guyana, 3, 198
Post, Ken, 121n.32
Poverty: in Jamaica, 27; and political activism, 203
PPP. *See* People's Progressive Party (PPP)
Pseudosocialism, 210–212, 215, 223, 233
PSP (Partido Socialista Popular), 180n.4
Puerto Rico, 143

Queen's College, 6–10, 193
Queen's College Magazine. See *lictor*.

Race: and African diaspora, 61–63; and anticolonial movement, 170; and black power, 108; and Burnham, 205, 220, 239–240; and capitalism, 168; and class, xvi, 4, 105, 109, 222, 256; and colonialism, 54–55, 71, 75–76; economic competition between races, 196; Great Britain's racism, 27, 31, 33, 34, 39; in Guyana, 3, 4, 197–198, 203, 206, 218, 221–222; and Haitian Revolution, 82n.3; in Jamaica, xiii, 28, 88, 89–95, 114, 123n.58, 222, 254–255; Jamaicans' attitude towards racism, 27, 88, 118n.8; and left, 106; and Marxism, 105, 221; and middle class, 210; and mulattoes, 28, 52, 62, 68, 95, 118n.8; and multiracial politics, 2, 4, 218; Nyerere on, 139; and People's National Congress, 95, 203, 249n.15; and People's Progressive Party, 204; political implications of, 35; racial riots of 1963–64, 4; racism's ideological basis, 84n.17; racist constructions of African history, 54–55, 76, 78–79, 82n.3, 84n.17; and Rodney family discussions, 5; and slave trade, 62; and social segmentation, 197; United States' racism, 178; and working class, 195, 197; and Working People's Alliance, 4, 203–204, 217–222, 230
Radicals: and *Abeng*, 208; in Africa, 170; and anti-imperialist regimes, 213; and Burnham, 212; in Caribbean, 115, 117, 203; in Guyana, 224; and intellectual tradition, xv; in Jamaica, 109–110; and liberation movements, 172; of London School of Economics, 39; and Marxism, xv; in middle class, 94; political parties of, 209; Rodney's links with, 209; and *Transition*, 216; of University of Dar es Salaam, 128; of University of the West Indies at Mona, 158–159, 209
Rain-Queen, 82n.6
Ramkissoon, Peter, 184–185
Ramoutar, Donald, 251n.32
Rampersaud, Arnold, 220–221, 251n.30
Ramsammy, Josh, 207, 229
Ranger, T.O., 43, 44, 128, 161
Rastafarian movement: and African repatriation, 101, 106; and black consciousness, 183; and colonialism, 28; cultural force of, xviii; and economic development, 116; and Henry protest, 119n.10; influence of youth, 98, 103, 107, 120n.17; and middle class, 88; and Moore, 30n.12; and Negus, 100–101; and race, 88, 95; and Rastafarian creativity, 102–103; report on, 28–29; repression of, 90, 100; Rodney's association with, 102, 118n.2, 255; Rodney's debate on, 19; and Selassie's visit, 90–91; and socialism, 28–29; and working class, 93, 94
Ratoon, 115, 208, 215, 218, 219
Reagan, Ronald, 247
Recolonisation, xvii. *See also* Neo-colonialism
Reed, John, 180n.3
Referendum, 225–226, 231
Reggae music, 121n.37, 183
Regional Union of West Indies Students (RUWIS), 20
Regional universities, 13, 17, 127, 134
Reid, Ptolemy, 227
Revolution: and capitalism, 64; in Jamaica, 111; James on, 36; localisation of, 186; and Marxism, 20, 39; middle class revolutionary leaders, 22–23; and neocolonialism, 210; and Pan-Africanism, 176; revolutionary idealism, 220. *See also* specific revolutions
Rhodesia, 125
Rice farming, 198
Riots, 4, 89, 90, 194
Rjkumar, Bisson, 229
Robinson, Cedric, xv
Rodney, Asha, 127, 182
Rodney, Donald, 1, 5, 6, 243–245
Rodney, Eddie, 4–5, 31–32, 45n.1
Rodney, Edward Percival: and boxing, 5; career of, 1; and church, 32; and People's Progressive Party, 2, 116, 203; and Walter Rodney's academic success, 4; role of, in family, 5
Rodney, Hubert, 1, 5

Rodney, Kanini, 127, 182
Rodney, Kathleen, 1, 5–6
Rodney, Keith, 1, 5
Rodney, Lawrence Albert, 1
Rodney, Pat Henry: Jessica Burnham as influence on, 10; family background of, 10–11; on Guyana, 182, 186; lifestyle of, 86, 108; marriage and family life of, 11, 32–33, 87, 115–116, 127, 165n.12, 183, 200n.1; nursing career of, 10, 31, 127, 164–165n.11; and Rodney's assassination, 243, 245; and Pauline Rodney's treatment of Walter, 4; on Tanzania, 44
Rodney, Pauline: and Anglican Church, 5; career of, 1, 5; and People's Progressive Party, 2; and Walter Rodney's academic success, 4; and Rodney's assassination, 245
Rodney, Shaka: family life of, 87, 115, 127, 165n.12, 182; and Rodney's assassination, 247–248
Rodney, Walter: academic success of, 4–7, 9, 11, 15, 20–21, 30n.13, 86; awards of, 7, 199, 248; and debating team, 7–8, 11, 18–19, 20, 30n.13, 193; doctoral work in African history, 26, 31, 40–45, 48, 49, 78; early years of, 1–12; foreign language mastery of, 7, 42; legacy of, 247; marriage and family life of, 11, 32–33, 87, 115–116, 127, 165n.12, 183, 187, 200n.1; memorial events for, 246–247; obituary of, 42; poetic tributes to, 246, 253n.54; and Queen's College, 6–10, 193; scholars' studies of, xiv-xvi; undergraduate education of, 7, 8, 11, 13, 14, 18–25, 95
—as historian: and African history, xiii, 11–12, 26, 39, 47–63, 69–70, 78, 107, 188, 199, 247, 254–256; and Caribbean history, 11–12, 39, 48, 187–200, 254–256; and decolonisation, xiv, 11, 54, 69, 81, 183, 256; Guyanese history, 183–184, 187–200, 200n.2, 220; and James' study group, 37; and Marxism, 12, 20, 26, 39, 48–50, 54, 70, 81, 137, 168; and political role, 11, 54, 69–70, 76, 81, 150–151, 163, 168, 199, 254; slavery research of, 25–26, 99, 254; social sciences' role, 24, 70, 78; and studies at University of the West Indies at Mona, 18; Tanzanian history, 159–160, 188, 199, 254; and University of Dar es Salaam, 44, 48, 69–70, 78, 127–131, 161–163
—political activism: and arson arrest, 189, 200n.5, 229, 234, 238; assassination of, 240–248; Burnham critique of, 76, 208, 235–236, 248n.3; and Burnham's 1961 election, 10; as Burnham's opponent, 10, 208, 224, 233, 235–237, 241, 243, 255; in Guyana, xiv, xvi-xviii, 1, 39, 183, 185, 187–189, 200n.2, 213–216, 225–248, 254; and Henry protest, 119n.10; and historian's role, 11, 54, 69–70, 76, 81, 150–151, 163, 168, 199, 254; ideology of, 111–112; in Jamaica, xiii, 85, 87–88, 93–97, 100, 117, 188, 254–255; and James' influence, 97; and middle class, 76; moral imperative in, 186–187; political crisis of 1978–1980, 225–243; and political role, xvi-xvii; public speaking of, 31, 33–34; on race, 218–222, 250n.29; and Rastafarian movement, 102, 107–112, 255; Rodney's lifestyle and, 86–89; and Rudie culture, 103–107; in Tanzania, xiii, 130–131, 136–137, 163, 188, 254; and ultra-leftist classification, 225, 250n.25, 255; and Working People's Alliance victimisation, 207
—political thought: on Africa, xiv; on African diaspora, xiv, xvii; on Caribbean, xiii, xiv, xv, 210; evolution of, xiii-xvii, 2–3; on Guyana, xvii, 2–3; on Jamaica, xvii, 85; and James' study group, 37; and London, xvii; on Marxism, xv, 15, 33–40, 70, 137, 224, 250n.29, 254; on Pan-Africanism, xv, xvi, 167–179, 254; and revolutionary pedagogy, 154–159; on Tanzania, xvii, 137–145, 147, 148–153, 165–166n.22; and victimisation, 9
—works: *Adriaan Henriks: Out of Holland*, 199; 'Africa in Europe and the Americas', 56, 61–63, 188; 'African History and Development Planning', 78; 'African History in the Service of Black Revolution', 54, 107; 'African Slavery and Other Forms of Social Oppression on the Upper Guinea Coast in the Context of the Atlantic Slave Trade', 49; 'Aspects of the International Class Struggle in Africa, the Caribbean and America', 170, 180n.7; 'Barbadian Immigration into British Guiana 1863-1924, 189; *Black Struggles,* 115; 'British Guiana — Some New Dimensions', 25; *Cambridge History of Africa* essays, 42, 48, 56–63, 188; 'Century of Development in Africa', 78–79; 'Class Contradictions in Tanzania', 151; 'Colonial Economy: Observations on British Guiana and Tanganyika', 188; 'Contemporary Political Trends in the English-speaking Caribbean', 209; 'Education in Africa and Contemporary Tanzania', 154; 'European Activity and African Reaction in Angola', 66, 128; *Fung-A-Fat: Out of China,* 199; *Groundings With My Brothers,*

54, 94, 99, 107, 111, 117, 222; 'Guinea Coast', 56, 60, 188; *Guyanese Sugar Plantations in the late Nineteenth Century,* 189; 'Historical Roots of African Underdevelopment', 78; *History of the Guyanese Working People 1881–1905,* 18, 48, 187, 189–190, 198–200, 216, 231; *History of the Upper Guinea Coast, 1545–1800,* 42, 49–54; 'Ideology of the African Revolution', 172–173; Immigrants and Racial Attitudes in Guyanese History', 188; 'In Defence of Arnold Rampersaud', 250n.30; 'Internal and External Constraints on the Development of the Guyanese Working Class', 216; *Joao Gomes: Out of Madeira,* 199; *Kofi Baadu Out of Africa,* 199; *Lakshmi: Out of India,* 199; 'Marx in the Liberation of Africa', 181n.10; 'Marxism as a Third World Ideology', 181n.10; 'Masses in Action', 188, 198; 'Message to Afro-Jamaica Associations', 96–97, 109; 'Migrant Labour and the Colonial Economy', 161; *Migrant Labour in Tanzania During the Colonial Period,* 162, 188; 'Negro Slave', 25–26; *One Hundred Years of Development in Africa,* 162; *People's Power No Dictator,* 235–236; 'Policing the Countryside in Colonial Tanganyika', 161; 'Political Economy of Colonial Tanganyika, 1890–1939', 161; 'Political Economy of Guyana, 1880–1939, 187; 'Portuguese Attempts at Monopoly on the Upper Guinea Coast', 44, 49; 'Reconsideration of the Mane Invasions of Sierra Leone', 49–50; 'Recruitment of Askari in Colonial Tanganyika 1920–1961, 161; 'Resistance and Accommodation in Ovimbundu/ Portuguese Relations', 64–65; 'Role of the Historian in the Developing West Indies', 24; 'Slavery and Underdevelopment', 189; 'Some Implications of the Question of Disengagement from Imperialism', 147; 'Some Political Aspects of Independence', 21–23; 'Strategies of Development', 69; 'Subject Races and Class Contradictions in Guyanese History', 188; 'Tanzania Ujamaa and Scientific Socialism', 139–140; 'Tanzanian Revolution', 108, 137; 'Transition', 216; 'West Africa and the Atlantic Slave Trade', 55; 'What Price Patriotism?', 9; 'World War II and the Tanzanian Economy', 161; 'Year 1895 in Southern Mozambique: African Resistance to the Imposition of European Colonial Rule', 63–64
—*How Europe Underdeveloped Africa:* and Babu, 164n.4; and colonialism, 73–74; critical reception of, 79–81; and economic development approach, 70–71, 73, 76, 78; and external African factors, 56; gender question in, 52, 82–83n.6; history/social sciences relationship, 24; and James' study group, 38; and Marxism, 54; and Marxist theory, 72; nationalist versus materialist historical reconstruction, 56; notoriety of, xiii, 69, 188, 254; polemical character of, 189; and political activism, 69–70; and slave trade, 50, 51, 70–71, 81n.1; themes of, 76–77; writing of, 36, 48, 70, 160, 199–200

Rodriquez, Carlos Rafael, 180n.4
Rodway, Brian, 199, 216
Rohee, Clement, 251n.32
Rohlehr, Gordon: career of, 12n.4; on dread, 252n.49; and educational opportunities, 6–7, 9; and James, 45n.3; and nationalism, 6; and Queen's College, 6; on Rastafarian creativity, 102; and Rodney's assassination, 246; and Rodney's ban from Jamaica, 115, 246; and Rodney's marriage, 32; and Rodney's social attitudes, 110–111; and turbulence of 1950s, 8–9; and University College of the West Indies, 8; and University of Birmingham, 31
Rohlehr, John, 223
Roopnarine, Rupert: arson arrest/trial of, 229, 234, 238; father's political activism, 203–204; and *Georgetown Review,* 216; Guyanese revolutionary situation, 228; return to Guyana, 187; and Rodney's blocked professorship, 208; and Working People's Alliance, 230, 231, 251n.36
Roy, M.N., 205, 249n.12
Royal Hampshires, 119n.10
Rudie culture, 103–107
Russian Revolution: and capitalism's decline, 147; and Cuban Revolution, 180n.4; and James, 40, 169; and James' study group, 37; Rodney's lectures on, 20, 38, 39–40, 131, 167–169, 179–180n.3; and Rodney's Marxism, 39
Rusticated students, 136
RUWIS (Regional Union of West Indies Students), 20
Rwanda, 126
Rweyemamu, Justinian, 160

Sago, Laurent, 162, 188
Said, Edward, 122n.41
St Lucia, 14, 17

St Stephen's Church of Scotland School, 6
St Vincent, 14, 115
Salkey, Andrew, 17, 35, 204, 205, 218, 253n.54
Sandinistas, 187
Sartre, Jean-Paul, 179n.2
Saul, John, 128, 147, 160
Sawyer, Aki, 129
Scandinavian socialism, 126, 164n.6
Schlesinger, Arthur, 206–207
Scholarships, 5, 6–8, 13, 33
Scholes, Theophilus, xviii
School of Oriental and African Studies (SOAS), 26, 31, 40–45, 48, 49, 78
Scott, Dennis, 18
Seaga, Edward, 114, 119n.12, 202, 248n.3
Second World War, xvii, 2
Secret societies, 59
Sekiapu, 59
Selassie, Haile, 90–91, 98, 101, 119–120n.15, 122n.42
Selvon, Samuel, 17–18
Senegal, 175
Senghor, Léopold, 140, 144, 165n.18
Shah, Raffique, 117
Shamuyarira, Nathan, 129
Shearer, Hugh: ban on Rodney, 100, 105, 113; constituency of, 97; and International Year for Human Rights, 120n.19; and Michael Manley, 119n.12
Shenton, Robert, 80, 83n.10
Shepperson, George, 54
Sherlock, Sir Philip, 8, 16, 123n.58
Shivji, Issa: and class, 149, 160; and Common Course, 160; intervention of, 145–148; and Rodney's involvement with students, 131, 136; and Rodney's role, 170; and student protests, 134; and Ujamaa, 139
Sierra Leone, 49–50, 101
Simango, U., 129
Singapore, 143
Singh, Rickey, 246
Singham, A.W., xvi, 23
Single, Ras, 97, 107, 120n.26
Sixth Pan-African Congress, 170–171, 180–181n.7
Ska music, 103–104, 121n.37
Slater, Henry, 161
Slave raiding, 56, 58–60, 66–67
Slave trade: and African history, 47, 81n.1; and African ruling groups, 50–53, 55–56, 58, 66; and African state building, 56; and Africa's political fragmentation, 61; and capitalism, 51, 52, 55, 143; and class, 51, 53, 83n.11;

and colonialism, 48, 71–72, 79, 143; and economic development, 72; and economics, 66; political economy of, xiv; and Portugal, 66–69; and race, 62; Rodney's work on, 48, 99, 254
Slaves and slavery: and economic development, 191; expanding slave market, 52; and humanisation of Guyana's coastal landscape, 191; and industrial capitalism, 68; Jamaican slave revolts, 27; Native American subjugation compared to, 63; research focus on, 83n.8; Rodney's historical interest in, 25–26, 99, 254; and Spain, 61; and underdevelopment, 200n.3; and working people, xv
Small, Hugh, 28, 32, 88
Small, Richard: and *Abeng,* 121n.32; and Guyana arson trial, 88; and James' study group, 37, 88; in London, 32; Rodney's meeting of, 20, 88
Small, Robin: and *Abeng,* 121n.32; and Ethiopian World Federation, 97; and International Year for Human Rights, 93; and Negus, 99–100; publications of, 98–99; and Rastafarian movement, 102; Rodney's association with, 87–88, 94, 107; and Rodney's writings, 107; and Selassie's visit, 91–92
Smith, Gregory, 243–244, 245
Smith, Ian, 125
Smith, M.G., 28
Smith, Michael, 23
Smith, Raymond, 23
SNCC (Student Nonviolent Coordinating Committee), 89
SOAS (School of Oriental and African Studies), 26, 31, 40–45, 48, 49, 78
Soba, 67
Social democracy, 2, 126, 164n.6, 202
Social differentiation: in Africa, 50–51, 56–57, 68, 82n.5; in Caribbean, 27; in Jamaica, 27–28. *See also* Class
Social sciences, 24, 70, 78
Social Scientist, 108
Socialism: of Africa, 140–141, 179; and black nationalism, 105; of British Labour Party, 22; and Burnham, 195, 204, 208, 223, 228, 248n.3; in Caribbean, 213–214; and decolonisation, 142; democratic socialism, 29, 90, 94, 203, 209; in Eastern Europe, 71, 176; and education, 154–155; and ethnicity, 218–219; European, xvi; in Guyana, 204, 213, 225, 233; ideology of, 134; and imperialism, 216–217; and independence, 75, 224; Italian, xv–xvi; and Jagan, 25, 195, 204, 217; James on, 35, 217; and Pan-Africanism, 176; and People's National Party, 29, 94; and People's Progressive Party, 2,

223; pseudosocialism, 210–212, 215, 233; and Rastafarian movement, 28–29; relations with socialist countries, 143–144; and Rodney's historical perspective, 71; of Scandinavia, 126; in Soviet Union, 71, 134, 169; and Tanzania, 125, 126, 139–145, 163; and Third World, 75, 216, 228; and University of Dar es Salaam, 128
Socialist Club, 131, 135
Somalia, 217
Somoza, Anastasio, 187, 228
Sossos, 67
South Africa, 116, 139
South West Africa People's Organisation (SWAPO), 125, 180n.7
Southern Africa: Caribbean solidarity with, 179; Cuban efforts in, 178; labour needs in, 77; liberation movements of, 175, 176, 178, 180n.7; liberation struggles of, 94; and Portuguese rule, 40, 65–66, 116; and Russian Revolution, 169
Southern Mozambique, 63–64
South-West Africa, 139
Soviet Union: and Burnham, 208, 212, 248n.3; and China, 142; Cold War interests of, 52; Communist Party of the Soviet Union, 46n.6, 140, 168, 203, 223, 224; and Cuban Revolution, 20; Czechoslovakian invasion, 131; dissolution of, 212; and economic development, 75; and ethnicity, 218; and Guyana, 213; and Jagan, 248n.3; and Jamaica's publications ban, 112; and Marxism, 39; relations with, 143; Rodney's visit to, 113; and Second World War, 2; socialism in, 71, 134, 169; and Third World, 178, 181n.12; and Workers' Party of Jamaica, 38, 46n.6
Soyinka, Wole, xvii, 170
Spain, 43, 61–62
Spanish language, 7, 42
Stalin, Joseph, 40, 167, 179–180n.3
Stalinism, 39, 40, 171
State Trading Corporation, 153
Stone, Carl, 92–93
Strickland, William, 221
Strikes, 227–228, 229, 238
Structuralist theory, 148
Student Nonviolent Coordinating Committee (SNCC), 89
Sugar estates, 14
Sugar industry, 212, 214, 238
Sugar Producers' Association, 184
Suriname, 108, 240

Swai, Bonaventure, xiv
SWAPO (South West Africa People's Organisation), 125, 180n.7
Sylvester-Williams, Henry, xvii
Syrians, 28, 211
Szentes, Tamas, 147, 148, 165n.13

Tactical Service Unit, 236
Tambila, Kapepwa, 162, 188
Tandon, Yash, 129, 165n.21
Tanganyika, 124, 137
Tanganyika African Association, 124
Tanganyika African National Union (TANU): and Arusha Declaration, 152; and Nyerere, 124; opposition to, 151; Youth League of, 132, 136, 173, 177
Tanzania: Arusha Declaration in, 44; class in, 48, 146, 148–151; compulsory national service in, 132–133; decolonisation in, 40; economic development in, 70, 138, 142–143, 147; education in, 70, 154; independence of, 124–126, 127, 135; and liberation movements, 125, 129, 163; political activism in, 134–136; political economy of, 48; political leadership of, 71; Rodney's activism in, xiii; and Rodney's criticism of African political leadership, 173; and Rodney's grassroots appeal, 86, 110, 160; Rodney's historical approach to, 159–160, 188, 199, 254; and Rodney's memorial events, 246; Rodney's political activism in, xiii, 130–131, 136–137, 163, 188, 254; and Rodney's political thought, xvii, 137–145, 147, 148–153, 165–166n.22; Rodney's return to, 115–116, 164n.9, 240; Rodney's study groups in, 38; Rodney's teaching in, 43; and Russian Revolution, 169
Tanzania Publishing House, 81
Tanzania-Zambia Railway, 125
Taylor, Leroy, 112, 113
Technology: and colonialism, 66; and Pan-Africanism, 176
Temu, A., 128, 161
Third World: Burnham's legitimacy in, 228; and colonialism, 150; communist influence in, 145; and global economic system, 48, 77–78, and localisation of revolution, 186; and Marxism, 39, 168, 177, 181n.10, 224; neocolonialism in, 211; radical nationalism in, 213; and socialism, 75, 216, 228; and Soviet Union, 178, 181n.12
Thomas, C.Y.: and bauxite workers, 238; and Grenadian Revolution, 233; Jamaica ban on, 112; and New Jewel Movement, 232; and *Ratoon,* 208; and *Transition,* 216; and

University of Dar es Salaam, 160, 165n.13; victimisation of, 207; and Working People's Alliance, 229, 230
Thomas, Eddy, 18
Thomas, Ewart: in London, 31; and Queen's College, 7–8; and Rodney's marriage, 32; and Rodney's revolution studies, 39–40, 167–168; and Rodney's support for Burnham, 10; scholarships of, 8; and University of the West Indies at Mona, 18
Thomas, J.J., 69
Thompson, E.P., 168
Thorne, A.A., 194
Thornton, John, 80
Thunder, 233
Thwaites, Ronald, 121n.32
Tobago: Black Power revolt in, 212; independence of, 16, 21; James in, xvi; and United States, 178–179; University of the West Indies at Mona students from, 14; and Williams, 54
Torchlight, 231
Tosh, Peter, 102, 104, 120n.15, 121–122n.38
Trade unions, 209, 227, 253n.55
Transition, 216, 250n.26
Trevor-Roper, Hugh, 78–79
Trinidad: February Revolution of, 115, 202, 212; independence of, 16, 21, 249n.20; Indian population of, 108; Jamaica compared to, 26; James in, xvi, 34, 35; middle class of, 210–211; People's National Movement in, 23, 202; and political activism, 34, 35, 249n.14; and Rodney's ban from Jamaica, 117; and United States, 178–179; University of the West Indies at Mona students from, 14; and West Indian intellectual tradition, 69; West Indian writers from, 17; and Williams, 54
Trotsky, Leon, 37, 40, 167, 169, 180n.3
Trotskyites, 39, 40
Ture, Kwame, 253n.55. *See also* Carmichael, Stokely
Twelve Tribes, 88, 118n.7

UF. *See* United Force (UF)
Uganda, 127
Ujamaa, 139–141, 144–145
Ulyanovsky, Rostislav, 46n.6, 224
Umma Party, 164n.4
Undesirable Publications Law, 112
UNESCO General History of Africa, 48
United Force (UF): and coalition government with People's National Congress, 206, 217–218; and election of 1973, 207; and People's National Congress, 223
United Labour Front of Trinidad and Tobago, 253n.55
United States: and African history, 47–48; and Burnham, 4, 10, 206, 208, 227, 241, 248n.3; and Caribbean diplomatic relations with Cuba, 202; Caribbean political involvement of, 5; civil rights movement in, 31; Cold War interests of, 6, 25; communist party in, 167; and Cuba in Angola, 178–179, 181n.12; Cuban blockade of, 249n.21; and Grenada, 233, 247; and Guyana's human rights violations, 252n.48; and Guyana's racial issues, 203; and Jonestown tragedy of 1978, 226–227; and liberation movements, 178; and lumpenisation, 177–178; and Nyerere, 124–125; and People's National Congress, 223; and political elites' ideology, 145; and Rodney's memorial events, 246; and Second World War, 2
Universal Negro Improvement Association, 101
University of Dar es Salaam: and African diaspora course, 61; Akivaga crisis, 135–136; and Common Course, 159–160, 161; and Gray, 42; masters programme, 161–162; opening of, 127–128; radicals of, 128–130, 135; and Eddie Rodney, 31; and Rodney as historian, 44, 48, 69–70, 78, 127–131, 161–163; Rodney on intellectuals' role, 23, 133–134; Rodney's comparative revolution studies, 39; and Rodney's criticism of African political leadership, 172–173; Rodney's impact on students, 131–137; Rodney's political role in, 130; and Rodney's Russian Revolution lectures, 20, 167–169, 179–180n.3; Rodney's teaching career at, 43
University of East Africa, 127
University of Guyana: and Burnham's control, 206; Rodney's application to, 184–185; Rodney's professorship denied, 44, 185, 208, 220; strike actions of, 227–228
University of Hamburg, 76, 78
University of London, 13, 18, 40–41
University of Michigan, 127
University of the West Indies at Cave Hill, 14, 209, 253n.55
University of the West Indies at Mona: and British institutions' role in Caribbean, 14–15, 29n.2; establishment of, 13–14; radical scholars of, 158–159, 209; and Rodney on intellectuals' role, 23; Rodney's attendance at, 7, 8, 11, 13, 14, 18–25, 95; Rodney's graduation from, 14, 95; and Rodney's qualification for doctoral

study, 40–41; Rodney's scholarship to, 7, 8; and Rodney's teaching career, 43–44, 86, 95
University of the West Indies at St Augustine, 14, 209, 253n.55
University Students African Revolutionary Front (USARF), 131–132, 135–136
University Students Association of East Africa, 173

Van Sertima, Ivan, 69
Vansina, Jan, 47–48
Victimisation: Africa as passive victim, 80; of Afro-Guyanese, 221; and bauxite workers' education, 238; and Burnham, 11, 235; and education, 41; in Guyana, 186–187; and neo-colonialism, 210; of People's Progressive Party, 207; and Rodney's assassination, 243; and Rodney's ban from Jamaica, 113; Rodney's fear of, 9; of students, 132; of Working People's Alliance, 207, 240–241
Vietnam, 145, 178
Vietnam War, 147, 178

Wabenzi, 148, 166n.25
Wailer, Bunny, 102, 122n.38
Walcott, Derek, 17, 18, 35, 45n.3
Wallerstein, Immanuel, 80
Walter, Selwyn, 18, 19
Ward, June, 180n.6
Warner, Carlton, 45n.4
Washington, Rabbi, 236, 252n.42
Wa'Thiongo, Ngugi, 166n.26
West Germany, 124–125
West Indian intellectual tradition: and economic development, 116; intellectuals' role, 23, 159; and Jamaica, 112–116; and James, xv–xvi, 15, 23, 35, 45n.3, 69, 188; and Lewis, 15–16, 149; and Rodney, xv, 15–16, 69, 188, 247, 256; and Williams, 15, 17, 188
West Indian Federal Labour Party, 34
West Indian Regiment, 119n.10
West Indian Society for the Study of Social Issues, 24–25
West Indian Students Union, 31
West Indies Federation, 15–16, 29n.2, 119n.11
Western political alignment, xvii
White, Garth, 88, 103–104, 118n.6
White paternalism, 93
Whylie, Marjorie, 18
Williams, Denis, 69
Williams, Eric: and educated populace, 21; and industrial capitalism, 68; and James, 34–35, 45n.2, 45n.4; on racism, 62; and People's National Movement, 202; Rodney's following in intellectual tradition of, 15, 54; Rodney's introduction to writings of, 8; and scholarships, 13; and slave trade, 81n.1; and University of West Indies' mission, 16–17; and West Indian Caribbean intellectual tradition, 69, 188
Williams, Lavinia, 18
Williams, Robert, 112
Windward Islands, 115
WLL (Workers' Liberation League), 209, 212, 249n.23
Wolf, Eric, 80
Women: and colonialism, 82–83n.6; and Rastafarian movement, 106; role of, in Africa, 82n.6
Woodford Square, 21
Workers' Liberation League (WLL), 209, 212, 249n.23
Workers' Party of Jamaica (WPJ), 114, 116; Burnham's demobilisation of, 207; communist links of, 202–203, 209; and Henry, 90; and Leninism, 251n.38; and Manley, 212; and Marxism, 224; and Rastafarian movement, 94; and Rodney's assassination, 253n.55; and Soviet Union, 38, 46n.6
Working class/people: in Africa, 74–75; and business cycles, 191; communists uncritical attitude toward, 178; and democratic rights, 232; and differentiation of class, 196; and education, 157; and environment, 190–191; ethnic divisions within, 192; of Guyana, 224, 226; and Jagan, 204; in Jamaica, 27, 28, 93, 94; and labour as commodity, 77; lumpenisation of, 177–178; and Marxism, 196, 237; and Pan-Africanism, 177; and peasantry, 192–193, 198–199; and People's Progressive Party, 2; perspective of, 173; political activism of, 203; political mobilisation of, 193–194; and race, 195, 197, 198; Rodney's class orientation to, 134; Rodney's commitment to, 117, 157, 199, 216, 243, 256; and Rodney's lifestyle, 33, 110; self-emancipation of, xiv–xv; social transformation of, 3; and socialism, 141; in Tanzania, 152, 153; of Trinidad, 210; in United States, 178; University of Dar es Salaam students from, 134; West Indians in London, 33–34
Working People's Alliance (WPA): Andaiye's work for, 187; and arson trial, 232, 234, 252n.41; as Burnham's opposition, 212, 229; burning of People's National Congress building, 229–230, 231; and Committee in Defence of

Democracy, 225–226; communication needs of, 253n.51; and Grenadian Revolution support, 232; and Guyanese revolution, 228; leadership arrangements of, 229–230, 251n.36; and multiracial political unity, 4; and People's Progressive Party alliance, 239; as political party, 229–231, 239; and political risks, 186–187; and race, 4, 203–204, 217–222, 230; and radicals, 209; and Rodney's funeral, 253n.53; Rodney's involvement in, 1, 45, 183, 186, 203–204, 219; and Rodney's work with bauxite workers, 237–238, 252n.43; as social movement, 230; ultra-leftist classification of, 215, 250n.25; victimisation of, 207, 240–241
Working People's Vanguard Party, 218, 219
World Bank, 75
World Marxist Review, 224, 251n.32
WPA. *See* Working People's Alliance (WPA)
WPJ. *See* Workers' Party of Jamaica (WPJ)
Wright, Richard, xv
Wynter, Sylvia, 45n.3

Yorubas, 56–57, 69
Young Socialist League: and Davis, 122n.48; ideology of, 22; and Rodney, 118n.1; and Hugh Small, 28, 88; and West Indies Federation, 15
Yulimo group, 115

Zaire, 152
Zanzibar, 124, 137
Zanzibar Revolution, 163–164n.4
Zimbabwe, 139, 240, 252n.44
Zimbabwe African National Union (ZANU), 125, 173, 180n.7
Zimbabwe African People's Union (ZAPU), 125, 173, 180n.7